Bloom's Shakespeare Through the Ages

HENRY V

Edited and with an introduction by
Harold Bloom
Sterling Professor of the Humanities
Yale University

Volume Editor
Albert Rolls

BLOOM'S
LITERARY CRITICISM
An imprint of Infobase Publishing

Bloom's Shakespeare Through the Ages: Henry V
Copyright © 2010 by Infobase Publishing
Introduction © 2010 by Harold Bloom

Bloom's Literary Criticism
An imprint of Infobase Publishing
132 West 31st Street
New York NY 10001

Library of Congress Cataloging-in-Publication Data
Henry V / edited and with an introduction by Harold Bloom ; volume editor, Albert
Rolls.
    p. cm.—(Bloom's Shakespeare through the ages)
  Includes bibliographical references and index.
  ISBN 978-1-60413-718-7 (hardcover)
  1. Shakespeare, William, 1564–1616. Henry V.   2. Henry V, King of England,
1387–1422—In literature.   3. Kings and rulers in literature.   I. Bloom,
Harold.   II. Rolls, Albert.
  PR2812.H46 2010
  822.3'3—dc22

                                    2009047625

Bloom's Literary Criticism books are available at special discounts when purchased in
bulk quantities for businesses, associations, institutions, or sales promotions. Please call
our Special Sales Department in New York at (212) 967-8800 or (800) 322-8755.

You can find Bloom's Literary Criticism on the World Wide Web at
http://www.chelseahouse.com

Text design by Erika A. Arroyo
Cover design by Ben Peterson
Composition by IBT Global, Troy NY
Cover printed by IBT Global, Troy NY
Book printed and bound by IBT Global, Troy NY
Date printed: April 2010
Printed in the United States of America

10 9 8 7 6 5 4 3 2 1

This book is printed on acid-free paper.

All links and Web addresses were checked and verified to be correct at the time of
publication. Because of the dynamic nature of the Web, some addresses and links
may have changed since publication and may no longer be valid.

CONTENTS

SERIES INTRODUCTION

Shakespeare Through the Ages presents not the most current of Shakespeare criticism, but the best of Shakespeare criticism, from the 17th century to today. In the process, each volume also charts the flow over time of critical discussion of a particular play. Other useful and fascinating collections of historical Shakespearean criticism exist, but no collection that we know of contains such a range of commentary on each of Shakespeare's greatest plays and at the same time emphasizes the greatest critics in our literary tradition: from John Dryden in the 17th century, to Samuel Johnson in the 18th century, to William Hazlitt and Samuel Coleridge in the 19th century, to A.C. Bradley and William Empson in the 20th century, to the most perceptive critics of our own day. This canon of Shakespearean criticism emphasizes aesthetic rather than political or social analysis.

Some of the pieces included here are full-length essays; others are excerpts designed to present a key point. Much (but not all) of the earliest criticism consists only of brief mentions of specific plays. In addition to the classics of criticism, some pieces of mainly historical importance have been included, often to provide background for important reactions from future critics.

These volumes are intended for students, particularly those just beginning their explorations of Shakespeare. We have therefore also included basic materials designed to provide a solid grounding in each play: a biography of Shakespeare, a synopsis of the play, a list of characters, and an explication of key passages. In addition, each selection of the criticism of a particular century begins with an introductory essay discussing the general nature of that century's commentary and the particular issues and controversies addressed by critics presented in the volume.

Shakespeare was "not of an age, but for all time," but much Shakespeare criticism is decidedly for its own age, of lasting importance only to the scholar who wrote it. Students today read the criticism most readily available to them, which means essays printed in recent books and journals, especially those journals made available on the Internet. Older criticism is too often buried in out-of-print books on forgotten shelves of libraries or in defunct periodicals. Therefore, many students, particularly younger students, have no way of knowing that some of the most profound criticism of Shakespeare's plays was written decades or centuries ago. We hope this series remedies that problem, and more importantly, we hope it infuses students with the enthusiasm of the critics in these volumes for the beauty and power of Shakespeare's plays.

INTRODUCTION BY HAROLD BLOOM

❧

The Life of Henry the Fifth does not enjoy much critical esteem in comparison with Shakespeare's other mature histories, but it is a remarkable play if one allows its ironies their full scope. The absence of Falstaff is the largest presence in this drama, since Hal is thereby absent also. Patriotic bombast abounds, and even a touch of Falstaff (or Hal) would destroy that rhetoric of gorgeous deception essential to the celebration of English prowess against the overdressed French. If we shipped Falstaff from Shrewsbury to Agincourt and the fat knight went into the battle there, carrying a bottle of sack instead of a pistol in his case or holster, would not the play break apart? *Henry V* can scarcely sustain its few overt references to Falstaff and dares not bring him on stage even to die before us. "The King has kill'd his heart," says Mistress Quickly, and the otherwise hyperbolical Pistol adds, in all truth: "His heart is fracted and corroborate." I do not read that last word as an error for "corrupted," but as a sad indication that Falstaff so loves Hal that he has agreed to his own rejection and so wills to die.

Nothing else in *Henry V* touches the sublimity and pathos of Mistress Quickly and Falstaff's followers recounting his final moments:

Bardolph: Would I were with him, wheresome'er he is, either in heaven or in hell!
Hostess: Nay sure, he's not in hell; he's in Arthur's bosom, if ever man went to Arthur's bosom. 'A made a finer end, and went away and it had been any christom child. 'A parted ev'n just between twelve and one, ev'n at the turning o' th' tide; for after I saw him fumble with the sheets, and play with flowers, and smile upon his finger's end, I knew there was but one way; for his nose was as sharp as a pen, and 'a [babbl'd] of green fields. "How now, Sir John?" quoth I, "what, man? be a' good cheer." So 'a cried out, "God, God, God!" three or four times. Now I, to comfort him, bid him 'a should not think of God; I hop'd there was no need to trouble himself with any such thoughts yet. So 'a bade me lay more clothes on

his feet. I put my hand into the bed and felt them, and they were as cold as any stone; then I felt to his knees, and so up'ard and up'ard, and all was as cold as any stone.

Nym: They say he cried out of sack.

Hostess: Ay, that 'a did.

Bardolph: And of women.

Hostess: Nay, that 'a did not.

Boy: Yes, that 'a did, and said they were dev'ls incarnate.

Hostess: 'A could never abide carnation—'twas a color he never lik'd.

Boy: 'A said once, the dev'l would have him about women.

Hostess: 'A did in some sort, indeed, handle women; but then he was rheumatic, and talk'd of the whore of Babylon.

Boy: Do you not remember, 'a saw a flea stick upon Bardolph's nose, and 'a said it was a black soul burning in hell?

Bardolph: Well, the fuel is gone that maintain'd that fire. That's all the riches I got in his service.

>   (2.3.7–44)

This is a broken Falstaff, facing the four last things of death, judgment, heaven, and hell, not as Dives, the purple-clad glutton of Luke 16:22ff., but as a beggar and a child, playing with flowers, smiling in a second innocence, and poignantly crying out against sack and women—but in vain, for who can envision Sir John Falstaff without a wench and a bottle? The boy reminds us of the knight's preternatural wit and its butt, Bardolph, reminds us of his master's hand-to-mouth economy of existence. Does Mistress Quickly's "rheumatic" mean "lunatic," and does the greatest of wits die as his true descendant Oscar Wilde died, as a repentent sinner, near madness? I think not. Rather, Shakespeare gives us an outrageous Falstaff, who dies as he has lived, but in a finer tone, his bed crowded with apocalyptic visions, not of Doll Tearsheet, but of the Whore of Babylon. She is the emblem of royal power, of every earthly tyranny however popular, and so a version of the goddess of war. That Falstaff, ironic subverter of royal pomp and power, should die discoursing about her is a very oblique but highly apposite commentary upon the royal crusade of Henry V against France.

If that seems excessive, since Henry V manifestly is a patriotic hero, precursor to the great Elizabeth, then consider the king's threats to Harfleur, complete with "naked infants spitted upon pikes," and his fairly consistent record of systematic brutality, including a shrugging-off that sends poor Bardolph, an old crony, to execution. No, Shakespeare knew better what he did than we tend to acknowledge, and his portrait of Henry V is both ironic and celebratory, but not in a balance. If you are Rudyard Kipling, then Henry V is a demigod of war, victory, splendor, and British superiority, but if you are William Hazlitt, then the great warrior is "a very amiable monster." He is an exemplary Christian king, hard and shrewd, who murders prisoners without remorse and seems to see through everything and everyone, himself presumably included. But that returns us to one of Shakespeare's greatest powers, the representation of change in the psyche. Long after he has rejected his teacher Falstaff, Hal benefits from the great ironist's lesson, which is to keep your freedom by seeing through every idea of order or code of moral behavior. Poor Falstaff was right to babble of the Whore of Babylon, because his pupil ends as a more efficient Bolingbroke, free of his father's guilt—a new and greater Fortinbras rather than another Hamlet.

Still, if we can see the Earl of Essex in the character of Fortinbras or Henry V, though not in Hamlet, then the hero of Shakespeare's play might as well have been Essex had not Essex come to a very bad end. Hamlet and Falstaff are counter-Machiavels, but Henry V is the perfect prince as sketched by Machiavelli. So large and profound are Shakespeare's ironies that Henry V in the context of his own play could not be bettered as a hero. His play is anything but a critique of the hero. The world without Falstaff is not a world without imagination, but its largest being, Henry V, is only as large as life. Henry V is not how meaning gets started. He does not overflow, has no excess of vitality that can give more life to others. But he knows always exactly what he says and what he does, as he knew exactly what he was doing when he banished Falstaff, and Prince Hal with him.

As in the much greater *Antony and Cleopatra*, Shakespeare lets you read yourself in him without seeking to alter you, whoever you are. If you are a reductionist, then Antony is in his dotage and Cleopatra is and will be always what she was, an imperial strumpet. If you yield to imagination, then Antony is a more generous Hercules and Cleopatra a prophetess of the Sublime, who fuses herself into her own immortal longings. So is it in *Henry V*; the reduction gets the ideal warrior-king, while the person who knows that the imagination wishes to be indulged ends with a nostalgia for the young man who sojourned in the taverns and on the highways with Falstaff. That sojourn was itself Machiavellian, a counterfeiting that taught excellence in counterfeiting, but the playgoer or reader learns what Henry V could not afford to know, which is that "to die is to be a counterfeit . . . but to counterfeit dying, when a man thereby liveth, is to be no counterfeit, but the true and perfect image of life indeed," which is to be Falstaff.

BIOGRAPHY OF WILLIAM SHAKESPEARE

William Shakespeare was born in Stratford-on-Avon in April 1564 into a family of some prominence. His father, John Shakespeare, was a glover and merchant of leather goods, who earned enough to marry the daughter of his father's landlord, Mary Arden, in 1557. John Shakespeare was a prominent citizen in Stratford, and at one point, he served as an alderman and bailiff.

Shakespeare presumably attended the Stratford grammar school, where he would have received an education in Latin, but he did not go on to either Oxford or Cambridge universities. Little is recorded about Shakespeare's early life; indeed, the first record of his life after his christening is of his marriage to Anne Hathaway in 1582 in the church at Temple Grafton, near Stratford. He would have been required to obtain a special license from the bishop as security that there was no impediment to the marriage. Peter Alexander states in his book *Shakespeare's Life and Art* that marriage at this time in England required neither a church nor a priest or, for that matter, even a document—only a declaration of the contracting parties in the presence of witnesses. Thus, it was customary, though not mandatory, to follow the marriage with a church ceremony.

Little is known about William and Anne Shakespeare's marriage. Their first child, Susanna, was born in May 1583, and twins, Hamnet and Judith Shakespeare, in 1585. Later on, Susanna married Dr. John Hall, but the younger daughter, Judith, remained unmarried. When Hamnet died in Stratford in 1596, the boy was only eleven years old.

We have no record of Shakespeare's activities for the seven years after the birth of his twins, but by 1592 he was in London working as an actor. He was also apparently well-known as a playwright, for reference is made of him by his contemporary, Robert Greene, in *A Groatsworth of Wit*, as "an upstart crow."

Several companies of actors were in London at this time. Shakespeare may have had connection with one or more of them before 1592, but we have no record that tells us definitely. However, we do know of his long association with the most famous and successful troupe, the Lord Chamberlain's Men. (When James I came to the throne in 1603, after Elizabeth's death, the troupe's name changed to the King's Men.) In 1599 the Lord Chamberlain's Men provided the financial backing for the construction of their own theatre, the Globe.

The Globe was begun by a carpenter named James Burbage and finished by his two sons, Cuthbert and Robert. To escape the jurisdiction of the Corporation of London, which was composed of conservative Puritans who opposed the theatre's "licentiousness," James Burbage built the Globe just outside London, in the Liberty of Holywell, beside Finsbury Fields. This also meant that the Globe was safer from the threats that lurked in London's crowded streets, like plague and other diseases, as well as rioting mobs. When James Burbage died in 1597, his sons completed the Globe's construction. Shakespeare played a vital role, financially and otherwise, in the construction of the theater, which was finally occupied some time before May 16, 1599.

Shakespeare not only acted with the Globe's company of actors, he was also a shareholder and eventually became the troupe's most important playwright. The company included London's most famous actors, who inspired the creation of some of Shakespeare's best-known characters, such as Hamlet and Lear, as well as his clowns and fools.

In his early years, however, Shakespeare did not confine himself to the theatre. He also composed some mythological-erotic poetry, such as *Venus and Adonis* and *The Rape of Lucrece*, both of which were dedicated to the earl of Southampton. Shakespeare was successful enough that in 1597 he was able to purchase his own home in Stratford, which he called New Place. He could even call himself a gentleman, for his father had been granted a coat of arms.

By 1598 Shakespeare had written some of his most famous works, *Romeo and Juliet, The Comedy of Errors, A Midsummer Night's Dream, The Merchant of Venice, Two Gentleman of Verona*, and *Love's Labour's Lost*, as well as his historical plays *Richard II, Richard III, Henry IV*, and *King John*. Somewhere around the turn of the century, Shakespeare wrote his romantic comedies, *As You Like It, Twelfth Night*, and *Much Ado about Nothing*, as well as *Henry V*, the last of his history plays in the Prince Hal series. During the next ten years he wrote his great tragedies, *Hamlet, Macbeth, Othello, King Lear*, and *Antony and Cleopatra*.

At this time, the theatre was burgeoning in London; the public took an avid interest in drama, the audiences were large, the plays demonstrated an enormous range of subjects, and playwrights competed for approval. By 1613, however, the rising tide of Puritanism had changed the theatre. With the desertion of the theatres by the middle classes, the acting companies were compelled to depend more on the aristocracy, which also meant that they now had to cater to a more sophisticated audience.

Perhaps this change in London's artistic atmosphere contributed to Shakespeare's reasons for leaving London after 1612. His retirement from the theatre is sometimes thought to be evidence that his artistic skills were waning. During this time, however, he wrote *The Tempest* and *Henry VIII*. He also wrote the "tragicomedies," *Pericles, Cymbeline*, and *The Winter's Tale*. These were thought to be inspired by Shakespeare's personal problems, and have sometimes been considered proof of his greatly diminished abilities.

However, so far as biographical facts indicate, the circumstances of his life at this time do not imply any personal problems. He was in good health, financially secure, and enjoyed an excellent reputation. Indeed, although he was settled in Stratford at this time, he made frequent visits to London, enjoying and participating in events at the royal court, directing rehearsals, and attending to other business matters.

In addition to his brilliant and enormous contributions to the theatre, Shakespeare remained a poetic genius throughout the years, publishing a renowned and critically acclaimed sonnet cycle in 1609 (most of the sonnets were written many years earlier). Shakespeare's contribution to this popular poetic genre are all the more amazing in his break with contemporary notions of subject matter. Shakespeare idealized the beauty of man as an object of praise and devotion (rather than the Petrarchan tradition of the idealized, unattainable woman). In the same spirit of breaking with tradition, Shakespeare also treated themes which hitherto had been considered off limits—the dark, sexual side of a woman as opposed to the Petrarchan ideal of a chaste and remote love object. He also expanded the sonnet's emotional range, including such emotions as delight, pride, shame, disgust, sadness, and fear.

When Shakespeare died in 1616, no collected edition of his works had ever been published, although some of his plays had been printed in separate unauthorized editions. (Some of these were taken from his manuscripts, some from the actors' prompt books, and others were reconstructed from memory by actors or spectators.) In 1623, two members of the King's Men, John Hemings and Henry Condell, published a collection of all the plays they considered to be authentic, the First Folio.

Included in the First Folio is a poem by Shakespeare's contemporary Ben Jonson, an outstanding playwright and critic in his own right. Jonson paid tribute to Shakespeare's genius, proclaiming his superiority to what previously had been held as the models for literary excellence—the Greek and Latin writers. "Triumph, my Britain, thou hast one to show / To whom all scenes of Europe homage owe. / He was not of an age, but for all time!"

Jonson was the first to state what has been said so many times since. Having captured what is permanent and universal to all human beings at all times, Shakespeare's genius continues to inspire us—and the critical debate about his works never ceases.

Summary of Henry V

Act 1

Henry V opens with the appearance of a Chorus, a typically male character who returns to preface each act. He provides a patriotic voice and an idealistic view of Henry V throughout the play. During his initial appearance, he concentrates on the inadequacy of the dramatic arts, belittling the stage on which such a noble figure as Henry V and such a noble action as the English success at Agincourt are to be portrayed, as well as the inability of the actors to cram two kingdoms and two armies' soldiers into the "wooden O" that is the stage of the playhouse. To make up for the defects of the theater and the performers, the audience is encouraged to use its imagination and "deck our kings, / Carry them here and there, jumping o'er times, / Turning accomplishment of many years / Into an hour-glass." The Chorus aids the audience's imagining of the historical lives portrayed before them and allows Shakespeare to introduce elements of Henry V's history that the limitations of the stage would not permit him to include.

Scene 1 opens in the second year of Henry V's reign and serves to reintroduce us to the character of the king, whom Shakespeare last presented when Henry assumed the throne at the end of *Henry IV, Part 2*. The king does not appear onstage, but the contrast between his youthful wildness and his royal seriousness is described as the Archbishop of Canterbury and the Bishop of Ely discuss a bill that had originally been proposed during Henry IV's reign and that is now set to be voted on in Parliament.

If the bill is passed, temporal lands, that is, lands that have been bequeathed to and used by the church to earn money through secular means, will be seized to raise funds not only to aid in the defense of the kingdom but also to help its most impoverished members. The religious leaders are, of course, opposed to the bill and hope that they can count on the king to prevent it from being enacted. It is within this context that Henry V is described as a "lover of the church" even though "The courses of his youth promised it not. / The breath no sooner left his father's body, / But that his wildness, mortified in him, / Seem'd to die too."

Canterbury goes on to praise the king's accomplishments in divinity and policy as well as to describe his former follies in more detail. As the conversation progresses, however, another contrast—between acting in good faith or in one's self-interest, irrespective of the consequences—begins to reveal itself.

When he had discussed the issue of the bill with the king, Canterbury had appealed not to Henry's love of the church to prevent the seizure of its lands but to Henry's need for funds, offering a greater donation to the realm than any religious figure in England had ever offered. Henry, at least in Canterbury's mind, suggested that helping justify the planned invasion of France might also be useful. Canterbury was eager to oblige him but had been interrupted by the French ambassador's petition for an audience with the king.

In the scene, Canterbury seems to serve as a counter-chorus, one that more successfully sets the tone of the play, for he simultaneously presents Henry V as an ideal—"the mirror of all Christian kings," as the Chorus describes him in act 2—while at the same time suggesting that he is a self-serving hypocrite, someone willing to offer rewards for being told what he wants to hear.

Scene 2 opens with the king searching for Canterbury, whom he will see before giving an interview to the French ambassador. The issue Henry wants resolved is whether or not France's Salic law, which bars women (and those whose claim to the throne derives from a maternal line, as Henry's does, from Phillip IV of France's daughter Isabella, who was the mother of Edward III of England) from taking the French throne. He warns Canterbury to "justly and religiously unfold" the truth, contradicting the suggestion Canterbury had made in the previous scene that he is more concerned with having his claim legitimized, although the first scene may suggest that Henry's virtue here is part of a performance. Canterbury's argument, in any case, apparently will determine whether or not Henry invades France.

Canterbury denies the legitimacy of the Salic law, first asserting that Salic is in Germany between Sala and Elbe, where Charles the Great, or Charlemagne, set up a French settlement and established the law to prevent the progeny of German women from assuming the throne. Furthermore, the archbishop goes on to argue, the legendary Pharamond, whom the French claim established the law, reigned more than 400 years before the French came to possess the land of Salic. Finally, other French kings—Pepin, Hugh Capet, Louis IX, as well as the present-day kings—have legitimized their claim through maternal descent.

Henry again asks if he may claim the French throne in good conscience, and Canterbury further asserts that the book of Numbers states, "When a man dies, let the inheritance, / Descend unto the daughter." He urges the king to claim his right and follow the warlike example of Edward III, who had waged successful war against the French. Ely, the duke of Exeter, and the earl of Westmorland join Canterbury in pressing the proposed action. Henry then raises the issue of the Scottish, who must first be defeated if France is to be claimed, and

Canterbury advises that the English forces be divided into four quarters, with one segment of them sent to France, while the others remain home to defend England's border, a plan Henry seems to accept.

Having settled the issue over his right to France, Henry calls in the French ambassadors, who have been sent by the Dauphin, the French king's heir. After being given leave to relate their message without fear, they present to Henry a barrel of tennis balls, a gift the Dauphin offers in lieu of the French dukedoms that Henry has already claimed as rightfully his. The frivolity of the gift is meant to comment on the frivolity of Henry's youthful reputation. Playing tennis, the French suggest, is a more suitable activity for the king than demanding dukedoms in France.

The king is measured in his reply at first, but he grows more intense as it proceeds. He thanks the Dauphin for the gift and acknowledges the "barbarous license" of his youth, attributing it to his being away from home, that is, in France, alluding to the proverb, "Don't foul your own nest." He warns that he will now keep his state and "Be like a king and shew my sail of greatness," specifically when he invades France and comes to possess the French crown. The act concludes with Henry urging his nobles to prepare everything that will be needed for the impending French campaign.

Act 2

The Chorus—transporting the audience from London, the setting of the first act, to Southampton, where Henry holds his council, and then on to France—describes England as a unified body with all of its members "on fire" in preparation for the coming war. The speech soon turns to dissent, though, revealing that the French, worried about England's strength, has paid traitors—Richard Earl of Cambridge, Henry Lord Scroop of Masham, and Sir Thomas Grey—to kill Henry and end the conflict before it begins.

Scene 1, concluding the action occurring in London, takes place in Eastcheap, the area where Henry earned his reputation for wildness. The associates of Falstaff, Henry's former companion, make their first appearance near where the famous tavern scenes take place in *Henry IV, Parts 1* and *2*. Corporal Nym and Lieutenant Bardolph first take the stage, discussing the conflict between Nym and Pistol over Nell Quickly, the hostess of the tavern. Bardolph wants to heal the rift between the two, which has arisen because Nym had been betrothed to Hostess Quickly, but she married Pistol instead. Pistol and the Hostess enter, and he and Nym, after sparring verbally, draw their swords and prepare to fight. Bardolph, however, stops them, drawing his sword and threatening to kill the first man to make a move.

The scene belies the vision of an England unified in its preparation for war with France by showing conflict already among those heading off to it. Such divisions and rivalries will appear throughout. The present one is resolved not by the soldiers' desire to follow their king but by the appearance of the Boy, Falstaff's page, who announces that Falstaff is sick and bedridden. The event reminds the audience of the cruelty Henry had shown when he rejected Falstaff, a point that is emphasized more strongly when Hostess Quickly, concluding the scene, notes, "The King has killed his heart."

Scene 2 shifts the setting to Southampton and opens with Exeter, Westmorland, and the duke of Bedford discussing the king's knowledge of Cambridge, Scroop, and Grey's treachery. The planned assassination of the king will not be successful, though Bedford is surprised at the apparent trust Henry continues to place in the three traitors.

Henry enters with Cambridge, Scroop, and Grey and asks about their thoughts on England's prospect for victory in France. Scroop replies that victory is certain "if each man do his best." Henry, mirroring the chorus, expresses certainty that such will be the case, for all English hearts are one with his own, a sentiment that Cambridge and Grey echo. Even here, there is evidence of discord among the English: Henry tells Exeter to free a man who had been arrested the day before for railing against the king.

Cambridge, Scroop, and Grey object to Henry showing the prisoner mercy, warning that such leniency may encourage others to question his authority. Henry is exposing their hypocrisy, before revealing to them that he is aware that they are in league with the French. Henry, after insisting the man should be pardoned, states that he is ready to name his commissioners and hands Scroop, Cambridge, and Grey papers, which they think are their commissions but which reveal that he has evidence of their intention to assassinate him. They appeal for mercy, but Henry, noting their recent calls for harshness, denies them any, observing that they deserve death not for their crimes against him personally—as the crimes of the man who was pardoned were—but for their crimes against the kingdom, which would have become subjected to the French had they succeeded.

Scene 3 returns the action to Eastcheap. Falstaff is dead, and Hostess Quickly describes his passing. (See the "Key Passages" section for the full speech and detailed commentary.) Framing the scene in which Henry uncovers treason with scenes announcing Falstaff's sickness and death is an odd choice in a play that, at least as the Chorus portrays it, is about the glorification of Henry V. The king had noted in his condemnation of the three conspirators that they were among his most trusted friends, while Falstaff had placed his trust just as strongly in Henry. Our view of the actions of the three conspirators is thus colored by the reminder that Henry has formerly renounced his friendship with Falstaff. Self-interest, even for the king, may be more important than the bonds of friendship.

Scene 4 takes place in the French court. The French king, Charles VI, orders his dukes, Berry, Britain, Brabant, and Orleans, as well as the Dauphin, to prepare for the defense of his realm. The Dauphin, while agreeing with the wisdom of his father's decision to prepare for the worst, discounts the threat Henry poses, asserting that he is a capricious ruler who they need not take seriously. The Constable, Charles Delabreth, contradicts the Dauphin, noting the change that Henry has undergone, a transformation made evident by his treatment of the French ambassador in act 1. The Dauphin maintains his position, but Charles remains cautious. He recalls the battle of Cressy, when Edward, the Black Prince of Wales, defeated the French as his father, Edward III, watched; Charles fears that Henry, who comes from the same bloodline as the Black Prince, is as dangerous as his ancestor.

The scene concludes with Charles giving an audience to Exeter, who is serving as an English ambassador. Exeter, using an argument that mirrors others that Henry makes, tells the French king to give up his throne or he will be responsible for the blood that will be shed on the battlefield. Charles promises to give his answer the next day. Exeter then turns to the Dauphin, informing him that he will regret mocking the king with the barrel of tennis balls. Finally, Exeter tells the king to give his answer quickly because Henry and his forces have already arrived in France.

Act 3

The Chorus, asking the audience to imagine what cannot be shown, describes the English forces boarding the ships, sailing across the English Channel, and arriving at Harfleur in France. The French king's answer to Henry's demand for him to give up his crown is also revealed. Henry has been offered Charles's daughter Katherine and "Some petty and unprofitable dukedoms." The offer is rejected, and the war begins.

Scene 1 opens in the middle of the battle for Harfleur. The English have already breached the wall and been beaten back. Henry cries "Once more unto the breach . . ." (See the "Key Passages" section for the full speech and detailed commentary) and urges his men to fight on, appealing to the example of their fathers, who "like so many Alexanders / Have in these parts from morn till even fought," and to the honor of their mothers.

Scene 2 takes places at another part of the field. Bardolph, echoing the king, urges Nym, Pistol, and the Boy to the breach, but his command is countered by Nym, who says he would rather live than die. The boy proclaims he would rather be in an alehouse in London. Captain Fluellen arrives and sends them into battle, leaving the Boy behind to denounce Bardolph, Pistol, and Nym as thieves and cowards and to declare his intention of finding a better master.

Captain Gower then meets Fluellen, telling him to go to the mines—tunnels that the English dug under Harfleur's walls during the siege—where Gloucester needs to speak with him. The request prompts Fluellen to denounce the value of creating the tunnels, as the French have created their own underground network. Gower blames the strategy on the Irishman Captain Macmorris, who is responsible for devising it. As Fluellen denounces Macmorris, Macmorris enters with Captain Jamy, a Scotsman, for whom Fluellen shows respect. The two have been forced to retreat from the mines, something Macmorris blames on the bad management of the project. An argument breaks out, again undermining the unified vision of Henry's forces that the Chorus has presented, when Fluellen refers to Macmorris's nation. Macmorris asks, "What ish my nation," challenging anyone who would suggest he is not a member of Henry V's realm. The need to fight the French, in the end, unites the four characters and, by extension, the four realms—England, Wales, Scotland, and Ireland. Still, the underlying tension remains as the scene closes with Fluellen promising to take up the matter when there is a better opportunity.

Scene 3 stages the surrender of Harfleur, beginning with the appearance of the French on the walls. Henry says the parley that the French have sought will be the last one that he will hold and promises that if he must renew the fight, he will burn Harfleur to the ground. He further warns that he will not be able to contain his men, who will slaughter the innocent and force themselves on the town's women. The blame will rest with the men of Harfleur, he goes on to assert, and urges them to surrender to avoid their destruction. The governor agrees, blaming the Dauphin's unpreparedness for their defeat, and the English enter the town.

Scene 4, which is largely in French, introduces the audience to Katherine, Charles's daughter, who is being taught English by an old gentlewoman, Alice.

The perspective of the French is again shown in scene 5. Charles, who is holding court at Rouen, reveals that Henry has already passed the Somme River on his march toward Calais. The noblemen present, as well as the Dauphin, express shock at the effectiveness of the British. The Dauphin and the Duke of Britain go on to observe that the women have begun to mock the French, saying "they will give / Their bodies to the lust of English youth" and "bid us to the English dancing-schools." The king is more focused on what is to be done, ordering his noblemen to stop Henry, whose forces, the Lord Constable says, have been depleted, while the soldiers that remain are ill and famished.

Scene 6 presents a skirmish between the English and the French as Henry's army crosses a river. Fluellen informs Gower of the valor of Exeter, who has been aided by Pistol, in defending the bridge the British must use. Gower says he does not know Pistol, who at that point appears on the scene. Pistol asks Fluellen to intercede with Exeter on behalf of Bardolph, who has stolen a pax—a religious object often depicting the Crucifixion and made of gold or another precious material—and has been sentenced to death. Fluellen refuses Pistol's request, praising the justice of the sentence and observing that executing Bardolph will instill discipline in the troops. Gower finally recalls Pistol, telling Fluellen that he is a thief and a coward who has merely come to France for the opportunities that having been a soldier will afford him in London upon his return.

The exchange is followed by the entrance of Henry, who learns from Fluellen the outcome of the skirmish, a victory that Exeter has secured without losing a man. Fluellen, however, treats Bardolph as a casualty, remarking that he has been condemned to death for "robbing a church." Henry acknowledges the justice of the sentence, adding that any other soldiers found to be stealing or abusing the French people should also be executed so that the French do not come to regard the English as cruel conquerors.

The scene concludes with a meeting between Henry and Montjoy, the French herald, who informs Henry that the French will now meet him with all their power and that he should consider the price of his ransom—what he will pay the French king to allow him and his army to return home without having to engage the French in further battle. The ransom will have to be enough, Montjoy explains, to make up not only for all that France has lost but also for the shame it has endured while incurring those losses.

Henry, expressing a desire not to fight until he reaches Calais, confirms Lord Constable's account of the weakness of the English, though he insists that they will meet the French forces and defeat them. After Montjoy departs, Gloucester expresses a wish that the French wait to attack, as Henry asserts, "We are in God's hand, brother, not theirs."

Scene 7 takes place the night before the battle of Agincourt in the French camp. The Constable, Orleans, and the Dauphin discuss the value of their armor and horses as they eagerly wait for morning, when they expect to slaughter the English, who are only 1,500 paces from the French camp and who, as the Constable says, are not eagerly anticipating the dawn. The contrast between Henry's frivolity before he assumed the throne and his behavior since becoming king is now reflected in the contrast between the frivolous French army, the first to be appear onstage in the buildup to Agincourt, and the English army, which arrives on the scene at the beginning of the next act.

Act 4

The Chorus, reiterating the close proximity of the two camps and confirming the overconfidence of the French, discusses the mood of the English camp, noting that the soldiers are sitting quietly by their fires, ruefully awaiting the morning like "So many horrid Ghosts." Henry, meanwhile, goes from tent to tent to lift the spirits of his men, perhaps in the disguise he assumes in the act, and the Chorus promises that we will soon see "A little touch of Harry in the night," that is, the king mixing with the common people on equal footing.

Scene 1 opens with Henry discussing the situation with Gloucester and Bedford, but the king does not express regret for placing his army in such danger and instead explains that the immensity of the threat should only increase their courage. Thomas Erpingham appears, assuring Henry that he is content to be in France rather than at home, and Henry borrows Erpingham's cloak, telling the others to gather all the princes in his tent so that he can be alone for a few moments.

Now in disguise, Henry proceeds to mingle with the common soldiers, first meeting Pistol, who professes love for Henry, though in terms that suggest he is thinking of the madcap prince rather than the serious king. Henry gives his name as Harry le Roy, French for "the king," and says that he is Welsh, which leads Pistol to ask about Fluellen, whom he promises to attack with the leek that Fluellen will be wearing on St. Davy's Day, the festival of the patron Saint of Wales. Henry claims kinship with Fluellen, and Pistol curses him and exits. Henry then overhears Fluellen telling Gower the proper rules of war, as gleaned from his study of "the wars of Pompey." Henry, while acknowledging Fluellen's pedantic nature, praises his valor.

The heart of the scene takes place after the arrival of three soldiers, John Bates, Alexander Court, and Michael Williams, with whom Henry engages in debate. These soldiers most clearly illustrate the anxiety of the English, as they suggest that they will not likely be alive by the day's end and wish they were in England. Bates also complains about the unwillingness of Henry to be ransomed, an act that would save lives, and Williams declares that the king will be responsible for the souls of those who die and should answer for their sins at Judgment Day. Henry discounts the validity of Williams's line of reasoning, even though it bears a resemblance to arguments that he has used earlier in the play, particularly when he was warning Canterbury to be honest about the justness of his claim to the throne. Williams, in any case, acquiesces to Henry's point but goes on to say that the king, despite his denials, will allow himself to be ransomed when his soldiers are lying dead and the battle has been lost. Henry replies that if the king allows himself to be ransomed, he will never trust a word the king says thereafter, a statement that leads William to mock him. The two then exchange gloves, and Williams promises to give Henry a box in the ear the next day.

Left alone on the stage, Henry delivers his only soliloquy (See the "Key Passages" section for the full speech and detailed commentary), a speech in which he addresses the burdens subjects place on monarchs. Erpingham enters and calls to Henry, who says he will shortly go to his tent and meet with his nobles.

Left alone again, Henry prays for God to give his soldiers strength and to forget "the fault / My father made in compassing the crown," that is, Henry IV's usurpation of Richard II. Showing contrition for his father's misdeeds, Henry has given Richard II the respect he deserved—giving him a proper burial and providing money to the poor to pray for him daily—and now promises to do more.

Scene 2 takes place in the French camp the next morning. The Dauphin, Orleans, and the Constable are again praising their horses, and a messenger arrives to tell them that the English have taken the field. After more boasting about their certain victory, they head off to battle.

Scene 3 returns the action to the more somber English camp, where the English noblemen await the arrival of their king. Westmoreland points out that there are 60,000 French, making them outnumbered, Exeter says, five to one. Westmoreland, just as Henry is arriving, wishes that there were an additional 10,000 Englishmen with them, and Henry remarks, "No, my fair cousin: / If we are marked to die, we are enough / To do our country loss, and if to live, / The fewer men, the greater share of honour." He goes on to proclaim that any man who "hath no stomach to fight" may leave the field, for he would not die in such a man's company.

Henry then delivers the St. Crispin Day speech, exclaiming that those who live to tell how the English defeated the French will be remembered for their deeds on St. Crispin's Day each year. (See the "Key Passages" section for the full speech and detailed commentary.) Salisbury arrives to hurry the king into battle, but before they can go, Montjoy appears, again asking Henry if he would like to admit defeat and pay a ransom. Henry refuses, and after giving York the command of the vanguard, prays: "And how thou pleases, God, dispose the day!"

In scene 4, Pistol subdues a French soldier, Le Fer, who speaks no English, and threatens to kill him, unless he pays a ransom, a message he is able to get across with the help of the Boy. Le Fer, in direct contrast to Henry V, agrees to give Pistol 200 crowns if Pistol spares his life. As the scene closes, the Boy condemns Pistol as a coward—an observation that emphasizes the failure of the French, since we have just seen Pistol procure a ransom for the safety of Le Fer—and notes that Bardolph and Nym, who has also been executed, were braver.

In scene 5 the Constable, Orleans, Bourbon, the Dauphin, and Rambures meet on the battlefield, lamenting the disarray of the French forces and the fact that they appear to have lost the day. Bourbon proclaims that it would be better to die in battle than to live with the shame they have suffered. Orleans argues that they could still, if order could be returned to their forces, smother the English with French corpses, to which Bourbon replies, "The devil take order now! I'll to the throng. / Let life be short, else shame will be too long."

Exeter reports the deaths of York and Suffolk to Henry in scene 6. An alarum is sounded from the French, indicating that they are regrouping their men, and Henry orders that all the prisoners be killed.

In scene 7, Fluellen and Gower report that some of the French fleeing the battle have killed, against the law of arms, the boys transporting the luggage, stealing and burning it, as the Boy had predicted they would. Gower explains that Henry ordered that the prisoners be killed in retaliation for that crime, and Fluellen proceeds to offer a comparison between Henry and Alexander the Great, which he concludes by noting that Alexander killed "his best friend Cleitus." Gower objects that Henry is not like Alexander in that respect, but Fluellen reminds him that Henry turned away Falstaff, thereby recalling Hostess Quickly's declaration that the king killed Falstaff's heart.

Henry enters with Bourbon, being held prisoner, and complains about French horsemen who remain on a hill but who refuse to engage the English or leave the field. Angry, Henry orders someone to ride up to them and demand that they fight or flee, promising to cut the throats of his prisoners and bring the fight to them if they do neither. Montjoy, however, arrives to ask permission to collect the French dead and sort the commoners from the nobility and assures Henry that the battle has been won. Fluellen proceeds to remind Henry of his ancestors' victories in France, as well as the part the Welsh had played in them and the fact that the Welsh had fought for the English in a leek garden, which is why the leek is a symbol of a Welsh soldier.

Williams then appears, and Henry asks about the glove Williams is wearing and is told about the swaggering soldier with whom Williams exchanged words and the promise that he made. Sending Williams to find Gower, Henry gives Fluellen the other glove and explains that it was taken from Duke Alencon and that anyone who challenges him for wearing it should be arrested. After dispatching Fluellen to find Gower, Henry sends Gloucester and Warwick after him to make sure no one is harmed when Williams and Fluellen meet.

Williams and Fluellen encounter each other in scene 8. Williams strikes the Welshman. As Fluellen accuses Williams of treason, Henry arrives and informs Williams that it was he who had been abused the night before. Taking the glove, Henry has Exeter fill it with coins and return it to Williams. Fluellen offers twelve pence more, though Williams refuses to take it.

A herald enters with a paper that lists the number of French dead, 10,000 in all. The English losses, by contrast, include only four noblemen and twenty-five others. Henry, however, asks his men not to take pride in the victory and proclaims that any man boasting of it will be executed. God deserves the praise for England's success.

Act 5

The Chorus explains that from Agincourt Henry goes to Calais and then home to England, where he is met on the beach and in London by throngs of people who celebrate his triumphant return. The event is compared to what will happen when Robert Devereux, Earl of Essex, returns victorious from Ireland, where he was sent in March 1399 to repress Tyrone's rebellion. (Essex, however, returned defeated in September 1399.) The Chorus goes on to note that Henry would return to France, although it leaves the false impression that he remained in England until his meeting with the French king in 1420, which is dramatized in scene 2 of the act. Henry was in France for much of the English campaigns between 1417 and 1419.

Scene 1 opens with Gower and Fluellen discussing the Welsh tradition of placing leeks in their hats on St. Davy's Day, which took place the previous day. Fluellen is still wearing his because Pistol had mocked the tradition, demanding that Fluellen eat the leek he was wearing. Having been unable to confront Pistol when the incident had occurred, Fluellen decides to wear his leek until he sees Pistol again.

Pistol enters and again mocks the leek, which Fluellen now orders him to eat. Pistol refuses, and Fluellen beats him with a cudgel until he eats it. Left alone onstage, Pistol reveals that Hostess Quickly has died of the "malady of France," that is, a venereal disease, and that he will now return to England, again become a thief, and brag about how the wounds Fluellen gave him were received in battle.

Scene 2 stages the negotiations of peace between England and France. The Duke of Burgundy observes that France, "this best garden of the world," has been left untended in the war and needs peace to reign in order for the nation to become productive again. Henry promises peace as soon as the French king meets his demand, which Charles says he will need to examine more closely. Henry allows his nobles to go with Charles to negotiate the terms of the treaty and remains alone with Charles's daughter, Katherine, whom he calls "our capital demand." Despite knowing that Katherine will be required to marry him, Henry woos her, quite clumsily in fact, asking her to teach him terms "Such as will enter at a lady's ear." She eventually accepts his marriage proposal, on the condition that her father agrees to the match. Charles returns, peace having been established, and the act concludes with Henry declaring "Prepare we for our marriage."

The Chorus then appears and delivers the epilogue, explaining that Henry VI, who became king of England and France while still an infant, lost everything his father had won due to the mismanagement of his affairs. Civil war then broke out in England.

KEY PASSAGES IN HENRY V

Prologue to act 1, 1–35

Chorus: O for a Muse of fire, that would ascend
The brightest heaven of invention,
A kingdom for a stage, princes to act
And monarchs to behold the swelling scene!
Then should the warlike Harry, like himself,
Assume the port of Mars; and at his heels,
Leash'd in like hounds, should famine, sword and fire
Crouch for employment. But pardon, and gentles all,
The flat unraised spirits that have dared
On this unworthy scaffold to bring forth
So great an object: can this cockpit hold
The vasty fields of France? or may we cram
Within this wooden O the very casques
That did affright the air at Agincourt?
O, pardon! since a crooked figure may
Attest in little place a million;
And let us, ciphers to this great accompt,
On your imaginary forces work.
Suppose within the girdle of these walls
Are now confined two mighty monarchies,
Whose high upreared and abutting fronts
The perilous narrow ocean parts asunder:
Piece out our imperfections with your thoughts;
Into a thousand parts divide one man,
And make imaginary puissance;
Think when we talk of horses, that you see them
Printing their proud hoofs i' the receiving earth;
For 'tis your thoughts that now must deck our kings,
Carry them here and there; jumping o'er times,
Turning the accomplishment of many years

Into an hour-glass: for the which supply,
Admit me Chorus to this history;
Who prologue-like your humble patience pray,
Gently to hear, kindly to judge, our play.

The Chorus's opening speech at once inflates the subject of *Henry V* and deflates
the performance that is about to be presented, positing a separation between a
historical ideal and present-day reality and asking the audience to bridge the
gap between the two. To adequately address the subject of *Henry V*, the Chorus
summons the "Muse of fire"—a muse connected to the highest, because the
lightest, and most spiritual of the four elements—asking it to ascend to the
"brightest heavens of invention," from which vantage point kingdoms will seem
mere stages and the princes, actors.

Such a muse will not come to the playwright's aid. Summoning it is a wish,
not a possibility, so the Chorus turns the audience's attention to the scene at hand,
specifically the theater and the "unraised spirits," that is, the dull, or earthly,
actors, within it. From the vantage point of the heavens, kingdoms might be
mere stages, but from our earthbound view, a stage and an acting company will
have to substitute for a kingdom and its principal members, a reality and an
artistic compromise that will debase the original, historical figures, whom the
audience will have to re-create for itself.

The speech, however, implies something more complex. Divided into three
parts—the first ending with the half line "Crouch for employment," the second
ending with the line "On your imaginary forces work," and the third taking
up the rest of the passage—the prologue starts in the heavens and progresses
downward, touching on monarchies and King Henry V, then the real stage,
and finally the audience. What the members of that audience are asked to
do suggests that an opposite progression, from the earthly to the heavenly
realms, is possible. The audience is charged with reversing the hierarchical
presentation and mentally lifting the action the play is about to present—and,
by association, the physical space within the "wooden O"—to the heights of
heavenly invention. The audience, if it does as the playwright asks, will take
the place of the heavenly muse.

The Chorus's use of "gentles all" is thus much more than a polite address.
Employing the phrase indicates that, for the playwright to find success, the
distinction between those of noble birth, or gentles, and commoners must be
removed and those watching the play must become the monarchs referred to
in the prologue's first section beholding the action. This collective involvement
transforms mundane things—a mere man and an inadequate stage and troupe of
actors—into heroic ideals, transcending the restrictions placed on the playwright
who attempts to conjure epic realms albeit with limited means.

Act 1, 1, 60–98

Canterbury: The king is full of grace and fair regard.
Ely: And a true lover of the holy church.
Canterbury: The courses of his youth promised it not.
The breath no sooner left his father's body,
But that his wildness, mortified in him,
Seem'd to die too; yea, at that very moment
Consideration, like an angel, came
And whipp'd the offending Adam out of him,
Leaving his body as a paradise,
To envelop and contain celestial spirits.
Never was such a sudden scholar made;
Never came reformation in a flood,
With such a heady currance, scouring faults
Nor never Hydra-headed wilfulness
So soon did lose his seat and all at once
As in this king.
Ely: We are blessed in the change.
Canterbury: Hear him but reason in divinity,
And all-admiring with an inward wish
You would desire the king were made a prelate:
Hear him debate of commonwealth affairs,
You would say it hath been all in all his study:
List his discourse of war, and you shall hear
A fearful battle render'd you in music:
Turn him to any cause of policy,
The Gordian knot of it he will unloose,
Familiar as his garter: that, when he speaks,
The air, a charter'd libertine, is still,
And the mute wonder lurketh in men's ears,
To steal his sweet and honey'd sentences;
So that the art and practic part of life
Must be the mistress to this theoric:
Which is a wonder how his grace should glean it,
Since his addiction was to courses vain,
His companies unletter'd, rude and shallow,
His hours fill'd up with riots, banquets, sports,
And never noted in him any study,
Any retirement, any sequestration
From open haunts and popularity.

The Archbishop of Canterbury and the Bishop of Ely have just been discussing a bill that is before Parliament that will strip from the church its temporal lands, "the better half of our possession." The exchange, which introduces the character of the reformed Henry V, is made in the context of the religious officials expressing their hope of preventing the bill from passing and, therefore, suggests the king's reformation can be used in the secular interests of the church.

Canterbury alludes to the theory of the king's two bodies—a concept that postulated that a monarch has two bodies, a physical human body and a political body, or the body of the realm in a communal and a metaphysical sense. The archbishop notes, "Consideration, like an angel, came / And whipp'd the offending Adam out of him [Henry],/ Leaving his body as a paradise." After all, according to this theory, monarchs, when functioning in their capacity as the body politic, were free from imperfections. Those who subscribed to the dual-body concept often assumed a strong relationship between the monarch's body and the realm's so that a discussion of one implied a consideration of other. Canterbury's praise of the king, then, is also directed toward the commonwealth. The absence of the type of rebellion that Henry IV had to battle against implies that a "Hydra-headed willfulness" has been cleansed from the realm as well as the king.

The two bodies theory is further suggested by Canterbury's list of the king's accomplishments, which gesture toward the idea that Henry has the abilities, to a higher degree, of various other members of his realm. It is significant that the archbishop expresses his astonishment at the king's accomplishments in relation to Henry's mastery of the languages of divinity, commonwealth affairs, war, and policy. Mastery of a realm's language is, in a number of Shakespeare plays, a sign of a monarch's possession of two bodies.

The Cardinal's intent to take advantage of Henry's apparent devotion to the church and the motives the Cardinal has for discrediting the Salic law also reveals a doubleness at the heart of Henry V's court. Both the king's physical body and the body politic are duplicitous by nature. As Hamlet says about women, whom "God hath given you one face and you make yourselves another," the Cardinal unwittingly implies about Henry V and his realm.

Act 2, 3, 4–36

Pistol: Falstaff he is dead, and we must yearn therefore.
Bardolph: Would I were with him, wheresome'er he is, either in heaven or in hell!
Hostess: Nay, sure, he's not in hell: he's in Arthur's bosom, if ever man went to Arthur's bosom. A' made a finer end and went away an it had been any christom child; a' parted even just between twelve and one, even at the turning o' the tide: for after I saw him fumble with the sheets and play with flowers and smile upon his fingers' ends, I

knew there was but one way; for his nose was as sharp as a pen, and a'
babbled of green fields. 'How now, sir John!' quoth I 'what, man! be o'
good cheer.' So a' cried out 'God, God, God!' three or four times. Now
I, to comfort him, bid him a' should not think of God; I hoped there
was no need to trouble himself with any such thoughts yet. So a' bade
me lay more clothes on his feet: I put my hand into the bed and felt
them, and they were as cold as any stone; then I felt to his knees, and
they were as cold as any stone, and so upward and upward, and all was
as cold as any stone.

Nym: They say he cried out of sack.

Hostess: Ay, that a' did.

Bardolph: And of women.

Hostess: Nay, that a' did not.

Boy: Yes, that a' did; and said they were devils incarnate.

Hostess: A' could never abide carnation; 'twas a colour he never liked.

Boy: A' said once, the devil would have him about women.

Hostess: A' did in some sort, indeed, handle women; but then he was
rheumatic, and talked of the whore of Babylon.

Boy: Do you not remember, a' saw a flea stick upon Bardolph's nose, and
a' said it was a black soul burning in hell-fire?

Bardolph: Well, the fuel is gone that maintained that fire: that's all the
riches I got in his service.

The scene of Falstaff's death, as described in this exchange, is as full of contrar-
ies as the knight's life had been. Falstaff laments his failure to embrace proper
order but continues to exhibit some of the qualities that enabled him to escape
such order. The Boy's recounting of his reaction to a flea on Bardolph's nose is
evidence that Falstaff does not abandon his wit, though it has perhaps become
a little feeble. He is repentant, or ready to accept what heaven requires, and
unrepentant, or unwilling to leave behind the life he has forged for himself, a
contradictory state perhaps best revealed by Hostess Quickly when she places
him in Arthur's rather than Abraham's bosom, signifying heaven. Falstaff, she
unwittingly seems to say, remains tied not to Christianity but to the culture of
English folklore, the tradition from which his character emerged, and he even
dies "at the turning o' the tide," as folk belief dictated he should.

Falstaff, however, also participates in a strain of Western tradition associated
with high culture, becoming in a sense an imitator of Socrates. Hostess Quickly's
description of the knight's dying, after all, paraphrases Plato's description of
Socrates's last moments, suggesting an analogous relationship between the two
figures. That relationship is perhaps unnoticeable at first. Almost everything we are
told about Falstaff's death scenes contrasts with Socrates' final moments. Falstaff
dies in the mixed company of Hostess Quickly, the Boy, and Bardolph, who laments

not Falstaff's passing but the lack of "riches [he] got in [Falstaff's] service." Socrates sends the women and boys away, "to avoid [the] unseemliness" of their weeping, and dies surrounded by adult male friends, who truly lament his passing. Furthermore, Socrates dies with the comfort that he has lived a good life and is assured a happy afterlife, while Falstaff dies fearing eternal punishment, condemning sack (a kind of wine or sherry), women, and everything else he had pursued.

The one element that is shared is the effect of death on the bodies of the two men. Hostess Quickly put her "hand into the / bed and felt them [Falstaff's feet], and they were as cold as any / stone. Then [she] felt to his knees, and so up'ard and / up'ard, and all was as cold as any stone." Plato writes, "The man who had given [Socrates] poison touched his body, and after a while tested his feet and legs, pressed hard upon his foot and asked him if he felt this, and Socrates said no. Then he pressed his calves, and made his way up his body and showed us that it was cold and stiff. He felt it himself and said that when the cold reached his heart he would be gone."

The transformation of Socrates into a cold and stiff or stonelike body points toward his transformation into a symbol of Hellenic order; the body turned to stone becomes an emblem of the dead luminary's status as the ideal philosopher. In the context of the Falstaffian milieu, turning to stone carries a different significance, one that undermines the inherent quality that makes the knight larger than life: in Falstaff's world, to be stonelike is to be worthless, for the fluidity of his character is what has allowed Falstaff to master his environment.

Act 4, 1, 210–63

Henry V: Upon the king! 'Let us our lives, our souls,
Our debts, our careful wives,
Our children and our sins lay on the king!'
We must bear all. O hard condition,
Twin-born with greatness, subject to the breath
Of every fool, whose sense no more can feel
But his own wringing! What infinite heart's-ease
Must kings neglect, that private men enjoy!
And what have kings, that privates have not too,
Save ceremony, save general ceremony?
And what art thou, thou idol ceremony?
What kind of god art thou, that suffer'st more
Of mortal griefs than do thy worshippers?
What are thy rents? what are thy comings in?
O ceremony, show me but thy worth!
What is thy soul of adoration?
Art thou aught else but place, degree and form,
Creating awe and fear in other men?

Wherein thou art less happy being fear'd
Than they in fearing.
What drink'st thou oft, instead of homage sweet,
But poison'd flattery? O, be sick, great greatness,
And bid thy ceremony give thee cure!
Think'st thou the fiery fever will go out
With titles blown from adulation?
Will it give place to flexure and low bending?
Canst thou, when thou command'st the beggar's knee,
Command the health of it? No, thou proud dream,
That play'st so subtly with a king's repose;
I am a king that find thee, and I know
'Tis not the balm, the sceptre and the ball,
The sword, the mace, the crown imperial,
The intertissued robe of gold and pearl,
The farced title running 'fore the king,
The throne he sits on, nor the tide of pomp
That beats upon the high shore of this world,
No, not all these, thrice-gorgeous ceremony,
Not all these, laid in bed majestical,
Can sleep so soundly as the wretched slave,
Who with a body fill'd and vacant mind
Gets him to rest, cramm'd with distressful bread;
Never sees horrid night, the child of hell,
But, like a lackey, from the rise to set
Sweats in the eye of Phoebus and all night
Sleeps in Elysium; next day after dawn,
Doth rise and help Hyperion to his horse,
And follows so the ever-running year,
With profitable labour, to his grave:
And, but for ceremony, such a wretch,
Winding up days with toil and nights with sleep,
Had the fore-hand and vantage of a king.
The slave, a member of the country's peace,
Enjoys it; but in gross brain little wots
What watch the king keeps to maintain the peace,
Whose hours the peasant best advantages.

This soliloquy, the only one that Henry V delivers, is spoken immediately after John Bates, Alexander Court, and Michael Williams exit. The speech gives us our only access to Henry's private thoughts in the entire play and fittingly hinges on a monarch's need to relinquish his private needs for the public good.

In a discussion with Harry La Roy—Henry's persona while he is disguised in Thomas Erpingham's robes—Williams has charged the king with responsibility for the lives, souls, debts, wives, and sins of the men who die in his service on the battlefield, particularly if the king's cause is unjust. Henry reiterates the charge here, apparently uneasy with the argument he had made to convince Williams that each man is responsible for himself and lamenting the difficulty and burdens of being king. The king must give up his personal concerns for the sake of his public responsibilities, a topic Henry returns to at the close of the speech when he refers to the watch that "kings keep to maintain the peace." (The reference to maintaining the peace does seem odd, as Henry is in the midst of the war with France, but he is likely referring to peace in England and, therefore, alluding to Henry IV's advice "to busy giddy minds / With foreign quarrels," or put an end to rebellion at home.)

Henry goes on to discount the perceived difference between a monarch and a subject, revisiting the statement that he had earlier made to Bates: "I think the king is but a man, as I am . . . his ceremonies laid by, in his nakedness he appears but a man." In the soliloquy, however, there is a greater emphasis placed on the worthlessness of ceremony, now called "idol ceremony," as it is a false god, intended for one who is idle, as the homonymic pun on "idol," as well as its failure to produce any real value, suggests. To Henry, all that ceremony seems capable of producing is grief for itself and fear in those who lack it.

The ceremonious order to which Henry refers seems empty. He goes on to deny possessing one of the abilities that monarchs were said to have because of their sacred character, that is, the ability to cure certain illnesses, particularly scrofula (a form of tuberculosis) by means of the royal touch. He is able to command a beggar to kneel, but he is unable to command him to be healthy, a fact that has a direct bearing on Henry's current worries. After all, his army's weakness is, in part, due to his soldiers' sickness, and he wishes he could command them to be healthy as much as he "could be willing to march on to Calais / Without impeachment" (act 3, scene 6).

Ceremony, in fact, is all show, intended for outward appearance, and such trappings of kingship as the scepter, the crown, and the title have little to do with the order they represent. It is rather the concern and toil of the person wearing the crown that maintains that order, such concern robbing the king of the peace enjoyed by his subjects, making his condition worse than "the wretched slave" whose hard work is profitable and is over at the day's end, when he "sleeps in Elysium." Ultimately, worthless ceremony is all that differentiates a king's life from a slave's.

Act 4, 3, 42–69

Henry V: This day is called the feast of Crispian:
He that outlives this day, and comes safe home,
Will stand a tip-toe when the day is named,
And rouse him at the name of Crispian.

He that shall live this day, and see old age,
Will yearly on the vigil feast his neighbours,
And say 'To-morrow is Saint Crispian:'
Then will he strip his sleeve and show his scars.
And say 'These wounds I had on Crispin's day.'
Old men forget: yet all shall be forgot,
But he'll remember with advantages
What feats he did that day: then shall our names,
Familiar in his mouth as household words,
Harry the king, Bedford and Exeter,
Warwick and Talbot, Salisbury and Gloucester,
Be in their flowing cups freshly remember'd.
This story shall the good man teach his son;
And Crispin Crispian shall ne'er go by,
From this day to the ending of the world,
But we in it shall be remember'd;
We few, we happy few, we band of brothers;
For he to-day that sheds his blood with me
Shall be my brother; be he ne'er so vile,
This day shall gentle his condition:
And gentlemen in England now a-bed
Shall think themselves accursed they were not here,
And hold their manhoods cheap whiles any speaks
That fought with us upon Saint Crispin's day.

These lines, spoken in response to Westmorland's wish that the English had 10,000 more men when clashing with the French at Agincourt, are among the most famous uttered in *Henry V*. They address the complex themes of remembrance and fellowship. Henry's assertion that "This day shall gentle [the] condition" of even the lowest born of his men is deemed to be the speech's most spurious element. That view seems to be validated later, when Henry reads the list of the English dead at the end of the day and refers to the twenty-five commoners who were killed as "None else of name."

The first portion of the speech, however, is about mythmaking not historical realities: the day will be remembered "with advantages," not as it actually and factually played out. This notion is reflected in the scars Pistol will show when he returns to London, erroneously claiming he received them while in battle. Henry, in pursuing this notion of exaggerating or misrepresenting the facts of the conflict, imagines that each soldier will place himself among the nobles, whose names will be as "Familiar in his mouth as household words / Harry the king, Bedford and Exeter,/ Warwick and Talbot, Salisbury and Gloucester." Note that Henry here becomes Harry, the name the English use to present the king as a communal figure.

After naming himself and the other prominent nobles, Henry goes on to refer to each man who will tell the story. Then he says "we shall be remembered; / We few, we happy few, we band of brothers." Through the use of the plural pronoun, each man comes to be included in the list of nobles and, therefore, secures a place in the historical myth that will grow around the day's battle and become part of the national story. The band of brothers, then, is something to be forged in retrospect, and those men back home in England will think themselves accursed for their inability to include themselves in that unifying "we." The pronoun may also suggest the "royal we," which the king would use speaking as the body politic, an act that in itself unifies the communal body of the nation into a single flawless entity.

Henry's words, of course, remain rhetorical and can be seen as ambiguous in their relationship to the rest of the play. The king's ideal of the warrior—at least as expressed outside the gates of Harfleur when he exhorts his men to "imitate the action of the tiger; / Stiffen the sinews, summon up the blood, / Disguise fair nature with hard-favour'd rage"—does not suggest a band of men fighting in unison but a horde of individuals caught up in the rage of the moment. The speech, whatever one thinks of the cause it is made in support of, effectively showcases the rhetorical abilities of a leader taxed with embodying and furthering the success of a kingdom and its individual members.

Act 4, 7, 8–46

Gower: . . . O, 'Tis a gallant king!
Fluellen: Ay, he was born at Monmouth, Captain Gower. What call you the town's name where Alexander the Pig was born!
Gower: Alexander the Great.
Fluellen: Why, I pray you, is not pig great? the pig, or the great, or the mighty, or the huge, or the magnanimous, are all one reckonings, save the phrase is a little variations.
Gower: I think Alexander the Great was born in Macedon; his father was called Philip of Macedon, as I take it.
Fluellen: I think it is in Macedon where Alexander is porn. I tell you, captain, if you look in the maps of the 'orld, I warrant you shall find, in the comparisons between Macedon and Monmouth, that the situations, look you, is both alike. There is a river in Macedon; and there is also moreover a river at Monmouth: it is called Wye at Monmouth; but it is out of my prains what is the name of the other river; but 'tis all one, 'tis alike as my fingers is to my fingers, and there is salmons in both. If you mark Alexander's life well, Harry of Monmouth's life is come after it indifferent well; for there is figures in all things. Alexander, God knows, and you know, in his rages, and his furies, and his wraths, and his cholers, and his moods, and his displeasures, and his indignations, and

also being a little intoxicates in his prains, did, in his ales and his angers,
look you, kill his best friend, Cleitus.
Gower: Our king is not like him in that: he never killed any of his friends.
Fluellen: It is not well done, mark you now take the tales out of my
mouth, ere it is made and finished. I speak but in the figures and
comparisons of it: as Alexander killed his friend, being in his ales
and his cups; so also Harry Monmouth, being in his right wits and
his good judgments, turned away the fat knight with the great belly-
doublet: he was full of jests, and gipes, and knaveries, and mocks; I
have forgot his name.
Gower: Sir John Falstaff.
Fluellen: That is he: I'll tell you there is good men porn at Monmouth.

The exchange here comes immediately after Henry's order to kill all the French
prisoners, an act that is against the rules of war as Holinshed notes in his history. Fluellen, following the Renaissance habit of seeking parallels between the
past and the present, as well as Plutarch's practice of finding commonalities
among historical figures, develops an analogy between Alexander the Great's
life and Henry V's to illustrate a profound affinity between the two figures.
The comparison is meant to offer a positive view of the king. If such praise was
directed effusively and solely at the sovereign, it would seemingly be summoned
in order to counterbalance the negative impression that the king's order leaves
at the end of the previous scene. Fluellen's speech, however, is prevented from
serving such a purpose because of the Welsh captain's pronunciation problems,
most notably his pronouncing *b* as *p* and his pushing the analogy too far. The
attempt at praise becomes unwitting satire.

By calling the ancient Macedonian leader Alexander the Pig, Fluellen
undercuts the positive impact of his comparison from the start, for the blunder—
itself a part of Fluellen's inattention to connotative differences among such terms
as "the pig, or the great, or the mighty, or the huge, or the magnanimous"—
makes it hard for Shakespeare's audience not to associate Alexander, and by
extension Henry, with a pig. Portrayed as a gluttonous beast, it is territory, rather
than food, that these voracious leaders devour. The very thing that brings glory
to Alexander or Henry also renders each piglike.

Fluellen goes on to suggest that God seems to have modeled Henry's life on
Alexander's, for the perceived similarity between the two figures' birthplaces,
that there are rivers flowing through both regions that are as "alike as my fingers
is to my fingers" gestures toward the idea that divine signs have been inscribed
in the heart of the two figures' biographies to call our attention to the presence
of a significant analogy.

Fluellen's next observation, however, reemphasizes the beastliness of the men
he would compare. Alexander killed his best friend, Cleitus. Gower, seeing the

possible negative tenor of the comparison, objects, saying "Our king is not like him in that." Fluellen forges ahead, nonetheless, noting that as Alexander killed his friend in a drunken rage, Henry "turned away" Falstaff "being in his right wits and his good judgments," a fact that would seem to make Henry more cruel than Alexander, especially since the connection between Falstaff's rejection and his death has been established by Hostess Quickly, who observes of the knight, "the king has killed his heart." The question the audience is asked to determine is not whether Alexander's behavior was worse than Henry's, as Gower would surely tell us, but whether killing a friend while in one's right mind is worse than killing one while one is intoxicated.

The early twentieth-century critic C. H. Herford observed that Fluellen "partially compensates for [Falstaff's] loss," though he cannot replace the knight, "with his quaint Welsh jests." Fluellen is intent on raising his king to heroic stature, but he finds, just as Falstaff had, that the king is not the man he wants him to be.

LIST OF CHARACTERS IN HENRY V

Henry V, the English king, is the play's principal, albeit ambiguous, figure. He can be regarded as an idealized larger-than-life character, "the mirror of all Christian kings." That particular aspect is established through the contrast between his present self and his former younger, wilder persona, whom Shakespeare featured in the two *Henry IV* plays. Canterbury, for example, remarks that Henry's wildness disappeared the moment he put on the crown, and the Dauphin mistakenly regards Henry as unchanged, even though others at the French court know otherwise. Another aspect of Henry's character, however—his manipulative, self-interested nature—seems to undermine his idealized status. This dimension is most evident in his apparent self-serving reasons for going to war. His father, Henry IV, had told him, in *Henry IV, Part 2,* "to busy giddy minds / With foreign quarrels." No one ascribes that motive to Henry V, but the idea is presented that alternative, Machiavellian motives are behind the war. Moreover, the blame Henry assigns to others—the Archbishop of Canterbury, the Dauphin, and the governor of Harfleur—as to the war's potential injustices as well as the ruthlessness he sometimes displays reveals an ability to distance himself from the implications of what he is doing. What he needs for himself and his own success comes before all else.

Chorus, a man who in Elizabethan performances most likely wore a long, black cloak, is a major character, even though his role places him outside the main action of the play. He calls attention to the inability of the stage to completely and sufficiently present the events of the play, telling the audience to use its imagination to provide what is missing. The Chorus aids that imaginative flight, filling in gaps in the dramatic version of the story that is being performed. He describes the mood in England and France after Henry's decision to go to war, the king and his army's deployment to France, and the greeting Henry received in England upon his return from the battle of Agincourt. The Chorus also offers summaries of the action that is staged, providing a patriotic perspective on the events that are shown and on the character of Henry V.

29

Cambridge, Scroop, and Grey, once trusted advisers to the king, turn traitorous, accepting money from the French to assassinate Henry. As they are about to be arrested for their crime, they are tricked into acknowledging and endorsing the justice of their being executed: Henry pardons a man who "railed against" him the day before, and they advise Henry to punish the man harshly.

The **Archbishop of Canterbury** and the **Bishop of Ely**, the two religious representatives in the play, attest to the ideal character that Henry has exhibited since becoming king, despite his behavior and actions as prince. They are in favor of England's going to war with France, if only because it will take Parliament's mind off moving forward with a bill that would take profitable lands away from the church. Canterbury provides the legal ground for Henry's claim to the French crown, thereby providing the king with justification for going to war.

The Dauphin, the eldest son to the French king, establishes himself as Henry's foil. He sends Henry tennis balls to mock his frivolous nature as a young man and dismisses the value of the English's threat to the French. The Dauphin, however, proves to be overconfident and somewhat frivolous himself, one who spends his time the night before the battle of Agincourt discussing the excellence of his horse and bragging about the number he will kill on the battlefield.

Katherine is the French king's daughter. She does not play a major role in the main action of the play, but she does have a significant part in the overall story that is presented, one that at first glance seems to indicate her secondary status. Her father offers her as a bride, along with some dukedoms, to Henry to appease him and put a stop to the English invasion. Also, she appears in a scene—when her attendant, Alice, helps her learn English—intended for comic relief and placed between the battle of Harfleur and Agincourt. In the final scene, Henry woos her in order to get her to acquiesce to marrying him, even though her father has again offered her hand in marriage, this time as an element of the peace treaty between France in England. Henry, thereby, grants her a degree of power over him, something that is made particularly evident by his asking her "to teach a soldier terms" used to speak of love. This wish suggests that his power, whether or not it is wielded prudently and judiciously, is based on his mastery of the language of a variety of discourses.

Fluellen, a Welsh captain, is introduced, along with the English captain Gower, the Irish captain Macmorris, and the Scottish captain Jamy, to represent the unity of the four nations of Great Britain and their backing of Henry V's campaign, even though that fraternity splinters, if only momentarily, as a result of the tension that builds between Fluellen and Macmorris. Fluellen, who is consistently in the company of Gower, develops into a rounded character, despite his retaining such stereotypical Welsh behavior as his different accent and his pedantic interest in history, both with regard to his establishing the rules of war and his overzealous observing of the tradition of wearing the leek. He helps Henry carry out his magnanimous joke on Michael Williams, one of the soldiers that Henry exchanges words with the night before the battle of Agincourt, He also exposes Pistol to be a coward.

Pistol, who had been introduced in *Henry IV, Part 2* as a member of Falstaff's company, continues to exhibit the characteristics of the cowardly bully. Quick to abuse and threaten those he confronts, he invariable fails to act on his words. In the end, he is beaten by Fluellen, promising to return to London and exploit to full advantage his membership in Henry V's army, despite his having avoided battle as much as possible. He is the only one of Falstaff's company to remain alive, as Bardolph and Nym are each hanged for theft.

Hostess Quickly, who was known as Mistress Quickly in the *Henry IV* plays, has married Pistol, although she had been betrothed to Nym. She owns the Boar's Head Tavern, which is where Henry V, as the younger man referred to as Hal, gave free reign to his madcap, dissolute ways. She now serves as the attendant at Falstaff's deathbed, describing the knight's final moments and thereby helping Shakespeare, if only through a report, fulfill his promise, made in the epilogue to *Henry IV, Part 2,* to "continue the story, with Sir John [Falstaff] in it." She dies, Pistol tells us in the last act, of a venereal disease.

CRITICISM THROUGH THE AGES

HENRY V IN THE
SEVENTEENTH CENTURY
❧

During the sixteenth century, Henry V was a popular figure, one celebrated in history, poetry, and drama. It is therefore hard to determine what influence Shakespeare had, if any, on appraisals and views of Henry V during the subsequent century. Judging from the critical commentary on his play, he likely had very little. Raphael Holinshed—the historian whose *Chronicles of England, Scotland, and Ireland* (1577; 1587, second edition) was, along with Edward Hall's *The Union of the Two Noble and Illustre Families of Lancaster and York* (1548), Shakespeare's primary source for the play—described the king, after discussing the wildness of Henry's princely days, in these terms: "This Henrie was a king, of life without spot; a prince whome all men loved, and of none disdained; a capteine against whome fortune never frowned, nor mischance once spurned; whose people him so severe a iusticer both loved and obeied, (and so humane withall,) that he left no offense unpunished, nor freendship unrewarded; a terrour to rebels, and suppressour of sedition; his vertues notable, his qualities most praise-worthie." Holinshed here captures, as well as helps to fashion, the idea of Henry as a great warrior and leader, the type of monarch that Michael Drayton celebrated when he asked at the conclusion of his poem "The Battle of Agincourt," "when shall . . . / England breed again / Such a King Harry."

As a dramatic subject, Henry V had been put onstage numerous times from the 1580s to the end of the century, probably starting with the anonymous *The Famous Victories of Henry the Fifth: Containing the Honourable Battell of Agincourt,* which was almost certainly performed earlier than 1588, was entered into the Stationers' Registry in 1594, and appeared in a quarto edition in 1598. Other now lost Henry V plays may also have existed. Thomas Nashe, for example, describes a scene from one that does not appear in *The Famous Victories,* at least as it has come down to us, observing that for "some shallow braind censurers . . . [, a]ll Artes . . . are vanitie: and, if you tell them what a glorious thing it is to have *Henrie* the fifth represented on the Stage, leading the French King prisoner, and forcing both him and the Dolphin to sweare fealty, I, but (will they say) what do we get by it?"

The full title of the anonymous play and the scene that Nashe writes about attest to the popularity of the image of Henry as a warrior king, but his value as a stage character also rested on his youthful reputation for wildness, as the period of his life before he assumed the throne gave a playwright comic material to please audiences who, after all, were coming to the theater for entertainment. The first half of *The Famous Victories* had dealt with Henry's youth, as had the two Shakespeare plays, *Henry IV, Parts 1* and *2*, in the tetralogy that began with *Richard II* and concluded with *Henry V*. Shakespeare had approached his three plays in which Henry appears in light of that earlier work, which he knew so well that James Shapiro has asserted that he had acted in it in one of its numerous revivals during the mid-1590s. Even if he did not, however, Shakespeare knew it well enough to supplement his two main sources with material from the play when composing *Henry IV, Parts 1* and *2*—both of which were written before *The Famous Victories* appeared in print—and *Henry V*. The scenes in the latter play in which Henry receives the Daulphin's gift of tennis balls; in which Pistol secures a ransom from Le Fer, the French soldier; and in which Henry woos the French princess, Katherine, are all reworkings of, and improvements on, episodes in *The Famous Victories*.

Whether Shakespeare's original audience found his *Henry V* to be more satisfying than *The Famous Victories* cannot be known for certain. No full-length contemporary consideration of either play exists, yet we might conjecture that Shakespeare's audience enjoyed Pistol's character, as the full title of the first quarto of the play, which appeared in 1600, was *The Cronicle History of Henry the fift, with his battell fought at Agin Court in France. Together with Auntient Pistoll.* The text was reprinted in 1602 and again in 1619, an edition that is incorrectly dated 1608 and that suggests that *Henry V* had a degree of popularity in the period, though not as much as other Shakespeare histories, *Henry IV, Part 1*, for example, of which six quarto editions were published prior to the appearance of the First Folio in 1623.

The earliest extant comment on *Henry V*, in any case, was negative. Writing in the prologue that was added to his *Everyman in His Humour* (1598) after *Henry V* appeared, Ben Jonson "prays" his audience "will be pleas'd to see / One such to-day, as other plays should be; / Where neither chorus wafts you o'er the seas." Jonson is critiquing Shakespeare's ignoring of the classical or, to be more exact, the neoclassical unities of place, time, and action, which stipulated that a play should be confined to one location, cover a period of no more than 24 hours, and consist of a single action. Jonson's criticism, however, does not explain why Shakespeare's *Henry V* did not generate the same type of interest as his other works did, for Elizabethan audiences cared little for tidy unities. The more popular history plays, as well as the majority of Shakespeare's other works, also ignored them.

The only other reference to *Henry V* by one of Shakespeare's contemporaries is in John Fletcher's *The Noble Gentleman*, which was most likely written about ten years after Shakespeare's death, though some scholars have argued that it could have been written in collaboration with Francis Beaumont as early as 1606. Fletcher parodies the Cardinal's discussion of the Salic law, but the criticism implied by the parody is leveled not so much against Shakespeare as it is against the ideology of legitimate kingship that the Cardinal relies on to substantiate Henry V's right to the French throne. This reaction may be an early expression of a particular strain of critical response, which did not begin in earnest until the twentieth century, that questions the legitimacy of Henry V's war. The parody is put into the mouth of the madman Shattillion, who is asserting that he is rightfully the French king. Marine, a gentleman who aspires to become a great courtier, wisely if uncharacteristically so, asks, "Is not his majesty [the present King] possess'd in peace, And justice executed in his name?" Marine is suggesting that the peacefulness of the reign, even if its hereditary legitimacy is questionable, is its most important feature.

The same suggestion is made in Beaumont and Fletcher's *A King and No King* (1611) when Arbaces, the accidental king of Iberia in that work, argues that his right to his throne, even though it is technically illegitimate, derives from the love his people bear him, telling his subjects, "By you I grow: 'Tis your united love / That lifts me to this height." Both Marine and Arbaces accept the common notion that a monarch, as Mervyn James explains in *Society, Politics and Culture: Studies in Early Modern England*, requires reverence from his "subjects because his authority rested on divine, as well as human, election." A monarch's ability to retain the love of his subjects and thus to rule peacefully, in this view, gives his reign legitimacy irrespective of another potential ruler's more valid hereditary claim. Fletcher's parody of *Henry V* in *The Noble Gentleman* thus seems to call attention to a faulty claim Henry makes to the French throne, one that even he acknowledges when he warns Canterbury, "God forbid, my dear and faithful lord, / That you should fashion, wrest, or bow your reading, / Or nicely charge your understanding soul / With opening titles miscreate, whose right / Suits not in native colors with the truth." If a claim to a throne held by a monarch reigning in peace is untruthful, the foundation on which Henry's heroic stature is built crumbles.

Margaret Cavendish makes, in passing, the one early positive reference to *Henry V* during the century. Defending Shakespeare in *Sociable Letters* (1664), Cavendish lauds his ability to develop characters from all classes and of all kinds of dispositions. Shakespeare presents his characters so effectively, she goes on to write, "one would think he had been Transformed into every one of those Persons he hath Described. . . . [W]ho would not think he had been Harry the Fifth?

Cavendish's praise of the characterization of Henry V aside, the play does not appear to have been well regarded. It was not revived during the Restoration, when Charles II returned to England, in 1660, and reestablished the theaters after they had been closed for 18 years under parliamentary rule, even though Henry V's legend had its specific applications to the monarchy of Charles II, whose own youthful indiscretions, contemporaries hoped, would not mar or qualify his reign. The criticism Jonson had leveled against the play had become more common, and it would not be until the eighteenth century that a revival of *Henry V*, the first of which involved a text that had been considerably rewritten to accommodate neoclassical tastes, would be staged. John Dryden, discussing Shakespeare's histories in general, states the prevailing view, observing in his "An Essay of Dramatic Poesy" (1668)

> if you consider the historical plays of Shakespeare, they are rather so many chronicles of kings, or the business many times of thirty or forty years, cramped into a representation of two hours and a half; which is not to imitate or paint Nature, but rather to draw her in miniature, to take her in little; to look upon her through the wrong end of a perspective, and receive her images not only much less, but infinitely more imperfect than the life: this, instead of making a play delightful, renders it ridiculous.

Restoration audiences preferred a neoclassical version of the legend, and when *Henry V* was put on stage during the period, it was Roger Boyle, Earl of Orrery's *The History of Henry the Fifth* (1664) that was performed. It was this play that the diarist Samuel Pepys saw "well done by the Duke's people, and in most excellent habit" in 1666, a play that he had written, in 1664, was "most full of height and raptures of wit and sense." Unlike Shakespeare's version, most of the episodes in Orrery's version are described rather than staged.

Shakespeare's plays, nonetheless, were recognized for their poetic brilliance, and even Dryden, who at times severely criticized them, noted in his "An Essay of Dramatic Poesy," "Shakspeare was the Homer, or father of our dramatick poets; Jonson was the Virgil, the pattern of elaborate writing; I admire him, but I love Shakspeare." His enduring reputation, thus, led to fresh consideration of *Henry V*. In the last decade of the century, Gerard Langbaine, who was the first to inquire into Shakespeare's sources, dated the play, noting for the first time that the reference to the Earl of Essex in the Chorus of the fifth act clearly placed its date of composition in 1599. Jeremy Collier, despite condemning the theaters for their corrupting influence on English morals, also found positive words for *Henry V* in his *A Short View of the Immorality and Profaneness of the English Stage*, observing that the pleasure Falstaff had supplied in the *Henry IV* plays did not absolve him of his guilt, so he was rightly left to die offstage.

Whatever value today's readers are likely to find in the work of these last two critics, they do lay the groundwork for the two main strains of Shakespearean criticism that was to follow. One group of eighteenth-century critics took it upon themselves to establish an editorial tradition, which involved tracking down sources and correcting corrupt or misunderstood passages that were allowed to stand in the four folio editions of Shakespeare's work published in the seventeenth century. Another group of readers, meanwhile, sought to establish the moral worth of the plays, even when doing so involved expurgating some of the racy passages that Shakespeare had written.

1616—Ben Jonson. Prologue to *Everyman in His Humour*

The poet and playwright Ben Jonson (1572–1637) was, in his youth, the student of William Camden, a classical scholar at the Westminster School. His family could not afford to send him to university, so he pursued his stepfather's trade, bricklaying, a life from which he escaped by becoming a soldier during England's conflict in Flanders. After returning to London, he turned to acting and writing, and during the seventeenth century, he was considered by many to be the preeminent playwright of his age because of his masterly employment of the classical unities of time and place. The following piece criticizes contemporary plays, particularly Shakespeare's histories, for ignoring such structural and genre requirements. The "chorus wafts you o'er the seas" refers to *Henry V,* which was first performed a year after *Everyman in His Humour.* This prologue was added later, perhaps specifically for Jonson's 1616 *Works.*

Though need make many poets, and some such
   As art and nature have not better'd much;
   Yet ours for want hath not so loved the stage,
   As he dare serve the ill customs of the age,
   Or purchase your delight at such a rate,
   As, for it, he himself must justly hate:
   To make a child now swaddled, to proceed
   Man, and then shoot up, in one beard and weed,
   Past threescore years; or, with three rusty swords,
   And help of some few foot and half-foot words,
   Fight over York and Lancaster's long jars,
   And in the tyring-house bring wounds to scars.
   He rather prays you will be pleas'd to see
   One such to-day, as other plays should be;

Where neither chorus wafts you o'er the seas,
Nor creaking throne comes down the boys to please;
Nor nimble squib is seen to make afeard
The gentlewomen; nor roll'd bullet heard
To say, it thunders; nor tempestuous drum
Rumbles, to tell you when the storm doth come;
But deeds, and language, such as men do use,
And persons, such as comedy would choose,
When she would shew an image of the times,
And sport with human follies, not with crimes.
Except we make them such, by loving still
Our popular errors, when we know they're ill.
I mean such errors as you'll all confess,
By laughing at them, they deserve no less:
Which when you heartily do, there's hope left then,
You, that have so grac'd monsters, may like men.

1625—John Fletcher. From *The Noble Gentleman*

John Fletcher (1579–1625), the son of a minister who rose to the position of bishop of London, is among the most celebrated playwrights of
the Jacobean period. Probably best known for such plays as *Philaster,
or Love Lies a-Bleeding* (1609), *The Maid's Tragedy* (1611), and *A King and
No King* (1611), which he wrote with his chief collaborator, Francis
Beaumont (1584–1616), with whom he worked between 1606 and
1613, Fletcher also worked with Philip Massinger and Shakespeare,
whom he replaced as the primary playwright of the King's Men.

From Act III, Scene iv

Marine and Shattillion.

Marine. In that chair take your place; I in this:
    Discourse your title now.
Shattillion. Sir, you shall know,
    My Love's true title, mine by marriage;
    Setting aside the first race of French kings,
    Which will not here concern us, as Pharamond,
    With Clodius, Meroveus, and Chilperick,
    And to come down unto the second race,

Which we will likewise slip—
Mar. But take me with you!
Shat. I pray you give me leave! Of Martel Charles,
   The father of king Pepin, who was sire
   To Charles, the great and famous Charlemain;
   And to come to the third race of French kings,
   Which will not be greatly pertinent in this cause
   Betwixt the king and me, of which you know
   Hugh Capet was the first;
   Next his son Robert, Henry then, and Philip,
   With Lewis, and his son a Lewis too,
   And of that name the seventh, but all this
   Springs from a female, as it shall appear—
Mar. Now give me leave! I grant you this your title,
   At the first sight, carries some show of truth;
   But if ye weigh it well, ye shall find light.
   Is not his majesty possess'd in peace,
   And justice executed in his name?
   And can you think the most Christian king
   Would do this, if he saw not reason for it?
Shat. But had not the tenth Lewis a sole daughter?
Mar. I cannot tell.
Shat. But answer me directly.
Mar. It is a most seditious question.
Shat. Is this your justice?
Mar. I stand for my king.
Shat. Was ever heir-apparent thus abused!
   I'll have your head for this!
Mar. Why, do your worst!
Shat. Will no one stir to apprehend this traitor?
   A guard about my person! Will none come?
   Must my own royal hands perform the deed?
   Then thus I do arrest you.   [*Seizes him.*]
Mar. Treason! help!
Enter Lady, Longueville, Beaufort, and Gentleman.
Lady. Help, help, my lord and husband!
Mar. Help the duke!
Long. Forbear his grace's person!
Shat. Forbear you
   To touch him that your heir apparent weds!
   But, by this hand, I will have all your heads. [*Exit.*]
Gent. How doth your grace?

Mar. Why, well.
Gent. How do you find his title?
Mar. 'Tis a dangerous one,
    As can come by a female.
Gent. Ay, 'tis true;
    But the law Salique cuts him off from all.
Long. I do beseech your grace how stands his title?
Mar. Pho! nothing! the law Salique cuts him off from all.

1664—Margaret Cavendish. From *Sociable Letters*

Margaret Cavendish (1623–73) was born into an aristocratic family that encouraged her interest in learning. Supporting the royalist
cause during the midcentury revolution, she lived in exile during the
Interugnum, when she married William Cavendish, a royalist general
who became duke of Newcastle after the Restoration. He, too, encouraged her intellectual interests, helping to see into print her prolific
output, a body of work that includes plays, poems, fiction, scientific
essays, an autobiography, and a biography of her husband.

Madam,

I Wonder how that Person you mention in your Letter, could either have the
Conscience, or Confidence to Dispraise *Shakespear's* Playes, as to say they were
made up onely with Clowns, Fools, Watchmen, and the like; But to Answer
that Person, though *Shakespear's* Wit will Answer for himself, I say, that it
seems by his Judging, or Censuring, he Understands not Playes, or Wit; for to
Express Properly, Rightly, Usually, and Naturally, a Clown's, or Fool's Humour,
Expressions, Phrases, Garbs, Manners, Actions, Words, and Course of Life, is
as Witty, Wise, Judicious, Ingenious, and Observing, as to Write and Express
the Expressions, Phrases, Garbs, Manners, Actions, Words, and Course of Life,
of Kings and Princes; and to Express Naturally, to the Life, a Mean Country
Wench, as a Great Lady, a Courtesan, as a Chast Woman, a Mad man, as a
Man in his right Reason and Senses, a Drunkard, as a Sober man, a Knave,
as an Honest man, and so a Clown, as a Well-bred man, and a Fool, as a Wise
man; nay, it Expresses and Declares a Greater Wit, to Express, and Deliver to
Posterity, the Extravagancies of Madness, the Subtilty of Knaves, the Ignorance
of Clowns, and the Simplicity of Naturals, or the Craft of Feigned Fools, than
to Express Regularities, Plain Honesty, Courtly Garbs, or Sensible Discourses,
for 'tis harder to Express Nonsense than Sense, and Ordinary Conversations,
than that which is Unusual; and 'tis Harder, and Requires more Wit to Express

a Jester, than a Grave Statesman; yet Shakespear did not want Wit, to Express to the Life all Sorts of Persons, of what Quality, Profession, Degree, Breeding, or Birth soever; nor did he want Wit to Express the Divers, and Different Humours, or Natures, or Several Passions in Mankind; and so Well he hath Express'd in his Playes all Sorts of Persons, as one would think he had been Transformed into every one of those Persons he hath Described; and as sometimes one would think he was Really himself the Clown or Jester he Feigns, so one would think, he was also the King, and Privy Counsellor; also as one would think he were Really the Coward he Feigns, so one would think he were the most Valiant, and Experienced Souldier; Who would not think he had been such a man as his Sir Iohn Falstaff? and who would not think he had been Harry the Fifth? & certainly Iulius Cæsar, Augustus Cæsar, and Antonius, did never Really Act their parts Better, if so Well, as he hath Described them, and I believe that Antonius and Brutus did not Speak Better to the People, than he hath Feign'd them; nay, one would think that he had been Metamorphosed from a Man to a Woman, for who could Describe Cleopatra Better than he hath done, and many other Females of his own Creating, as Nan Page, Mrs. Page, Mrs. Ford, the Doctors Maid, Bettrice, Mrs. Quickly, Doll Tearsheet, and others, too many to Relate? and in his Tragick Vein, he Presents Passions so Naturally, and Misfortunes so Probably, as he Peirces the Souls of his Readers with such a True Sense and Feeling thereof, that it Forces Tears through their Eyes, and almost Perswades them, they are Really Actors, or at least Present at those Tragedies. Who would not Swear he had been a Noble Lover, that could Woo so well? and there is not any person he hath Described in his Book, but his Readers might think they were Well acquainted with them; indeed Shakespear had a Clear Judgment, a Quick Wit, a Spreading Fancy, a Subtil Observation, a Deep Apprehension, and a most Eloquent Elocution; truly, he was a Natural Orator, as well as a Natural Poet, and he was not an Orator to Speak Well only on some Subjects, as Lawyers, who can make Eloquent Orations at the Bar, and Plead Subtilly and Wittily in Law-Cases, or Divines, that can Preach Eloquent Sermons, or Dispute Subtilly and Wittily in Theology, but take them from that, and put them to other Subjects, and they will be to seek; but Shakespear's Wit and Eloquence was General, for, and upon all Subjects, he rather wanted Subjects for his Wit and Eloquence to Work on, for which he was Forced to take some of his Plots out of History, where he only took the Bare Designs, the Wit and Language being all his Own; and so much he had above others, that those, who Writ after him, were Forced to Borrow of him, or rather to Steal from him; I could mention Divers Places, that others of our Famous Poets have Borrow'd, or Stoln, but lest I should Discover the Persons, I will not Mention the Places, or Parts, but leave it to those that Read his Playes, and others, to find them out. I should not have needed to Write this to you, for his Works would have Declared the same Truth: But I believe, those that Dispraised his Playes, Dispraised them more out of

Envy, than Simplicity or Ignorance, for those that could Read his Playes, could not be so Foolish to Condemn them, only the Excellency of them caused an Envy to them. By this we may perceive, Envy doth not Leave a man in the Grave, it Follows him after Death, unless a man be Buried in Oblivion, but if he Leave any thing to be Remembred, Envy and Malice will be still throwing Aspersion upon it, or striving to Pull it down by Detraction. But leaving *Shakespear's* Works to their own Defence, and his Detractors to their Envy, and you to your better Imployments, than Reading my Letter, I rest,
Madam,
Your faithful Friend and humble Servant

1691—Gerard Langbaine. "William Shakespear," from *An Account of the English Dramatick Poets*

Gerard Langbaine (1656-92), whose father was the provost of Queen's College Oxford, is remembered for tracing, in a scholarly fashion, the sources of Renaissance and Restoration plays as well as for writing critical biographies of their authors. He followed these pursuits while leading a life of leisure. In 1690, he became yeoman bedel in arts at Oxford and then, in 1691, esquire bedel of law and architypographus, a printer who was also expected to serve in an editorial capacity.

One of the most Eminent Poets of his Time; he was born at *Stratford* upon *Avon in Warwickshire;* and flourished in the Reigns of Queen *Elizabeth,* and *King James* the First. His Natural Genius to *Poetry* was so excellent, that like those Diamonds,[1] which are found in *Cornwall,* Nature had little, or no occasion for the Assistance of Art to polish it. The Truth is, 'tis agreed on by most, that his Learning was not extraordinary; and I am apt to believe, that his Skill in the *French* and *Italian* Tongues, exceeded his Knowledge in the *Roman* Language: for we find him not only beholding to *Cynthio Giraldi* and *Bandello,* for his Plots, but likewise a Scene in *Henry* the Fifth, written in *French,* between the Princess *Catherine* and her Governante: Besides *Italian* Proverbs scatter'd up and down in his Writings. Few Persons that are acquainted with *Dramatick 'Poetry,* but are convinced of the Excellency of his Compositions, in all Kinds of it: and as it would be superfluous in me to endeavour to particularise what most deserves praise in him, after so many Great Men that have given him their several Testimonials of his Merit; so I should think I were guilty of an Injury beyond pardon to his Memory, should I so far disparage it, as to bring his Wit in competition with any of our Age. 'Tis true Mr. *Dryden*[2] has censured him very severely, in his Postscript to *Granada;* but in cool Blood, and when the *Enthusiastick* Fit was past, he has acknowledged him Equal at least, if not Superiour, to Mr. *Johnson in Poesie*. I shall not here repeat what has been before urged in his behalf, in that Common Defence of the Poets of that Time, against Mr. *Dryden's* Account of *Ben. Johnson;* but shall take the Liberty to speak my Opinion, as my predecessors have done, of his Works; which is this, That I esteem his Plays beyond any that have ever been published in our Language: and tho' I extreamly admire *Johnson* and *Fletcher*; yet I must still aver, that when in competition with *Shakespear*, I must apply to them what *Justice Lipsius* writ in his Letter to *Andraeas Schottus*, concerning *Terence* and *Plautus* when compar'd; *Terentium amo, admirer, sed Plautum magis.*

He has writ about Forty six Plays [counting a number of plays attributed to Shakespeare that are known to have been written by other hands], all which except three, are bound in one Volume in Fol. printed *Lond.* 1685. The whole Book is dedicated to the Earls of *Pembroke* and *Montgomery:* being usher'd into the World with several Copies of Verses; but none more valued than those Lines made by *Ben Johnson*; which being too long to be here transcribed, I shall leave them to be perus'd by the Reader, with his Works, of which I shall give some Account as follows.

. . .

Henry the Fifth. His Life. This Play is likewise writ and founded on History, with a Mixture of Comedy. The Play is continued from the beginning of his Reign, to his Marriage with *Katherine* of *France*. For Historians, see as before, *Harding, Caxton, Walsingham, &c.* This Play was writ during the time that *Essex* was General in *Ireland*, as you may see in the beginning of the first Act; where our Poet by a pretty Turn, compliments *Essex*, and seems to foretell Victory to Her Majesties Forces against the Rebels.

. . .

I have now no more to do, but to close up all, with an Account of his Death; which was on the 23^d of *April, Anno Dom.* 1616. He lyeth Buried in the Great Church in *Stratford* upon *Avon*, with his Wife and Daughter *Susanna*, the Wife of Mr. *John Hall*. In the North Wall of the Chancel, is a Monument fixed which represents his true Effigies, leaning upon a Cushion, with the following Inscription.

Ingenio Pylum, genio Socratem, arte Maronem,
Terra tegit, Populus maeret, Olympus habet.
Stay, Passenger, why dost thou go so fast?
Read, if thou canst, whom. envious'Death has plac't

Within this Monument, Shakespear, with whom
Quick Nature died, whose Name doth deck the Tomb
Far more than cost, Since all that he hath writ
Leaves living Art, but Page, to serve his Wit.

    Obiit An. Dom. 1616.
    Æt 53. die 23. Apr.

Near the Wall where this Monument is Erected, lyeth a plain Free-stone, underneath which, his Body is Buried, with this Epitaph.

Good Friend, for Jesus sake, forbear
To dig the Dust enclosed here.
Blest be the Man that spares these Stones,
And curs'd be he that moves my Bones.

NOTES
1. Dr. Fuller in his Account of *Shakespear.*
2. See Mr. *Dryden's* Account.

1698—Jeremy Collier. From *A Short View of the Immorality and Profaneness of the English Stage*

Jeremy Collier (1650–1726) was a member of the nonjurors, individuals who would not take the oath of allegiance after James II was dethroned during the Glorious Revolution. He was ordained a bishop of that schismatic group in 1713. By that time, he had written a number of moral tracts, including his well-known condemnation of the theater in which he applauds Shakespeare's rejection of Falstaff.

Ben Johnson's Fox is clearly against Mr. *Dryden.* And here I have his own Confession for proof. He declares the *Poets end in this Play was the Punishment of Vice and Essay of the Reward of Virtue. Ben* was forced to strain for this piece of Justice, and break through the *Unity of Design.* This Mr. *Dryden* remarks upon him: However, he is pleased to commend the Performance, and calls it an excellent *Fifth Act.*

    Ben Johnson shall speak for himself afterwards in the Character of a Critick. In the mean time I shall take a Testimony or two from *Shakespear.* And here we may observe the admir'd *Falstaffe* goes off in Disappointment. He is thrown out of Favour as being a *Rake,* and dies like a Rat behind the Hangings. The Pleasure he had given would not excuse him. The *Poet* was not so partial as to let his Humour compound for his Lewdness. If 'tis objected that this remark is wide of the Point, because *Falstaffe* is represented in Tragedy, where the Laws of Justice are more strickly observ'd: To this I answer that you may call *Henry* the Fourth and Fifth Tragedies if you please. But for all that, *Falstaffe* wears no *Buskins;* his Character is perfectly Comical from end to end.

HENRY V IN THE
EIGHTEENTH CENTURY
☙

In the eighteenth century, serious and scholarly editions of Shakespeare's plays began to appear, increasing the amount of commentary that they received. *Henry V* was given more attention as a result, and while the most important critical remarks made about it for the majority of the century are in the form of passing observations in prefaces and notes, eighteenth-century views on the play are also discernable from the editorial practices that were observed.

Nicholas Rowe, who was the first to take on the task of producing an authoritative text of Shakespeare's work (he used only the folio texts to create his edition, ignoring the quartos that appeared during Shakespeare's life), merely comments, when discussing *Henry V,* on the value of Hostess Quickly's description of Falstaff's death. Rowe does something else, however, important to helping Shakespeare's reputation grow in stature. He asks that his readers judge Shakespeare by the aesthetic values of his own age rather than by those that had become accepted in the second half of the seventeenth century.

Rowe is not above referring to such elements as the mixing of tragedy and comedy, which neoclassicists frowned on, and the overuse of wordplay as faults, but he adds that Shakespeare was following the common practice of his day and goes so far as to assert that keeping the unities was something that Shakespeare "valu'd himself least upon, since his Excellencies were all of another Kind." Rowe thereby suggests that the best elements of Shakespeare's works could have been lost if he had confined himself to the rules and conventions of dramatic structure. Rowe attests to a budding recognition that aesthetic values other than those derived from Greek drama or, to be more exact, Aristotle's description of it, could have merit.

Charles Gildon, who wrote an extended commentary on the plays for a volume that was added to Rowe's 1709 edition the following year, took up the idea that Shakespeare should not be entirely condemned for his failure to follow neoclassical standards. Gildon approaches the issue in a different way from Rowe. He argues, using the Chorus in *Henry V* as evidence, that Shakespeare realized that developing the action of a play over a period of many years and in a number of different places was preposterous, but he was not, Gildon maintains, familiar with dramatic works that demonstrated the proper use of the unities. Gildon was wrong about Shakespeare's knowledge of the unities, which he followed in *A Comedy of Errors* and *The Tempest*, but his approach to the issue, like Rowe's, seems to acknowledge that alternative aesthetic traditions, albeit in his opinion preposterous ones, existed. The divide between the positions of Rowe and Gildon lasted into the second half of the century.

Samuel Johnson, who is regarded by many critics as the preeminent Shakespearean scholar of his century, also put his stamp on the issue of judging Shakespeare by neoclassical standards. Disregarding the problem of Shakespeare's familiarity with the rules, Johnson considered the effect of Shakespeare's aesthetic on audiences, which neoclassicists believed would find works not adhering to the unities unrealistic. He noted, "Imitations produce pain or pleasure, not because they are mistaken for realities, but because they bring realities to mind. . . . We are agitated in reading the History of *Henry* the Fifth, yet no man takes his book for the field of *Agencourt*. A dramatick exhibition is a book recited with concomitants that encrease or diminish its effect." He argues, in other words, that we are as capable of imagining characters moving across oceans or through the years when we are watching a play as we are when we are reading a book.

The editorial work that was carried out throughout the century, with collections of complete plays being produced by Alexander Pope, Lewis Theobald, Thomas Hanmer, William Warburton, Samuel Johnson, Edward Capell, George Steevens, and Edmund Malone, added to the understanding of Shakespeare in other ways, even though the choices that the editors made sometimes tell us more about their preconceptions concerning Shakespeare or his works than about his texts. Pope, for example, proposed restoring the texts to their original beauty, however, he followed his taste too often, removing or improving lines that he felt unworthy of Shakespeare. The practice led not to an original text but to one that demonstrates Shakespeare's growing reputation as a genius. He was, in Pope's view, beyond compare and any flaws in his work must have been introduced by another hand.

The inadequacy of Pope's practice, nonetheless, led others, particularly Lewis Theobald, to look more carefully at the texts. The benefit of Theobald's review of Pope's work can be observed by examining his handling of what has since become the most famous textual problem in *Henry V*. In her description of Falstaff's death, according to the first folio, Hostess Quickly recalls, "his Nose was as sharpe as a Pen, and a Table of greene Fields." The line had been left to stand in the succeeding folios that were published in the seventeenth century, but Pope found it unintelligible and went about to correct it. His solution involved the following conjecture:

> This nonsense got into all these editions [the folios] by a pleasant
> mistake of the stage-editors, who printed from the common piece-meal
> written parts in the play-house. A table was here directed to be brought

in, (it being a scene in a tavern where they drink at parting,) and this direction crept into the text from the margin. Greenfield was the name of the property-man in that time, who furnish'd implements, &c. for the actors. A Table of Greenfield's.

When Theobald, whose knowledge of Elizabethan drama far surpassed Pope's, discussed the same line in his *Shakespeare Restor'd* (1726), he acknowledged that Pope was correct about the presence of an error, but objected to Pope's conjecture that the name of the property man and a direction to bring a table on stage would have been written down next to the play's text in the middle of a scene. Theobald countered that *a* was a mistake for *a'*, which Elizabethans commonly used for *he*, and that the *t* in *table* was a transcriber's error for *b*, making the line read, "*his Nose was as sharp as a Pen, and* a' babled *of green Fields.*" The emendation is the one that editors accept today, even though alternative solutions to the textual error have been offered on occasion.

Theobald's practice of finding historically viable solutions to the problems found in Shakesperean texts was not always followed by the editors who came after him nor did they always accept Rowe and Gildon's suggestion that Shakespeare's aesthetic values should not be determined by the standards that dominated dramatic criticism during the Restoration and early eighteenth century. Thomas Hanmer, whose edition appeared in 1744, accepted Pope's editorial judgment, keeping Pope's deletions and making others. Perhaps the most startling correction that Hanmer made was his cutting the scene in which Katherine, the French princess, studies English with Alice in *Henry V.*

Hamner was in one sense following the neoclassical stipulation that high and low should not be mixed, but he was also making a moral judgment; he considers the scene too vulgar and thus decides that it must have been added by someone other than Shakespeare, along with a number of other vulgar passages that he believed were inserted into the original plays for the sake of the groundlings, the members of Elizabethan audiences who paid the least and stood throughout the performance. Such morality was often behind the criticism of the period but is most clearly manifested in Griffith's work, which set out to demonstrate how the plays provide us with "observations and reflections . . . [on] the general economy of life and manners, respecting prudence, polity, decency, and decorum; or relative to the tender affections and fond endearments of human nature; more especially regarding those moral duties which are the truest source of mortal bliss—domestic ties, offices, and obligations."

The editorial activities, however inadequate they may have been at times, led to an increased interest in Shakespeare's sources, something Langbaine had begun to seek out at the end of the previous century. Rowe had largely ignored the need to look for the relationship between the plays and their sources, having portrayed Shakespeare as an original genius who developed his art from nature.

Theobald, by contrast, had recognized the similarities between *The Famous Victories* and Shakespeare's *Henry IV* plays and *Henry V*, commenting on them in a note to *Henry IV, Part 1*. The most extensive effort to document Shakespeare's sources was carried out by the novelist Charlotte Lennox, whom Johnson both aided and encouraged in the endeavor, in the early 1750s. Her work went further than any of her predecessors', though she does not mention *The Famous Victories*, perhaps because her primary interest was nondramatic sources, mainly prose fiction and some histories, and she was not familiar with that play. She instead speculated that the tennis ball episode in *Henry V* derived from a ballad that had been printed in *A Collection of Old Ballads: Corrected from the Best and Most Ancient Copies Extant* (1723), probably edited and introduced by the poet Ambrose Philips, along with a prefatory introduction relating Henry V's legend. (More recently Ross W. Duffin has traced the ballad to an early seventeenth-century broadside, ca. 1614, attributed to S.W., perhaps making Shakespeare's play or *The Famous Victories* a source for it.) Despite the occasional missteps that Lennox made, her work proved a valuable resource, one that Johnson, for example, liberally used in his notes for his Shakespeare edition.

Another source of attention for *Henry V* was the status Shakespeare was gaining as a national poet, a status that gave patriotic value to his works. That aspect of Shakespeare's reputation during the period is apparent at the beginning of the century in one of Richard Steele's *Tatler* essays. Steele builds an analogy between the Duke of Marlborough and Henry V, drawing on Shakespeare's play to give force to the comparison, much as Shakespeare had compared Essex to Henry. More frequently, the play was appropriated to develop the contrast between the French and English national character, a practice followed by Aaron Hill, both in his adaption of the play, *K. Henry V, or, the Conquest of France by the English* (1723), and in his *Prompter* essay. Even Johnson indulges in such criticism in his notes, remarking that "Throughout the whole scene [in which Katherine and Alice study English] there may be found *French* servility, and *French* vanity."

The patriotic use of *Henry V* also helped to establish its place in the repertoire of Shakespeare plays that were put on the stage. Unlike a number of Shakespeare's other works, *Henry V*'s reputation did not benefit from the emergence of strong performance history until the second half of the century, when John Kemble took on the role of the king. He was not the first eighteenth-century actor to play the part, but he was the first since the time of Shakespeare, as James N. Loehlin writes, "to place a real stamp on" it. Before Kemble, the value it was thought to have as a performance piece is perhaps best revealed by the fact that David Garrick, the preeminent Shakespearean actor in the middle of the century, never played the role of Henry—though he did appear as the Chorus in a production in 1747. The play, in fact, seems to have been treated as a propaganda piece. Revivals, after the first one in 1738, were generally mounted during times of conflict between England and France, for instance, after the French-supported Jacobite rebellion in the mid-1740s and during the Seven Years' War (1756–1763), a conflict in which an alliance that included Britain was pitted against one that included France. Even Kemble's production, which lacked elements that showed Henry in a bad light, was staged for patriotic reason between 1789 and 1806. In his adaptation, Aaron Hill felt the need to produce a version more reflective of neoclassical tastes. Critics may have, at times, called attention to the closed-mindedness of judging all literature by Greek standards, but most were inclined to regard them as the correct ones. Gildon's position—that other standards existed but they were inferior—was the predominate one for those interested in explaining earlier writers' lack of adherence to the rules.

1709—Nicholas Rowe. From "Some Account of the Life of Shakespeare"

Nicholas Rowe (1674–1718) was a poet and playwright who is best remembered as the editor of the earliest critical edition of Shakespeare's works, *The Works of Mr. William Shakespear; Revis'd and Corrected* (1709), and for the Shakespeare biography that introduced it.

His Plays are properly to be distinguish'd only into Comedies and Tragedies. Those which are called Histories, and even some of his Comedies, are really Tragedies, with a run or mixture of Comedy amongst 'em. That way of Trage-Comedy was the common Mistake of that Age, and is indeed become so agreeable to the *English* Tast, that tho' the severer Critiques among us cannot bear it, yet the generality of our Audiences seem to be better pleas'd with it than with an exact Tragedy. *The Merry Wives of Windsor, The Comedy of Errors,* and *The Taming of the Shrew* are all pure Comedy; the rest, however they are call'd, have something of both Kinds. 'Tis not very easie to determine which way of Writing he was most Excellent in. There is certainly a great deal of Entertainment in his Comical Humours; and tho' they did not then strike at all Ranks of People, as the Satyr of the present Age has taken the Liberty to do, yet there is a pleasing and a well-distinguish'd Variety in those Characters which he thought fit to meddle with. *Falstaff* is allow'd by every body to be a Master-piece; the Character is always well-sustain'd, tho' drawn out into the length of three Plays; and even the Account of his Death, given by his Old Landlady Mrs. *Quickly,* in the first Act of *Henry V.* tho' it be extremely Natural, is yet as diverting as any Part of his Life. If there be any Fault in the Draught he has made of this lewd old Fellow, it is, that tho' he has made him a Thief, Lying, Cowardly, Vainglorious, and in short every way Vicious, yet he has given him so much Wit as to make him almost too agreeable; and I don't know whether some People have not, in remembrance of the Diversion he had formerly afforded 'em, been sorry to see his Friend *Hal* use him so scurvily, when he comes to the Crown in the End of the Second Part of *Henry* the Fourth.

1709—Richard Steele. From *The Tatler*

Primarily remembered for collaboratoring with his friend Joseph Addison (1672-1719) on the periodicals *The Tatler* and *The Spectator*, Richard Steele (1672-1729), who was knighted by George I, was a journalist, a member of Parliament for a time, a playwright, and a theater manager. He, along with Addison, is responsible for developing the periodic essay, which for them were moralistic works meant to improve their readers' minds by stressing the value of moderation, reasonableness, and other values.

St. James's Coffee-house, February 22.

There arrived a messenger last night from Harwich, who left that place just as the duke of Marlborough was going on board. The character of this important general going out by the command of his queen, and at the request of his country, puts me in mind of that noble figure which Shakspeare gives Harry the Fifth upon his expedition against France. The poet wishes for abilities to represent so great a hero:

> 'Oh for a muse of fire!
> Then should the warlike Harry, like himself,
> Assume the fort of Mars, and at his heels,
> Leash'd in, like hounds, should famine, sword and fire
> Crouch for employments.'

A conqueror drawn like the god of battle, with such a dreadful leash of hell-hounds at his command, makes a picture of as much majesty and terror as is to be met with in any poet.

Shakspeare understood the force of this particular allegory so well, that he had it in his thoughts in another passage, which is altogether as daring and sublime as the former. What I mean, is in the tragedy of *Julius Caesar*, where Antony, after having foretold the bloodshed and destruction that should be brought upon the earth by the death of that great man, to fill up the horror of his description, adds the following verses:

And Caesar's spirit ranging for revenge,
With Ate by his side, come hot from Hell,
Shall in these confines, with a monarch's voice,
Cry 'Havoc'; and let slip the dogs of war.

I do not question but these quotations will call to mind, in my readers of learning and taste, that imaginary person described by Virgil with the same spirit. He mentions it upon the occasion of a peace which was restored to the Roman Empire, and which we may now hope for from the departure of that great man who has given occasion to these reflections. The Temple of Janus, says he, shall be shut, and in the midst of it *military* Fury shall sit upon a pile of broken arms, loaded with a hundred chains, bellowing with madness, and grinding his teeth in blood.

Claudentur belli portae; Furor impius intus,
Saeva sedens super arma, et centum vinctus ahenis
Post tergum nodis, fremit horridus ore cruento.

    Virg. Aen. i. 298

Janus himself before his fane shall wait,
And keep the dreadful issues of his gate,
With bolts and iron bars. Within remains
Imprisoned Fury bound in brazen chains;
High on a trophy raised of useless arms,
He sits, and threats the world with vain alarms

    Dryden

1710—Charles Gildon. From "Remarks on the Plays of Shakespeare"

Charles Gildon (1665-1724), a prolific writer who penned early biographies of Daniel Defoe and Aphra Benn, numerous critical works, plays, fiction, and poetry, is remembered for being an enemy of Jonathan Swift and for being satirized by Pope in *The Dunciad* and in "Epistle to Dr. Arbuthnot." He, nonetheless, also holds the distinction of being the first critic to write an extended commentary on Shakespeare's body of work.

The Life of Henry V.

The Prologue to this Play is as remarkable as any thing in *Shakespear*, and is a Proof that he was extremely sensible of the Absurdity, which then possess'd the Stage, in bringing in whole Kingdoms, and Lives, and various Actions, in one Piece; for he apologizes for it, and desires the Audience to persuade their Imaginations to help him out, and promises a Chorus to help their Imagination.

> *For 'tis your Thought t (says he) that now must deck our Kings,*
> *Carry them here and there, jumping o'er Times;*
> *Turning the Accomplishments of many years*
> *Into an Hour-Glass: for the which supply*
> *Admit me Chorus to this History.*

He here, and in the foregoing Lines, expresses how preposterous it seem'd to him and unnatural, to huddle so many Actions, so many Places, and so many Years into one Play, one Stage, and two Hours. So that it is not to be doubted but that he wou'd have given us far more noble Plays, if he had had the good Fortune to have seen but any one regular Performance of this Nature. The Beauty of Order wou'd have struck him immediately, and at once have made him more correct, and more excellent; and I do not at all doubt but that he wou'd have been the *Sophocles* of *England*, as he is now but little more than the *Thespis*, or at most the *Æschylus*. Tho Tragedy in Greece was founded on Religion, and came early under the Care of the Magistrate; yet by what I can discover, the Stage was as rude as our's, till *Æschylus* gave it Majesty. But in *England* it had no such advantageous Foundation, nor any such nourishing Influence; yet *Shakespear* by his own Genius brought it so far, as to leave it some Beauties, which have never since been equall'd.

The Character of *Henry V.* given by the Bishop of Canterbury, is very noble. His Discourse of the Salique Law, is a Proof, that Shakespear was well acquainted with the History of modern Times, and that very Controversy; which was an Argument of his Application to reading, and will not let me think, that having some Foundation of *Latin*, he should totally neglect that.

Obedience and Order,

> *Therefore doth Heaven divide*
> *The State of Man in divers Functions, &c.*

The fine Description of the State of the Bees is worth a careful Observation in this same Speech. The King's Answer to the French Ambassadors, on the *Dauphine*'s Present, is not only fine, but shews that *Shakespear* understood Tennis very well, and was perfect in the Terms of the Art. The *Chorus* is forc'd to come in to fill up the Gap of Time, and help the Imagination of the Audience with a Narration of what is not represented. In this Chorus are a few Lines of good Morals to the English, and therefore I transcribe them.

O! England: Model to thy inward Greatness,
Like a little Body with a mighty Heart:
What mightst thou do, that Honour wou'd thee do,
Were all thy Children kind and natural?

King Henry Vth's Speech to Scroop, &c. from this Line, is very fine.

Oh! how hast thou with Jealousy infected,
The Sweetness of Affiance—

The latter end of the Constable of *France*'s Speech, and part of the *French* King's, is worth perusing, as giving a noble Character of two *English* Kings; and *Exeter*'s Anawer to the *French* in the next Page, shews the Spirit of en *English* Nobleman. The *Chorus* is necessitated to come in again, to tell all that must be suppos'd to connect the Representation before to that which follows. King Henry's Encouragement of his Men contains a great many fine Lines. Another *Chorus* begins the third Act, to help out the Lameness of the Representation; and I wonder when *Shakespear* was sensible of the Absurdity of the bringing a Battle on the Stage, he shou'd in some measure do it not-withstanding.

Were OI (for Pity) we shall much disgrace
With four or five most vile and ragged Foils
(Right ill-dispos'd in Brawl ridiculous)
The Name of Agin-Court, &c.

A King but a Man.

—*I think the King is but a Man, as I am. The Violet smells to him as it does to me,* &c.—Tho the Dizcourses of the King to *Williams, &c.* are very good, and full of Reason and Morality, yet contain they nothing Dramatic, and are indeed fitter for a Philosopher, than a King.

On a King and Greatness.

Upon the King, &c.
Oh! hard Condition, twin-born with Greatness
Subject to the Breath of every Fool.

Of Ceremony.

And what art thou, thou Idol Ceremony? &c.

See *Grandpree*'s Description of the low Condition of the *English* Army.

What I have already said of *Shakespear*'s being sensible of the Defect of these historical Representations, is confirm'd plainly in the *Chorus* of the fifth Act.

> *I humbly pray them to admit th' excuse*
> *Of Time, of Numbers, and due Course of things'*
> *Which cannot in their huge and proper Life*
> *Be here presented.*

He shows how sensible he is of this in the short Chorus that ends this Play, zaying.

> *Thus far with rough, and all-unable Pen,*
> *Our bending Author hath pursued the Story,*
> *In little Room confining mighty Men;*
> *Mangling by Starts the full Course of their Glory.*

And indeed all that can be done in these Cases, is only a Collection of so many Themes of different Subjects: As in *Burgundy*'s Speech, the Description of *Peace*, and its Advantages.

The Character of *Fluellen* is extremely comical, and yet so very happily touch'd, that at the same time when he makes us laugh, he makes us value his Character. The Scene of Love betwixt *Henry V.* and Catherine, is extravagantly silly and unnatural; for why he should not allow her to speak in *English,* as well as all the other *French* I cannot imagine, since it adds no Beauty, but gives a patch'd and pye-bald Dialogue of no Beauty or Force.

1726—Lewis Theobald. From *Shakespeare Restor'd*

Lewis Theobald (1688-1744) was a poet, dramatist, translator, and editor who served as the hero in Alexander Pope's first version of *The Dunciad,* largely because he earned Pope's ire for correcting the errors Pope had made in his edition of Shakespeare. Theobald, nonetheless, was the better editor, and his solutions to some textual problems in the extant Shakespearean texts continue to be followed by those who edit the playwright.

> *For after I saw him fumble with the Sheets, and play with Flowers, and smile upon his Finger's End, I knew there was but one way; for his nose was as sharp as a Pen.*

*His nose was as sharp as a pen, and a table of green fields.

These Words, and a table of green fields, *are not to be found in the old Editions of* 1600 *and* 1608. *This nonsense got into all the following Editions by a pleasant mistake of the Stage-Editors, who printed from the common piece-meal written Parts in the Play-house. A Table was here directed to be brought in, (it being a scene in a tavern where they drink at parting,) and this Direction crept into the text from the margin.* Greenfield *was the name of the Property-man in that time who furnish'd implements,* &c. *for the actors.* A Table *of* Greenfield's.

So far, the Note of the EDITOR. Something more than *Ingenuity* is wanting, as I said before, to make these Conjectures pass current; and That is, a *competent Knowledge* of the *Stage* and its *Customs.* As to the History of *Greenfield* being then Property-Man, whether it was really so, or it be only a *gratis dictum,* is a Point which I shall not contend about. But allowing the marginal Direction, and supposing that a *Table* of *Greenfield's* was wanting; I positively deny that it ever was customary (or, that there can be any Occasion for it) either in the *Prompter's* Book, or piece-meal Parts, where any such Directions are marginally inserted for the *Properties,* or *Implements* wanted, to add the *Property-Man's* Name whose Business it was to provide them. The Stage-Necessaries are always furnish'd between the *'Property-Man* and the *Scene-Keeper;* and as the Direction is for the *Prompter's* Use, and issued from him, there can be no Occasion, as I said, for inserting the Names either of the one, or the other.

But there is a stronger Objection yet against this Conjecture of the *Editor's,* in the Manner he supposes it: Which he must have foreseen, had he had that Acquaintance with Stage- Books, which it has been my Fortune to have. Surely, Mr. POPE cannot imagine, that when Implements are wanted in any Scene, the Direction for them is mark'd in the Middle of that Scene, tho' the Things are to be got ready against the Beginning of it. No; the Directions for *Entrances,* and *Properties* wanting, are always mark'd in the Book at about a Page in Quantity before the *Actors* quoted are to enter, or the *Properties* be carried on. And therefore GREENFIELD's *Table* can be of no Use to us for this Scene.

I agree, indeed, with *Mr. Pope,* that these Words might be a *Stage-Direction, and so* crept into the Text from the Margin: But, I insist, that they must be a Direction then for the *subsequent* Scene, and not for the Scene *in Action.* I don't care therefore if I venture my Conjecture too upon the Passage: I'll be sure at least, if it be not altogether right, it shall not be liable to the *Absurdity* of the *Objection* last struck at. I suppose, with the Editor, that over-against the Words of the Text, there might be this Marginal Quotation so close to them, that the Ignorance of the Stage-Editors might easily give them Admittance into the Text.

——— h*is Nose was as sharp as a Chairs,* and a Table off. Green
Pen. Fields.

The Scene in Action is part of Dame *Quickly*, the Hostess, her House; and Chairs and Table were here necessary: The following Scene carries us into the *French* Dominions. I therefore believe This was intended as a Direction to the *Scene-Keepers*, to be ready to remove the *Chairs* and *Table* so soon as the *Actors* went off; and to shift the Scene, from the *Tavern*, to a Prospect of *green Fields*, representing Part of the *French* Territories.

But what if it should be thought proper to retract both Mr. Pope's and my own Conjecture, and to allow that these Words, corrupt as they now are, might have belong'd to the Poet's Text? I have an Edition of *Shakespeare* by Me with some Marginal Conjectures of a Gentleman sometime deceas'd, and he is of the Mind to correct this Passage thus;

for his Nose was as sharp as a Pen, and a' talked *of green Fields.*

It is certainly observable of People near Death, when they are delirious by a Fever, that they talk of moving; as it is of Those in a Calenture, that they have their Heads run on green Fields. The Variation from *Table* to *talked* is not of a very great Latitude; tho' we may still come nearer to the Traces of the Letters, by restoring it thus;

for his Nose was as sharp as a Pen, and a' babled *of green Fields.*

To *bable*, or *babble*, is to mutter, or speak indiscriminately, like Children that cannot yet talk, or dying Persons when they are losing the Use of Speech.

. . .

Will. *Under what Captain serve you?*
K. Hen. *Under Sir* JOHN Erpingham.
Will. *A good old Commander*, &c.

Here again History and our Poet's Text are made to disagree; nor was there any such Gentleman as Sir *John Erpingham* in Being in K. *Henry* Vth's Reign:

Restore it, as it ought
to be;

Will. *Under what Captain serve you?*
K. Hen. *Under Sir* THOMAS Erpingham, &c.

This is one of the Characters introduced in the Play; and he entring but three Pages before, the King salutes him thus;

Good Murrow, old Sir THOMAS Erpingham:
A good soft Pillow for that good white Head
Were better than a churlish Turf of France.

That this was his Name, we have the Authority of our Chronicles; and They, and our Poet from them, in his *Richard* II., tell us, that Sir *"Thomas Erpingham was One of those who embark'd from Bretagne to espouse the Interest of Bolingbroke* the Father of K. *Henry* V.

XLIII. *The Like.*

> Alarum. *Enter K.* Henry *and* BOURBON *with Prisoners, Lords,* &c.

This is likewise an Error transmitted from the Old to the Modern Editions; *Bourbon* was one of the *French* Party, and therefore could not make a Part of K. *Henry's* Train. Restore it;

> Alarm, *Enter K.* Henry *and* GLOUCESTER, *with Prisoners,* &c.

But may it not be said, that *Bourbon* is brought in here amongst the *French* Prisoners? To This, I reply, that our Poet would hardly have introduc'd a Character of that Dignity, crowded him amongst the common Prisoners, and neither made him speak to the King, nor the King to him. Besides, I have another Exception yet stronger to add, why *Bourbon* cannot be supposcd to enter here: In a few Pages after, the King asks the Duke of *Exeter* (who enter'd with him, and had been all along in the Prefence) what Prisoners of Rank were taken, and *Exeter* replies;

> Charles *Dukc of* Orleans, *Nephew to the King;*
> John *Duke of* BOURBON, *and Lord* Bouchiquald.

I submit it therefore to the most common Judgments, whether 'tis probable, if *Bourbon* was among the Prisoners introduc'd in the King's Train, that the Duke of *Exeter* could have been guilty of such an Absurdity, to tell the King that *Bourbon* was taken Prisoner.

. . .

LXXV. K. Henry V.

> *High Dukes, great Princes, Barons, Lords and* KINGS.

The *French* King is speaking here to the Great Lords of his Court, and Army, in all these pompous Titles. But why, *Kings?* There was not one King amongst them besides the Speaker. Tho' this Error runs thro' all the Copies, correct it,

> *High Dukes, great Princes, Barons, Lords, and* KNIGHTS.

When the Battle is over, and we come to have an Account of the Loss on the *French* Side, we find that they had 500 Knights dubb'd but the Day before the Battle: And that in the 10000 Men, which they lost, there were but 1600 who fought for Pay. The rest, as the Poet tells us, Page 481, were

Princes, Barons, Lords, KNIGHTS, *Squires,*
And Gentlemen of Blood and Quality.

1735—Aaron Hill. From *The Prompter*

Aaron Hill (1685–1750), in addition to writing numerous poems, was an important figure in theatrical circles during the first half of the eighteenth century. He co-wrote, at the age of 26, the opera *Rinaldo,* which introduced Handel to England as well as popularized opera in the country, and later wrote original plays, an adaptation of *Henry V* and translations of Voltaire's *Zaire* and *Alzire.* He also served as a stage manager and published *The Prompter,* a theatrical journal. He is probably best known today for being ridiculed by Alexander Pope in *The Dunciad.*

Mark, in these French, *and* English, *here,* oppos'd,
The different Genius *of the* Realms *disclos'd:*
There, *the* French Levity, *vain—boastful,—loud—*:
Dancing, *in* Death!—*gay, wanton, fierce, and proud!*
Here, *with a* silent *Fire, a* temper'd *Heat;*
Calmly Resolv'd, *our* English *Bosoms beat.*

    Prol. to King *Henry* the Vth.

I felt myself *blush,* the other Day, under Sense of the *Weakness* of human *Vanity,* in the narrow, *national Prejudices,* which incline Every People under the Sun to prefer *Themselves, and* THEIR *Country,* above all the Rest of the World: whereby Every Nation, by Turns, *ridicules,* and is *ridicul'd by,* Another.

The Occasion of this Reflexion arose from such an Instance of Partiality, in one of our own *Historical* Writers, who, speaking of our *Success,* in a Battle, He has been describing, is pleas'd to conclude, with this sagacious Remark, to the Honour of his Country-men—"In fine, The *English,,* in This Day's Action, behav'd themselves, like *English-men,* fighting against *French-men*—THAT is,— like Men, Born, to Conquer."

However laudable the *Motive* of this Judgment, I was shock'd at the *insult* of it; and, throwing aside any Author, for Another, who lay next him, happened to take up a *French-man*, in his stead:—And, the first Paragraph I open'd upon, was the following Instance of that Gentleman's Respect, for the *Ladies*, of His Country.

"Of *Women*, I say nothing: but shall imitate *Lycurgus*, and *Aristotle; who* conceiv'd it *impossible* to restrain *them*, by Rules, because so *imperious, and willful.*—This, indeed, in FRENCH-WOMEN, is more pardonable than *in others*, since It is *Their Due* to be *Mistresses*, who have the *Glory of giving Birth*, to Men, whose *Valour*, and *Great qualities*, have accomplish'd them for *Conquerors of All the Earth!*"

By this Time, I *absolv'd* the *English-man's* Partiality: and looking forward, a few Leaves, where the Author in my Hand was instructing the *French King*, his Master, how to become Powerful *at Sea*, and *humble the Insolence of* the People of *Tunis, Algiers, Holland*, and ENGLAND (for in this Order, he puts us together!) I met with a second Demonstration, that *Vanity*, might (as justly as *Ingratitude)* have been call'd, by the Poet,

"——*The Growth, of* Every *Clime*.

"These, All, (says He) are *Petty States*, yet, *dare* measure their Force, with *Great Monarchs.*—The Former of them, but *Turkish Slaves*, the others, *Revolted Burghers:*—And, how *insolent* soever the ENGLISH are, They must confess, that All their *Islands* together equal not *Half* of *our Continent:* either in Extent, in Fertility, in Commodiousness of Situation, or in Number of Men, Wealth, Valour, Industry, or Undemanding.—Yet, they fear not to affirm themselves *Sovereigns of the Sea.*—But, had they cast up the *Battles* they have *lost;* had they well examin'd our *Ports;* In fine, had they *compar'd the Coasts of* FRANCE *with those of* ENGLAND, They would *be asham'd of their Vanity*.

"As for Matter of the *English*, (continues He, in another Place) They have not any Friends: They are a Sort of People, without *Faith*, without *Religion*, without *Honesty*, without any *Justice at all;* of the greatest *Levity* that can be; Cruel, Impatient, Gluttonous, Proud, Audacious, Covetous fit for handy Strokes, and a sudden Execution; but *unable to carry on a War, with Judgment* Their Country is good enough for Sustenance of Life, but not rich enough to afford them Means for issuing forth, and making any Conquest: Accordingly, they never conquer'd any thing, but *Ireland*, whose inhabitants are *weak*, and *ill Soldiers*. On the contrary, the *Romans* conquer'd *Them;* then, the *Danes*, and the *Normans;* in such a Manner, too, that their present Kings are the *Heirs* of a *Conqueror*. They *hate one Another*, and are in *continual Division*, either about Religion, or about the Government. A War of *France* for three or four Years upon them, would *totally ruin them*. So, it seems reasonable, that we should make *no Peace* with them, but upon Conditions of *greatest Advantage for us*.

"In *fine*, if we had a Mind to *ruin the English*, we need but oblige them to *keep an Army on foot;* and there is no Fear, that they should make any Invasion upon *France;* That would be their undoubted *Ruin*, if they be not call'd in by some Rebels.—Now, if they have an *Army*, they will, infallibly, *make War upon one another*, and so, *ruin* THEMSELVES.—You must put them upon making *great Expences;* and, for this End, raise a Jalousy for them in the Isles of *Jersey*, and *Guernsey*, of *Wight*, and *Man*, for the *Cinque Ports*, and *Ireland;* and, by that Means, oblige them to keep strong Garisons, in all those Places; This will create a Belief in the People, that the *King* forms great Projects *against their Liberty;* and, while He is in *Arms*, his Subjects will *hate* Him.

THEY must be wrought to Distrusts of one another, by writing Letters, in *Cypher* to some Particular Persons, and causing them to be intercepted: For (being *Suspicious*, and *Imprudent)* they will soon be persuaded, that the Letters were *seriously written:*—Some Forces should be landed in *Ireland*, and in other Parts. The *Irish* may be induced to *revolt*, as having a mortal *Hatred* for the *English:* The *Scots* also will not neglect to set themselves at *Liberty:*—FACTIONS muft be raised, and the Sects favour'd, against One another; especially the *Catholicks;* among whom the *Benedictine Monks*, in particular, should be secretly promis'd, on the *King of England's* Behalf, (wherein it will be easy to *deceive* them) that they shall be *restor'd to all the Estates*, which they once possess'd in the Island, according to the *Monasticon*, there printed.—Upon This, the *Monks* will move Heaven, and Earth, and the *Catholicks* DECLARE themselves; and, so, All will fall into utter Confusion, and the *English Monarchy* be in Case to be *divided.*"

Thus far, the Author of a Treatise, call'd *The Politics of France:* and the Use I wou'd make of the *Quotation*, is to recommend a Detestation of this *Self-preference*, in our *own Ideas*, which, in those of Another, makes so ridiculous a Figure.

The unreflecting Vivacity of Spirit, so natural to a *French-Man*, is some Excuse for his most ill-grounded Partialities: But, we *English-Men* are *unpardonable*, in our *Vanities*, because they are *heavy*, and *serious* ones.—There is the same kind of Difference, too, in the *Virtues* of these Nations—They are, *Both*, remarkable for *Courage:* But, the Courage of the One is *precipitate;* of the Other, *progressive*, and *lasting.*—Our excellent Countryman, *Shakespear*, in that *Tragedy*, from which I have taken my *Motto*, has given us a View of this *Contraste*, in the strongest, and most beautiful Light, from the different Behaviour of the *Dauphin*, and other *French* Generals, compar'd with that of the *English King*, in the Night that preceded the *Battle of Agincourt*.

SCENE, *a Tent, in the* French *Camp.*
The *Dauphin*, with the Dukes *of Orleans* and *Bourbon.*
Bourb. Nay, never go about to dispute it: 'tis the best *Armour* in the World.
Orl.—The Armour is Excellent:—But, then, rob not *my Horse* of his Due.
Dauph.—Will it never be Morning?—My Lords, of *Orleans*, and *Bourbon*, You talk, of Horse, and Armour: I'll not change *my* Horse, for a *Diadem.*—Cha ha,—Cha ha—He bounds from the Earth, as if his Entrails were *Hairs!*—He's the Horse of the *Muses:* the *Pegasus!* with

Nostrils of Fire!—When I once get astride him, I *soar!* I'm a *Hawk!*—
He trots through the *Air;* The Earth *sings* when he touches it: And the
basest Horn of his Hoof is more Musical than the *Harp of Apollo!*
Orl. He's of the Colour of .a Nutmeg.
Dauph.—And of the *Heat* of the Ginger!—'Tis a Beast for a *Perseus!*
pure *Air*, and *Fire!* The dull Elements of *Water*, and *Earth*, never appear
in him, but only in patient Stillness while I mount him.—He is indeed
a *Horse:* and All Others, of his Kind, You may *call Jades.*
Bourb.—Indeed my Lord, It is a most absolute and excellent Horse.
Dauph.—He is the *Prince of Palfreys!* His Neigh is like the *Bidding* of a
Monarch! and his Countenance enforces *Homage!*
Orl.—Well—but, enough of him, Cousin.
Dauph.—Psha! the Man has *no Wit*, who can't, from the Rising of the
Lark, to the Lodging of the Lamb, *vary* deserv'd Praises, on *my Palfry.*
The Theme is as fluent as the *Sea!*—Turn the *Sands* into elegant *Tongues,*
and MY HORSE will be Argument for 'em all.————Will it never be
Day?—I will trot him, to-morrow, a Mile and a Half; and my Way shall
be *pav'd* with *English-Mens Faces!*
Orl.—I would it were Morning: for I would fain be about the Ears of
the *English.*
Bourb.—Who'll go to *Hazard* with me, for *Twenty Prisoners?*
Dauph.—Alas! *Poor Harry!* He longs not for the Morning, as We do.—
What a wretched, peevish Fellow is This King of *England*, to mope, with
his fat-brain'd Followers, so far out of his Knowledge!
Orl.—If the *English* had any Apprehension, they Wou'd *run away.*
Bourb.—That Island of *England* breeds very valiant *Mastiffs.*
Dauph.—Foolish Curs! that run, winking, into the Mouth of a *Bear,*
and get their Heads crush'd, like a *Rotten Apple!*—You may e'en as well
say, 'tis a valiant *Flea*, that dares breakfast on the *Lip* of a *Lyon.*
Orl.—Just! Just!—And the Men too, are a-kin to the *Mastiffs:* rough,
and roburst, in coming on.—But, they leave all their *Wit* with their
Wives!—And, then, give 'em great Meals of *Beef;*—and *Iron* and *Steel:*
and they'll *eat like Wolves, and fight like Devils.*
Dauph.—Ay—but *These English* are shrewdly *out of Beef.*—Come—now
we'll *in.*—'tis about two o'Clock: and—let me see—

By Ten,

We shall have, Each, a Hundred English-Men. [Ex.
Enter King Henry, *as discovering the* French *Camp, at some Distance.*
K.Hen.—The Night wears off, with *slow*, and *heavy*
Now, creeping *Murmur*, and the poring *Dark*, [Pace.
Fill the wide Vessel of the Universe.———.
From Camp, to Camp, thro' the *thick Shade of Night,*

The *Hum* of either Army, *stilly,* sounds!——
The out-fix'd *Centinels* almost receive
The *secret Whispers* of Each Other's *Watch.*
Fire answers Fire: and thro' their *paly* Flames,
Each *Battle* sees the *other's umber'd Face!*
Steed threatens Steed, in high, and boastful, Neigh;
Piercing thc Night's dull Ear.—And, from the Tents,
The *Armourers,* accomplishing the Chiefs,
With Clink of Hammers, closing *Rivets up,*
Give dreadful *Note,* of Preparation.——
The Country *Cocks* crow round us.—Mournful *Bells,*
From Distance, *swing* their flow, and solemn, *Sound!*
—The lusty *French* invite the drowsy Morning:
Proud of their Number, and secure in Soul,
They, the low-rated *English* play at *Dice* for.——
—My poor, condemn'd, and *thoughtful* Followers
Sit, *patiently,* round their small, watchful, Fires,
And *inly ruminate* the Morning's Danger.
Their lank, lean, Cheeks, sad Air, and war-worn Coats,
Present them, to the distant-gazing *Moon,*
So many horrid *Ghosts!*—Oh!—*Thou,* SUPREAM!
Thou! in whose Hand alone lies *Victory!*
Thou MAKER of the *Soul,* that bows before thee!
Judge, 'twixt my *Foes,* and *Me.*—If Thou decreest
To bless me, with the *Power of blessing Others,*
Preserve *my Life,* for All my *People's* Safety.
—But, *if my Death* can free my dear-lov'd Country,
From any doom'd Distress, my Life must cause her
Oh! *then*—accept *Me,* as my Subject's *Sacrifice,*
And, Ihave *liv'd enough.*—.

————— ·∿∿∿· ——— ·∿∿∿· ——— ·∿∿∿· —————

1744—Thomas Hanmer. Preface to the Oxford Edition

Sir Thomas Hanmer (1677-1746), who spent a good part of his adult life as a member of Parliament where he also served for a time as the speaker of the House of Commons, is remembered for his 1744 edition of Shakespeare's works, a text in which he sought to amend irregularities of some of the verse and remove vulgarities he believed Shakespeare incapable of producing.

What the Publick is here to expect is a true and correct Edition of Shakespear's works cleared from the corruptions with which they have hitherto abounded. One of the great Admirers of this incomparable Author hath made it the amusement of his leisure hours for many years past to look over his writings with a careful eye, to note the obscurities and absurdities introduced into the text, and according to the best of his judgment to restore the genuine sense and purity of it. In this he proposed nothing to himself but his private satisfaction in making his own copy as perfect as he could: but as the emendations multiplied upon his hands, other Gentlemen equally fond of the Author desired to see them, and some were so kind as to give their assistance by communicating their observations and conjectures upon difficult passages which had occurred to them. Thus by degrees the work growing more considerable than was at first expected, they who had the opportunity of looking into it, too partial perhaps in their judgment, thought it worth being made publick; and he, who hath with difficulty yielded to their perswasions, is far from desiring to reflect upon the late Editors for the omissions and defects which they left to be supplied by others who should follow them in the same province. On the contrary, he thinks the world much obliged to them for the progress they made in weeding out so great a number of blunders and mistakes as they have done, and probably he who hath carried on the work might never have thought of such an undertaking if he had not found a considerable part so done to his hands.

From what causes it proceeded that the works of this Author in the first publication of them were more injured and abused than perhaps any that ever pass'd the Press, hath been sufficiently explained in the Preface to Mr. Pope's Edition which is here subjoined, and there needs no more to be said upon that subject. This only the Reader is desired to bear in mind, that as the corruptions are more numerous and of a grosser kind than can well be conceived but by those who have looked nearly into them; so in the correcting them this rule hath been most strictly observed, not to give a loose to fancy, or indulge a licentious spirit of criticism, as if it were fit for any one to presume to judge what *Shakespear* ought to have written, instead of endeavouring to discover truly and retrieve what he did write: and so great caution hath been used in this respect, that no alterations have been made but what the sense necessarily required, what the measure of the verse often helped to point out, and what the similitude of words in the false reading and in the true, generally speaking, appeared very well to justify.

Most of those passages are here thrown to the bottom of the page and rejected as spurious, which were stigmatized as such in Mr. Pope's Edition; and it were to be wished that more had then undergone the same sentence. The promoter of the present Edition hath ventured to discard but few more upon his own judgment, the most considerable of which is that wretched piece of ribaldry in King *Henry V.* put into the mouths of the *French* Princess and an old Gentlewoman, improper enough as it is all in *French* and not intelligible to an

English audience, and yet that perhaps is the best thing that can be said of it. There can be no doubt but a great deal more of that low stuff which disgraces the works of this great Author, was foisted in by the Players after his death, to please the vulgar audiences by which they subsisted: and though some of the poor witticisms and conceits must be supposed to have fallen from his pen, yet as he hath put them generally into the mouths of low and ignorant people, so it is to be remember'd that he wrote for the Stage, rude and unpolished as it then was; and the vicious taste of the age must stand condemned for them, since he hath left upon record a signal proof how much he despised them. In his Play of *The Merchant of Venice* a clown is introduced quibbling in a miserable manner, upon which one who bears the character of a man of sense makes the following reflection: *How every fool can play upon a word! I think the best grace of wit will shortly turn into silence, and discourse grow commendable in none but parrots.* He could hardly have found stronger words to express his indignation at those false pretences to wit then in vogue; and therefore though such trash is frequently interspersed in his writings, it would be unjust to cast it as an imputation upon his taste and judgment and character as a Writer.

There being many words in Shakespear which are grown out of use and obsolete, and many borrowed from other languages which are not enough naturalized or known among us, a Glossary is added at the end of the work, for the explanation of all those terms which have hitherto been so many stumbling-blocks to the generality of Readers; and where there is any obscurity in the text not arising from the words but from a reference to some antiquated customs now forgotten, or other causes of that kind, a note is put at the bottom of the page to clear up the difficulty.

With these several helps if that rich vein of sense which runs through the works of this Author can be retrieved in every part and brought to appear in its true light, and if it may be hoped without presumption that this is here effected; they who love and admire him will receive a new pleasure, and all probably will be more ready to join in doing him justice, who does great honour to his country as a rare and perhaps a singular Genius: one who hath attained an high degree of perfection in those two great branches of Poetry, Tragedy and Comedy, different as they are in their natures from each other; and who may be said without partiality to have equalled, if not excelled, in both kinds, the best writers of any age or country who have thought it glory enough to distinguish themselves in either.

Since therefore other nations have taken care to dignify the works of their most celebrated poets with the fairest impressions beautified with the ornaments of sculpture, well may our *Shakespear* be thought to deserve no less consideration: and as a fresh acknowledgment hath lately been paid to his merit, and a high regard to his name and memory, by erecting his Statue at a publick expence; so it is desired that this new Edition of his works, which hath cost some attention and care, may be looked upon as another small monument designed and dedicated to his honour.

1754—Charlotte Lennox. "*The Life of King Henry the Fifth*," from *Shakespeare Illustrated*

A member of Samuel Johnson's circle, Charlotte Lennox, née Ramsay (ca. 1730–1804), was a poet, novelist, and dramatist, as well as a Shakespearean scholar. Her contribution to Shakespearean studies was primarily to trace and illustrate, to a greater extent than anyone before her, the source material behind Shakespeare's plays. *Shakespeare Illustrated* thus stands as the first source study of the plays.

The Transactions comprised in this Historical Play, commence about the latter End of the first, and terminate in the eighth Year of this King's Reign, when he married the Princess *Catharine* of *France,* and put an End to the Differences betwixt *England* and that Crown.

The Siege and taking of *Harfleur,* the Battle of *Agincourt,* the Peace concluded between King *Henry* and the *French* King, with the Marriage of the former to the Princess of *France,* are the principal Actions of this Play, and are taken from *Holingshed's* Chronicle, after whom the Characters are likewise drawn, with very little Variation.

The Archbishop's Speech to King *Henry,* in the first Act, in which he explains his Title to the Crown of *France,* is closely copied from this Historian, *Page* 545. "Herein did he much enveie against the surmised and false fained Law *Salike,* which the *Frenchmen* allege ever against the Kings of *England* in barre of their just Title to the Crown of *France.* The verie Words of that supposed Law are these, *In terram Salicam Mulieres ne succedant.* That is to say, Into the Salike Land let not Women succeed. Which the *French* Glossers expound to be the Realme of *France,* and that this Law was made by King *Pharamond;* whereas yet their own Authors affirme, that the Land *Salike* is in *Germany* between the Rivers *Elbe* and *Sala,* and that when *Charles* the Great had overcome the *Saxons,* he placed there certain *Frenchmen,* which having in disdain the dishonest Manners of the *German* Women, made a Law that the Females should not succeed to any Inheritance within that Land, which at this Day is called *Meisen:* So that if this be true, this Law was not made for the Realme of *France,* nor the *Frenchmen* possessed the Land *Salike,* till four hundred and one and twenty Years after the Death of *Pharamond,* the supposed Author of this *Salike* Law; for this *Pharamond* deceased in the Year

426, and *Charles* the Great subdued the *Saxons* and placed the *Frenchmen* in
those Parts, beyond the River of *Sala,* in the Year 805.

Moreover, it appeareth by their own Writers, that King *Pepen* which deposed
Childerike, claimed the Crown of *France,* as Heir general, for that he was descended
of *Blithila* Daughter of King *Clothair* the first: *Hugh Capet* also, who usurped the
Crown upon *Charles* Duke of *Loraine,* the sole Heir-male of the Line and Stocke
of *Charles* the Great, to make his Title seem true, and appear good, though indeed
it was starke naught; conceived himself as Heir to the Ladie *Lingard,* Daughter
to King *Charlemain,* Sonne to *Lewis* the Emperor, that was Sonne to *Charles* the
Great: King *Lewis* also the tenth, otherwise also called Saint *Lewis* being verie
Heir to the Usurper *Hugh Capet,* could never be satisfied in his Conscience how
he might justly keep and possesse the Crowne of *France,* till he was persuaded
and fully instructed that Queene *Isabell* his Grandmother was lineally descended
of the Ladie *Ormengard* Daughter and Heir to the above named *Charles* Duke
of *Loraine;* by the which Marriage, the Blood and Line of *Charles* the Great was
again united and restored to the Crowne and Scepter of *France:* So that more
clear than the Sun, it openly appeareth, that the Title of King *Pepen,* the Claim
of *Hugh Capet,* the Possession of *Lewis;* yea, and the *French* Kings to this Day,
are derived and conveyed from the Heirs-female, though they would, under the
Colour of such a feigned Law, barre the Kings and Princes of this Realme of
England of their right and lawful Inheritance.

The Archbishop further alleged, out of the Book of *Numbers,* this Saying:
When a Man dieth without a Son, let the Inheritance descend to his Daughter. At
length having said sufficiently for the Proof of the King's just and lawful Title
to the Crown of *France,* he exhorted him to advance forth his Banner to fight
for his Right, to conquer his Inheritance, to spare neither Blood, Sword, nor
Fire, sith his War was just, his Cause good, and his Claim true; and to the
Intent his loving Chaplains, and obedient Subjects of the Spiritualtie might
shew themselves willing and desirous to aid his Majesty for the Recovery of
his ancient Right and true Inheritance, the Archbishop declared that, in their
Spiritual Convocation, they had granted to his Highness such a Summe of
Money, as never, by no spiritual Persons, was to any Prince before those Days,
given or advanced." *Holingshed.*

CANTERBURY.

Then hear me, gracious Sovereign, and you Peers
That owe your Lives, your Faith and Services
To this imperial Throne: There is no Bar
To make against your Highness' Claim to *France,*
But this which they produce from *Pharamond;*
In Terra Salicam Mulieres ne succedant;
No Woman shall succeed in *Salike* Land:

Which *Salike* Land the *French* unjustly gloze,
To be the Realm of *France,* and *Pharamond,*
The Founder of this Law and female Bar:
Yet their own Authors faithfully affirm,
That the Land *Salike* lies in *Germany,*
Between the Floods of *Sala* and of *Elve:*
Where *Charles* the Great, having subdued the *Saxons,*
There left behind and settled certain *French:*
Who holding in Disdain the *German* Women,
For some dishonest Manners of their Life,
Establish'd then this Law, to wit, no Female
Should be Inheretrix in *Salick* Land;
Which *Salick,* as I said, 'twixt *Elve* and *Sala,*
Is at this Day in *Germany* called *Meisens:*
Thus doth it well appear, the *Salick* Law
Was not devised for the Realm of *France;*
Nor did the *French* possess the *Salick* Land,
Untill four hundred one and twenty Years
After Defunction of King *Pharamond,*
(Idly suppos'd the Founder of this Law)
Who died within the Year of our Redemption
Four hundred twenty-six; and *Charles* the Great
Subdu'd the *Saxons,* and did seat the *French*
Beyond the River *Sala,* in the Year
Eight hundred five: Besides, their Writers say,
King *Pepen,* which deposed *Childerick,*
Did, as Heir-general (being descended
Of *Blithild,* which was Daughter to King *Clothair)*
Make Claim and Title to the Crown of *France.*
Hugh Capet also, who usurp'd the Crown
Of *Charles* the Duke of *Lorain, sole* Heir-male
Of the true Line and Stock of *Charles* the Great,
To fine his Title with some Shews of Truth
(Though, in pure Truth, it was corrupt and naught)
Convey'd himself, as Heir to th'Lady *Lingar*
Daughter to *Charlemain,* who was the Son
To *Lewis* the Emperor, which was the Son
Of *Charles* the Great. Also, King *Lewis* the Ninth,
Who was sole Heir to the Usurper *Capet,*
Could not keep Quiet in his Conscience,
Wearing the Crown of *France,* till satisfy'd
That fair Queen *Isabel,* his Grandmother,

Was lineal of the Lady *Ermengere,*
Daughter to *Charles,* the foresaid Duke of *Lorrain;*
By the which Match the Line of *Charles* the Great
Was re-united to the Crown of *France.*
So that, as clear as is the Summer's Sun,
King *Pepin's* Title, and *Hugh Capet's* Claim,
King *Lewis,* his Satisfaction, all appear
To hold in Right and Title of the Female:
So do the Kings of *France* until this Day.
Howbeit, they would hold up this *Salick* Law,
To bar your Highness, claiming from the Female,
And rather choose to hide them in a Net,
Than amply to unbare their crooked Titles,
Usurp'd from you and your Progenitors.

In *Shakespear,* when the Conspiracy of *Scroop, Cambridge,* and *Grey,* is discovered to the King, after expostulating with them on their Treachery, he gives them up to punishment and dismisses them from his Presence in the very Words of *Holingshed:*

Touching; our Person seek we no Revenge;
But we our Kingdom's safety must so tender,
Whose ruin you three sought, that to her Laws
We do deliver you. Go therefore hence,
Poor miserable Wretches to your Death;
The Taste whereof God of his Mercy give
You Patience to endure, and true Repentance
Of all your dear Offences! bear them hence.

"Revenge herein touching my Person, tho' I seek not; yet for the Safeguard of my dear Friends, and for due Preservation of all Sorts, I am by Office to cause Example to be shewed: Get ye hence, therefore, you poor miserable Wretches, to the receiving of your just Reward, wherein God's Majesty give you Grace of his Mercy, and Repentance of your heinous Offences." *Holingshed.*

In the Play, King *Henry,* after the taking of *Harfleur,* marches his Army, which was greatly reduced by Sickness and Fatigue, towards *Calais,* and is met by a Messenger from the *French* King; who, in his Master's Name, defies him to a Battle: *Shakespear,* in the latter Part of the Kings Answer, again copies the Words of *Holingshed,*

Go, bid thy Master well advise himself:
If we may pass we will; if we be hinder'd,

We shall your tawny Ground with your red Blood
Discolour, and so *Mountjoy* fare you well.
The Sun of all our Answer is but this:
We wou'd not seek a Battle as we are,
Yet, as we are, we say, we will not shun it.

"I will not seek your Master, at this Time, but, if he or his seek me, I will
meet with them, God willing: If any of your Nation attempt once to slop me in
my Journey towards *Calais*, at their Jeopardy be it; and yet wish I not any of you
so unadvised as to be the Occasion that I dye your tawny Ground with your red
Blood."- *Holingshed.*

Shakespear, throughout this Play, has copied many of the Sentiments and even
Words of *Holingshed*, sometimes almost literally, as in the above quoted Passages;
at others he has just taken Hints which the Force of his own Imagination
improves into the most striking Beauties, the following Passage of *Holingshed*
furnished him with some of the noblest Thoughts that ever animated the Mind
of a Heroe.

The Historian says, Page 553, that a little Time before the Battle of
Agincourt was fought, King *Henry* overheard a Soldier say to his Fellow: "I
would to God there were with us now so many good Soldiers as are at this
Hour within *England.*" To which the King replied: "I would not wish a Man
more here than I have; we are, indeed, in Comparison to the Enemies, but a
few; but if God, of his Clemency, do favour us and our just Cause (as I trust
he will) we shall Speed well enough: But let no Man ascribe Victory to our
own Strength and Might, but only to God's Assistance, to whom, I have no
doubt we shall worthily have Cause to give thanks therefore; and if so be that,
for our Offences Sakes, we shall be delivered into the Hands of our Enemies,
the less Number we be the less Damage shall the Realm of *England* sustain."
Holingshed.

This Passage is thus improved by *Shakespear:* The Earl of *Westmourland*
having been to take a View of the Enemies Forces, as they were drawn up in
Order of Battle, alarmed at the Superiority of their Numbers, cries out as the
King meets him,

Oh! that we now had here,
But one ten thousand of those Men in *England,*
That do no Work to Day!
        K. HENRY.
What's he that wishes so?
My Cousin *Westmourland?* No, my fair Cousin!
If we are marked to dye, we are enow
To do our Country loss; and if to live,

The fewer Men, the greater share of Honour.
God's Will, I pray thee wish not one Man more.
By Jove I am not covetous of Gold;
Nor care I, who doth feed upon my Cost;
It yerns me not, if Men my Garments wear;
Such outward Things dwell not in my Desire.
But, if it be a Sin to covet Honour,
I am the most offending Soul alive.
No, faith, my Lord, wish not a Man from *England;*
God's Peace, I would not lose so great an Honour
As one Man more, methinks would share from me,
For the best Hopes I have. Don't wish one more:
Rather proclaim it *(Westmourland)* through my Host,
That he, which hath no Stomach to this Fight,
Let him depart; his Passport shall be made,
And crowns for convoy put into his Purse:
We would not die in that Man's Company,
That fears his Fellowahip to die with us.

In the first Act of this Play the Dauphin of *France* sends an insulting Message to King *Henry* accompanied with a Present of Tennis Balls as a Reproach for the wild Sallies of his Youth.

There is no Foundation either in *Hall* or *Holingshed* for this Circumstance, *Shakespear* indeed took the out-lines of the Dauphin's Character from these Historians who represent him to be a light, arrogant, and vain-glorious Prince; but he has painted at full Length what they only drew in Miniture; and by adding, with great Propriety some of the Characteristic Follies of his Nation, given us a lively and numerous Picture of a Coxcomb Prince.

The absurdity of making the Princess *Catharine* the only Person in the *French* Court, who does not understand *English*, has been already taken Notice of: And it must be confessed that the great *Henry* makes but a miserable Figure as a Lover; no Language can be coarser than that in which he addresses the Princess, the first Time he sees her, *Do you like* me Kate, *&c.* Yet the Dialogue is not without wit, livliness, and humour; but so utterly void of Propriety that we lose all Idea of the Dignity of the Persons who manage it, and, are readier to imagine we hear a common Soldier making love to an aukward Country Girl, than a King of *England* courting a Princess of *France.*

Shakespear, it is probable, took the Hint of the *Dauphin's* Present of Tennis Balls from the following old Ballad.

A Council grave our King did hold,
  With many a Lord and Knight;

That they might truly understand,
  That *France* did hold his Right.

Unto the King of *France* therefore
  Ambassadors were sent,
That he might fully understand
  His Mind and his Intent:

Desiring him in friendly wise,
  His lawful Right to yield;
Or else he vow'd, by Dint of Sword
  To win the fame in Field.

The King of *France* with all his Lords,
  Which heard his Message plain,
Unto our brave Ambassadors
  Did answer in Disdain:

And feigned our King was yet too young,
  And of too tender Age;
Therefore we weigh not of his War,
  Nor fear we his Courage.

His Knowledge is in Feats of Arms
  As yet but very small;
His tender Joints much fitter were
  To toss a Tennis Ball.

A Tun of Tennis Balls therefore,
  In Pride and great Disdain,
He sent unto our Noble King,
  To recompence his Pain

Which Answer when our King did hear,
  He waxed wroth in Heart;
And said, he would such *Balls* provide,
  Should make all *France* to smart.

An Army then our King did raise,
  Which was both good and strong;
And from *Southampton* is our King
  With all his Navy gone.

In *France* he landed safe and sound,
   With all his warlike Train;
And to the Town of *Harfleur* strait
   He marched up a-main.

But when he had besieged the same,
   Against their fenced Walls,
To batter down their stately Towers,
   He sent his *English* Balls.

This done, our noble *English* King
   March'd up and down the Land;
And not a *Frenchman* for his Life
   Durst once his Force withstand.

Until he came to *Agincourt*;
   Where as it was his Chance
To find the King in Readiness
   With all his Power of *France*.

A mighty Host he had prepar'd
   Of armed Soldiers then;
Which were no less by just Account,
   Than Forty Thousand Men.

Which Sight did much amaze our King;
   For he and all his Host
Not passing Fifteen Thousand had,
   Accounted at the most.

The King of *France* which well did know
   The Number of our Men,
In vaunting Pride unto our Prince
   Did send a Herald then.

To understand what he would give
   For Ransom of his Life,
When he in Field should taken be
   Amidst their bloody Strife.

And then our King with chearful Heart,
   This Answer soon bid make;

And said, Before this comes to pass,
    Some of their Hearts shall quake.
And to their proud presumptuous Prince,
    Declare this Thing, quoth he,
Mine own Heart's Blood shall pay the Price;
    None else he gets of me.

With that bespoke the Duke of *York;*
    O Noble King, quoth he,
The Leading of this Battle brave
    Vouchsafe to give to me.

God a Mercy, Cousin *York,* quoth he,
    I grant thee thy Request;
Then march thou on courageously,
    And I will lead the rest.

Then came the bragging *Frenchmen* down
    With greater Force and Might;
With whom our Noble King began
    A hard and cruel Fight.

The Archers they discharged their Shafts,
    As thick as Hail from Sky;
That many a *Frenchman* in the Field
    That happy Day did die.

Ten Thousand Men that Day were slain
    Of Enemies in the Field;
And as many Prisoners
    That Day were forced to yield.

Thus had our King a happy Day,
    And Victory over *France;*
And brought them quickly under Foot,
    That late in Pride did prance.

The Lord preserve our Noble King,
    And grant to him likewise
The upper Hand and Victory
    Of all his Enemies.

1765—Samuel Johnson. "The Preface to Shakespeare" and "Notes on the Plays," from *The Plays of William Shakespeare*

Samuel Johnson (1709–84) was one of the greatest eighteenth-century English intellectuals and among the best of Shakespeare's critics from any period. Johnson's eight-volume collection, *The Plays of William Shakespeare* (1765), while not proving a definitive edition of Shakespeare's work, included a critical preface and many notes that have remained relevant to the study of Shakespeare more than two hundred years after they were first written.

Imitations produce pain or pleasure, not because they are mistaken for realities, but because they bring realities to mind. When the imagination is recreated by a painted landscape, the trees are not supposed capable to give us shade, or the fountains coolness; but we consider, how we should be pleased with such fountains playing beside us, and such woods waving over us. We are agitated in reading the History of *Henry* the Fifth, yet no man takes his book for the field of *Agencourt*. A dramatick exhibition is a book recited with concomitants that encrease or diminish its effect. Familiar comedy is often more powerful on the theatre, than in the page; imperial tragedy is always less. The humour of *Petruchio* may be heightened by grimace; but what voice or what gesture can hope to add dignity or force to the soliloquy of *Cato?*

Notes for The Life of King Henry V.

Prologue. (Chorus 3–4.).

——————————*Princes to act,*
And Monarchs to behold.

Shakespeare does not seem to set distance enough between the performers and spectators.

Prologue. (Chorus 13.)
Within this wooden O,

Nothing shews more evidently the power of custom over language, than that the frequent use of calling a circle an O could so much hide the meanness of the metaphor from *Shakespeare*, that he has used it many times where he makes his most eager attempts at dignity of stile.

Prologue. (Chorus 18).
Imaginary forces.

Imaginary for *imaginative*, or your powers of fancy. Active and passive words are by this authour frequently confounded.

Prologue. (Chorus 25.)
    And make imaginary puissance.

This passage shews that *Shakespeare* was fully sensible of the absurdity of shewing battles on the theatre, which indeed is never done but tragedy becomes farce. Nothing can be represented to the eye but by something like it, and *within a wooden O* nothing very like a battle can be exhibited.

Act I. Scene i. (I. i. 38.)
    Hear him but reason in divinity.

This speech seems to have been copied from King *James's* prelates, speaking of their *Solomon*; when Archbishop *Whitgift*, who, as an eminent writer says, *died soon afterwards, and probably doated then*, at the *Hampton-Court* conference, declared himself v*erily persuaded, that his* sacred *Majesty spake by the Spirit of God*. And, in effect, this scene was added after King *James's* accession to the crown: So that we have no way of avoiding its being esteemed a compliment to *him*, but by supposing it was a satire on *his bishops*.—Warburton.

    Why these lines should be divided from the rest of the speech and applied to king *James*, I am not able to conceive; nor why an opportunity should be so eagerly snatched to treat with contempt that part of his character which was least contemptible. King *James's* theological knowledge was not inconsiderable. To preside at disputations is not very suitable to a king, but to understand the questions is surely laudable. The poet, if he had *James* in his thoughts, was no skilful encomiast; for the mention of *Harry's* skill in war, forced upon the remembrance of his audience the great deficiency of their present king; who yet with all his faults, and many faults he had, was such that Sir *Robert Cotton* says, *he would be content that* England *should never have a better, provided that it should never have a worse.*

Act I. Scene i. (I. i. 47–48).
     When he speaks
  The air, a charter'd libertine, is still.

This line is exquisitely beautiful.

Act II. Scene iii. (II. ii. 126–27.)
    King Henry. *Oh, how hast thou with jealousy infected*
    The sweetness of affiance.

Shakespeare urges this aggravation of the guilt of treachery with great judgment. One of the worst consequences of breach of trust is the diminution of that confidence which makes the happiness of life, and the dissemination of suspicion, which is the poison of society.

Act II. Scene iii. (II. ii. 165.)
  Grey. *My fault, but not my body, pardon, Sovereign.*

One of the conspirators against Queen *Elizabeth,* I think *Parry,* concludes his letter to her with these words, a culpa, *but not* a poena; *absolve me most dear Lady.* This letter was much read at that time, and the authour doubtless copied it.

Act II. Scene iv. (II. iii. 13.)
  Turning o' the' Tide

It has been a very old opinion, which *Mead, de imperio solis,* quotes, as if he believed it, that nobody dies but in the time of ebb: half the deaths in London confute the notion; but we find that it was common among the women of the poet's time.

Act II. Scene iv. (II. iii. 16–17.)
  For his nose was as sharp as a pen, and a table of green-fields.

These words, *and a table of greenfields,* are not to be found in the old editions of 1600 and 1608. This nonsense got into all the following editions by a pleasant mistake of the stage editors, who printed from the common piece-meal-written parts in the play-house. A table was here directed to be brought in (it being a scene in a tavern where they drink at parting) and this direction crept into the text from the margin. *Greenfield* was the name of the property-man in that time who furnish'd implements, &c. for the actors, *A table of* Greenfield's. Pope.

So reasonable an account of this blunder *Mr. Theobald* would not acquiesce in. He thought *a table of Greenfield's* part of the text, only corrupted, and that it should be read, *he babbled of green fields,* because men do so in the ravings of a calenture. But he did not consider how ill this agrees with the nature of the Knight's illness, who was now in no *babling* humour: and *so* far from wanting cooling in *greenfields,* that his feet were cold, and he just expiring. Warburton.

Upon this pasage Mr. *Theobald* has a note that fills a page, which I omit in pity to my readers, since he only endeavours to prove, what I think every reader perceives to be true, that at this time no *table* could be wanted. Mr. *Pope,* in an appendix to his own edition in *twelves,* seems to admit *Theobald's* emendation, which we would have allowed to be uncommonly happy, had we not been prejudiced against it by a conjecture with which, as it excited merriment, we are loath to part.

Act II. Scene iv. (II. iii 27–8.)
   and all was as Cold as any stone.

Such is the end of *Falstaff,* from whom *Shakespeare* had promised us in his epilogue to *Henry* IV. that we should receive more entertainment. It happened to *Shakespeare* as to other writers, to have his imagination crowded with a tumultuary confusion of images, which, while they were yet unsorted and unexamined, seemed sufficient to furnish a long train of incidents, and a new variety of merriment, but which, when he was to produce them to view, shrunk suddenly from him, or could not be accommodated to his general design. That he once designed to have brought *Falstaff* on the scene again, we know from himself; but whether he could contrive no train of adventures suitable to his character, or could match him with no companions likely to quicken his humour, or could open no new vein of pleasantry, and was afraid to continue the same strain lest it should not find the same reception, he has here for ever discarded him, and made haste to dispatch him, perhaps for the same reason for which *Addison* killed Sir *Roger,* that no other hand might attempt to exhibit him.

Let meaner authours learn from this example, that it is dangerous to sell the bear which is yet not hunted, to promise to the publick what they have not written.

This disappointment probably inclined Queen *Elizabeth* to command the poet to produce him once again, and to shew him in love or courtship. This was indeed a new source of humour, and produced a new play from the former characters.

I forgot to note in the proper place, and therefore note here, that *Falstaff's* courtship, or *The Merry Wives of* Windsor, should be read between *Henry* IV. and *Henry* V.

Act III. Scene iii. Line (III. Ii. 82 foll.)
   It were to be wished that the poor merriment of this dialogue
   [between Macmorris and Jamy] had not been purchased with so much
   profaneness.

Act III. Scene v. (III. iv.)
   Catherine. *Alice, tu of etti en Angleterre,* &c-

I have left this ridiculous scene as I found it; and am sorry to have no colour left, from any of the editions, to imagine it interpolated. WARBURTON.

Sir *T. Hanmer* has rejected it. This scene is indeed mean enough, when it is read, but the grimaces of two *French* women, and the odd accent with which they uttered the *English*, made it divert upon the stage. It may be observed, that there is in it not only the *French* language, but the *French* spirit. *Alice* compliments the princess upon her knowledge of four words, and tells her that she pronounces like the *English* themselves. The princess suspects no deficiency in her instructress, nor the instructress in herself. Throughout the whole scene there may be found *French* servility, and *French* vanity.

I cannot forbear to transcribe the first sentence of this dialogue from the edition of 1608, that the reader who has not looked into the old copies may judge of the strange negligence with which they are printed.

Kate. Alice *venecia, vous aves cates en, vou parte fort bon Angloys englatara, Coman sae palla vou la main en francoy.*

Act III. Scene vi. (III. v. 40–45.)
Charles Delabreth, high constable of *France* &c.

Milton somewhere bids the *English* take notice how their names are mispelt by foreigners, and seems to think that we may lawfully treat foreign names in return with the same neglect. This privilege seems to be exercised in this catalogue of *French* names, which, since the sense of the authour is not asserted, I have left it as I found it.

Act III. Scene vi. (III. v. 50–52.)
Rush on his host, as doth the melted snow
Upon the vallies; whose low vassal seat
The Alps doth spit and void his rheum upon.

The poet has here defeated himself by passing too soon from one image to another. To bid the *French* rush upon the *English* as the torrents formed from melted snow stream from the Alps, was at once vehement and proper, but its force is destroyed by the grossness of the thought in the next line.

Act III. Scene viii. (III. vi. 114–15.)
Fluellen. His nose is executed, and his fire's out

This is the last time that any sport can be made with the red face of *Bardolph,* which, to confess the truth, seems to have taken more hold on *Shakespeare's* imagination than on any other. The conception is very cold to the solitary reader, though it may be somewhat invigorated by the exhibition on the stage. This poet is always more careful about the present than the future, about his audience than his readers.

Act III. Scene viii. (III. vi. 133–34.)
Now speak we on our cue.

In our turn. This phrase the authour learned among players, and has imparted it to kings.

Act IV. Scene i. (IV. Chorus. 2–3.)
The poring dark
Fills the wide vessel of the universe.

Universe for *horizon*: for we are not to think *Shakespear* so ignorant as to imagine it was night over the whole globe at once. He intimates he knew otherwise, by that fine line in *Midsummer Night's Dream.*

——*following darkness like a dream.*

Besides, the image he employs shews he meant but half the globe: the horizon round, which has the shape of a vessel or goblet. WARBURTON.

There is a better proof that Shakespeare knew the order of night and day in *Macbeth.*

Now o'er one half the world
Nature seems dead.

But there was no great need of any justification. The universe, in its original sense, no more means this globe singly than the circuit of the horizon; but, however large in its philosophical sense, it may be poetically used for as much of the world as falls under observation. Let me remark further, that ignorance cannot be certainly inferred from inaccuracy. Knowledge is not always present.

Act IV. Scene iv. (iv. i. 189–90.)
Every subject's duty is the King's, but every subject's soul is his own.

This is a very just distinction, and the whole argument is well followed, and properly concluded.

Act IV. Scene v. (iv. i. 250 foll.)
King Henry. *Upon the King! &c.*

There is something very striking and solemn in this soliloquy, into which the king breaks immediately as soon as he is left alone. Something like this, on less occasions, every breast has felt. Reflection and seriousness rush upon the mind upon the separation of a gay company, and especially after forced and unwilling merriment.

Act IV. Scene viii. (iv. iii. 24.)
King Henry. *By Jove, I am not covetous of gold.*

The king prays like a Christian, and swears like a heathen.

Act IV. Scene viii. (iv. iii. 50–51.)
They'll remember, with advantages,
What feats they did that day.

Old men, notwithstanding the natural forgetfulness of age, shall remember *their feats of this day*, and remember to tell them *with advantage*. Age is commonly boastful, and inclined to magnify past acts and past times.

Act IV. Scene viii. (IV. iii. 57–59.)
Crispin Crispian *shall ne'er go by,*
From this day to the ending of the world,
But me in it shall be remembered.

It may be observed that we are apt to promise to ourselves a more lasting memory than the changing state of human things admits. This prediction is not verified; the feast of *Crispin* passes by without any mention of *Agincourt*. Late events obliterate the former: the civil wars have left in this nation scarcely any tradition of more ancient history.

Act IV. Scene viii. (IV. iii. 41–67.)
. . . *Upon St Crispin's day*

This speech, like many others of the declamatory kind, is too long. Had it been contracted to about half the number of lines, it might have gained force, and lost none of the sentiments.

Act IV. Scene xiv. (IV. vii. 51–52.)
The fat Knight with the great belly-doublet.

This is the last time that *Falstaff* can make sport. The poet was loath to part with him, and has continued his memory as long as he could.

Act V. Scene ii. (v. i. 94.)
Exit Pistol.

The comick scenes of the history of *Henry* the fourth and fifth are now at an end, and all the comick personages are now dismissed. *Falstaff* and Mrs. *Quickly* are dead; *Nym* and *Bardolph* are hanged; *Gadshill* was lost immediately after the robbery; *Poins* and *Peto* have vanished since, one knows not how; and *Pistol* is now beaten into obscurity. I believe every reader regrets their departure.

Act V. Scene iv. (v. ii. 125 foll.)
King Henry. *I'faith, Kate, than wouldst find me such a plain King, &c.*

I know not why *Shakespeare* now gives the king nearly such a character as he made him formerly ridicule in *Percy*. This military grossness and unskilfulness in all the softer arts, does not suit very well with the gaieties of his youth, with the general knowledge ascribed to him at his accession, or with the contemptuous message sent him by the *Dauphin*, who represents him as fitter for the ball room than the field, and tells him that he is not *to revel into dutchies*, or win provinces *with a nimble galliard*. The truth is, that the poet's matter failed him in the fifth act, and he was glad to fill it up with whatever he could get; and not even *Shakespeare* can write well without a proper subject. It is a vain endeavour for the most skilful hand to cultivate barrenness, or to paint upon vacuity.

Act V. Scene v. (v. ii. 305–402.)
We have here but a mean dialogue for princes; the merriment is very gross, and the sentiments are very worthless.

End Note
This play has many scenes of high dignity, and many of easy merriment. The character of the King is well supported, except in his courtship, where he has neither the vivacity of *Hal*, nor the grandeur of *Henry*. The humour of *Pistol* is very happily continued; his character has perhaps been the model of all the bullies that have yet appeared on the *English* stage.

The lines given to the chorus have many admirers; but the truth is, that in them a little may be praised, and much must be forgiven; nor can it be easily discovered why the intelligence given by the chorus is more necessary in this play than in many others where it is omitted. The great defect of this play is the emptiness and narrowness of the last act, which a very little diligence might have easily avoided.

HENRY V IN THE
NINETEENTH CENTURY
❦

The beginning of the nineteenth century saw a shift in approaches to reading Shakespeare that, while taking hints from the past, determined the future of criticism as a discipline that became increasingly professionalized as the century progressed. Romantic critics, in one sense, rebelled against the eighteenth century and its lingering reliance on neoclassical ideas, but they expanded on suggestions that their predecessors had made. Thomas De Quincey's discussion of the mixture of the "pathetic and the humorous" in the scene in which Falstaff's death is described by Hostess Quickly, for example, calls to mind Rowe's remark that "even the Account of [Falstaff's] Death, given by his Old Landlady Mrs. Quickly . . . tho' it be extremely Natural, is yet as diverting as any Part of his Life." Whether De Quincy was thinking about Rowe cannot be determined with any certainty, but the contrast between how each critic addresses the same issue, despite the similarities in what they seem to be saying, illustrates the innovative approaches that had developed between Rowe and De Quincey not only for reading Shakespeare but also literary works in general. Rowe states; De Quincey explores.

August Wilhelm von Schlegel is among the most influential early romantic critics to take up the task of transforming Shakespeare studies into a more analytic discipline. He addressed, in his *Lectures on Dramatic Art and Literature* (1808), the issue of Shakespeare's aesthetic, which Rowe, Gildon, and Johnson among others, had suggested was an alternative to a neoclassical one. He also put forth the important notion that the unity of a work is developed organically from within rather than from a set of pre-established rules. Discussing *Henry V,* which Schlegel regarded as a part of a whole that consisted of all of Shakespeare's history plays, he observed that Shakespeare's difficulty when approaching the work was the problem of putting onstage a subject fit for epic, rather than dramatic, treatment. This characterization of the task Shakespeare faced when handling his subject would be reworked for well over a century. Schlegel regarded the Chorus as Shakespeare's solution, though not an entirely happy one, describing it as something "tacked" onto the beginning of each act.

The reading of *Henry V* in the *Lectures* is prescient of things to come in other ways, for Schlegel hinted at the ambiguous nature of the king's character. Calling Henry "Shakespeare's favourite hero in English history," Schlegel draws on and helps to establish further an approach to *Henry V* that finds in it a patriotic celebration of England's glorious past. The idea of Henry being a favorite hero was immediately influential. Schlegel, however, also suggests that there is a negative side to Shakespeare's presentation of the king's conquest, pointing out that "the secret springs of this undertaking" is Henry's desire to secure his place on the throne and the clergy's wish to distract the king from the bill that would deprive them of revenues. The latter element of his reading was, with a few exceptions, overlooked during the nineteenth century, but it has since become a major concern of critics dealing with the play.

Less than a decade after Schlegel gave his lectures and two years after they had appeared in English, William Hazlitt, who had reviewed them in 1816, published *Characters of Shakespears Plays* (1817), the first major study of that particular aspect of Shakespeare's works. Shakespeare's ability to develop striking individuals in his works had been praised since at least the time of Margaret Cavendish. In the eighteenth century, Rowe had asserted, "there is a pleasing and well-distinguisg'd Variety in those Characters which he though fit to meddle with," and Pope had remarked, "His *Characters* are so much Nature herself, that 'tis a sort of injury to call then by so distant a name as Copies of her. . . . [E]very single character in *Shakespear* is as much an Individual, as those in Life it self." There had been a few longer considerations of particular characters, but Hazlitt's work, which sees itself as developing remarks such as those made by Rowe and Pope to a greater degree, established a more modern approach to character study.

Hazlitt's consideration of the play has proved particularly important, becoming a central statement in the reception of *Henry V,* even though its influence was not felt strongly at first, except perhaps by Leigh Hunt, who argued that *Henry V* "is not a good acting play" and that the power it had possessed for its original audience was lost because of the cultural and ideological changes that had taken place in England between Elizabethan times and Hunt's own. Hazlitt had gone much further in condemning Henry. Foregrounding for the first and almost last time in the nineteenth century the Schlegel-influenced focus on the negative aspects of Henry and how they compromise his status as an ideal figure, Hazlitt condemned the king as well as prince Hal, whose dissolute life, in his view, anticipates the behavior of the conqueror king. His involvement in the robbery on Gadshill in *Henry IV, Part 1,* for instance, is treated as a precursor to his invasion of France: Both events illustrate the corrupt nature of the man. Hazlitt's ire, however, seems at times to be directed against the historical figure of the king and monarchs in general. When he begins to look more closely at the play, his stance becomes less certain. Hazlitt, who had echoed Schlegel's favorite-hero comment, finds much that is likable in Shakespeare's Henry and declares, "We like him in the play. There he is a very amiable monster." Henry then is simultaneously a good fellow and bad person.

Hazlitt's position, particularly its negative aspect, remained a marginal one for some time. The more conventional view throughout the century—the one, for example, that Nathan Drake presented in his *Shakespeare and His Times* (1817)—was that Henry was an ideal figure, the patriotic public placed on the stage during the eighteenth century who continued to find his way there in the nineteenth. Drake goes so far as to assert that Henry was always already an ideal, finding perfection in his princely behavior as well as his regal character. "In every situation ... he is evidently the darling offspring of his bard, whether we attend him to the frolic orgies in Eastcheap, to his combat with the never-daunted Percy, or, as in the play before us, to the immortal plains of Agincourt." Drake writes, illustrating his point at least in regard to Henry V, with analyses of the discovery of the traitors Cambridge, Gray, and Scroop just before Henry embarks for France; Henry's conduct before the walls of Harfleur; his soliloquy the night before Agincourt; and his playfulness in the episode with Fluellen and Williams.

The tradition of reading *Henry V* in a heroic light was continued in the Victorian period by such writers as Thomas Carlyle, Algernon Charles Swinburne, and Julia Wedgwood. Carlyle praises, in a passing reference to the play in *On Heroes, Hero-worship, and the Heroic in History,* the contrast between the French and English in the buildup to the battle of Agincourt and the valor of the English once it has begun. He lauds the play's "noble Patriotism." In a similar vein, the poet Charles Algernon Swinburne, in *A Study of Shakespeare* (1880), called Henry V the noblest of Shakespeare's "calculating statesmen-warriors" and compared him with such figures as Robert Clive (1725–74), who established the British presence in India in the eighteenth century, and Warren Hastings (1732–1818), who strengthened British power in that country in the early years of the nineteenth. Meanwhile, Wedgwood casts Henry as a figure whom Shakespeare fashioned for his play by drawing on his own pride in his country and to further the patriotism of the subjects of Elizabeth I.

Wedgwood's argument was greatly influenced by Georg Gottfried Gervinus, who, writing in mid-century Germany, a country in which Shakespeare had acquired the status of an almost national figure thanks in part to Schlegel's translation, posited the notion that Shakespeare's art arose in a period of national unity that was fostered because of the defeat of the Spanish Armada. The fleet's arrival constituted the great crisis that the English had united around in 1588 and saw themselves as successfully overcoming, just as Aeschylus' art, Gervinus implied and Wedgwood stated explicitly, had been created in the stable period after the battle of Salamis that was fought between an alliance of ancient Greek city states and the Persians.

For Gervinus, Shakespeare's history plays are an illustration of the playwright being "stirred by thoughts political and national, and not merely by moral ideas and psychological truths." When Gervinus turns his attention to *Henry V*, however, he changes tactics, although not without noting how Henry's own heroic stature has permeated the commonwealth, bringing together all social classes and British nations—that is, Scotland, Ireland, Wales, and England—in "heroic unity." *Henry V* is, it seems, too character centered to ignore the import of its eponymous figure: "The whole interest of our play lies in the development of the ethical character of the hero," he writes, and concentrates not on Henry's development from puerile youth to focused king, which was accomplished in *Henry IV, Parts 1* and *2*, but on the king's "many-sided nature," or his ability to accommodate himself to any occasion while always retaining his core humility and religious piety.

Gervinus's study assumes rather than demonstrates that Henry is an ideal. What Henry does and the reasons behind his actions are necessarily right. Following his father's advice "to busy giddy minds / With foreign quarrels" does not suggest that Henry has unjust motives for starting a war any more than the thought that Henry is following his ambition to compensate for his wasted youth does. That approach was common to Victorian critics, but occasionally an apparent flaw was reevaluated to illustrate the wisdom behind Henry's actions. Edward Dowden, for example, notes, "From the coldness, the caution, the convention, of his father's court (an atmosphere which suited well the temperament of John of Lancaster), Henry escapes to the teeming vitality of the London streets, and the tavern where Falstaff is monarch." The tavern world might not be the best place to be, but it is infinitely preferable to the coldness of the court, which would have been unsuitable for a personality whom "life breathed through." The apparent fault is rather an illustration of the strength of his character in an imperfect world.

More often than not, however, Dowden ignores, as did his contemporaries, unpleasant elements of Henry's character, presenting him as someone who is focused on the realities of life and who is able to master them. For him, the heart of the play lies in that element of Henry's character, and its import rests on what the work can teach us about conducting our own lives and what it reveals about Shakespeare's mind. Indeed, Dowden finds the history plays valuable for bringing to light biographical facts. *Henry V*, in particular, teaches us "Shakspere's convictions as to how the noblest practical success in life may be achieved" and "how Shakspere would endeavor to control, and in what directions he would endeavor to reinforce his own nature while in pursuit of a practical mastery over events and things."

Character analyses may have played an import part in nineteenth-century approaches to *Henry V*, but critics found other aspects of the play worth discussing as well. Denton J. Snider, for instance, while characterizing Henry as "the supreme type of national hero," takes up the issue of the play's form, finding it lacks an inherent unity and is rather "a series of heroic pictures" with the chorus providing a transition from one to the other. It can, however, "externally be divided into two movements" with each containing a serious and a comic thread: The first involves the preparation for the war in England and France and the second, the conflict and its conclusion.

Denton draws on Schlegel's distinction between mechanical and organic form not only to explain how *Henry V*'s material is held together to form a dramatic whole but also to determine its value as a work of art. "Form is mechanical when, through external force, it is imparted to any material merely as an accidental addition without reference to its quality . . . ," Schlegel writes, "Organical form . . . is innate; it unfolds itself from within." He goes on to argue that, for the great artist, "all genuine forms are organical, that is, determined by the quality of the work." Denton, then, is offering an explanation for the artistic inferiority of *Henry V* when compared to Shakespeare's best works, while at the same time demonstrating how Shakespeare manipulates his material to hold it together.

Considerations of *Henry V* during the nineteenth century had increased considerably. The commonly held opinion of the king was positive, but other voices besides those of Hazlitt's and Hunt's existed, most notably William Watkiss Lloyd, who condemned Henry in no uncertain terms in *Critical Essays on the Plays of Shakespeare* (1875). Lloyd finds no heroism in the king, seeing his aspiration for France in terms of his father's dying words to divert his subjects' attention and his constant references to God as religious hypocrisy. Lloyd's point of view, while of negligible significance in its day, would come to greater prominence in the twentieth century.

1809—August Wilhelm von Schlegel.
From *Lectures on Dramatic Art and Literature*

August Wilhelm von Schlegel (1767–1845) was a German romantic poet and a professor of art and literary history in Bonn. He had also served as the secretary to Jean Baptiste Jules Bernadotte before Bernadotte became Charles XIV of Sweden. Schlegel is best remembered as a critic and translator. His translation of Shakespeare's works, which was completed by others, was important in establishing Shakespeare's reputation in Germany.

King Henry the Fifth is manifestly Shakspeare's favourite hero in English history: he paints him as endowed with every chivalrous and kingly virtue; open, sincere, affable, yet, as a sort of reminiscence of his youth, still disposed to innocent raillery, in the intervals between his perilous but glorious achievements.

However, to represent on the stage his whole history subsequent to his accession to the throne, was attended with great difficulty. The conquests in France were the only distinguished event of his reign; and war is an epic rather than a dramatic object. For wherever men act in masses against each other, the appearance of chance can never wholly be avoided; whereas it is the business of the drama to exhibit to us those determinations which, with a certain necessity, issue from the reciprocal relations of different individuals, their characters and passions. In several of the Greek tragedies, it is true, combats and battles are exhibited, that is, the preparations for them and their results; and in historical plays war, as the *ultima ratio regum,* cannot altogether be excluded. Still, if we would have dramatic interest, war must only be the means by which something else is accomplished, and not the last aim and substance of the whole. For instance, in *Macbeth,* the battles which are announced at the very beginning merely serve to heighten the glory of Macbeth and to fire his ambition; and the combats which take place towards the conclusion, before the eyes of the spectator, bring on the destruction of the tyrant. It is the very same in the Roman pieces, in the most of those taken from English history, and, in short, wherever Shakspeare has introduced war in a dramatic combination. With great insight into the essence of his art, he never paints the fortune of war as a blind deity who sometimes favours one and sometimes another; without going into the details of the art of war, (though sometimes he even ventures on this), he allows us to anticipate the result from the qualities of the general, and their influence on the minds of the soldiers; sometimes, without claiming our belief for miracles, he yet exhibits the issue in the light of a higher volition: the consciousness of a just cause and reliance on the protection of Heaven give courage to the one party, while the presage of a curse hanging over their undertaking weighs down the other. In *Henry the Fifth* no opportunity was afforded Shakspeare of adopting the last mentioned course, namely, rendering the issue of the war dramatic; but he has skilfully availed himself of the first.—Before the battle of Agincourt he paints in the most lively colours the light-minded impatience of the French leaders for the moment of battle, which to them seemed infallibly the moment of victory; on the other hand, he paints the uneasiness of the English King and his army in their desperate situation, coupled with their firm determination, if they must fall, at least to fall with honour. He applies this as a general contrast between the French and English national characters; a contrast which betrays a partiality for his own nation, certainly excusable in a poet, especially when he is backed with such a glorious document as that of the memorable battle in question. He has surrounded the general events of the war with a fulness of individual, characteristic, and even sometimes comic features. A heavy Scotchman, a hot Irishman, a well-meaning, honourable, but pedantic Welchman, all speaking in their peculiar dialects, are intended to show us that the warlike genius of Henry did not merely carry the English with him, but also the other natives of the two islands, who were either not yet fully united or in no degree subject to him. Several good-for-nothing associates of Falstaff among the dregs of the army either afford an opportunity for proving Henry's strictness of discipline, or are sent home in disgrace. But all this variety still seemed to the poet insufficient to animate a play of which the subject was a conquest, and nothing but a conquest. He has, therefore, tacked a prologue (in the technical language of that day *a chorus)* to the beginning of each act. These prologues, which unite epic pomp and solemnity with lyrical sublimity, and among which the description of the two camps before the battle of Agincourt forms a most admirable night-piece, are intended to keep the spectators constantly in mind, that the peculiar grandeur of the actions described cannot be developed on a narrow stage, and that they must, therefore, supply, from their own imaginations, the deficiencies of the representation. As the matter was not properly dramatic, Shakspeare chose to wander in the form also beyond the bounds of the species, and to sing, as a poetical herald, what he could not represent to the eye, rather than to cripple the progress of the action by putting long descriptions in the mouths of the dramatic personages. The confession of the poet that "four or five most vile and ragged foils, right ill disposed, can only disgrace the name of Agincourt," (a scruple which he has overlooked in the occasion of many other great battles, and among others of that of Philippi,) brings us here naturally to the question how far, generally speaking, it may be suitable and advisable to represent wars and battles on the stage. The Greeks have uniformly renounced them: as in the whole of their theatrical system they proceeded on ideas of grandeur and dignity, a feeble and petty imitation of the unattainable would have appeared insupportable in their eyes. With them, consequently, all fighting was merely recounted. The principle of the romantic dramatists was altogether different: their wonderful pictures were infinitely larger than their theatrical means of visible execution, they were every where obliged to count on the willing imagination of the spectators, and consequently they also relied on them in this point. It is certainly laughable enough that a handful of awkward warriors in mock armour, by means of two or three swords, with which we clearly see they take especial care not to do the slightest injury to one another, should decide the fate of mighty kingdoms. But the opposite extreme is still much worse. If we in reality succeed in exhibiting the tumult of a great battle, the storming of a fort, and the like, in a manner any way calculated to deceive the eye, the power of these sensible impressions is so great that they render the spectator incapable of bestowing that attention which a poetical work of art demands; and thus the essential is sacrificed to the accessory. We have learned from experience, that whenever cavalry combats are introduced the men soon become secondary personages beside the four-footed players.' Fortunately, in Shakspeare's time, the art of converting the yielding boards of the theatre into a riding course had not yet been invented. He tells the spectators in the first prologue in *Henry the Fifth:*—

Think, when we talk of horses, that you see them
Printing their proud hoofs in the receiving earth.

When Richard the Third utters the famous exclamation,—A horse! a horse! my kingdom for a horse! it is no doubt inconsistent to see him both before and afterwards constantly fighting on foot. It is however better, perhaps, that the poet and player should by overpowering impressions dispose us to forget this, than by literal exactness to expose themselves to external interruptions. With all the disadvantages which I have mentioned, Shakspeare and several Spanish poets have contrived to derive such great beauties from the immediate representation of war, that I cannot bring myself to wish they had abstained from it. A theatrical manager of the present day will have a middle course to follow: his art must, in an especial manner, be directed to make what he shows us appear only as separate groups of an immense picture, which cannot be taken in at once by the eye; he must convince the spectators that the main action takes place behind the stage; and for this purpose he has easy means at his command in the nearer or more remote sound of warlike music and the din of arms.

However much Shakspeare celebrates the French conquest of Henry, still he has not omitted to hint, after his way, the secret springs of this undertaking. Henry was in want of foreign war to secure himself on the throne; the clergy also wished to keep him employed abroad, and made an offer of rich contributions to prevent the passing of a law which would have deprived them of the half of their revenues. His learned bishops consequently are as ready to prove to him his indisputable right to the crown of France, as he is to allow his conscience to be tranquillized by them. They prove that the Salic law is not, and never was, applicable to France; and the matter is treated in a more succinct and convincing manner than such subjects usually are in manifestoes. After his renowned battles, Henry wished to secure his conquests by marriage with a French princess; all that has reference to this is intended for irony in the play. The fruit of this union, from which two nations promised to themselves such happiness in future, was the weak and feeble Henry VI., under whom every thing was so miserably lost. It must not, therefore, be imagined that it was without the knowledge and will of the poet that a heroic drama turns out a comedy in his hands, and ends in the manner of Comedy with a marriage of convenience.

NOTES

1. The Greeks, it is true, brought horses on the tragic stage, but only in solemn processions, not in the wild disorder of a fight. Agamemnon and Pallas, in Aeschylus, make their appearance drawn in a chariot with four horses. But their theatres were built on a scale very different from ours.

1817—William Hazlitt. "Henry V," from *Characters of Shakespears Plays*

William Hazlitt (1778–1830), whose friends included William Wordsworth, Samuel Taylor Coleridge, and Charles Lamb, was an essayist and critic. He began making a name for himself writing theater criticism in the first half of the 1810s but shot to fame in 1817 as a result of publishing *Characters of Shakespears Plays,* which remains among the best commentaries on the playwright's work.

Henry V. is a very favourite monarch with the English nation, and he appears to have been also a favourite with Shakespear, who labours hard to apologise for the actions of the king, by shewing us the character of the man, as "the king of good fellows." He scarcely deserves this honour. He was fond of war and low company:—we know little else of him. He was careless, dissolute, and ambitious;—idle, or doing mischief. In private, he seemed to have no idea of the common decencies of life, which he subjected to a kind of regal licence; in public affairs, he seemed to have no idea of any rule of right or wrong, but brute force, glossed over with a little religious hypocrisy and archiepiscopal advice. His principles did not change with his situation and professions. His adventure on Gadshill was a prelude to the affair of Agincourt, only a bloodless one; Falstaff was a puny prompter of violence and outrage, compared with the pious and politic Archbishop of Canterbury, who gave the king *carte blanche,* in a genealogical tree of his family, to rob and murder in circles of latitude and longitude abroad—to save the possessions of the church at home. This appears in the speeches in Shakespear, where the hidden motives that actuate princes and their advisers in war and policy are better laid open than in speeches from the throne or woolsack. Henry, because he did not know how to govern his own kingdom, determined to make war upon his neighbours. Because his own title to the crown was doubtful, he laid claim to that of France. Because he did not know how to exercise the enormous power, which had just dropped into his hands, to any one good purpose, he immediately undertook (a cheap and obvious resource of sovereignty) to do all the mischief he could. Even if absolute monarchs had the wit to find out objects of laudable ambition, they could only "plume up their wills" in adhering to the more sacred formula of the royal prerogative, "the right divine of kings to govern wrong," because will is only then triumphant when it is opposed to the will of others, because the pride of power is only then shewn, not when it consults the rights and interests of others, but when it insults and tramples on all justice and all humanity. Henry declares his resolution "when France is his, to bend it to his awe, or break it all to pieces"—a resolution worthy of a conqueror, to destroy all that he cannot enslave; and what adds to the joke, he lays all the

blame of the consequences of his ambition on those who will not submit tamely
to his tyranny. Such is the history of kingly power, from the beginning to the
end of the world;—with this difference, that the object of war formerly, when the
people adhered to their allegiance, was to depose kings; the object latterly, since
the people swerved from their allegiance, has been to restore kings, and to make
common cause against mankind. The object of our late invasion and conquest of
France was to restore the legitimate monarch, the descendant of Hugh Capet,
to the throne: Henry v. in his time made war on and deposed the descendant of
this very Hugh Capet, on the plea that he was a usurper and illegitimate. What
would the great modern catspaw of legitimacy and restorer of divine right have
said to the claim of Henry and the title of the descendants of Hugh Capet?
Henry V. it is true, was a hero, a King of England, and the conqueror of the king
of France. Yet we feel little love or admiration for him. He was a hero, that is,
he was ready to sacrifice his own life for the pleasure of destroying thousands of
other lives: he was a king of England, but not a constitutional one, and we only
like kings according to the law; lastly, he was a conqueror of the French king,
and for this we dislike him less than if he had conquered the French people. How
then do we like him? We like him in the play. There he is a very amiable monster, a very splendid pageant. As we like to gaze at a panther or a young lion in
their cages in the Tower, and catch a pleasing horror from their glistening eyes,
their velvet paws, and dreadless roar, so we take a very romantic, heroic, patriotic,
and poetical delight in the boasts and feats of our younger Harry, as they appear
on the stage and are confined to lines of ten syllables; where no blood follows
the stroke that wounds our ears, where no harvest bends beneath horses' hoofs,
no city flames, no little child is butchered, no dead men's bodies are found piled
on heaps and festering the next morning—in the orchestra!

So much for the politics of this play; now for the poetry. Perhaps one of the
most striking images in all Shakespear is that given of war in the first lines of
the Prologue.

> "O for a muse of fire, that would ascend
> The brightest heaven of invention,
> A kingdom for a stage, princes to act,
> And monarchs to behold the swelling scene!
> Then should the warlike Harry, like himself,
> Assume the port of Mars, and *at his heels*
> *Leash'd in like hounds, should famine, sword, and fire*
> *Crouch for employment.*"

Rubens, if he had painted it, would not have improved upon this simile.

The conversation between the Archbishop of Canterbury and the Bishop
of Ely, relating to the sudden change in the manners of Henry V. is among the

well-known *Beauties* of Shakespear. It is indeed admirable both for strength and grace. It has sometimes occurred to us that Shakespear, in describing "the reformation" of the Prince, might have had an eye to himself—

> "Which is a wonder how his grace should glean it,
> Since his addiction was to courses vain,
> His companies unletter'd, rude and shallow,
> His hours fill'd up with riots, banquets, sports;
> And never noted in him any study,
> Any retirement, any sequestration
> From open haunts and popularity.
>   *Ely.* The strawberry grows underneath the nettle,
> And wholesome berries thrive and ripen best
> Neighbour'd by fruit of baser quality:
> And so the prince obscur'd his contemplation
> Under the veil of wildness, which no doubt
> Grew like the summer-grass, fastest by night,
> Unseen, yet crescive in his faculty."

This at least is as probable an account of the progress of the poet's mind as we have met with in any of the Essays on the Learning of Shakespear.

Nothing can be better managed than the caution which the king gives the meddling Archbishop, not to advise him rashly to engage in the war with France, his scrupulous dread of the consequences of that advice, and his eager desire to hear and follow it.

> "And God forbid, my dear and faithful lord,
> That you should fashion, wrest, or bow your reading,
> Or nicely charge your understanding soul
> With opening titles miscreate, whose right
> Suits not in native colours with the truth.
> For God doth know how many now in health
> Shall drop their blood, in approbation
> Of what your reverence shall incite us to.
> Therefore take heed how you impawn your person,
> How you awake our sleeping sword of war;
> We charge you in the name of God, take heed.
> For never two such kingdoms did contend
> Without much fall of blood, whose guiltless drops
> Are every one a woe, a sore complaint
> 'Gainst him, whose wrong gives edge unto the swords
> That make such waste in brief mortality.

Under this conjuration, speak, my lord;
For we will hear, note, and believe in heart,
That what you speak, is in your conscience wash'd,
As pure as sin with baptism."

Another characteristic instance of the blindness of human nature to
every thing but its own interests, is the complaint made by the king of "the
ill neighbourhood" of the Scot in attacking England when she was attacking
France.

"For once the eagle England being in prey,
To her unguarded nest the weazel Scot
Comes sneaking, and so sucks her princely eggs."

It is worth observing that in all these plays, which give an admirable picture
of the spirit of the *good old times*, the moral inference does not at all depend
upon the nature of the actions, but on the dignity or meanness of the persons
committing them. "The eagle England" has a right "to be in prey," but "the
weazel Scot" has none "to come sneaking to her nest," which she has left to
pounce upon others. Might was right, without equivocation or disguise, in that
heroic and chivalrous age. The substitution of right for might, even in theory, is
among the refinements and abuses of modern philosophy.

A more beautiful rhetorical delineation of the effects of subordination in a
commonwealth can hardly be conceived than the following:—

"For government, though high and low and lower,
Put into parts, doth keep in one concent,
Congruing in a full and natural close,
Like music.
————Therefore heaven doth divide
The state of man in divers functions,
Setting endeavour in continual motion;
To which is fixed, as an aim or butt,
Obedience: for so work the honey-bees;
Creatures that by a rule in nature, teach
The art of order to a peopled kingdom.
They have a king, and officers of sorts:
Where some, like magistrates, correct at home;
Others, like merchants, venture trade abroad;
Others, like soldiers, armed in their stings,
Make boot upon the summer's velvet buds;
Which pillage they with merry march bring home

To the tent-royal of their emperor;
Who, busied in his majesty, surveys
The singing mason building roofs of gold;
The civil citizens kneading up the honey ,
The poor mechanic porters crowding in
Their heavy burthens at his narrow gate;
The sad-eyed justice, with his surly hum,
Delivering o'er to executors pale
The lazy yawning drone. I this infer,—
That many things, having full reference
To one concent, may work contrariously:
As many arrows, loosed several ways,
Fly to one mark;
As many several ways meet in one town;
As many fresh streams meet in one salt sea;
As many lines close in the dial's centre;
So may a thousand actions, once a-foot,
End in one purpose, and be all well borne
Without defeat."

Henry V. is but one of Shakespear's second-rate plays. Yet by quoting passages, like this, from his second-rate plays alone, we might make a volume "rich with his praise,"

"As is the oozy bottom of the sea
With sunken wrack and sumless treasuries."

Of this sort are the king's remonstrance to Scroop, Grey, and Cambridge, on the detection of their treason, his address to the soldiers at the siege of Harfleur, and the still finer one before the battle of Agincourt, the description of the night before the battle, and the reflections on ceremony put into the mouth of the king.

"O hard condition; twin-born with greatness,
Subjected to the breath of every fool,
Whose sense no more can feel but his own wringing!
What infinite heart's ease must kings neglect,
That private men enjoy; and what have kings,
That privates have not too, save ceremony?
Save general ceremony?
And what art thou, thou idol ceremony?
What kind of God art thou, that suffer'st more
Of mortal griefs, than do thy worshippers?

What are thy rents? what are thy comings-in?
O ceremony, shew me but thy worth!
What is thy soul, O adoration?
Art thou aught else but place, degree, and form,
Creating awe and fear in other men?
Wherein thou art less happy, being feared,
Than they in fearing.
What drink'st thou oft, instead of homage sweet,
But poison'd flattery? O, be sick, great greatness,
And bid thy ceremony give thee cure!
Think'st thou, the fiery fever will go out
With titles blown from adulation?
Will it give place to flexure and low bending?
Can'st thou, when thou command'st the beggar's knee,
Command the health of it? No, thou proud dream,
That play'st so subtly with a king's repose,
I am a king, that find thee: and I know,
'Tis not the balm, the sceptre, and the ball,
The sword, the mace, the crown imperial,
The enter-tissu'd robe of gold and pearl,
The farsed title running 'fore the king,
The throne he sits on, nor the tide or pomp
That beats upon the high shore of this world,
No, not all these, thrice-gorgeous ceremony,
Not all these, laid in bed majestical,
Can sleep so soundly as the wretched slave;
Who, with a body fill'd, and vacant mind,
Gets him to rest, cramm'd with distressful bread,
Never sees horrid night, the child of hell:
But like a lacquey, from the rise to set,
Sweats in the eye of Phoebus, and all night
Sleeps in Elysium; next day, after dawn,
Doth rise, and help Hyperion to his horse;
And follows so the ever-running year
With profitable labour, to his grave:
And, but for ceremony, such a wretch,
Winding up days with toil, and nights with sleep,
Has the forehand and vantage of a king.
The slave, a member of the country's peace,
Enjoys it; but in gross brain little wots,
What watch the king keeps to maintain the peace,
Whose hours the peasant best advantages."

Most of these passages are well known: there is one, which we do not remember to have seen noticed, and yet it is no whit inferior to the rest in heroic beauty. It is the account of the deaths of York and Suffolk.

"*Exeter.* The duke of York commends him to your majesty.
    K. Henry. Lives he, good uncle? thrice within this hour,
I saw him down; thrice up again, and fighting;
From helmet to the spur all blood he was.
    Exeter. In which array (brave soldier) doth he lie,
Larding the plain: and by his bloody side
(Yoke-fellow to his honour-owing wounds)
The noble earl of Suffolk also lies.
Suffolk first died: and York, all haggled o'er,
Comes to him, where in gore he lay insteep'd,
And takes him by the beard; kisses the gashes,
That bloodily did yawn upon his face;
And cries aloud—*Tarry, dear cousin Suffolk!*
My soul shall thine keep company to heaven:
Tarry, sweet soul, for mine, then fly a-breast;
As, in this glorious and well-foughten field,
We kept together in our chivalry!
Upon these words I came, and cheer'd him up;
He smil'd me in the face, raught me his hand,
And, with a feeble gripe, says—*Dear my lord,*
Commend my service to my sovereign.
So did he turn, and over Suffolk's neck
He threw his wounded arm, and kiss'd his lips;
And so, espous'd to death, with blood he seal'd
A testament of noble-ending love."

But we must have done with splendid quotations. The behaviour of the king, in the difficult and doubtful circumstances in which he is placed, is as patient and modest as it is spirited and lofty in his prosperous fortune. The character of the French nobles is also very admirably depicted; and the Dauphin's praise of his horse shews the vanity of that class of persons in a very striking point of view. Shakespear always accompanies a foolish prince with a satirical courtier, as we see in this instance. The comic parts of *Henry V.* are very inferior to those of *Henry IV.* Falstaff is dead, and without him, Pistol, Nym, and Bardolph, are satellites without a sun. Fluellen the Welchman is the most entertaining character in the piece. He is good-natured, brave, choleric, and pedantic. His parallel between Alexander and Harry of Monmouth, and his desire to have "some disputations" with Captain Macmorris on the discipline of the Roman wars, in the heat of the battle, are never to be forgotten. His treatment of Pistol is as good as Pistol's treatment of his French prisoner. There are two other remarkable prose passages in this play: the conversation of Henry in disguise with the three sentinels on the duties of a soldier, and his courtship of Katherine in broken French. We like them both exceedingly, though the first savours perhaps too much of the king, and the last too little of the lover.

1817—Nathan Drake. "King Henry The Fifth: 1599," from *Shakespeare and His Times*

Nathan Drake (1766–1836) was a physician and essayist, and while he continued to serve as a doctor throughout his life, he made a name for himself as a literary critic, writing on such figures as Samuel Johnson, Joseph Addison, and Richard Steele. His most distinguished writing, however, was on Shakespeare, and *Shakespeare and His Times* was published in a German translation the year of his death and in a French translation two years later.

The chorus at the commencement of the fifth act, and the silence of Meres, too plainly point out the era of the composition of this play, to admit of any alteration depending on the bare supposition of subsequent interpolation, or on allusions too vague and general to afford any specific application.

No character has been pourtrayed more at length by our poet than that of Henry the Fifth, for we trace him acting a prominent part through three plays. In *Henry the Fourth*, until the battle of Shrewsbury, we behold him in all the effervescence of his madcap revelry; occasionally, it is true, affording us glimpses of the native mightiness of his mind, but first bursting upon us with heroic splendour on that celebrated field. In every situation, however, he is evidently the darling offspring of his bard, whether we attend him to the frolic orgies in Eastcheap, to his combat with the never-daunted Percy, or, as in the play before us, to the immortal plains of Agincourt.

The fire and animation which inform the soul of Henry when he rushes to arms in defence of his father's throne, are supported with unwearied vigour, with a blaze which never falters, throughout the whole of his martial achievements in France. Nor has Shakspeare been content with representing him merely in the light of a noble and chivalrous hero, he has endowed him with every regal virtue; he is magnanimous, eloquent, pious, and sincere; versed in all the arts of government, policy, and war; a lover of his country and of his people, and a strenuous protector of their liberties and rights.

Of the various instances which our author has brought forward for the exemplification of these virtues and acquirements, it may be necessary to notice two or three. Thus the detection of the treason of Cambridge, Gray, and Scroop, who had conspired to assassinate Henry previous to his embarkation, exhibits a rich display of the mental greatness and emphatic oratory of this warlike monarch. After reprobating the treachery of Cambridge and Gray, he suddenly turns upon Scroop, who had been his bosom-friend, with the following pathetic and soul- harrowing appeal:—

_____"But
What shall I say to thee, lord Scroop!—
Thou, that did'st bear the key of all ray counsels,
That knew'st the very bottom of my soul!—
May it be possible, that foreign hire
Could out of thee extract one spark of evil,
That might annoy my finger?—
O, how hast thou with jealousy infected
The sweetness of affiance!—
_____I will weep for thee;
For this revolt of thine, methinks, is like
Another fall of man."

Nor can we forbear distinguishing the dismissal of these traitors, as a striking example of magnanimity, and of justice tempered with dignified compassion:—

"God quit you in his mercy!—
Touching our person, seek we no revenge;
But we our kingdom's safety must so tender,
Whose ruin you three sought, that to her laws
We do deliver you. Get you therefore hence,
Poor miserable wretches, to your death:
The taste whereof, God, of his mercy, give you
Patience to endure, and true repentance
Of all your dear offences!"

In the fourth act, what a masterly picture of the cares and solicitudes of royalty is drawn by Henry himself, in his noble soliloquy on the morning of the battle, especially towards the close, where he contrasts the gorgeous but painful ceremonies of a crown with the profitable labour and the balmy rest of the peasant, who

_____" from the rise to set,
Sweats in the eye of Phoebus, and all night
Sleeps in Elysium!"

But the prayer which immediately follows is unrivalled for its power of impression, presenting us with the most lively idea of the amiability, piety, and devotional fervour of the monarch:—

"O God of battles! steel my soldiers' hearts!
_____ Not to-day, O Lord,
O not to-day, think not upon the fault
My father made in compassing the crown!
I Richard's body have interred anew;
And on it have bestow'd more contrite tears,
Than from it issued forced drops of blood.
Five hundred poor I have in yearly pay,
Who twice a day their *wither'd* hands hold up
Toward heaven, to pardon blood; and I have built
Two chantries, where the sad and solemn priests
Sing still for Richard's soul."

Of the *picturesque force* of an epithet, there is not in the records of poetry a more remarkable instance than what is here produced by the adoption of the term *withered,* through which the scene starts into existence with a boldness of relief that vies with the noblest creations of the pencil.

The address to Westmoreland, on his wishing for more men from England, is a fine specimen of military eloquence, possessing that high tone of enthusiasm and exhilaration, so well calculated to inflame the daring spirit of the soldier. It is in perfect keeping with the historical character of Henry, nor can we agree with Dr. Johnson in thinking that its reduction "to about half the number of lines," would have added, either to its force or weight of sentiment; so far, indeed, are we from coalescing with this decision, that we feel convinced not a clause could be withdrawn without material injury to the animation and effect of the whole.

Instances of the same impressive and energising powers of elocution, will be found in the King's exhortation to his soldiers before the gates of Harfleur; in his description of the horrors attendant on a city taken by storm; and in his replies to the Herald Montjoy; all of which spring naturally from, and are respectively adapted to the circumstances of the scene.

Nor, amid all the dangers and unparalleled achievements of the Fifth Henry, do we altogether lose sight of the frank and easy gaiety which distinguished the Prince of Wales. His winning condescension in sympathising with the cares and pleasures of his soldiers, display the same kindness and affability of temper, the same love of raillery and humour, reminiscences, as it were, of his youthful days, and which, in his intercourse with Williams and Fluellin, produce the most pleasing and grateful relief.

These touches of a frolic pencil are managed with such art and address, that they derogate nothing from the dignity of the monarch and the conqueror; what may be termed the truly comic portion of the play, being carried on apart from any immediate connection with the person of the sovereign.

As the events of warfare and the victories of Henry form the sole subjects of the serious parts of this piece, it was necessary for the sake of variety and dramatic effect, and in order to satisfy the audience of this age, that comic characters and incidents should be interspersed; and, though we arc disappointed in not seeing Falstaff, according to the poet's promise, again on the scene, we once more behold his associates, Bardolph, Pistol, and Hostess Quickly, pursuing their pleasant career with unfailing eccentricity and humour. The description of the death of Falstaff by the last of this fantastic trio, is executed with peculiar felicity, for while it excites a smile verging on risibility, it calls forth, at the same time, a sigh of pity and regret.

Of the general conduct of this play, it may be remarked, that the interest turns altogether upon the circumstances which accompany a single battle; consequently the poet has put forth all his strength in colouring and contrasting the situation of the two armies; and so admirably has he succeeded in this attempt, by opposing the full assurance of victory, on the part of the French, their boastful clamour, and impatient levity, to the conscious danger, calm valour, and self-devotedness of the English, that we wait the issue of the combat with an almost breathless anxiety.

And, in order that the heroism of Henry might not want any decoration which poetry could afford, the epic and lyric departments have been laid under contribution, for the purpose of supplying what the very confined limits of the stage, then in the infancy of its mechanism, had no means of unfolding. A preliminary chorus, therefore, is attached to each act, impressing vividly on the imagination what could not be addressed to the senses, and adding to a subject, in itself more epic than dramatic, all the requisite grandeur and sublimity of description.

1821—Thomas De Quincey.
From "John Paul Frederick Richter"

Thomas De Quincey (1785–1859), a friend of William Wordsworth and Samuel Taylor Coleridge, is best remembered for his *Confessions of an English Opium-Eater* (1821), but he was a prolific writer of critical essays

for such journals as *London Magazine* and *Blackwood's*. The following
comments on Falstaff's death were first published as part of a larger
consideration of John Paul Frederick Richter under the pseudonym
Grasmeriensis Teutonizans in *London Magazine* in December 1821.

[T]he pathetic and the humorous are but different phases of the same orb;
they assist each other, melt indiscernibly into each other, and often shine each
through each like layers of coloured chrystals placed one behind another. Take,
as an illustration, Mrs. Quickly's account of Falstaff s death:—here there were
three things to he accomplished; first, the death of a human being was to he
described; of necessity, therefore, to be described pathetically: for death being
one of those events which call up the pure generalities of human nature, and
remove to the background all individualities, whether of life or character, the
mind would not in any case endure to have it treated with levity: so that, if any
circumstances of humour are introduced by the poetic painter, they must be
such as will blend and fall into harmony with the ruling passion of the scene:
and, by the way, combining it with the fact, that humorous circumstances often
have been introduced into death-scenes, both actual and imaginary,—this
remark of itself yields a proof that there *is* a humour which is in alliance with
pathos. How else could we have borne the jests of Sir Thomas More after his
condemnation, which, as jests, would have been unseasonable from anybody
else: but being felt in him to have a root in his character, they take the dignity of
humorous traits; and do, in fact, deepen the pathos. So again, mere naiveté, or
archness, when it is felt to flow out of the cheerfulness of resignation, becomes
humorous, and at the same time, becomes pathetic: as, for instance, Lady Jane
Grey's remark on the scaffold—"I have but a little neck," &c. But to return: the
death of Falstaff, as the death of a man, was in the first place to be described
with pathos, and if with humour, no otherwise than as the one could be reconciled with the other: but, 2dly, it was the death, not only of a man, but also
of a Falstaff; and we could not but require that the description should revive
the image and features of so memorable a character; if not, why describe it at
all? The understanding would as little bear to forget that it was the death-bed
of a Falstaff, as the heart and affections to forget that it was the death-bed of
a fellow-creature. Lastly, the description is given, not by the poet speaking in
his own universal language, but by Mrs. Quickly,—a character as individually
pourtrayed, and as well known to us, as the subject of her description. Let me
recapitulate: first, it was to be pathetic, as relating to a man: 2dly, humorous,
as relating to Falstaff: 3dly, humorous in another style, as coming from Mrs.
Quickly.—These were difficulties rather greater than those of levelling hills,
filling up vallies, and arranging trees, in picturesque groups: yet Capability
Brown was allowed to exclaim, on surveying a conquest of his in this walk of
art—"Aye! none but your Browns and your G—Almighties can do such things

as these." Much more then might this irreverent speech be indulged to the gratitude of our veneration for Shakspeare, on witnessing such triumphs of his art. The simple words—"*and a' babbled of green fields,*" I should imagine, must have been read by many a thousand with tears and smiles at the same instant; I mean, connecting them with a previous knowledge of Falstaff and of Mrs. Quickly. Such then being demonstrably the possibility of blending, or fusing, as it were, the elements of pathos and of humor—and composing out of their union a third metal *sui generis,* (as Corinthian brass, you know, is said to have been the product of all other metals, from the confluence of melted statutes, &c., at the- burning of Corinth.) . . .

1830—Leigh Hunt. "King Henry V," from *The Tatler*

Leigh Hunt, the friend of such figures as Lord Byron, Percy Shelley, and John Keats, tried his hand at almost every mode of writing in vogue during his life, and despite wanting to be a poet, his most important role was as critic, one who sought to cultivate the literary tastes of the reading public. The following review of a production of *Henry V* was published on November 9, 1830.

The play of *Henry V.* was performed here last night, but to little purpose. It is a *rifacimento* of Shakspeare's play, partly taken out of *Henry IV.,* in order to increase the dramatic effect. But the secret must out. It is not a good acting play—at least not for these times. In every production of Shakspeare's there must be noble passages. There are fine lines in this, "familiar in our mouths" (to quote one of them) "as household words." But the historical plays of our great poet were written, not merely as dramas, but as chronicles. People in ordinary, in his time, were not so well informed as they are now. They went to the theatre, when one of these plays was performed, not merely to see a play as we do, but to receive an historical lesson, to hear about England and France, and take home the legend to their children, as we carry home now a piece of news. Besides, the feeling was not what it is now between the two countries. They affected then (as indeed they did up to a late period) to bully and undervalue one another: Henry V. was a popular prince with our ancestors, purely because he went to France, and read the Dauphin's insolence a terrible lesson. But these times are over now: the French (with illustrious reason) are no longer reckoned boasters: those even who conquered them but a little while since, may not be popular. The English care little for quarrels between kings: audiences at a play want something better than this prince and that stepping out alternately with a flourish of trumpets—then a little huddle of soldiers, which we are to take for an onset—then the English flag running in, and then the French flag—with an occasional speech between, about St. George or St. Denys—and a Welsh captain, who is proud because the King is a Welshman. In a word, the play of *Henry V.* was written to please the uninformed subjects of a despotic government two hundred years ago, and as it comprises little of the everlasting humanity that fills most of the plays of Shakspeare, it falls flat on the ears of an audience in these times of popular spirit! Of all the plays that could be selected, it struck us as one of the least fit to be performed on the eve of our present Lord Mayor's Day! and we found it so. Mr. Macready, though too loud in some parts, made a gallant and a gallant prince too (we allude to his courtship of Katharine), and Mr. Webster, in Captain Fluellen, sustained the reputation he acquired as Sir Hugh Evans:—but it would not do. The piece was as flat as the water in Tower Ditch, and about as noisy to no purpose as the beating to arms there.

1836—Samuel Taylor Coleridge. "Henry V," from *Lectures and Notes on Shakspere and Other English Poets*

The English poet and critic Samuel Taylor Coleridge (1772–1834) is now remembered for such poems as *The Rime of the Ancient Mariner* (1798) and "Kubla Khan" (1816) and for his role in establishing the English romantic movement with his friend William Wordsworth. During the second decade of the nineteenth century, he gave a series of lectures on important literary figures, including Shakespeare, that were posthumously published along with notes, some concerning *Henry V*, found in his copy of Shakespeare's works.

Act. I. sc. 2. Westmoreland's speech:—

They know your *grace* hath cause, and means, and might;
So hath your *highness;* never King of England
Had nobles richer, &c.

Does 'grace' mean the king's own peculiar domains and legal revenue, and 'highness' his feudal rights in the military service of his nobles?—I have sometimes thought it possible that the words 'grace' and 'cause' may have been transposed in the copying or printing;—

They know your cause hath grace, &c.

What Theobald meant, I cannot guess. To me his pointing makes the passage still more obscure. Perhaps the lines ought to be recited dramatically thus:

> They know your Grace hath cause, and means, and might:—
> So *hath* your Highness—never King of England
> *Had* nobles richer, &c.

He breaks off from the grammar and natural order from earnestness, and in order to give the meaning more passionately.

Ib. Exeter's speech:—

> Yet that is but a *crush'd* necessity.

Perhaps it may be 'crash' for 'crass' from. *crassus,* clumsy; or it may be 'curt,' defective, imperfect: anything would be better than Warburton's 'scus'd,' which honest Theobald, of course, adopts. By the by, it seems clear to me that this speech of Exeter's properly belongs to Canterbury, and was altered by the actors for convenience.

Act iv. sc. 3. K. Henry's speech:—

> We would not *die* in that man's company
> That fears his fellowship to die with us.

Should it not be 'live' in the first line?

Ib. sc. 5.

> *Const. O diable!*
> *Orl. O seigneur! le jour est perdu, tout est perdu!*
> *Dan. Mort de ma vie!* all is confounded, all!
> Reproach and everlasting shame
> Sit mocking in our plumes!—*O meschante fortune!*
> Do not run away!

Ludicrous as these introductory scraps of French appear, so instantly followed by good, nervous mother-English, yet they are judicious, and produce the impression which Shakspeare intended,—a sudden feeling struck at once on the ears, as well as the eyes, of the audience, that 'here come the French, the baffled French braggards!'—And this will appear still more judicious, when we reflect on the scanty apparatus of distinguishing dresses in Shakspeare's tyring-room.

1841—Thomas Carlyle. "The Hero as Poet," from
On Heroes, Hero-worship, and the Heroic in History

Thomas Carlyle (1795-1881) was a historical philosopher and essayist
who promoted the great man theory of history, that is, the notion that
history is essentially the story of its heroes. He is, however, best known
today for his vaguely veiled spiritual autobiography, *Sartor Resartus*. The
following commentary is from one of a series of lectures that Carlyle
gave in 1840 in which he clearly expressed his historical theory.

We have no room to speak of Shakspeare's individual works; though perhaps
there is much still waiting to be said on that head. Had we, for instance, all
his plays reviewed as *Hamlet,* in *Wilhelm Meister,* is! A thing which might, one
day, be done. August Wilhelm Schlegel has a remark on his Historical Plays,
Henry Fifth and the others, which is worth remembering. He calls them a
kind of National Epic. Marlborough, you recollect, said, he knew no English
History but what he had learned from Shakspeare. There are really, if we look
to it, few as memorable Histories. The great salient points are admirably seized;
all rounds itself off, into a kind of rhythmic coherence; it is, as Schlegel says,
epic;—as indeed all delineation by a great thinker will be. There are right beautiful things in those Pieces, which indeed together form one beautiful thing.
That battle of Agincourt strikes me as one of the most perfect things, in its sort,
we anywhere have of Shakspeare's. The description of the two hosts: the worn-
out, jaded English; the dread hour, big with destiny, when the battle shall begin;
and then that deathless valor: "Ye good yeomen, whose limbs were made in
England!" There is a noble Patriotism in it,—far other than the "indifference"
you sometimes hear ascribed to Shakspeare. A true English heart breathes,
calm and strong, through the whole business; not boisterous, protrusive; all the
better for that. There is a sound in it like the ring of steel. This man too had a
right stroke in him, had it come to that!

But I will say, of Shakspeare's works generally, that we have no full impress
of him there; even as full as we have of many men. His works are so many
windows, through which we see a glimpse of the world that was in him. All his
works seem, comparatively speaking, cursory, imperfect, written under cramping
circumstances; giving only here and there a note of the full utterance of the man.
Passages there are that come upon you like splendor out of Heaven; bursts of
radiance, illuminating the very heart of the thing: you say, "That is *true,* spoken
once and forever; wheresoever and whensoever there is an open human soul,
that will be recognized as true!" Such bursts, however, make us feel that the
surrounding matter is not radiant; that it is, in part, temporary, conventional.
Alas, Shakspeare had to write for the Globe Playhouse: his great soul had to
crush itself, as it could, into that and no other mould. It was with him, then, as

it is with us all. No man works save under conditions. The sculptor cannot set his own free Thought before us; but his Thought as he could translate it into the stone that was given, with the tools that were given. *Disjecta membra* are all that we find of any Poet, or of any man.

Whoever looks intelligently at this Shakspeare may recognize that he too was a *Prophet*, in his way; of an insight analogous to the Prophetic, though he took it up in another strain. Nature seemed to this man also divine; *un*speakable, deep as Tophet, high as Heaven; "We are such stuff as Dreams are made of!" That scroll in Westminster Abbey, which few read with understanding, is of the depth of any seer. But the man sang; did not preach, except musically. We called Dante the melodious Priest of Middle-Age Catholicism. May we not call Shakspeare the still more melodious Priest of a *true* Catholicism, the "Universal Church" of the Future and of all times? No narrow superstition, harsh asceticism, intolerance, fanatical fierceness or perversion: a Revelation, so far as it goes, that such a thousand-fold hidden beauty and divineness dwells in all Nature; which let all men worship as they can! We may say without offence, that there rises a kind of universal Psalm out of this Shakspeare too; not unfit to make itself heard among the still more sacred Psalms. Not in disharmony with these, if we understood them, but in harmony!—I cannot call this Shakspeare a "Sceptic," as some do; his indifference to the creeds and theological quarrels of his time misleading them. No: neither unpatriotic, though he says little about his Patriotism; nor sceptic, though he says little about his Faith. Such "indifference" was the fruit of his greatness withal: his whole heart was in his own grand sphere of worship (we may call it such); these other controversies, vitally important to other men, were not vital to him.

But call it worship, call it what you will, is it not a right glorious thing, and set of things, this that Shakspeare has brought us? For myself, I feel that there is actually a kind of sacredness in the fact of such a man being sent into this Earth. Is he not an eye to us all; a blessed heaven-sent Bringer of Light?—And, at bottom, was it not perhaps far better that this Shakspeare, every way an unconscious man, was *conscious* of no Heavenly message? He did not feel, like Mahomet, because he saw into those internal Splendors, that he specially was the "Prophet of God:" and was he not greater than Mahomet in that? Greater; and also, if we compute strictly, as we did in Dante's case, more successful. It was intrinsically an error that notion of Mahomet's, of his supreme Prophethood; and has come down to us inextricably involved in error to this day; dragging along with it such a coil of fables, impurities, intolerances, as makes it a questionable step for me here and now to say, as I have done, that Mahomet was a true Speaker at all, and not rather an ambitious charlatan, perversity and simulacrum; no Speaker, but a Babbler! Even in Arabia, as I compute, Mahomet will have exhausted himself and become obsolete, while this Shakspeare, this Dante may still be young;—while this Shakspeare may still pretend to be a Priest of Mankind, of Arabia as of other places, for unlimited periods to come!

Compared with any speaker or singer one knows, even with Aeschylus or Homer, why should he not, for veracity and universality, last like them? He is *sincere* as they; reaches deep down like them, to the universal and perennial. But as for Mahomet, I think it had been better for him *not* to be so conscious! Alas, poor Mahomet; all that he was *conscious* of was a mere error; a futility and triviality,—as indeed such ever is. The truly great in him too was the unconscious: that he was a wild Arab lion of the desert, and did speak out with that great thunder-voice of his, not by words which he *thought* to be great, but by actions, by feelings, by a history which *were* great! His Koran has become a stupid piece of prolix absurdity; we do not believe, like him, that God wrote that! The Great Man here too, as always, is a Force of Nature. Whatsoever is truly great in him springs up from the *in*articulate deeps.

Well: this is our poor Warwickshire Peasant, who rose to be Manager of a Playhouse, so that he could live without begging; whom the Earl of Southampton cast some kind glances on; whom Sir Thomas Lucy, many thanks to him, was for sending to the Treadmill! We did not account him a god, like Odin, while he dwelt with us;—on which point there were much to be said. But I will say rather, or repeat: In spite of the sad state Hero-worship now lies in, consider what this Shakspeare has actually become among us. Which Englishman we ever made, in this land of ours, which million of Englishmen, would we not give up rather than the Stratford Peasant? There is no regiment of highest Dignitaries that we would sell him for. He is the grandest thing we have yet done. For our honor among foreign nations, as an ornament to our English Household, what item is there that we would not surrender rather than him? Consider now, if they asked us, Will you give up your Indian Empire or your Shakspeare, you English; never have had any Indian Empire, or never have had any Shakspeare? Really it were a grave question. Official persons would answer doubtless in official language; but we, for our part too, should not we be forced to answer: Indian Empire, or no Indian Empire; we cannot do without Shakspeare! Indian Empire will go, at any rate, some day; but this Shakspeare does not go, he lasts forever with us; we cannot give up our Shakspeare!

Nay, apart from spiritualities; and considering him merely as a real, marketable, tangibly useful possession. England, before long, this Island of ours, will hold but a small fraction of the English: in America, in New Holland, east and west to the very Antipodes, there will be a Saxondom covering great spaces of the Globe. And now, what is it that can keep all these together into virtually one Nation, so that they do not fall out and fight, but live at peace, in brotherlike intercourse, helping one another? This is justly regarded as the greatest practical problem, the thing all manner of sovereignties and governments are here to accomplish: what is it that will accomplish this? Acts of Parliament, administrative prime-ministers cannot. America is parted from us, so far as Parliament could part it. Call it not fantastic, for there is much reality in it: Here, I say, is an English King, whom no time or chance, Parliament or combination of Parliaments, can dethrone! This King Shakspeare, does not he shine, in crowned sovereignty, over us all, as the noblest, gentlest, yet strongest of rallying-signs; *in*destructible; really more valuable in that point of view than any other means or appliance whatsoever? We can fancy him as radiant aloft over all the Nations of Englishmen, a thousand years hence. From Paramatta, from New York, wheresoever, under what sort of Parish-Constable soever, English men and women are, they will say to one another: "Yes, this Shakspeare is ours; we produced him, we speak and think by him; we are of one blood and kind with him." The most common-sense politician, too, if he pleases, may think of that.

Yes, truly, it is a great thing for a Nation that it get an articulate voice; that it produce a man who will speak forth melodiously what the heart of it means! Italy, for example, poor Italy lies dismembered, scattered asunder, not appearing in any protocol or treaty as a unity at all; yet the noble Italy is actually *one*: Italy produced its Dante; Italy can speak! The Czar of all the Russias, he is strong with so many bayonets, Cossacks and cannons; and does a great feat in keeping such a tract of Earth politically together; but he cannot yet speak. Something great in him, but it is a dumb greatness. He has had no voice of genius, to be heard of all men and times. He must learn to speak. He is a great dumb monster hitherto. His cannons and Cossacks will all have rusted into nonentity, while that Dante's voice is still audible. The Nation that has a Dante is bound together as no dumb Russia can be.—We must here end what we had to say of the Hero-Poet.

1850—Georg Gottfried Gervinus. "Henry V," from *Shakespeare's Commentaries*

Georg Gottfried Gervinus (1805–71), a German political and literary historian, served as a professor of history and literature at Göttingen in the mid-1830s, a position he lost due to his political activities. Later, he was made an honorary professor at Heidelberg. He is best known for his work as a historian, but his *Shakespeare's Commentaries,* published in 1849, 1850, and 1852, was reprinted in numerous German and English editions during the second half of the nineteenth century.

The history of Henry V., as we read it in the text of the folio edition of 1623, existed previously in a defective sketch, which has been preserved in three older quarto editions (1600, 1602, 1608), but unfortunately in such a disfigured form that it seems hardly possible to conceive a correct idea of the poet's first design; it is, therefore, venturesome and inadmissible to draw any conclusion whatever from their comparison, respecting their accurate relation to the improved play which will alone occupy our attention. In this last form the play appears to be written in immediate connection with the preceding histories. The epilogue to Henry IV. already announces the play; the chorus at the close of Henry V. looks back, at the conclusion of the great work of this tetralogy, to the earlier histories of Henry VI., 'which oft our stage hath shown.' The date of this piece is certified by the allusion of the chorus in the fifth act to the Earl of Essex's military expedition to Ireland. This passage must have been written between the April and October of 1599. In outward bearing, the piece resembles the second part of Henry IV. The choruses seem to announce that here the 'brightest heaven of invention' is to be ascended; yet this is reached rather in a patriotic and ethical sense than in an aesthetic one. The lack of all plot and the prose of the low scenes check the poetic flight; some of these scenes, such as that between Katharine and Alice, and that between Pistol and Le Fer, might even be well omitted. Here and there the poetry in this piece rises, it must be admitted, to the most lofty expression, and this especially in the choruses. This unequal form seems to reflect the deep nature of the subject displayed. Interpreters regarded these choruses as a means for investing the piece with an epic character, for which the simple battle material seemed to them more adapted. But these choruses are maintained in a bold, ardent, figurative diction, utterly opposed to the epic; Shakespeare rather employs this more elevated poetry to place the hero of his poem in the splendid heroic light in which from his unassuming nature he cannot place himself, and in which, when arrived at the height of his fame, he expressly wishes not to be seen by those around him. Garrick felt very justly that in representation these choruses ought not only not to be omitted, but that they ought to be placed most prominently forward: he spoke them himself.

The whole interest of our play lies in the development of the ethical character of the hero. After the poet has delineated his careless youthful life in the first part of Henry IV., and in the second part has shown the sting of reflection and consideration piercing his soul as the period of self-dependence approaches, he now displays Henry as arrived at the post of his vocation, and exhibits the king acting up to his resolutions for the future. At the very beginning of the play we are at once informed of the utter change which has passed over him. The sinful nature is driven out of him by reflection, the current of reformation has suddenly scoured away the old faults; as the wholesome strawberry ripens best 'neighboured by fruit of baser quality,' so his active practice, his intercourse with lower life and simple nature, has matured in him all those gifts which etiquette and court ceremony would never have produced in him, and which those now around him perceive in him with admiration. The poet expressly tells us, through the prelates who discuss the king in the first scene, that there are no miracles, either in his poetry or the world, and that the natural grounds for this wonderful change are to he sought for really in the unpromising school of this apparently untutored man. There this many-sidedness was developed, which now astonishes them in him, and on account of which he now appears equally acquainted with all things, ecclesiastical and secular, in the cabinet as in the field. He no longer squanders his now valuable time, but weighs it to the last grain; the curb of mildness and mercy is now placed on his passions, and even foreign lands conjecture that

> his vanities fore-spent
> Were but the outside of the Roman Brutus,
> Covering discretion with a coat of folly.

And *how* justly his systematic wickedness was calculated, how entirely according to his design the unexpected sunshine broke through the veil of clouds is excellently expressed in the scene in which the king first meets us again, discussing with his counsellors the important business of the wars with France. The force and courage of men, the success and the favour of Providence, is manifest in every word of this discussion. 'When once the mind,' says Bacon, 'has placed before it noble aims, it is immediately surrounded not only by the virtues, but by the gods!' Every one, in the suddenness of his gladly disappointed expectation, appears as if electrified. The thought of honour prevails in every breast. All classes are equally devoted to him in heroic unity; his family, his uncle and brothers, no less than the nobles, urge him to the war; the clergy give him the mightiest sum that they had ever granted to an English king; they depict to him the heroic age of the Edwards, and call him to renew their feats; everything breathes courage and good will. As if seized with a better spirit, even Bardolph, Nym, and Pistol seem to settle their quarrels among themselves, that as sworn brothers they may march against France. The Eumenides of the insurrection, who had disturbed and crossed the rule of Henry IV., are heard retreating in the distance. The Irish, who had rebelled against Richard II., and the Welsh and Scotch, with whom Henry IV. had to fight, appear together as countrymen in the king's army. The treachery of a few bribed nobles is easily frustrated. The words of the dying Henry IV. are fulfilled, that the crown seemed in him merely as 'an honour snatched with boisterous hand,' and the quarrel which arose in consequence was the argument of which his reign had been the scene. His death 'changed the mode.' The young king follows the home policy which his father had in dying commended to him; he leads those 'overproud with sap and blood' into foreign war, and turns their thoughts to new and greater things.

This policy urges Henry to the French war; he is urged to it by right and the well-grounded claim of which with religious conscientiousness he is convinced; he is urged to it by his ambition, which bids him compensate for his youth and its idleness by great deeds. His history, he desires, shall speak with full mouth freely of his acts, or else his grave 'shall have a tongueless mouth, not worship'd with a waxen epitaph.' The scorn of the enemy and the mocking taunt at his madly-spent youth excite his passion for the righteous war, which he has undertaken with steadfast resolve, and to this passion he gives vent in an ambition equally scornful:—he never valued 'this poor seat of England,' but when he rouses himself in his throne of France, for which he has laid by his majesty, he will 'rise there with so full a glory, that he will dazzle all the eyes of France.' It is in this war that he acknowledges himself the most offending soul alive if it be a sin to covet honour; for now he has the great object before him, as we have said before, in behalf of which it must seem to him noble to be roused. In his fight at Agincourt he has before him even to surpass the warlike Edwards, when, with a little, weak, famished band, he has to withstand the brilliant force of the French, at least fivefold more in number. And in this position he aspires truly after the wholly undiminished glory of a position so desperate; he prefers not to lose so much 'honour as one man more would share from him,' who should come to his assistance from England.

In these expressions somewhat of that strained nature may seem to lie, which we pointed out in Percy as opposed to Henry; and truly we see the king in this over-strained condition throughout the whole war. This would be a contradiction in his character, if anything were a contradiction in it; but we showed throughout that it belongs to his nature and essence to be everything when occasion calls him and necessity claims him. We found him indolent and idle amid the degeneracy of a corrupt period of peace; now that he is in the war he is a soldier, showing himself collected and eager, mighty and violent in word and deed, acquainted with the terrible ravages of war, and with unrestrained passions ready even at the right moment to unbridle them himself. In peace, he says himself, nothing so becomes a man as modest stillness and humility; but in war he must 'imitate the action of the tiger, stiffen the sinews, summon up the blood, and disguise fair nature with hard-favoured rage.' Just so, influenced less by principle than after his fashion by time and place, the king's behaviour at first towards the French ambassador is marked by resolute decision; he sends back defiance and contempt to the scornful Dauphin; he is announced by the French embassy as coming 'in thunder, and in earthquake, like a Jove;' and thus we see him before Harfleur, threatening the citizens with all the terrors of a besieged town. Once had *Prince* Henry said that he was 'not yet of Percy's mind,' but the *King* is so now. Just in the same way would Percy's impatient spirit have chafed before a besieged city; just in the same way as Henry does would Percy have broken out with boasting before the scornful French ambassadors, infected by the soil of the boastful nation; just in the same way did Vernon's words provoke Percy at Shrewsbury as the Dauphin's message now does the prince; and yet, at his subsequent wooing of Katherine, he is as entirely the soldier, as far from quibbling rhetoric and as free from all arts of verse and mincing as Percy ever could have appeared. The world now compares him, as the poet once had done Percy, to Caesar and to Alexander. He appears now wrathful and terrible as the war-god, when, in the battle of Agincourt, furious at the plunder and slaughter committed by the flying French, he commands the death of the prisoners. His ambition now also, like Percy's, imperceptibly passes into a thirst for honour, which, when in hasty impatience it desires to obtain an object, weighs not means and ways.

But that which at once obliterates all these similarities to Percy is the contrast of circumstances, which at once draw out in him those opposite qualities which Percy could not have possessed. Left to himself, and unprovoked, the braggart is all humility; in the pauses of rest the warlike tiger is peaceful and tame. He calls himself a man like every other, whose affections are indeed higher mounted, yet when they stoop they stoop with the like wing. Percy's affections did not do this. Never would he have been seen, least of all as king, in that condescension which marks Henry in his present position; never, in the moment of serious preparation for hot strife, would he have exhibited the tranquil repose which Henry manifested. In his courtship and on the day of battle Henry is just as plain a king as if he had 'sold his farm to buy his crown.' He has shaken off his old dissolute companions, but the remembrances of that simple intercourse are recalled to our mind at every moment. The same inclination to rove about with the common man in his army, the old mildness and familiarity, and the same love for an innocent jest, exist in him now as then, without derogating in the least from his kingly dignity. He leaves his nobles waiting in his tent, while he visits the posts of his soldiers; the old habit of night-watching is of use to him now; he sounds the disposition of individuals; he encourages them without high-sounding words; he fortifies them without ostentation; he can preach to them and solve moral scruples, and can make himself intelligible to them; he contrives a trick quite of the old kind in the moment of most gloomy suspense; like a brother, he borrows the cloak of the old Erpingham; he familiarly allows his countryman Fluellen to join freely in his conversation with the herald, and in his short appeal before the battle he declares all to be his brothers who on this Crispin's day shed their blood with him.

This contrast between his repose and calmness and his martial excitement, between his plain homely nature and the kingly heroic spirit which in the moment of action exercises dominion over him, is, however, not the only one in which the poet has exhibited him. The night before and the day during the battle, which form the centre of our play, is a period so prominent, and one in which such manifold moods, emotions, and passions are roused and crossed, that the best opportunity was here afforded to the poet for exhibiting to our view this many-sided man in all the richness and the diversity of his nature. When the mind is quickened, he himself says, 'the organs break up their drowsy grave, and newly move with casted slough and fresh legerity:' and thus is it with him in this great and decisive moment. We see him in a short time alternate between the most different emotions and positions, ever the same master over himself, or we may rather say, over the opportunity and the matter which lie for the moment before him. The French herald comes and challenges him to ransom himself from his unavoidable detention; he returns a proud bragging declaration; he repents it while he is speaking. He is seized with a moment of passion, as in that collision with the Chief Justice, but at once he is again master of himself; nor was he so forgetful, even in the moment of excitement, as in any way to neglect the truthfulness of his nature; imprudently he conceals not from the enemy the critical condition of his little army. At night, well knowing the danger of his position, we find him in the most serious mood: he desires no other company, he and his bosom will debate awhile. This debating is disturbed by contact with all sorts of people belonging to his camp. He hears the scorn of the boaster, he listens to the voice of the pedantic lover of discipline, and he talks with the apprehensive who are better and braver than their words. That truth so incapable of dissimulation speaks in him even here. What would it have cost him to boast of the king in the name of a third person, and to declare that he was cheerful and full of trust? But he does it not; he desires as little in the soldiers as in himself to extinguish the consciousness of danger, in order that he may spur them by the necessity to their utmost exertion. When he remarks this anxious expectation, he assures them truly that the king himself would not wish to be anywhere but where he is. The serious natures are occupied with the question as to whether they must answer with their souls for the possible injustice of the royal cause they fight for, or whether the king, if they die for him unprepared, will have to answer for their sins? He turns field preacher and explains to them; he falls into a quarrel on the matter with the coarse Williams; he takes up the jest as well as the edifying conversation, though the acting out of the matter is to be disturbed by the bloody seriousness of the battle. After the unexpected interruption and its half-constrained humorous turn the king sinks all the more completely into solemn deliberation with himself; meditation and seriousness overtake and overburden his soul. After the soldiers had just been laying their cares and burdens to the king's charge, how natural is the sequence of this same king's train of thought, that having known the happiness of private life he should recall it to his mind at this hour, when ceremony, the prerogative of kings from which he was ever escaping, must appear so empty to him. He, he says in the deepest self-consciousness of his real sterling value, he is a king who has found out this ceremony and its importance! How enviously (standing before the last pinnacle of his fame, as his father had done before in the moment of sickness and distress), how enviously he looks upon the healthful occupation of the peasant, who rises with the sun, 'sweats in the eye of Phoebus, and all night sleeps in Elysium'—and how affecting and striking is it, and how completely in the spirit of this king by merit, that in sight of this happy toil of the poor, returning to his former idea, he sees the vocation of the king in this, that he, conscious and vigilant, with *his own* labour and exertions, establishes that security of the state and that peace which the poor man enjoys in unconscious happiness. His meditation upon the ideas thus aroused is followed by the perfect collectedness of mind exhibited in that fervent prayer, in which he prays God 'not to-day' to think upon his father's fault. Then he rides forth to see the order of the battle. And as he meets his nobles, and hears Westmoreland's wish to have here 'one ten thousand of those men in England that do no work,' he shows how seriously he means to gain for himself, out of this very necessity, the highest prize of honour without further help. How popular after his old fashion, and at the same time how sublime, is his encouragement to the battle! How calm his last words to the French herald! How far is he from being over-hasty in giving credit to the victory! When he hears of the touching death of the noble York, how near is he to tears! and at the same moment, alarmed by a new tumult, how steeled to a bloody command! how impatiently furious at the last resistance! and at the moment when victory decides for him, how pious and how humble! And again, a short time after this solemn elevation of mind, he concludes his joke with Williams, careful even then that no harm should result from it. The poet has continued in the fifth act to show us to the very last the many-sided nature of the king. The terrible warrior is transformed into the merry bridegroom, the humorous vein again rises within him; yet he is not so much in love with his happiness, or so happy in his love, that in the midst of his wooing, and with all his jest and repartee, he would relax the smallest article of the peace which his policy had designed.

But how is it? Has not the poet forgotten that grand feature in Henry's character, that profound modesty, which formerly, as if willfully, veiled all his brilliant qualities? Is it only expressed in the serious mood before the battle, which is however natural, even in the coarse, quarrelsome Williams, when in a similiar position? Or was there no occasion to display this former characteristic of the prince, which appeared to us the very marrow of his virtue? Or did he cast it off for this once at this noble provocation for the exertion of all his powers. We saw him at the battle of Shrewsbury voluntarily yield one glorious deed to his inglorious friend; but here he has fought a battle, the whole glory of which falls on him alone, and which the poet with evident design has cast upon him alone, since he keeps the heroic forms of Bedford, Salisbury, and York so completely in the background. What turn does his modesty take, if it retains its old character of avoiding after its fashion this glaring light of fame? The answer is this: it deepens in the same degree as his fame becomes more exalted; it becomes humility, and gives the honour to God. This sentence will shock many of Shakespeare's worshippers, who discover in him nothing but aesthetic and moral free-thinking, and who regard him as a man of disorderly and wild genius. But to our mind the truth of the sentence and the truth of the delineation of the character can be little disputed. Throughout the whole play, throughout the whole bearing of the king, sounds the key-note of a religious composure, of a severe conscientiousness, and of an humble modesty. The Chronicle itself, which extols Henry so highly that it placed him before the poet as an historical favourite, praises the king's piety at home and at every page in his campaign; Shakespeare accepted this historical hint in no mechanical manner, but wrought it appropriately into the characteristics of his hero. The clergy, at the very beginning of the play, call him a true friend of the Church, and have reason to rejoice over his respect for it, as well as over his knowledge of sacred things. When he is occupied with the plan of war, he charges the Archbishop of Canterbury with a solemn oath to take heed in his counsel; he 'will believe in heart,' that what he speaks as to his right to this war is in his 'conscience washed as pure as sin with baptism.' When he has no thought but France, those to God alone 'run before' his business. He receives it as a promising ordinance from God that the treason lurking in his way is 'brought to light.' He delivers his 'puissance into the hand of God, putting it straight in expedition;' 'God before,' he says several times, he will come to take his right. He orders his old friend Bardolph to be pitilessly executed for robbing a church; he wishes all such offenders to be cut off; for he knows well that when 'lenity and cruelty play for a kingdom, the gentler gamester is the soonest winner.' We have seen him previous to the battle in solemn preparation, and engaged in edifying conversation with his soldiers. His first word on the certainty of the victory is—'Praised be God, and not our strength, for it!' When he reviews the greatness of the victory, he says again: 'Take it, God, for it is only thine!' And that this is in earnest, he orders even death to be proclaimed to any who may boast of it or take the honour from God. At his triumphal entry into London he forbids the sword and helm, the trophies of his warlike deeds, to be borne before him; and the poet says expressly of him, in the prologue, what once the prince had said of himself on that day at Shrewsbury over Percy's body—that he was 'free from vainness and self-glorious pride, giving full trophy, signal, and ostent, quite from himself to God.' The atonement which his father could not attain to, for want of energetic, persevering, inward stimulus, is accomplished by him. In his prayer to God before the battle, when he wishes that 'the sense of reckoning' may be taken from his soldiers and that his father's fault may not be thought upon, he declares that he has 'interred anew' Richard's body, has wept over it and has ordered masses to be said; that he has five hundred poor in yearly pay, 'who twice a day their withered hands hold up toward Heaven' for him. The poet, we see plainly, adheres to the character of the age, and invests Henry with all that outward work of repentance which in that day was considered necessary for the expiation of a crime. To many he will appear to have gone too far in this, both as regards his hero, who is otherwise of so unshackled a mind, and himself, rising as he does generally so far above the narrow views of his own, to say nothing of older times. But above this objection, also, the poet soars victoriously in those excellent words which he puts into the mouth of the king at the close of that penitential prayer:—

> More will I do;
> Though all that I can do is nothing worth,
> Since that my penitence comes after all,
> Imploring pardon.

Shakespeare has in no wise attributed to the king this pious humility and fear of God as an occasional quality, upon which he places no more value than upon any other; we see from the repeated reference to it, we see from the nature of the character and its consequent bearing in various circumstances, we see from the plan of the whole play, that this trait is intended to form the central point of the whole. The poet works with the same idea in which Aeschylus wrote his warlike pieces, the Persians and the Seven before Thebes: namely, that terrible is the warrior who fears God, and that on the other hand the blossom of pride ripens into the fruit of evil and the harvest of tears. For entirely in this sense has Shakespeare depicted the camp of the French and their princes, in Xerxes-like arrogance and crime, in opposition to the little troop of Britons and their intrepid pious hero. He shows this arrogance in their dividing the lion's skin before the hunt; in the French king wishing to bring the English prince in a chariot captive to Rouen; in the Dauphin, in derision of his youthful tricks, sending a tun of tennis-balls to the man who is pondering with such anxious conscientiousness his articles of war; in their playing at dice beforehand for 'the low-rated English;' in their bribing the English nobles with money to murder their king. Shakespeare's age designated that impious reliance on human power by the name of *security*, and this bold confidence in their number and this proud contempt of the enemy is imputed by the poet to the French camp. With arrogant desire they long for the day which the English are awaiting in suspense and doubt; they spend the night in noise and din which the English pass waking in uneasy calmness, and in edifying preparation; they sparkle with shining weapons, and they boast of splendid steeds, while 'the beggared host' of the Britons go in war-worn coats and ride famished horses; they look down with haughty boasting on the heads so heavily armed yet devoid of 'intellectual armour,' and compare their fool-hardy courage to that of their mastiffs; while the English, as if the king had imparted his soul to them, calm in their anxiety, gather rather fresh courage from necessity, self-respect, and fidelity. Among the French leaders there is hardly one who does not vie with another in empty boasting and bragging, not one who does not share the childish delight in dress and military decoration, not one whom the seriousness of things can draw away from insipid witticisms and vain debates, not one who showed even a tinge of the seriousness and of the calm courage and devotion of the English. But the Dauphin surpasses them all in shallow self-complacency, in frivolous arrogance, and in this merry bragging from natural narrowness of capacity. These scenes, if only from the broken French introduced, border on caricature; Shakespeare here, if anywhere, has fallen too easily into a weakness of the age. It seems to me more than probable that a jealous patriotic feeling actuated our poet in the entire representation of his Prince Henry: the intention, namely, of exhibiting by the side of his brilliant contemporary, Henry IV. of France, a Henry upon the English throne equal to him in greatness and originality. The greatness of his hero, however, would appear still more estimable if his enemies were depicted as less inestimable. It alone belonged to the ancients to honour even their enemies. Homer exhibits no depreciation of the Trojans, and Aeschylus no trace of contempt of the Persians, even when he delineates their impiety and rebukes it. In this there lies a large-hearted equality of estimation, and a nobleness of mind, far surpassing in practical morality many subtle Christian theories of brotherly love. That Shakespeare distorts the French antagonists, and could not even get rid of his Virgil-taught hatred against the Greeks, is one of the few traits which we would rather not see in his works; it is a national narrow-mindedness, with which the Briton gained ground over the man. The nations of antiquity, who bore a far stronger stamp of nationality than any modern people, were strangers to this intolerant national pride; even the Romans were so: on their triumphal arches they fashioned the statues of captive barbarian monarchs, noble in outward form, and showing in their whole bearing all the hostile defiance of independence.

Shakespeare has in this play also brought the popular king Henry into close contact with the people; his society is, however, now wholly different to that of his youth. At that time extravagance and idleness, thieving and loitering, were placed by his side, in order to make the contrast more sensible of his own occasional participation in the wantonness of the others; now the poet has found it necessary to present a wholly different contrast, designed to show us that his new moral severity and religious character rest not on the mechanism of an ecclesiastical habit, and that the free-spirited youth has in no wise become an old devotee. Shakespeare could not dare to exhibit the plain contrast of a religious bigot; the religious spirit and puritanical strictness of the age did not permit it; the whole English stage of the period never ventured, to my knowledge, to portray a character even slightly tinged with religious bigotry. Shakespeare therefore has rather exhibited by the side of the king the worldly aspect of an austerity and conscientiousness of this kind: he displays it as grown into a habit, respectable but not too accountable, so that we at once feel the contrast to the unshackled mind of his hero, in whom religious fervour, like each of his qualities, was developed according to the nature of circumstances: in whom it became apparent before, over the body of Percy, at the tidings of his father's illness, and as early as at that first soliloquy upon the crown; in whom it now blazes forth more brightly on the great occasion of a war between two mighty states, at an undertaking in which the boldest is reminded of his dependence on external powers. Among the more serious popular characters—the steady, worthy Gower, the rough Williams, and the dry Bates—the Welshman Fluellen, the king's countryman, is the central point. He is, as the king himself says, a man of 'much care and valour,' but 'out of fashion.' Compared with the former companions of the Prince, he is like discipline opposed to licence, like pedantry opposed to dissoluteness, conscientiousness to impiety, learning to rudeness, temperance to intoxication, and veiled bravery to concealed cowardice. Contrasted with those boasters, he appears at first a 'collier' who pockets every affront. In common with his royal countryman, he is not what he seems. Behind little caprices and awkward peculiarities is hidden an honest, brave nature, which should be exhibited by the actor, as it was by Hippisley in Garrick's time, without playfulness or caricature. Open and true, he suffers himself to be deceived for a time by Pistol's bragging, then he seems coldly to submit to insult from him, but he makes him smart for it thoroughly after the battle, and then gives him 'a groat to heal his broken pate.' He settles the business on which Henry sets him against Williams and which brings him a blow, and when the king rewards Williams with a glove full of crowns, he will not be behind in generosity, and gives him a shilling. He speaks good and bad of his superiors, ever according to truth, deeply convinced of the importance of his praise and blame, but he would do his duty under each. He is talkative in the wrong place, takes the word from the lips of others, and is indignant when it is taken from him; but in the night before the battle he knows how to keep himself quiet and calm, for nothing surpasses to him the discipline of the Roman wars, in which this is enjoined. The cold man flashes forth warmly like the king when the French commit the act, so contrary to the law of arms, of killing the soldiers' boys. At the time of his respect for Pistol, the latter begs him to intercede for the church-robber Bardolph, but he made his appeal to the wrong man. It is a matter of dicipline, in which Fluellen is inexorable. Indeed he especially esteems his countryman king for having freed himself of these old companions. This is the essential point to him in his learned comparison between Henry V. and Alexander the Great, that the latter killed his friends in his intoxication, while the former turned away his when he was in 'his right wits.' Since then his countryman is inscribed in his honest scrupulous heart, though before he had certainly made little of the dissolute fellow; now he cares not who knows that he is the king's countryman, he needs not to be ashamed of him 'so long as his majesty is an honest man.' Happy it is that the noble Henry can utter a cordial amen to this remark, 'God keep me so;' his captain Fluellen would at once renounce his friendship if he learned from him his first dishonourable trick. The self-contentedness of an integrity, unshaken indeed, but also never exposed to any temptation, is excellently designed in all the features of this character.

The pedantic-like discipline and love of order, the valour by line and level of the brave Fluellen, though it may appear in an old-fashioned light compared with the well-based and free virtue of the king, stands out on the other hand by its unassuming nature in advantageous contrast to the worthlessness of his boasting companions, Pistol, Nym, and Bardolph. The poet allows us through them to have another glimpse of the early intercourse of the prince. At the commencement of the important period they appear a little elevated, but circumstances again ruin them. Their seducer Falstaff is no longer with them; a better spirit accompanies them in the boy, whom we venture to take for the page in the second part of Henry IV., and who honourably falls in battle with the boys. He characterises his three companions, whom he thought of leaving, so distinctly that we require no other analysis. They are soon again 'sworn brothers in filching,' and Bardolph and Nym bring themselves to the gallows. As a proof that Shakespeare has not made the king act inconsiderately to Falstaff (who in the Chronicle also appears as a strict lover of justice), he makes him say expressly, at Bardolph's fall, that he 'would have all such offenders so cut off.' Pistol is not so bold a thief as they, and he is, therefore, dismissed with the more lenient lesson from Fluellen, who makes him eat his Welsh leek, and 'cudgels his honour' from his limbs. The poet did not again introduce the fat Falstaff; we hear only of his death. From the epilogue to Henry IV. it was undoubtedly Shakespeare's intention to let him appear in this piece also. During the work itself he must have discovered that this was no longer practicable. He could only have exhibited him in ever greater debasement, and this would have destroyed the symmetry and the great design of the play. The poet, however, by this omission, remained in debt, as it were, to the public; and he seized therefore an opportunity, not long afterwards, of liquidating it in another manner by writing the Merry Wives of Windsor, in which he once again, in strict ethical development of the character, makes 'plump Jack' appear as the principal figure.

1875—Edward Dowden. "The English Historical Plays" and "The Humour of Shakespeare," from *Shakspere: A Critical Study of His Mind and Art*

The Irish scholar Edward Dowden (1843–1913) was the first professor of English at University College, Dublin, a position to which he was appointed in 1867, four years after earning his degree from Trinity College, Dublin. He wrote studies of numerous European writers, but he was most influential as a Shakespearean scholar, publishing, in addition to *Shakspere: A Critical Study of His Mind and Art,* the student primer *Shakespere* (1877), *An Introduction to Shakespeare* (1900), as well as introductions to the 1884 Cambridge edition of the plays.

"The English Historical Plays"

Shakspere has judged Henry IV., and pronounced that his life was not a failure; still, it was at best a partial success. Shakspere saw, and he proceeded to show to others, that all which Bolingbroke had attained, and almost incalculably greater possession of good things, could be attained more joyously by nobler means. The unmistakable enthusiasm of the poet about his Henry V. has induced critics to believe that in him we find Shakspere's ideal of manhood. He must certainly be regarded as Shakspere's ideal of manhood in the sphere of practical achievement—the hero and central figure, therefore, of the historical plays.

The fact has been noticed that with respect to Henry's youthful follies, Shakspere deviated from all authorities known to have been accessible to him. "An extraordinary conversion was generally thought to have fallen upon the Prince on coming to the crown—insomuch that the old chroniclers could only account for the change by some miracle of grace or touch of supernatural benediction."[1] Shakspere, it would seem, engaged now upon historical matter, and not the fantastic substance of a comedy, found something incredible in the sudden transformation of a reckless libertine (the Henry described by Caxton, by Fabyan, and others) into a character of majestic force, and large practical wisdom. Rather than reproduce this incredible popular tradition concerning Henry, Shakspere preferred to attempt the difficult task of exhibiting the Prince as a sharer in the wild frolic of youth, while at the same time he was holding himself prepared for the splendid entrance upon his manhood, and stood really aloof in his inmost being from the unworthy life of his associates.

The change which effected itself in the Prince, as represented by Shakspere, was no miraculous conversion, but merely the transition from boyhood to adult years, and from unchartered freedom to the solemn responsibilities of a great ruler. We must not suppose that Henry formed a deliberate plan for concealing the strength and splendor of his character, in order, afterwards, to flash forth upon men's sight, and overwhelm and dazzle them. When he soliloquizes (1 Henry IV., act i., sc. 2), having bidden farewell to Poins and Falstaff,

> "I know you all, and will awhile uphold
> The unyoked humor of your idleness:
> Yet herein will I imitate the sun,
> Who doth permit the base contagious clouds
> To smother up his beauty from the world,
> That, when he please again to be himself,
> Being wanted, he may be more wondered at,
> By breaking through the foul and ugly mists
> Of vapors, that did seem to strangle him."

—when Henry soliloquises thus, we are not to suppose that he was quite as wise and diplomatical as he pleased to represent himself, for the time being, to his own heart and conscience.[2] The Prince entered heartily, and without reserve, into the fun and frolic of his Eastcheap life; the vigor and the folly of it were delightful; to be clapped on the back, and shouted for as "Hal," was far better than the doffing of caps and crooking of knees, and delicate, unreal phraseology of the court. But Henry, at the same time, kept himself from subjugation to what was really base. He could truthfully stand before his father (1 Henry IV., act iii., sc. 2) and maintain that his nature was substantially sound and untainted, capable of redeeming itself from all past, superficial dishonor.

Has Shakspere erred? Or is it not possible to take energetic part in a provisional life which is known to be provisional, while at the same time, a man holds his truest self in reserve for the life that is best and highest and most real? May not the very consciousness, indeed, that such a life is provisional enable one to give one's self away to it, satisfying its demands with scrupulous care, or with full and free enjoyment, as a man could not if it were a life which had any chance of engaging his whole personality, and that finally? Is it possible to adjust two states of being, one temporary and provisional, the other absolute and final, and to pass freely out of one into the other? Precisely because the one is perfect and indestructible, it does not fear the counter life. May there not have been passages in Shakspere's own experience which authorized him in his attempt to exhibit the successful adjustment of two apparently incoherent lives?[3]

The central element in the character of Henry is his noble realisation of fact. To Richard II., life was a graceful and shadowy ceremony, containing beautiful and pathetic situations. Henry IV. saw in the world a substantial reality, and he resolved to obtain mastery over it by courage and by craft. But while Bolingbroke, with his caution and his policy, his address and his ambition, penetrated only a little way among the facts of life, his son, with a true genius for the discovery of the noblest facts, and of all facts, came into relation with the central and vital forces of the universe, so that, instead of constructing a strong but careful life for himself, life breathed through him, and blossomed into a glorious enthusiasm of existence. And therefore from all that was unreal, and from all exaggerated egoism, Henry was absolutely delivered. A man who firmly holds, or, rather, is held by, the beneficent forces of the world, whose feet are upon a rock, and whose goings are established, may with confidence abandon much of the prudence and many of the artificial proprieties of the world. For every unreality Henry exhibits a sovereign disregard—for unreal manners, unreal glory, unreal heroism, unreal piety, unreal warfare, unreal love. The plain fact is so precious it needs no ornament.

From the coldness, the caution, the convention, of his father's court (an atmosphere which suited well the temperament of John of Lancaster), Henry escapes to the teeming vitality of the London streets, and the tavern where Falstaff is monarch. There, among ostlers, and carriers, and drawers, and merchants, and pilgrims, and loud robustious women, he at least has freedom and frolic. " If it be a sin to covet honor," Henry declares, "I am the most offending soul alive." But the honor that Henry covets is not that which Hotspur is ambitious after:

"By heaven, methinks it were an easy leap
To pluck bright honor from the pale-faced moon."[4]

The honor that Henry covets is the achievement of great deeds, not the words of men which vibrate around such deeds. Falstaff, the despiser of honor, labors across the field, bearing the body of the fallen Hotspur, the impassioned pursuer of glory, and, in his fashion of splendid imposture or stupendous joke, the fat Knight claims credit for the achievement of the day's victory. Henry is not concerned, on this occasion, to put the old sinner to shame. To have added to the deeds of the world a glorious deed is itself the only honor that Henry seeks. Nor is his heroic greatness inconsistent with the admission of very humble incidents of humanity:

"*Prince.* Doth it not show vilely in me to desire small beer?
Poins. Why, a prince should not be so loosely studied as to remember so weak a composition.
Prince. Belike, then, my appetite was not princely got; for, by my troth, I do now remember the poor creature, small beer. But indeed these humble considerations make me out of love with my greatness."[5]

Henry, with his lank frame and vigorous muscle (the opposite of the Danish Prince, who is "fat, and scant of breath"), is actually wearied to excess, and thirsty, and he is by no means afraid to confess the fact; his appetite, at least, has not been pampered. "Before God, Kate," such is Henry's fashion of wooing, "I cannot look greenly, nor gasp out my eloquence, nor I have no cunning in protestation; only downright oaths, which I never use till urged, nor never break for urging. . . . I speak to thee plain soldier; if thou canst love me for this, take me; if not, to say to thee that I shall die, is true; but for thy love, by the Lord, no; yet I love thee, too."

And, as in his love there is a certain substantial homeliness and heartiness, so is there also in his piety. He is not harassed like his son, the saintly Henry, with refinements of scrupulosity, the disease of an irritable conscience, which is delivered from its irritability by no active pursuit of noble ends. Henry has done what is right; he has tried to repair his father's faults; he has built "two chantries, where the sad and solemn priests still sing for Richard's soul." He has done his part by God and man, will not God, in like manner, stand by him and perform what belongs to God? Henry's freedom from egoism, his modesty, his integrity, his joyous humor, his practical piety, his habit of judging things by natural and not artificial standards—all these are various developments of the central element of his character, his noble realisation of fact.

But his realisation of fact produces something more than this integrity, this homely honesty of nature. It breathes through him an enthusiasm which would be intense if it were not so massive. Through his union with the vital strength of the world, he becomes one of the world's most glorious and beneficent forces. From the plain and mirth-creating comrade of his fellow-soldiers, he rises into the genius of impassioned battle. From the modest and quiet adviser with his counsellors and prelates, he is transformed, when the occasion requires it, into the terrible administrator of justice. When Henry takes from his father's pillow the crown, and places it upon his own head, the deed is done with no fluttering rapture of attainment. He has entered gravely upon his manhood. He has made very real to himself the long, careful, and joyless life of the father who had won for him this "golden care." His heart is full of tenderness for this sad father, to whom he had been able to bring so little happiness. But now he takes his due, the crown, and the world's whole force shall not wrest it from him:

> "Thy due from me
> Is tears and heavy sorrows of the blood,
> Which nature, love, and filial tenderness
> Shall, O dear father, pay thee plenteously:
> My due from thee is this imperial crown,
> Which, as immediate from thy place and blood,
> Derives itself to me. Lo, here it sits,
> Which God shall guard; and put the world's whole strength
> Into one giant arm, it shall not force
> This lineal honor from me."

Here is no aesthetic feeling for the "situation," only the profoundest and noblest entrance into the fact.

The same noble and disinterested loyalty to the truth of things renders it easy, natural, and indeed inevitable that Henry should confirm in his office the Chief Justice who had formerly executed the law against himself, and equally inevitable that he should disengage himself absolutely from Falstaff and the associates of his provisional life of careless frolic. To such a life an end must come; and, as no terms of half-acquaintance are possible with the fat Knight, exorbitant in good-fellowship as he is, and inexhaustible in resources, Henry must become to Falstaff an absolute stranger:

> "I know thee not, old man: fall to thy prayers:
> How ill white hairs become a fool and jester!"

Henry has been stern to his former self, and turned him away forever; therefore he can be stern to Falstaff. There is no faltering. But at an enforced distance of ten miles from his person (for the fascination of Falstaff can hardly weave a bridge across that interval) Falstaff shall be sufficiently provided for:

> "For competence of life I will allow you
> That lack of means enforce you not to evil:
> And as we hear you do reform yourselves,
> We will, according to your strengths and qualities,
> Give you advancement."[6]

Shortly before the English army sets sail for France, the treason of Cambridge, Scroop, and Grey is disclosed to the King. He does not betray his acquaintance with their designs. Surrounded by traitors, he boldly enters his council-chamber at Southampton (the wind is sitting fair, and but one deed remains to do before they go abroad). On the preceding day a man was arrested who had railed against the person of the King. Henry gives orders that he be set at liberty:

> "We consider
> It was excess of wine that set him on;
> And on his more advice we pardon him."

But Scroop, and Grey, and Cambridge interpose. It would be true mercy, they insist, to punish such an offender. And then, when they have unawares brought themselves within the range of justice, Henry unfolds their guilt. The wrath of Henry has in it some of that awfulness and terror suggested by the Apocalyptic reference to "the wrath of the Lamb." It is the more terrible because it transcends all egoistic feeling. What fills the King with indignation is not so much that his life should have been conspired against by men on whom his bounty has been bestowed without measure, as that they should have revolted against the loyalty of man, weakened the bonds of fellowship, and lowered the high tradition of humanity:

> "O, how hast thou with jealousy infected
> The sweetness of affiance! Show men dutiful?
> Why so didst thou: seem they grave and learned?
> Why so didst thou: come they of noble family?
> Why so didst thou: seem they religious?
> Why so didst thou: or are they spare in diet,
> Free from gross passion, or of mirth or anger,
> Constant in spirit, not swerving with the blood,
> Garnish'd and deck'd in modest complement,

Not working with the eye without the ear,
And but in purged judgment trusting neither?
Such and so finely bolted didst thou seem:
And thus thy fall hath left a kind of blot
To mark the full-fraught man and best indued
With some suspicion. I will weep for thee;
For this revolt of thine, methinks, is like
Another fall of man."

No wonder that the terrible moral insistence of these words can subdue consciences made of penetrable stuff; no wonder that such an awful discovery of
high realities of life should call forth the loyalty that lurked within a traitor's
heart. But though tears escape Henry, he cannot relent:

"Touching our person seek we no revenge;
But we our kingdom's safety must so tender,
Whose ruin you have sought, that to her laws
We do deliver you. Get you therefore hence,
Poor miserable wretches, to your death,
The taste whereof God of his mercy give
You patience to endure, and true repentance
Of all your dear offences!"

And, having vindicated the justice of God and purged his country of treason,
Henry sets his face to France with the light of splendid achievement in his
eyes.

On the night before the great battle, Henry moves among his soldiers, and
passes disguised from sentinel to sentinel. He is not, like his father, exhausted
and outworn by the careful construction of a life. If an hour of depression comes
upon him, he yet is strong, because he can look through his depression to a
strength and virtue outside of and beyond himself. Joy may ebb with him, or
rise, as it will; the current of his inmost being is fed by a source that springs
from the hard rock of life, and is no tidal flow. He accepts his weakness and his
weariness as part of the surrender of ease and strength and self which he makes
on behalf of England. With a touch of his old love of frolic, he enters on the
quarrel with Williams, and exchanges gages with the soldier. When morning
dawns, he looks freshly, and "overbears attaint" with cheerful semblance and
sweet majesty:

"A largess universal like the sun
His liberal eye doth give to every one,
Thawing cold fear."

With a prayer to God he sets to rights the heavenward side of his nature, and there leaves it. In the battle Henry does not, in the manner of his politic father, send into the field a number of counterfeit kings to attract away from himself the centre of the war. There is no stratagem at Agincourt. It is " plain shock and even play of battle." If Henry for a moment ceases to be the skilful wielder of resolute strength, it is only when he rises into the genius of the rage of battle:

> "I was not angry since I came to France
> Until this instant. Take a trumpet, herald;
> Ride thou unto the horsemen on yon hill:
> If they will fight with us, bid them come down,
> Or void the field; they do offend our sight:
> If they do neither, we will come to them,
> And make them skirr away as swift as stones
> Enforced from the old Assyrian slings;
> Besides we'll cut the throats of those we have,
> And not a man of them that we shall take
> Shall taste our mercy."

It is in harmony with the spirit of the play and with the character of Henry that it should close with no ostentatious heroics, but with the half-jocular, whole-earnest wooing of the French princess by the English king. With a touch of irony, to which one of the critics of the play has called attention, we are furnished with a hint as to the events which must follow Henry's glorious reign. "Shall not thou and I," exclaims the King, in his unconventional manner of winning a bride, "Shall not thou and I, between Saint Denis and Saint George, compound a boy, half French, half English, that shall go to Constantinople and take the Turk by the beard?" This boy, destined to go to Constantinople and confront the Turk, was the helpless Henry VI.

The historical plays are documents written all over with facts about Shakspere. Some of these facts are now discernible. We have learned something about Shakspere's convictions as to how the noblest practical success in life may be achieved. We know what Shakspere would have tried to become himself if there had not been a side of his character which acknowledged closer affinity with Hamlet than with Henry. We can in some measure infer how Shakspere would endeavor to control, and in what directions he would endeavor to reinforce his own nature while in pursuit of a practical mastery over events and things.

"Humour of Shakespeare"

Sir John, although, as he truly declares, "not only witty in himself, but the cause that wit is in other men," is by no means a purely comic character. Were he no more than this, the stern words of Henry to his old companion would be unendurable. The central principle of Falstaff's method of living is that the facts and laws of the world may be evaded or set at defiance, if only the resources of inexhaustible wit be called upon to supply by brilliant ingenuity whatever deficiencies may be found in character and conduct. Therefore Shakspere condemned Falstaff inexorably. Falstaff the invulnerable endeavours . . . to coruscate away the realities of life. But the fact presses in upon Falstaff at the last relentlessly. Shakspere's earnestness here is at one with his mirth; there is a certain sternness underlying his laughter. Mere detection of his stupendous unveracities leaves Sir John just where he was before; the success of his lie is of less importance to him than is the glory of its invention. "There is no such thing as totally demolishing Falstaff; he has so much of the invulnerable in his frame that no ridicule can destroy him; he is safe even in defeat, and seems to rise, like another Antaeus, with recruited vigour from every fall." It is not ridicule, but some stern invasion of fact—not to be escaped from—which can subdue Falstaff. Perhaps Nym and Pistol got at the truth of the matter when they discoursed of Sir John's unexpected collapse:—

Nym. The king hath run bad humours on the knight; that's the even of it.
Pistol. Nym, thou hast spoke the right;
   His heart is fracted and corroborate.

In the relation by Mrs Quickly of the death of Falstaff pathos and humour have run together and become one. "A' made a finer end and went away an it had been any christom child; a' parted even just between twelve and one, even at the turning o' the tide: for after I saw him fumble with the sheets, and play with flowers and smile upon his fingers' ends, I knew there was but one way; for his nose was as sharp as a pen, and a' babbled of green fields." Here the smile and the tear rise at the same instant. Nevertheless, the union of pathos with humour as yet extends only to an incident; no entire pathetic-humourous character has been created like that of Lear's Fool.

   Pathetically, however, the fat knight disappears, and disappears for ever. The Falstaff of *The Merry Wives of Windsor* is another person than the Sir John who is "in Arthur's bosom, if ever man went to Arthur's bosom." The epilogue to the second part of Henry IV. (whether it was written by Shakspere or not remains doubtful) had promised that "our humble author will continue the story with Sir John in it." But our humble author decided (with a finer judgment than Cervantes in the case of his hero) that the public was not to be indulged in laughter for laughter's sake at the expense of his play. The tone of the entire play of Henry V. would have been altered if Falstaff had been allowed to appear in it. During the monarchy of a Henry IV. no glorious enthusiasm animated England. It was distracted by civil contention. Mouldy, Shallow, and Feeble were among the champions of the royal cause. Patriotism and the national pride of England could not under the careful policy of a Bolingbroke burst forth as one ascending and universal flame. At such a time our imagination can loiter among the humours and frolics of a tavern. When the nation was divided into various parties, when no interest was absorbing and supreme, Sir John might well appear upon his throne at Eastcheap, monarch by virtue of his wit, and form with his company of followers a state within the state. But with the coronation of Henry V. opens a new period, when a higher interest animates history, when the national life was unified, and the glorious struggle with France began. At such a time private and secondary interests must cease; the magnificent swing, the impulse and advance of the life of England occupy our whole imagination. It goes hard with us to part from Falstaff, but, like the king, part from him we must; we cannot be encumbered with that tun of flesh; Agincourt is not the battle-field for splendid mendacity. Falstaff, whose principle of life is an attempt to coruscate away the facts of life, and who was so potent during the Prince's minority, would now necessarily appear trivial. There is no place for Falstaff any longer on earth; he must needs find refuge "in Arthur's bosom."

NOTES

1. Hudson, "Shakespeare: his Life, Art, and Characters," vol. ii., p. See also C. Knight's "Studies of Shakspere," bk. iv., ch. ii., p. 164.

2. Kreyssig, "Vorlesungen uber Shakespeare" (ed. 1874), vol. i., p. 212. R. Genee, "Shakespeare, sein Leben und seme Werke," p. 202.

3. Rümelin, who argues that Shakspere wrote to please the *jeunesse dorée* of the period, suggests that the character of the Prince was drawn from that of the Earl of Southampton! The originals of many of Shakspere's historical personages, Rümelin supposes, sat upon the side-seats of the stage, and are, alas! irrecoverably lost. (With such conjectures must "realist" criticism buttress up its case!) "Shakespeare-Studien" (ed. 1874), p. 127.

4. 1 Henry IV., act i., sc. 3. Kreyssig contrasts Hotspur's passion for honor with Falstaffs indifference to it. "Can honor set to a leg or an arm? no: or take away the grief of a wound? no." Henry, in this matter, is equally remote from Falstaff and from Hotspur ("Vorlesungen iiber Shakespeare," vol. i., pp. 244, 245).

5. Jack Cade, in his aspiration after greatness, announces, "I will make it a felony to drink small beer . . . when I am king, as king I will be." Henry's desire would seem, then, to be inexpressibly humiliating.

6. It is noteworthy that although we meet Sir John so often in 2 *Henry IV.*, we find the Prince only on a single occasion in his company; and it would be beyond human nature to deny himself the delight and edification of such a spectacle as the fat knight cuddling and kissing Doll Tearsheet: Henry *must* go.

1886—Julia Wedgwood. "Aeschylus and Shakespeare," from *The Contemporary Review*

Julia Wedgwood (1833–1913) began her career by writing two novels, the pseudonymously published *Framleigh Hall* (1858) and the anonymously published *An Old Debt* (1859). She turned to nonfiction thereafter, publishing books on religion, evolution, and other topics as well as numerous essays in periodicals. The following remarks on *Henry V* are from an essay concerned primarily with *Hamlet* that first appeared in January 1886.

The Greek and the Englishman had something in common beside genius. The roseate glow that comes in the dawn of a nation's life was around them both. Aeschylus lived in that brief gleam of splendour between the war which made Greeks discover that Greece was a unity, and the war in which they forgot it. Shakespeare lived in that steady, increasing radiance when England first awoke to feel her power and delight in her freedom. Both were animated by an awakening national life, both sung the glories of their country. But how strikingly the resemblance brings out the difference! We may take Henry V. as a sort of symbol of Shakespeare's pride in England; the hero king shines forth as a type of all that should gather up the loyalty, the patriotism of a subject of Elizabeth; his portrait is painted in Shakespeare's richest hues, and set in his clearest light. The whole play is full of a glowing pride in England, and defiance to her enemies, and this feeling finds its focus in the conqueror of Agincourt; the glory of England is summed up in the glory of an Englishman. But, when we turn to the play in which the like sense of a nation's triumph bursts forth in the verse of Aeschylus—like, but infinitely greater, for even the new sense of freedom, when the black thundercloud of the Armada rolled away, must have been feeble in comparison with the raptures that succeeded Salamis—when we turn to the play in which that rapture of relief is commemorated, we remark with surprise, that while it is filled with the names of Persians, real or invented, Aeschylus has studiously avoided the name of a single Greek. That concrete embodiment of national pride, which was indispensable to the Englishman, was abhorrent to the Athenian. He is absorbed by a religious sense of the invisible bond which made his people one, of the Divine power which had fought on their side. "Who is their shepherd and their master? who leads them to the fight?" asks the mother of Xerxes, and we can imagine what an overpowering thrill of emotion went through the crowd of spectators as they heard the answer given by the humbled foes of Greece, "They are subjects of no man." Loyalty was a feeling which would have roused nothing but dread in an Athenian. The subject of reverence was the city, the invisible would endure no rivalry on the part of the visible. Aeschylus was recounting the events in which he had borne a part: and doubtless the honour of the warrior was dearer to him than the honour of the poet. Yet all the more he felt that the interest of the drama of the deliverance of Greece must centre in a throne filled by no visible form. Shakespeare makes the most of Henry V.; Aeschylus does not take cognizance of the very existence of Miltiades or Themistocles.

The different ideals which come out in these two national dramas are visible whenever we contrast the life of the modern and the ancient world. In some sense we are forced to realize this difference whenever we look backwards. We see not merely that the Greek was a different kind of being from the Englishman, but that he was trying to be something different. The ideal state of the wisest Greek would have revolted the practical moral standard of the least virtuous Englishman. Men are separated, not by their ideal of what is good, but by their ideal of what is best; for by the correlation of moral force the whole of life is altered when we alter its hierarchy of reverence. It is of no avail that two men should agree that individual life is sacred, and that membership in a State is sacred, if they differ as to which is to come first. From the ancient point of view goodness was invisible in the individual, the group was the smallest organism in which it could be discerned. Hence all that belonged to individual relation was comparatively uninteresting. The one strong emotion which forms almost the theme of modern art, which every one thinks he can draw from imagination and most people have known by experience, had a subordinate place on the Athenian stage. The love of man for woman, so far as it ever appears there, is something quite secondary, something more or less to be kept out of sight. In the guilty love of Clytemnestra for Aegisthus there is indeed something pathetic and tender, but it is hardly allowed to appear at all; we are made to feel that she hates her husband much more than that she loves her paramour; the sense of destiny is a much stronger element in the murder than the sense of choice. In the classical ideal man's love for woman is almost nothing. In the chivalric idea it is almost everything. In Hamlet we see the chivalric ideal stamped by the individuality of a great original genius. Hamlet thinks, on the tomb of the drowned Ophelia, that he loved her more than twenty thousand brothers. Ah, how like human nature! We seemed to have loved so passionately when we have lost. We *do* so love what is gone out of reach. While Ophelia was living, to be chilled or warmed by Hamlet's love, he took very little thought of her. Other feelings were not stronger than his love of her, perhaps, but quite as strong, and there were many of them. What a wonderful knowledge of the human heart lies in that combination of the cool lover and the passionate mourner! We know no other delineation of man's love that can be put by its side. An inferior artist would have painted so slight a love as Hamlet's for Ophelia only in the portrait of a slight character. Shakespeare knew that a love may be indestructible, and rooted in a deep nature, and yet in itself may be a small thing; for he knew the heart of man. We fancy that those words are the mere equivalent of the statement that he was a great poet. But we are now comparing Shakespeare with a poet as great as he was, and surely more original, who did not know the heart of man, and did not care to know it. He was not studying the springs of individual character. He cared only for that which was universal.

1889—Denton J. Snider. "Henry the Fifth," from *The Shakespearian Drama*

Denton J. Snider (1841–1925), who was born in Mount Gilead, Ohio, was a prolific writer, publishing more than forty books, including novels; biographies of Lincoln, Emerson, and Shakespeare; and critical commentaries on authors such as Goethe and Dante as well as Shakespeare. The following consideration of *Henry V* is a slightly modified version of a commentary first published in *System of Shakespeare's Dramas* (1877).

Henry the Fourth, with its two parts, was occupied with the internal affairs of England; it portrays the great national transition from revolution triumphant to revolution suppressed—from civil discord to domestic harmony. The dynasty has been changed and the country has acquiesced. A great ruler has spent his lifetime in this long, wearisome, and painful struggle, the right of which and the wrong of which have torn his mind with their ever-recurring contradictions. But the work is done, and is well done; England is now a unit within herself, and not a mass of warring fragments; the spirit of rebellion has been extinguished in the blood of its noblest and most powerful representatives; no such personage as the gallant Hotspur will again arise to make it attractive with beauty and chivalrous daring.

The result is that a new national life has appeared, whose vigor is pulsating through the whole land with unparalleled energy. England is fired with the hope and ardor of youth; her inward impulse is driving her forward to some higher destiny; a narrow, insular existence has become too limited for her mighty aspiration. The nation is loudly calling for a great enterprise abroad, wherein it may realize this new spirit by enlarging the country with new territory, and may give expression, by deeds of valor, to the awakened impulse of nationality.

But the nation is chiefly fortunate in the present turn of affairs on account of having a leader, a man who embodies, in the full sense of the word, the national regeneration. Henry the Fifth is now seated on the throne; he, along with his country, has passed through the political and the moral fire which burns, yet purifies; both are one in character and aspiration. The father, Henry the Fourth, could hardly have been the successful leader of a foreign enterprise; his great vocation was to put down domestic revolution—to effect which, cunning as well as violence had to be employed. The function of the subtle politician has ended with his life; the immoral taint which infected his character must also be cleansed from the land. Henry the Fifth steps forth, the warlike champion and purified man; he has overthrown Hotspur on the one hand, and has cast off Falstaff on the other; both conquests are equally necessary to make him the true representative of his people—the outer and inner conquests of an heroic soul.

England, therefore, is seen marching under his leadership to the subjugation of a foreign foe. Nothing remains to be done at home adequate to the national ambition which is bursting forth on all sides; the pent-up energy must find a vent outwards. Into what channel will it thrust itself? Just across a narrow strip of water lies France, the hereditary enemy of the nation; on France, therefore, the storm will be likely to fall. Many an old score is now to be settled between the two peoples. Each has always been a barrier to the other; cannot that barrier be swept down by us, the English? No, not permanently, so one may give the answer here; for it is just that barrier that makes you both just what you are—two distinct nations, England and France. Remove it, and England will suffer in the end quite as much as France; indeed, if she be successful in breaking down all national boundaries, she will lose the very thing which she is so vehemently maintaining, namely, nationality.

But this reflection lies beyond the play—in fact, beyond the consciousness of the Poet. To him, Henry the Fifth seems to be the supreme type of the national hero, and the conquest of France the highest national object. Thus the Lancastrian Tetralogy comes to an end; it portrays the truly constructive epoch of English History according to the conception of Shakespeare, showing the glorious rise of the country from rebellion at home to the subjection of its ancient enemy abroad. Herein, therefore, the loftiest pinnacle of nationality is reached, and the poetical work must conclude. The Yorkian Tetralogy was written first, though it follows the Lancastrian in historical order; the Poet has, in consequence, not developed the inner ground of the Wars of the Roses. The play of *Henry the Fifth* is, hence, the culminating point of the English Historical series.

The structure of *Henry the Fifth* is without its like in Shakespeare. The employment of choruses or prologues to precede every Act, as is the case here, is unknown in any of his other works, if we except the doubtful play of *Pericles*. The object of these choruses seems, in the main, twofold; they announce the subject of the Acts which are to follow, and mark with some care the large gaps of time which are to be passed over by the mind. Thus they try to connect somewhat more closely the disjointed parts of the drama. The Poet himself clearly sees the loose texture of his work; he is full of apologies, which imply his own judgment of its main weakness. He appears to feel that he has transcended quite the limits of Dramatic Art—the theme is too extensive for representation on a petty stage; he seems almost afraid of turning it into ridicule. Hence he is continually begging the spectator to use his imagination and forget the apparent caricature. In no other play is he seen to struggle so hard with his artistic form as here; he surges and frets against its bounds on every side. The great exploits of his hero are in danger of appearing farcical on the stage.

The whole action is of the moving, spectacular kind; it is a series of historical pictures selected from one great campaign, with a chorus to explain the general movement and to supply the omitted links. The play, therefore, is closely tied to the external realities of place and time, and is governed to a less extent than usual by an inner controlling thought; hence criticism, whose function it is to unfold this thought, has no very profound task at present. The result is that *Henry the Fifth,* judged by the Shakespearian standard, must be considered as one of the lesser stars of the Poet's dramatic constellation; it is lacking in unity, in concentration, in organic completeness. Still, it must not be esteemed too lightly. As the play moves in the external details of history, much has to be omitted, since the dramatic form is too narrow; such a manner of treatment demands the fullness and diversity of the Epic or of the Novel. The dramatic work must compress all into the one central, glowing point; only those events are to be taken, and only those things are to be said, which embody directly the thought.

As might be inferred from its spectacular character, the play has no inherent division into movements; indeed, the structure indicates that it is made up of five separate pictures, each of which is preceded by an explanatory prologue. Yet the entire action tends to one supreme event—the battle of Agincourt— in which single effort the conquest of France was accomplished. The drama may be externally divided into two movements. First, the preparation at home on both sides, comprising the first two Acts; secondly, the conflict and its results, terminating in the overwhelming success of Henry the Fifth. England, united within after a slight ripple of opposition, prepares herself for the struggle, passes over to the territory of her enemy, subjugates the country, and tries to confirm its possession by an alliance of marriage with the royal family of France.

The division into threads is, however, strictly maintained; they were called in *Henry the Fourth,* and still may be called, the elevated or serious thread, and the low or comic thread. The first subdivides itself, according to nationality, into two groups—the French and the English—between whom lies the conflict, which is the main theme of the play. Here we must seek for the political elements which control the work. England claims the right to the throne of France, and makes good the claim by force of arms. The second or comic thread has not less than four groups; there are the remnants of the old Falstaffian company; the three English common soldiers who have the little intrigue with the King; the group of officers representing the several British nationalities—Welsh, Scotch, Irish, English; to these must be added the French Princess in her conversation with her attendant, Alice, and with the English King. The superabundance here is manifest; it branches out into so many directions that the unity of the work is in danger of being lost— the central thought seems not to be able to control the dramatic luxuriance springing out of the subject.

I

1. Beginning with the English side of the first thread, we notice at once the remarkable change in the life of the King. He is no longer the wild Prince Harry of Eastcheap, companion of thieves and revelers, but he has become a religious man; he has truly received the new birth, which has left "his body as a paradise to envelop and contain celestial spirits." The caprice of youthful wantonness, "hydra-headed willfullness," has been completely laid aside, and there has been a full submission to the established order of the world. It is clergymen who are speaking; they praise especially his holy demeanor, and wonder at his sudden reformation. Indeed, the play throughout exalts the piety of the King as one of his main characteristics, and there is, perhaps, no other personage in Shakespeare's dramas who comes so near being a religious hero. The associate of Falstaff has, therefore, fully redeemed his promise of amendment.

His intellectual gifts, which were never dim, seem to be wonderfully brightened and quickened by his moral change. "Hear him but reason in divinity," says the admiring Archbishop, "you would desire the King were made a prelate;" he speaks of matters of policy with the knowledge and skill of the veteran statesman. But, when he comes to his supreme vocation, "list to his discourse of war, and you shall hear a fearful battle rendered you in music." Still greater is his genius for action; he is the true practical man, who strikes boldly, yet at the same time thinks. In fine, he is the all-sufficient hero in whom intellect and will, the speculative and the active principles of man, are blended in the happiest harmony. Neither of these powers paralyzes the other, as is often the case, but each supports and intensifies the other to a supreme degree. And also he is the stronger and better for having passed through a wild period in his youth. "Wholesome berries thrive and ripen best, neighbored by fruit of baser quality," says the worthy Bishop of him, a clerical authority to which we may reasonably submit, though not without some surprise at the source.

Next there is revealed the chief object of his ambition, the object for which his whole career has been a long preparation—in fact, the object in which the Lancastrian Tetralogy culminates, namely, the conquest of France. But he will not proceed to it without being first assured of the justice of his cause. Accordingly he calls around himself his learned religious advisers, who state in full the grounds of his claim, and vindicate his title against the French doctrine of succession. The Clergy thus requite his favors to the Church; they even urge him to conquest, who needed no incitement; the Archbishop of Canterbury addresses him: "Stand for your own, unwind your bloody flag," and bids him take as a pattern his noble ancestors who once did "forage in blood of French nobility." So speaks the primate of all England, the chief apostle of peace and good-will among men in the British isles.

It is manifest that the nation is for war; it is not merely sustaining, but even pushing, Henry to the struggle. Yet he is fired with the same ambition; he, therefore, most truly represents the spirit of the country. The Nobles are with him, the People have been always with him, now the Clergy have become the most urgent advisers of an invasion of France. All classes are in harmony; then there is the furious energy resulting from a common aspiration. It is a national enterprise, at the head of which is marching the national Hero; the outlook is ill for the object which offers resistance to their purpose.

The King organizes rapidly his powers, wisely leaving a bulwark against the Scot "who hath been still a giddy neighbor to us." Then the reply of France is heard; to a denial of the royal claim is added a wanton insult. More impatient, then, is the cry for war. Yet even here in England there is manifested a slight reaction against the general tendency of the nation; this reaction culminates in a conspiracy against the life of the King. Still some embers of revolt remain and give out sparks; thus the old spirit of insurrection will once more appear. Three nobles, most intimate friends of Henry, were ready to thrust a dagger into his heart; but the plot is discovered and the conspirators punished. It is only a momentary gleam, passing into speedy darkness. Rebellion has been put down in the previous reign with vigor and vengeance; it cannot rise now, for other business is on hand to occupy the life of Henry the Fifth. But, after his death, will not the spirit of rebellion dart up again in the face of his successor, and will not the question of title arise once more for settlement? But let us suppress the premonition which the event excites. At present, after this slight reaction, the union is firmer than ever; England—consolidated, as it were, into one body—is eager to be hurled across the channel into the heart of France, shouting with her monarch the popular war cry:—

No King of England if not King of France.

The French group, on the other hand, are introduced discussing the threatened invasion. Their monarch, with the circumspection of age, manifests no little anxiety; he recalls the many examples of English valor enacted on the soil of his own realm. But the Dauphin, with the impetuosity of youth, is eager for the conflict, having no fear of England now, because "she is so idly kinged." But the clear-headed Constable gives a well-timed warning to the young Prince; he has carefully noted the great transformation of King Henry's character, whose

> Vanities forespent
> Were but the outside of the Roman Brutus,
> Covering discretion with a coat of folly.

Of course the French emphatically reject the claims of England, and the messenger departs with the declaration of war. Thus we are prepared for the shock of armies which is to follow—two great nations are about to grapple in a terrific struggle—though the English predilection of the Poet has given a distinct hint of the result. Such is the faint outline of the leading French characters.

2. Passing now to the comic thread, we behold the Falstaffian group without Falstaff. At the first view this omission seems quite surprising, since the Poet has distinctly promised the reappearance of the jolly Fat Knight, at the end of *Henry the Fourth*. Why he is dropped can be only conjectured; but it is manifest that the Poet changed his mind only after mature deliberation. A little reflection on the part of the reader will fully justify the same conclusion; in fact, the dramatic possibilities of the character had been exhausted in the previous plays—nothing could well be added to the portraiture. Besides, some repugnance to Falstaff must have been manifested by the more decent and moral portion of the audience, inasmuch as there are not a few persons of the present day who cannot endure his appearance and behavior. Personally, we would like to have seen his enormous bulk again on the stage and heard some of his monstrous lies, but, upon the second thought, it is well as it is; we, too, like the Prince, have had enough of his society for our own good, and should now consent to a permanent separation. Only the death of poor Jack is told; it looks as if he had experienced a hard struggle in his last hours, wrestling with repentance; and we repeat involuntarily the sigh of Prince Henry on the field of Shrewsbury: "I could have better spared a better man."

The remaining members of this comic group are brought forward from *Henry the Fourth*, and need not be characterized in detail. It is still the reverse side of society—the immoral element—in the present case transmitted to a happier era from a period of civil discord. Its importance is much diminished; still, it is here, following in the track of war, and the whole company is about to cross the channel with the army, not for the purpose of patriotism, but of plunder. The contrast to the general feeling of the nation is most clearly seen in this group of debauched camp-followers. Every great enterprise, however righteous it may be, always has such vermin clinging to it on the outside, and trying to reach its vital juices, but they must be brushed off with the strong hand of merciless justice. The fate of these people in the present undertaking will be the same as that of the external enemy—the French.

II

In the second movement of the play, which now follows, the scene changes to France, where the struggle at once begins. The key-note is struck by the King in his famous address to his soldiers—the fierce blast of the English war bugle:—

Once more unto the breach, dear friends, once more,
Or close the wall up with our English dead.

The sublime theme of the speech throughout is nationality, of which Henry is the most glorious representative in English History. The same spirit permeates this entire series of plays; here is its culmination. Hitherto England had been able to master her internal difficulties; now she is to measure herself with another nation, which it is her weighty enterprise to conquer. If she succeeds, then the English nationality has won the laurel among peoples. The strong appeal is, therefore, to Englishmen, their glory and superiority; it is a battle-prologue, nerving for the conflict which is to follow.

1. Great stress is laid by the Poet upon the behavior of the two armies just before the struggle comes on. The haughty confidence and fatuitous arrogance of the French are brought out in the strongest colors. It is, indeed, the only tragic ground of their fate; they seem to defy Heaven itself to keep them from their prey; on the pinnacle of insolence they are placed, to be hurled down by an avenging Nemesis. Even the cautious Constable gives way to arrogant boasting. A herald is sent to King Henry demanding ransom before the battle is fought; the common soldiers play at dice for English captives that are not yet taken. To the entire French army the victory seems to be won before the engagement; their camp is a scene of wild frolic and impatience. Very necessary and skillful is this motive of impious arrogance, in order to detach the sympathy of the hearer or reader from the side of the French, for they are really defending their nationality, while the English are assailing it; their cause is in every way the more rightful. Indeed, the English are not only committing a wrong against a neighboring nation, but against themselves; they are logically destroying their own supreme principle in the present conflict, namely, nationality. All of which is felt by the Poet, and its effects artfully guarded against by introducing an old Greek tragic motive—human arrogance humbled by a leveling Nemesis.

In the strongest contrast to the action of the French is the conduct of the English; from the noble down to the private soldier there is a feeling of humility—indeed, of depression, though not of despair. They all think that the result will be very doubtful; gloomy forebodings haunt them; still, the staunchest resolution pervades the host. But there is one Englishman who is animated by the most exalted hope, who sees in the present emergency the greatest opportunity of his life or of his century—it is King Henry himself. He moves around among his soldiers, giving a word of encouragement to all; he is full of religious fervor—prayer is often on his lips; nor, on the other hand, does he forget even in the most trying hour of his life to play a good joke on a common soldier. He still has some of the former Prince Hal peering out of his conduct; he has not lost his sportiveness. Once, however, in a sudden fit of anger, he gives the most cruel order that every soldier should slay his prisoners—a fact which can be reconciled with his general character only by reflecting that his highest principle is the victory and supremacy of his nation, and whatever jeopardizes this supreme end must be removed at any cost. The day of Agincourt is won;

King Henry the Fifth comes out of the battle the greatest of English national heroes; at one blow he utterly overwhelms and subjugates the ancient enemy of his country. For France naught remains but submission; one people passes under the yoke of another. It has already been frequently stated that such a condition of affairs violates in the deepest manner the principle of nationality; there can result from it only perennial strife and calamity to both States. To avoid the difficulty inherent in the situation, to cement the bond between the two nations by domestic affection, the Family is now introduced into the political relation. Henry marries Catherine, daughter of the French King; but the royal woman is not here, as is often the case, made a sacrifice to the State. The famous wooing scene shows that their marriage had its true basis of love, notwithstanding the strong comic features. But the domestic ties of the Monarchs cannot control the destinies of two great people; the Family is a very imperfect bulwark against the Nation. The political object of the present matrimonial alliance is manifest from the beautiful expressions of the Queen-mother, who gives the true ground of royal intermarriage, in her earnest appeal to the happy pair:—

As man and wife, being two, are one in love, So be there 'twixt your kingdoms such a spousal That never may ill office or fell jealousy, Which troubles oft the bed of blessed marriage, Thrust in between the paction of these kingdoms, To make divorce of their incorporate league, That English may as French, French Englishmen, Received each other.

2. The comic thread of the second movement breaks up into four distinct groups. The first is composed of the old associates of Falstaff; they now meet the fit retribution of their deeds. The immoral company seems to be pretty much wiped out in the course of the war; Nym and Bardolph have been hung; "Nell is dead in the spital;" Pistol, ranter and coward, steals back in shame and punishment to England. Thus debauchery from its first prominence in *Henry the Fourth* is quite brought to an end under the heroic King at the same time with his great national victory.

A second and new comic group is made up of representatives from the four British peoples—Welsh, Scotch, Irish, and English. They are all working for the common cause, though they have their little bickerings among themselves; they show how the heroic King had united every kind of subjects in his great foreign enterprise. In compliment to the birthplace and blood of Henry, the pedantic but valorous Welshman, Fluellen, is here the leading figure. The comic effect rests mainly upon the pronunciation of the English tongue in a different fashion by each of these persons, thus indicating with a laugh the checkered variety of speech and men in the English army—a motley gathering, but with the deepest purpose.

Another group is that of the three English soldiers, quite sober when talking together of the prospect of the battle, and not at all very comic figures at any time. But the King comes along in disguise, and they converse with him reprovingly; the result is, he exchanges gloves with one of them in token of a future settlement. From this incident springs a little comic intrigue, which ends in the King discovering himself to the soldier, who is overcome with confusion, but who receives a reward for his manly behavior generally. It is such a simple story as would be told among the common people of their beloved leader.

One more comic group can be distinguished, of which the French Princess, with her broken English, is the chief character. She makes the fourth person employing a brogue in the play. This slender comic instrumentality is quite worked to death; the tendency thereby is to drop down into a farce. In this respect the present play touches the *Merry Wives of Windsor*, in which broken English, spoken by a Welshman and a Frenchman, is the source of much of the fun.

These four groups, composing the second thread, have no very rigid central thought; they manifest rather the appearance of capricious diversity. Yet they all celebrate the internal or domestic triumphs of Henry, while the great battle of Agincourt, given in the first thread, celebrates the external or national triumph of the heroic King. It will hardly be questioned, however, that four comic groups here are too many; confusion results from excessive multiplicity always, and the feeling of the artistic Whole is obscured—or, even lost—in a labyrinth of details.

Such is the conclusion of the Lancastrian Tetralogy. Indeed, the present play, as was before said, may be considered as the culminating point of the whole Historical Drama of Shakespeare; it delineates the ideal ruler in his personal, civil, and military character, and it portrays the ideal England in harmony at home and in supremacy abroad. This Tetralogy is, in the highest sense, a positive work, having a happy outcome; it begins with a revolution and passes through to final reconstruction. A Drama of the Nation it may be called, as distinct from the Drama of the Individual; for here it is a nation which after many conflicts and obstacles, reaches a happy destiny, at least for the time being.

Looking back at the entire Tetralogy, we notice that the poet has seized the essence of Universal History, and put it into a poem which rounds itself into unity. He has shown the cycle of a nation's development, taking it, so to speak, out of Time and making it eternal as a typical experience of national life. It is the account of a particular period of a particular people, but it images all peoples of all periods, past, present, and future. Thus the work is poetic in the highest sense; it has an universal meaning, which gleams out of its particular shape.

The poet has taken a time of revolution, of civil war—the most important of all wars in the development of the modern State. Such a war is not a war of conquest, not a war of glory; it is rather inglorious, whichever way it may fall out, and the nation engaged in it can only succeed in whipping itself. But this is just the interest and the worth of civil war; it is a grand discipline of the people, which they take unwillingly enough, but they have to take it anyhow; it is the process by which the nation in tears and blood has to free itself of some weak, guilty, or inadequate phase of its life. The right of rebellion and the wrong of rebellion, are two halves which, put together, make the cycle of this poem, ending in a grand total outburst of the united national spirit.

Every people at some time has to go through this discipline, in order that it may take its step in advance. Not long after Shakespeare's death, England had to pass through this process again—the process of rebellion triumphant and rebellion defeated. Our own national life is made up of these two phases; American History opens with rebellion triumphant, and its last great act has been rebellion defeated. The two oscillations are finally one—the pulse and ebb of historic heart of the world. The rebellion of 1776 and the rebellion of 1861 are the two halves of the one entire cycle of our national discipline; they together make really one revolution, of which the two rebellions are but moieties, which complete themselves through each other, being the positive and negative phases of the same ultimate principle. The North must digest the fact that George Washington was a rebel as well as Jefferson Davis; the South must digest the fact that the one rebel was the father of his country and triumphed, the other rebel was, as far as his deed went, the destroyer of his country and had to be put down.

Thus the deepest experience in our own national life is but another manifestation of Shakespeare's Lancastrian Tetralogy. The poem is universal, belongs to all time, yet has its setting in a certain period of time. The forms which truth takes are temporal, the truth itself is eternal. Yet it must have these forms in order to manifest itself. And the manifestation also is in a process. In the present poem feudalism is the outer setting; feudal rebellion against the head of the State on the part of the powerful lord gets a death-blow in the person of Hotspur. But the greatest English rebellion, the one not long after Shakespeare's time, proceeded not from the nobility, but from the people, against the King. The double movement of this Tetralogy may well be called the systole and diastole of Time's heart, eternally repeating itself like our own heart-beat, but also eternally moving forward to the higher goal with each pulsation.

The character of Bolingbroke is this double synthesis of rebellion; he is the right rebel, and the right destroyer of the rebel. He is the genetic character; from him springs Hotspur, the image of his political violation carried to the extreme, as well as Falstaff, the image of his moral violation carried to the extreme. But his own son, Prince Henry, completes his work by putting down political rebellion in Hotspur and moral rebellion in Falstaff, thus overarching his father and becoming the hero of the Tetralogy.

In this way we behold here portrayed two grand cycles of experience: that of the nation, England, and that of the individual Prince Henry. Both have a certain correspondence; both show an alienation, a rebellion, a fall, through which both have to pass, for the sake of discipline, whereby they attain to harmony—harmony, both national and individual, with the divine order.

But there is, behind the bright skies of *Henry the Fifth* a dark, concealed background. A violation has taken place which will in its own time bring the penalty. Nationality is the spirit of England, of these English Historical plays of Shakespeare, of the modern world as distinguished from the Roman Empire, which sought to absorb all nations. But after the anguish and struggle of a thousand years, nationality has been restored to Europe, which now consists, not of one all-devouring Empire, but of a family of Nations, of which England and France have grown to be two members, independent, self-contained, with the same ultimate right, namely, that of nationality. It is this right which England assails in assailing France; it is the highest of all rights, above the right of inheritance specially to which the counselors of Henry appeal, but which cannot stand in the way of the nation, as Shakespeare himself has shown in two revolutionary plays, *King John* and *Richard the Second.* The political principle of modern times, the World-Spirit itself, is violated. The irony of the deed at once begins to show itself; England, in the pride of nationality, marches forth to destroy nationality, and thus aims a blow at herself, at her own greatest right and achievement. She obtains a transcendent victory which in the end will turn out a terrible defeat; Agincourt is really the loss of her own deepest principle. Such is the danger lurking in all victory; in the irony of history it is apt to change to the very opposite of itself. Only a national recognition and charity can avert such a fate.

Such is the transition from the Lancastrian to the Yorkian Tetralogy in idea, though this idea transcends the consciousness of the poet, who manifestly places *Henry the Fifth* on the pinnacle of his English Histories. But we, looking back through the perspective of three hundred years, must rise above the consciousness of the poet in order to understand him.

Instinctively he wrote the Yorkian before the Lancastrian series; but we must see how the former, in thought as well as in historic continuity, comes after the latter. In *Henry the Fifth* there is a violation of the World-Spirit which Shakespeare did not consciously realize, but the penalty must be paid all the same, as we see in *Henry the Sixth.* Later in life the poet will rise into this conception of the World-Spirit as the supreme ruling power of History; such we behold it in the Roman plays, but hardly in the English ones, where the national Spirit is the highest. Success has again brought guilt, and guilt will call down retribution not only upon the individual, but also upon the nation.

HENRY V IN THE TWENTIETH CENTURY
℘

The characterization of Henry V as an ideal king, which dominated nineteenth-century criticism, continued to be put forward at the beginning of the twentieth century by such critics as Sir Sidney Lee, who argued in the introduction to his 1908 edition that "*Henry V* is the author's confession of faith in what he deems to be the best and most distinctive type of English character." Lee detects a note of criticism, not of Henry's ethical character but of the robust manner in which the English conduct themselves, or their "rough coming on" and their love of "great meals of beef," as the French Constable puts it. Those phrases were meant to be laughed at in Lee's view, and Shakespeare included them to satirize English manners and show those in his audience that they were not above improvement. Such criticism aside, Lee sees the play as a "heroic biography" of Henry. Other perspectives, which found early expression in the criticism of A. C. Bradley and William Butler Yeats, began to emerge, complicating the idea of Henry V. By the end of the century, an ambiguous view of him came to dominate the critical response.

Bradley, who brought more resonance to Henry V's rejection of Falstaff than any critic before him, acknowledges the value of positive readings of the king, portraying him as modest, genuinely religious, and charming. He "is treated as a national hero" and "is deservedly a favorite" with audiences. Bradley, however, denies that Henry represents Shakespeare's ideal of manhood. In Bradley's eyes, Henry's strengths are inescapably entwined with his faults, something that is clearly seen in his treatment of Falstaff. The episode in which the king turns away the knight is, for Bradley, simultaneously a fine and a nasty moment in Henry's progress toward Agincourt.

We should expect the rejection, Bradley argues, and see it as the inevitable conclusion to an association that we "wish" from the start Henry will end once he assumes the throne. The problem is its public nature and Henry's manner, which pains us and leaves us feeling resentful. Henry could have found another way, one that Bradley imagines would separate him from the friend his responsibility as king prevents him from keeping. Shakespeare, however, chooses to make the rejection public, illustrating that Henry shares qualities with his brother John of

Lancaster and his father: cold heartedness and a willingness to subordinate all considerations to policy. Those same qualities also impact the French campaign.

Bradley's influence was almost immediate and continued to be felt for some time. The year after "The Rejection of Falstaff" was published, Yeats, who favored the character of Richard II over Henry V, seems to have picked up some hints from it. Finding Henry's story to be one of "tragic irony," Yeats sees the king as a "vessel of clay" who "has the gross vices, the coarse nerves, of one who is to rule among violent people." Henry is, Yeats continues, "so little 'too friendly' to his friends that he bundles them out of doors when their time is over." Similarly, Benedetto Croce sounds a Bradleian note when he observes, "Aesthetically speaking, Falstaff did not deserve such treatment, or at least Henry V, who inflicts it upon him, should not be given the credit of possessing an admirable moral character, which he does not possess, for it cannot be maintained that he is a great man, lofty in heart and mind, when he shows us that he has failed to understand Falstaff."

Despite the critiques that marked some of the commentary of the twentieth century, positive interpretations of Henry's character and his play continued to hold force with many critics as well as with those putting the play on the stage or on film, a technological advance that enhanced the presentation of performances of Shakespeare's work and led to the development of a critical industry in its own right. As in the eighteenth century, heroic productions of the play were staged at times of war to stir the patriotism of British audiences. The most famous of the war productions is Laurence Olivier's 1944 film, which leaves out scenes that put Henry in a bad light and, to avoid any suggestion that Great Britain was less than unified, the lines concerning the potential threat of the Scottish. Productions not made during wars have also often put a positive spin on Henry. Kenneth Branagh's celebrated 1989 film, although it uses scenes that undermine an entirely positive presentation of Henry and presents war in a manner that led some critics to regard it as an antiwar film, nonetheless portrays the king as a man who heroically faces his duty in difficult circumstances. Not all twentieth century directors maintained the tradition of presenting a heroic king. Michael Bogdanov, for example, famously produced a version in 1986 in which Henry is portrayed as a coldhearted villain as commentary on the British war in the Falkland Islands earlier in the decade as well as on Margaret Thatcher's Britain.

Among the most important critics to argue that Shakespeare intended Henry to be taken as a hero were E.M.W. Tillyard in *Shakespeare's History Plays* (1944) and John Dover Wilson in his introduction to the 1947 Cambridge edition of the play. Tillyard and Wilson, despite agreement over Henry's character, have different views of the play. Tillyard finds it to be a mechanical conclusion, full of artistic failures, to *Henry IV, Part 1* and *2*, regarding it as a play Shakespeare felt compelled to write in order "to show Henry in his traditional part of perfect king." Wilson defends the artistic merit of the work and tries to reestablish Henry as a heroic figure, defending him as a man of action against those who condemn him. Wilson, for example, characterizes the brutality of Henry's speech to the governor of Harfleur as a pose used to put an end to a battle being fought by an army of sick soldiers, whereas his true character is on display when he tells Exeter, whom he temporarily leaves in charge, to "Use mercy to them all."

Tillyard's position proved more influential, if only because of the way it places the play in a larger interpretation of Elizabethan culture. Tillyard is only tangentially interested in Henry's status as an ideal king, assuming it rather than proving it; his real concern is to demonstrate how the history plays reflect "the thought-idiom of [Shakespeare's] age," or "the Elizabethan World Picture," which posited a divinely ordained hierarchical political order with the monarch on top and the commoners at the bottom. If that order was disrupted, divine justice would follow, as it did after Henry IV usurped Richard II's throne, in the form of rebellions during Henry IV's reign; the civil war in the fifteenth century known as the War of the Roses, which Shakespeare dealt with in his *Henry VI* plays; and the villainous reign of Richard III, about which Shakespeare also wrote a play. Tillyard's disappointment with *Henry V* stems from its not fitting neatly in with the providential view of history that assumed God would curse a commonwealth in which his order had been subverted, for the history of Henry's reign only allows Shakespeare to "keep alive the theme of civil war . . . more faintly than in any other of his History Plays."

In the second half of the century, critics began to look for ways to rise above the debate about whether Henry should be viewed as a positive or negative character. Marilyn L. Williamson, for example, complains, "We have been so busy deciding whether Shakespeare's portrait of Henry is satiric or heroic that we have not bothered to look closely at some of the complexity Shakespeare has put into the figure of Henry." She proceeds to demonstrate the psychological depth that can be found in Shakespeare's portrayal of the king in the episode in which the disguised Henry confronts Williams. A more interesting approach to the problem is offered in Norman Rabkin's "Rabbits, Ducks, and *Henry V*." Rabkin argues that the critics' penchant for depicting the play either as patriotic or ironic is an effect of the complexity of *Henry V* and its relationship to the two previous plays in the tetralogy. When the play is positioned as a sequel to *Henry IV, Part 1*, Henry is a positive figure, but when it is positioned as a sequel to *Henry IV, Part 2*, Henry is a negative figure. "Shakespeare," he writes, "creates a work whose ultimate power is precisely the fact that it points in two opposite directions, virtually daring us to choose one of the two opposed interpretations it requires."

In the last quarter of the twentieth century, historical critics began to reevaluate the methodology of Tillyard and his contemporaries. Those earlier historicists had treated literary works as reflections of the dominant thought of the period in which they were written, while such critics as Stephen Greenblatt, Jonathan Dollimore and Alan Sinfieland sought to demonstrate how literary texts not only reflect but also engage, either unconsciously or consciously, the orthodoxies of their age. The ambiguity of Rabkin's Henry V came to dominate, though that ambiguity is often reconfigured in terms of whether or not the play upholds or undermines the orthodoxies of the age. Greenblatt, in his influential essay "Invisible Bullets," depicts a play that tests and records a subversive hypothesis, Machiavelli's. Dollimore and Sinfield, in their "History and Ideology: The Instance of *Henry V*," find a play that reveals the ideological processes that work to legitimate the social order, while simultaneously revealing the anxieties involved in keeping that order unified.

Perspectives other than those of the newer historical critics were articulated during the last decades of the twentieth century. Harold Bloom, in particular, has served as a contrary voice to historically focused critics, insisting on the importance of a literary work's aesthetic value. In the essays included in this section, Paul M. Cubeta and Grace Tiffany ignore the ideological debates of the 1980s and 1990s. Cubeta assumes a Goddardian view of Henry V, but his interest is in Falstaff's deathbed scene, not Henry's character. The characterization of Henry and its relationship to Elizabethan political orthodoxy is not even a secondary concern. Tiffany leaves ideological concerns of the play in the background of her argument, though her characterization of Hal/Henry V as a Dionysian figure calls into question the idea that Shakespeare's king represents a straightforward figure of orthodoxy. Bloom's, Cubeta's, and Tiffany's voices can then be seen as alternatives that refuse to be contained by the thought that has dominated their contemporaries.

1902—A. C. Bradley. From "The Rejection of Falstaff"

A. C. Bradley (1851–1935) is among the most important Shakespeare critics of the twentieth century, bringing into prominence the issue of Falstaff's rejection in the essay from which the following excerpt has been taken. His influence continues to exert itself on critics today, evident in the fact that his *Shakespearean Tragedy* (1904) and *Oxford Lectures on Poetry* (1909) remain in print.

Of the two persons principally concerned in the rejection of Falstaff, Henry, both as Prince and as King, has received, on the whole, full justice from readers and critics. Falstaff, on the other hand, has been in one respect the most unfortunate of Shakespeare's famous characters. All of them, in passing from the mind of their creator into other minds, suffer change; they tend to lose their harmony through the disproportionate attention bestowed on some one feature, or to lose their uniqueness by being conventionalized into types already familiar. But Falstaff was degraded by Shakespeare himself. The original character is to be found alive in the two parts of *Henry IV.*, dead in *Henry V.*, and nowhere else. But not very long after these plays were composed, Shakespeare wrote, and he afterwards revised, the piece called *The Merry Wives of Windsor*. Perhaps his company wanted a new play on a sudden, or, perhaps, as one would rather believe, the tradition may be true that Queen Elizabeth, delighted with the Falstaff scenes of *Henry IV.*, expressed a wish to see the hero of them again, and to see him in love. Now it was no more possible for Shakespeare to show his own Falstaff in love than to turn twice two into five. But he could write in haste—the tradition says, in a fortnight—a comedy or farce differing from all his other plays in this, that its scene is laid in English middle-class life, and that it is prosaic almost to the end. And among the characters he could introduce a disreputable fat old knight with attendants, and could call them Falstaff, Bardolph, Pistol, and Nym.

And he could represent this knight assailing, for commercial purposes, the virtue of two matrons, and in the event baffled, duped, treated like dirty linen, beaten, burnt, pricked, mocked, insulted, and, worst of all, repentant and didactic. It is horrible. It is almost enough to convince one that Shakespeare himself could sanction the parody of Ophelia in the *Two Noble Kinsmen*. But it no more touches the real Falstaff than Ophelia is degraded by that parody. To imagine the real Falstaff befooled like the Falstaff of the *Merry Wives* is like imagining Iago the gull of Roderigo, or Becky Sharp the dupe of Amelia Osborne. Before he had been served the least of these tricks he would have had his brains taken out and buttered, and have given them to a dog for a New Year's gift. I quote the words of the impostor, for after all Shakespeare made him and gave to him a few sentences worthy of Falstaff himself. But they are only a few—one side of a sheet of note-paper would contain them. And yet critics have solemnly debated at what period in his life Sir John endured the gibes of Master Ford, and whether we should put this comedy between the two parts of *Henry IV.*, or between the Second Part and *Henry V.* And the Falstaff of the general reader, it is to be feared, is an impossible conglomerate of two distinct characters, while the Falstaff of the mere playgoer is certainly much more like the impostor than the true man.

The separation of these two has long ago been effected by criticism, and is insisted on in almost all competent estimates of the character of Falstaff. I do not propose to attempt a full account either of his character or of that of Prince Henry, but shall connect the remarks I have to make on them with a question which does not appear to have been satisfactorily discussed—the question of the rejection of Falstaff by the Prince on his accession to the throne. What do we feel, and what are we meant to feel, as we witness this rejection? And what does our feeling imply as to the characters of Falstaff and the new King?

Sir John, you remember, is in Gloucestershire, engaged in borrowing £1,000 from Justice Shallow; and here Pistol, riding helter-skelter from

London, brings him the great news that the old King is as dead as nail in door, and Harry the Fifth is the man. Sir John, in wild excitement, taking any man's horses, rushes to London and carries Shallow with him, for he longs to reward all his friends. We find him standing with his companions just outside Westminster Abbey in the crowd that is waiting for the King to come out after his coronation. He himself is stained with travel and has had no time to spend any of the £1,000 in buying new liveries for his men. But what of that? His haste only shows his earnestness in affection, his devotion, how he thinks of nothing else but to see Henry, puts all affairs else in oblivion, as if there were nothing else to be done but to see him. There is a shout within the Abbey like the roaring of the sea, and a clangor of trumpets, and the doors open and the procession streams out.

> *Fal.* God save thy grace, King Hal! my royal Hal!
> *Pist.* The heavens thee guard and keep, most royal imp of fame!
> *Fal.* God save thee, my sweet boy!
> *King.* My Lord Chief Justice, speak to that vain man.
> *Ch. Just.* Have you your wits? Know you what 'tis you speak?
> *Fal.* My King! my Jove! I speak to thee, my heart!
> *King.* I know thee not, old man: fall to thy prayers;
> How ill white hairs become a fool and jester!
> I have long dream'd of such a kind of man,
> So surfeit-swell'd, so old and so profane;
> But being awaked I do despise my dream.
> Make less thy body hence, and more thy grace;
> Leave gormandizing; know the grave doth gape
> For thee thrice wider than for other men.
> Reply not to me with a fool-born jest:
> Presume not that I am the thing I was;
> For God doth know, so shall the world perceive,
> That I have turn'd away my former self;
> So will I those that kept me company.
> When thou dost hear I am as I have been,
> Approach me, and thou shalt be as thou wast,
> The tutor and the feeder of my riots:
> Till then, I banish thee, on pain of death,
> As I have done the rest of my misleaders,
> Not to come near our person by ten mile.
> For competence of life I will allow you,
> That lack of means enforce you not to evil:
> And, as we hear you do reform yourselves,
> We will, according to your strength and qualities,

Give you advancement. Be it your charge, my lord,
To see perform'd the tenor of our word.
Set on.

The procession passes on, but Falstaff and his friends remain. He shows no resentment. He comforts himself, or tries to comfort himself—first, with the thought that he has Shallow's £1,000, and then, more seriously, I believe, with another thought. The King, he sees, must look thus to the world; but he will be sent for in private when night comes, and will yet make the fortunes of his friends. But even as he speaks, Prince John and the Chief Justice return, and the Chief Justice says to his officers:

"Go, carry Sir John Falstaff to the Fleet;
Take all his company along with him."

Falstaff breaks out: "My lord, my lord," but he is cut short and hurried away; and after a few words between the Prince and the Chief Justice, the scene closes and with it the drama.

What are our feelings during this scene? They will answer to our feelings about Falstaff. If we have not keenly enjoyed the Falstaff scenes of the two plays, if we regard Sir John chiefly as an old reprobate, not only a sensualist, a liar, and a coward, but a cruel and dangerous ruffian, I suppose we enjoy his discomfiture and consider that the King has behaved magnificently. But if we *have* keenly enjoyed the Falstaff scenes, if we have enjoyed them as Shakespeare surely meant them to be enjoyed, and if, accordingly, Falstaff is not to us solely or even chiefly a reprobate and ruffian, we feel, I think, during the King's speech, a good deal of pain and some resentment, and when, without any further offence on Sir John's part, the Chief Justice returns and sends him to prison we stare in astonishment. These I believe, are, in greater or less degree, the feelings of most of those who enjoy the Falstaff scenes (I am aware that many readers do not). Nor are these feelings diminished when we remember the end of the whole story, as we find it in *Henry V.*, where we learn that Falstaff quickly died, and died, according to the testimony of persons not very sentimental, of a broken heart. Suppose this merely to mean that he sank under the shame of his public disgrace, and it is pitiful enough: but the words of Mrs. Quickly, "The king has killed his heart"; of Nym, "The king hath run bad humors on the knight; that's the even of it"; of Pistol, "Nym, thou hast spoke the right, His heart is fracted and corroborate," surely point to something more than wounded pride; they point to wounded affection, and remind us of Falstaff's own answer to Prince Hal's question, "Sirrah, do I owe you a thousand pound?" "A thousand pound, Hal? a million: thy love is worth a million: thou owest me thy love."

Now why did Shakespeare end his play with a scene which, though undoubtedly striking, leaves an impression so unpleasant? I will venture to put aside without discussion the idea that he meant us throughout the two plays to regard Falstaff with disgust or indignation, so that we naturally feel nothing but pleasure at his fall; for this idea implies that kind of inability to understand Shakespeare with which it is idle to argue. And there is another and a much more ingenious suggestion which must equally be rejected as impossible. According to it, Falstaff, having listened to the King's speech, did not seriously hope to be sent for by him in private; he fully realized the situation at once, and was only making game of Shallow; and in his immediate turn upon Shallow when the King goes out, "Master Shallow, I owe you a thousand pound," we are meant to see his humorous superiority to any rebuff, so that we end the play with the delightful feeling that Henry has done the right thing, and yet Falstaff, in his outward overthrow, has still proved himself inwardly invincible. This suggestion comes from a critic who understands Falstaff, and in the suggestion itself shows that he understands him. But it provides no solution, because it wholly ignores, and could not account for, that which follows the short conversation with Shallow. Falstaff's dismissal to the Fleet, and his subsequent death, prove beyond doubt that his rejection was meant by Shakespeare to be taken as a catastrophe which not even his humor could enable him to surmount. Moreover, these interpretations, even if otherwise admissible, would still leave our problem only partly solved. For what troubles us is not only the disappointment of Falstaff, it is the conduct of Henry. It was inevitable that on his accession he should separate himself from Sir John, and we wish nothing else. It is satisfactory that Sir John should have a competence and the hope of promotion in the highly improbable case of his reforming himself. And if Henry could not trust himself within ten miles of so fascinating a companion, by all means let him be banished that distance: we do not complain. These arrangements would not have prevented a satisfactory ending: the King could have communicated his decision, and Falstaff could have accepted it, in a private interview rich in humor and merely touched with pathos. But Shakespeare has so contrived matters that Henry could not send a private warning to Falstaff even if he wished to, and in their public meeting Falstaff is made to behave in so outrageous and infatuated a manner that great sternness on the King's part was unavoidable. And the curious thing is that Shakespeare did not stop here. If this had been all we should have felt pain for Falstaff, but not, perhaps, resentment against Henry. But two things we do resent. Why, when this painful incident seems to be over, should the Chief Justice return and send Falstaff to prison? Can this possibly be meant for an act of private vengeance on the part of the Chief Justice, unknown to the King? No, for in that case Shakespeare would have shown at once that the King disapproved and cancelled it. It must have been the King's own act. This is one thing we resent; the other is the King's sermon. He had a right to turn away his former self and his old companions with it, but he had no right to talk all of a sudden like a clergyman; and surely it was both ungenerous and insincere to speak of them as his "misleaders," as though in the days of Eastcheap and Gadshill he had been a weak and silly lad. We have seen his former self, and we know that it was nothing of the kind. He had shown himself, for all his follies, a very strong and independent young man, deliberately amusing himself among men over whom he had just as much ascendancy as he chose to exert. Nay, he amused himself not only among them, but at their expense. In his first soliloquy—the place we ought always to look to for the key to a Shakespearian character—he declares that he associates with them in order that, when at some future time he shows his true character, he may be the more wondered at for his previous aberrations. You may think he deceives himself here; you may believe that he frequented Sir John's company out of delight in it and not merely with this cold-blooded design; but at any rate he *thought* the design was his one motive. And, that being so, two results follow. He ought in honor long ago to have given Sir John clearly to understand that they must say goodbye on the day of his accession. And, having neglected to do this, he ought not to have lectured him as his misleader. It was not only ungenerous, it was dishonest. It looks disagreeably like an attempt to buy the praise of the respectable at the cost of honor and truth. And it succeeded. Henry *always* succeeded.

You will see what I am suggesting for the moment as a solution of our problem. I am suggesting that our fault lies not in our resentment at Henry's conduct, but in our surprise at it; that if we had read his character truly in the light that Shakespeare gave us, we should have been prepared for a display both of hardness and of policy at this point in his career. And although this suggestion does not suffice to solve the problem before us, I am convinced that in itself it is true. Nor is it rendered at all improbable by the fact that Shakespeare has made Henry, on the whole, a fine and very attractive character, and that here he makes no one express any disapprobation of the treatment of Falstaff; for in similar cases Shakespeare is constantly misunderstood. His readers expect him to mark in some distinct way his approval or disapproval of that which he represents; and hence where *they* disapprove and *he* says nothing, they fancy that he does *not* disapprove, and they blame his indifference, like Dr. Johnson, or at the least are puzzled. But the truth is that he shows the fact and leaves the judgment to them. And again, when he makes us like a character we expect the character to have no faults that are not expressly pointed out, and when other faults appear we either ignore them or try to explain them away.

This is one of our methods of conventionalizing Shakespeare. We want the world's population to be neatly divided into sheep and goats, and we want an angel by us to say, "Look, that is a goat and this is a sheep," and we try to turn Shakespeare into this angel. His impartiality makes us uncomfortable: we cannot bear to see him, like the sun, lighting up everything and judging nothing. And this is perhaps especially the case in his historical plays, where we are always trying to turn him into a partisan. He shows us that Richard II. was unworthy to be king, and we at once conclude that he thought Bolingbroke's usurpation justified, whereas he shows merely, what under the conditions was bound to exist, an inextricable tangle of right and unright. Or, Bolingbroke being evidently wronged, we suppose Bolingbroke's statements to be true, and are quite surprised when Bolingbroke, after attaining his end through them, mentions casually on his death-bed that they were lies. Shakespeare makes us admire Hotspur heartily, and so when we see Hotspur discussing with others how large his particular slice of his mother country is to be, we either fail to recognize the monstrosity of the proceeding, or, recognizing it, we complain that Shakespeare is inconsistent. Prince John breaks the last remains of rebellion by practising a detestable fraud on the rebels. We are against the rebels, and have heard high praise of Prince John, but we cannot help seeing that this fraud is detestable, so we say indignantly to Shakespeare: "Why, you told us he was a sheep"; whereas, in fact, if we had used our eyes we should have known beforehand that he was the brave, determined, loyal, cold-blooded, pitiless, unscrupulous son of a usurper whose throne is in danger.

To come, then, to Henry. Both as prince and king he is deservedly a favorite, and particularly so with English readers, being, as he is, perhaps, the most distinctively English of all Shakespeare's men. In *Henry V.* he is treated as a national hero. In this play he has lost much of the wit which in him seems to have depended on contact with Falstaff, but he has also laid aside the most serious faults of his youth. He inspires in a high degree fear, enthusiasm, and affection; thanks to his beautiful modesty he has the charm which is lacking to another mighty warrior, Coriolanus; his youthful escapades have given him an understanding of simple folk, and sympathy with them; he is the author of the saying, "There is some soul of goodness in things evil"; and he is much more obviously religious than most of Shakespeare's heroes. Having these and other fine qualities, and being without certain dangerous tendencies which mark the tragic heroes, he is, perhaps, the most *efficient* character drawn by Shakespeare, unless Ulysses, in *Troilus and Cressida,* is his equal. And so he has been described as Shakespeare's ideal man of action; nay, it has even been declared that here for once Shakespeare plainly disclosed his own ethical creed and showed us his ideal, not simply of a man of action, but of a man.

But Henry is neither of these. The poet who drew Hamlet and Othello can never have thought that even the ideal man of action would lack that light upon the brow which at once transfigures them and marks their doom. It is as easy to believe that, because the lunatic, the lover, and the poet are not far apart, Shakespeare would have chosen never to have loved and sung. Even poor Timon, the most inefficient of the tragic heroes, has something in him that Henry never shows. Nor is it merely that his nature is limited: if we follow

Shakespeare and look closely at Henry, we shall discover with the many fine traits a few less pleasing. Henry IV. describes him as the noble image of his own youth; and, for all his superiority to his father, he is still his father's son, the son of that "vile politician, Bolingbroke," as Hotspur calls him. Henry's religion, for example, is genuine, it is rooted in his modesty; but it is also superstitious—an attempt to buy off supernatural vengeance for Richard's blood, and it is also in part political, like his father's projected crusade. Just as he went to war chiefly because, as his father told him, it was the way to keep factious nobles quiet and unite the nation, so when he adjures the Archbishop to satisfy him as to his right to the French throne, he knows quite well that the Archbishop *wants* the war because it will defer and perhaps prevent what he considers the spoliation of the Church. This same strain of policy is what Shakespeare marks in the first soliloquy in *Henry IV.*, where the prince describes his riotous life as a mere scheme to win him glory later. It implies that readiness to use other people as means to his own ends, which is a conspicuous feature in his father; and it reminds us of his father's plan of keeping himself out of the people's sight while Richard was making himself cheap by his incessant public appearances. And if I am not mistaken there is a further likeness. Henry is kindly and pleasant to every one as Prince, to every one deserving as King, and that not out of policy as with his father: but there is no sign in him of a strong affection for any one, such an affection as we recognize at a glance in Hamlet and Horatio, Brutus and Cassius, and many more. We do not find this in *Henry V.*, not even in the noble address to Lord Scroop, and in *Henry IV.* we find, I think, a liking for Falstaff and Poins, but no more: there is no more, for instance, in his soliloquy over the supposed corpse of his fat friend, and he never speaks of Falstaff to Poins with any affection. The truth is, that the members of the family of Henry IV. have love for one another, but they cannot spare love for any one outside their family, which stands firmly united, defending its royal position against attack and instinctively isolating itself from outside influence.

Thus I would suggest that Henry's conduct in his rejection of Falstaff is in perfect keeping with his character on its unpleasant side as well as on its finer; and that, so far as Henry is concerned, we ought not to feel surprise at it. And on this view we may even explain the strange Incident of the Chief Justice being sent back to order Falstaff to prison (for there is no sign of any such uncertainty in the text as might suggest an interpolation by the players). Remembering his father's words about Henry, "Being incensed, he's flint," and remembering in *Henry V.* his ruthlessness about killing the prisoners when he is incensed, we may imagine that, after he had left Falstaff and was no longer influenced by the face of his old companion, he gave way to anger at the indecent familiarity which had provoked a compromising scene on the most ceremonial of occasions and in the presence alike of court and crowd, and that he sent the Chief Justice back to take vengeance. And this is consistent with the fact that in the next play we find Falstaff shortly afterwards not only freed from prison, but unmolested in his old haunt in Eastcheap, well within ten miles of Henry's person. His anger had soon passed, and he knew that the requisite effect had been produced alike on Falstaff and on the world.

But all this, however true, will not solve our problem. It seems, on the contrary, to increase its difficulty. For the natural conclusion is that Shakespeare *intended* us to feel resentment against Henry. And yet that cannot be, for it implies that he meant the play to end disagreeably; and no one who understands Shakespeare at all will consider that supposition for a moment credible. No, he must have meant the play to end pleasantly, although he made Henry act consistently. And hence it follows that he must have intended our sympathy with Falstaff to be so far weakened when the rejection-scene arrives that his discomfiture should be satisfactory to us; that we should enjoy this sudden reverse of enormous hopes (a thing always ludicrous if sympathy is absent), that we should approve the moral judgment that falls on him, and so we should pass lightly over that disclosure of unpleasant traits in the King's character which Shakespeare was too true an artist to suppress. Thus our pain and resentment, if we feel them, are wrong, in the sense that they do not answer to the dramatist's intention. But it does not follow that they are wrong in a further sense. They may be right because the dramatist has missed what he aimed at. And this, though the dramatist was Shakespeare, is what I would suggest. In the Falstaff scenes he overshot his mark. He created so extraordinary a being, and fixed him so firmly on his intellectual throne, that when he sought to dethrone him he could not. The moment comes when we are to look at Falstaff in a serious light and the comic hero is to figure as a baffled schemer; but we cannot make the required change, either in our attitude or in our sympathies.

We wish Henry a glorious reign and much joy of his crew of hypocritical politicians, lay and clerical; but our hearts go with Falstaff to the Fleet, or, if necessary, to Arthur's bosom or wheresoever he is.

. . .

As I said, in the creation of Falstaff he overreached himself. He was caught up on the wind of his own genius, and carried so far that he could not descend to earth at the intended spot. It is not a misfortune that happens to many authors, nor is it one we can regret, for it costs us but a trifling inconvenience in one scene, while we owe to it perhaps the greatest comic character in literature. For it is in this character and not in the judgment he brings upon Falstaff's head, that Shakespeare asserts his supremacy. To show that Falstaff's freedom of soul was in part illusory, and that the realities of life refused to be conjured away by his humor—this was what we might expect from Shakespeare's unfailing sanity but it was surely no remarkable achievement beyond the power of lesser men. The achievement was Falstaff himself and the conception of that freedom of soul, a freedom illusory only in part, and attainable only by a mind which had received from Shakespeare's own that inexplicable touch of infinity which he bestowed on Hamlet and Macbeth and Cleopatra, but denied to Henry the Fifth.

1903—William Butler Yeats. "At Stratford-on-Avon," from *Ideas of Good and Evil*

W. B. Yeats (1865–1939), who was awarded the Nobel Prize for literature in 1923, was an Irish poet and dramatist. Throughout his career, he published numerous critical essays, among them the following essay on Shakespeare, a slightly longer version of which first appeared in *The Speaker: A Liberal Review* on May 11 and 18, 1901. The essay has influenced the way critics such as Harold Bloom see *Henry V*.

I

I have been hearing Shakespeare, as the traveller in *News from Nowhere* might have heard him, had he not been hurried back into our noisy time. One passes through quiet streets, where gabled and red-tiled houses remember the Middle Age, to a theatre that has been made not to make money, but for the pleasure of making it, like the market houses that set the traveller chuckling; nor does one find it among hurrying cabs and ringing pavements, but in a green garden by a river side. Inside I have to be content for a while with a chair, for I am unexpected, and there is not an empty seat but this; and yet there is no one who has come merely because one must go somewhere after dinner. All day, too, one does not hear or see an incongruous or noisy thing, but spends the hours reading the plays, and the wise and foolish things men have said of them, in the library of the theatre, with its oak-panelled walls and leaded windows of tinted glass; or one rows by reedy banks and by old farmhouses, and by old churches among great trees. It is certainly one's fault if one opens a newspaper, for Mr. Benson gives one a new play every night, and one need talk of nothing but the play in the inn-parlour, under the oak beams blackened by time and showing the mark of the adze that shaped them. I have seen this week *King John, Richard II.*, the second part of *Henry IV., Henry V.*, the second part of *Henry VI.*, and *Richard III.* played in their right order, with all the links that bind play to play unbroken; and partly because of a spirit in the place, and partly because of the way play supports play, the theatre has moved me as it has never done before. That strange procession of kings and queens, of warring nobles, of insurgent crowds, of courtiers, and of people of the gutter has been to me almost too visible, too audible, too full of an unearthly energy. I have felt as I have sometimes felt on grey days on the Galway shore, when a faint mist has hung over the grey sea and the grey stones, as if the world might suddenly vanish and leave nothing behind, not even a little dust under one's feet. The people my mind's eye has seen have too much of the extravagance of dreams, like all the inventions of art before our crowded life had brought moderation and compromise, to seem more than a dream, and yet all else has grown dim before them.

In London the first man one meets puts any high dream out of one's head, for he will talk to one of something at once vapid and exciting, some one of those many subjects of thought that build up our social unity. But here he gives back one's dream like a mirror. If we do not talk of the plays, we talk of the theatre, and how more people may be got to come, and our isolation from common things makes the future become grandiose and important. One man tells how the theatre and the library were at their foundation but part of a scheme the future is to fulfil. To them will be added a school where speech, and gesture, and fencing, and all else that an actor needs will be taught, and the council, which will have enlarged its Festivals to some six weeks, will engage all the chief players of Shakespeare, and perhaps of other great dramatists in this and other countries. These chief players will need to bring but few of their supporters, for the school will be able to fill all the lesser parts with players who are slowly recovering the lost tradition of musical speech. Another man is certain that the Festival, even without the school, which would require a new endowment, will grow in importance year by year, and that it may become with favouring chance the supreme dramatic event of the world; and when I suggest that it may help to break the evil prestige of London he becomes enthusiastic.

Surely a bitter hatred of London is becoming a mark of those that love the arts, and all that have this hatred should help anything that looks like a beginning of a centre of art elsewhere. The easiness of travel, which is always growing, began by emptying the country, but it may end by filling it; for adventures like this of Stratford-on-Avon show that people are ready to journey from all parts of England and Scotland and Ireland, and even from America, to live with their favourite art as shut away from the world as though they were 'in retreat,' as Catholics say. Nobody but an impressionist painter, who hides it in light and mist, even pretends to love a street for its own sake; and could we meet our friends and hear music and poetry in the country, none of us that are not captive would ever leave the thrushes. In London, we hear something that we like some twice or thrice in a winter, and among people who are thinking the while of a music-hall singer or of a member of parliament, but there we would hear it and see it among people who liked it well enough to have travelled some few hours to find it; and because those who care for the arts have few near friendships among those that do not, we would hear and see it among near friends. We would escape, too, from those artificial tastes and interests we cultivate, that we may have something to talk about among people we meet for a few minutes and not again, and the arts would grow serious as the Ten Commandments.

II

I do not think there is anything I disliked in Stratford, beside certain new houses, but the shape of the theatre; and as a larger theatre must be built sooner or later, that would be no great matter if one could put a wiser shape into somebody's head. I cannot think there is any excuse for a half-round theatre, where land is not expensive, or no very great audience to be seated within earshot of the stage; or that it was adopted for a better reason than because it has come down to us, though from a time when the art of the stage was a different art. The Elizabethan theatre was a half-round, because the players were content to speak their lines on a platform, as if they were speakers at a public meeting, and we go on building in the same shape, although our art of the stage is the art of making a succession of pictures. Were our theatres of the shape of a half-closed fan, like Wagner's theatre, where the audience sit on seats that rise towards the broad end while the play is played at the narrow end, their pictures could be composed for eyes at a small number points of of view, instead of for eyes at many points of view, above and below and at all sides, and what is no better than a trade might become an art. With eyes watching from the sides of a half-round, on the floor and in the boxes and galleries, would go the solid-built houses and the flat trees that shake with every breath of air; and we could make our pictures with robes that contrasted with great masses of colour in the back cloth and such severe or decorative forms of hills and trees and houses as would not overwhelm, as our naturalistic scenery does, the idealistic art of the poet, and all at a little price. Naturalistic scene-painting is not an art, but a trade, because it is, at best, an attempt to copy the more obvious effects of nature by the methods of the ordinary landscape-painter, and by his methods made coarse and summary. It is but flashy landscape-painting and lowers the taste it appeals to, for the taste it appeals to has been formed by a more delicate art. Decorative scene-painting would be, on the other hand, as inseparable from the movements as from the robes of the players and from the falling of the light; and being in itself a grave and quiet thing it would mingle with the tones of the voices and with the sentiment of the play, without overwhelming them under an alien interest. It would be a new and legitimate art appealing to a taste formed by itself and copying nothing but itself. Mr. Gordon Craig used scenery of this kind at the Purcell Society performance the other day, and despite some marring of his effects by the half-round shape of the theatre, it was the first beautiful scenery our stage has seen. He created an ideal country where everything was possible, even speaking in verse, or speaking in music, or the expression of the whole of life in a dance, and I would like to see Stratford-on-Avon decorate its Shakespeare with like scenery. As we cannot, it seems, go back to the platform and the curtain, and the argument for doing so is not without weight, we can only get rid of the sense of unreality, which most of us feel when we listen to the conventional speech of Shakespeare, by making scenery as conventional. Time after time his people use at some moment of deep emotion an elaborate or deliberate metaphor, or do some improbable thing which breaks an emotion of reality we have imposed upon him by an art that is not his, nor in the spirit of his. It also is an essential part of his method to give slight or obscure motives of many actions that our attention may dwell on what is of chief importance, and we set these cloudy actions among solid-looking houses, and what we hope are solid-looking trees, and illusion comes to an end, slain by our desire to increase it. In his art, as in all the older art of the world, there was much make-believe, and our scenery, too, should remember the time when, as my nurse used to tell me, herons built their nests in old men's beards! Mr. Benson did not venture to play the scene in *Richard III.* where the ghosts walk, as Shakespeare wrote it, but had his scenery been as simple as Mr. Gordon Craig's purple back cloth that made Dido and Aeneas seem wandering on the edge of eternity, he would have found nothing absurd in pitching the tents of Richard and Richmond side by side. Goethe has said, 'Art is art, because it is not nature!' It brings us near to the archetypal ideas themselves, and away from nature, which is but their looking-glass.

III

In *La Peau de Chagrin* Balzac spends many pages in describing a coquette, who seems the image of heartlessness, and then invents an improbable incident that her chief victim may discover how beautifully she can sing. Nobody had ever heard her sing, and yet in her singing, and in her chatter with her maid, Balzac tells us, was her true self. He would have us understand that behind the momentary self, which acts and lives in the world, and is subject to the judgment of the world, there is that which cannot be called before any mortal Judgment seat, even though a great poet, or novelist, or philosopher be sitting upon it. Great literature has always been written in a like spirit, and is, indeed, the Forgiveness of Sin, and when we find it becoming the Accusation of Sin, as in George Eliot, who plucks her Tito in pieces with as much assurance as if he had been clockwork, literature has begun to change into something else. George Eliot had a fierceness one hardly finds but in a woman turned argumentative, but the habit of mind her fierceness gave its life to was characteristic of her century, and is the habit of mind of the Shakespearian critics. They and she grew up in a century of utilitarianism, when nothing about a man seemed important except his utility to the State, and nothing so useful to the State as the actions whose effect can be weighed by the reason. The deeds of Coriolanus, Hamlet, Timon, Richard II. had no obvious use, were, indeed, no more than the expression of their personalities, and so it was thought Shakespeare was accusing them, and telling us to be careful lest we deserve the like accusations. It did not occur to the critics that you cannot know a man from his actions, because you cannot watch him in every kind of circumstance, and that men are made useless to the State as often by abundance as by emptiness, and that a man's business may at times be revelation, and not reformation. Fortinbras was, it is likely enough, a better King than Hamlet would have been, Aufidius was a more reasonable man than Coriolanus, Henry V. was a better man-at-arms than Richard II., but after all, were not those others who changed nothing for the better and many things for the worse greater in the Divine Hierarchies? Blake has said that 'the roaring of lions, the howling of wolves, the raging of the stormy sea, and the destructive sword are portions of Eternity, too great for the eye of man,' but Blake belonged by right to the ages of Faith, and thought the State of less moment than the Divine Hierarchies. Because reason can only discover completely the use of those obvious actions which everybody admires, and because every character was to be judged by efficiency in action, Shakespearian criticism became a vulgar worshipper of Success. I have turned over many books in the library at Stratford-on-Avon, and I have found in nearly all an antithesis, which grew in clearness and violence as the century grew older, between two types, whose representatives were Richard II., 'sentimental,' 'weak,' 'selfish,' 'insincere,' and Henry V., 'Shakespeare's only hero.' These books took the same delight in abasing Richard II. that school-boys do in persecuting some boy of fine temperament, who has weak muscles and a distaste for school games. And they had the admiration for Henry V. that school-boys have for the sailor or soldier hero of a romance in some boys' paper. I cannot claim any minute knowledge of these books, but I think that these emotions began among the German critics, who perhaps saw something French and Latin in Richard II., and I know that Professor Dowden, whose book I once read carefully, first made these emotions eloquent and plausible. He lived in Ireland, where everything has failed, and he meditated frequently upon the perfection of character which had, he thought, made England successful, for, as we say, 'cows beyond the water have long horns.' He forgot that England, as Gordon has said, was made by her adventurers, by her people of wildness and imagination and eccentricity; and thought that Henry V., who only seemed to be these things because he had some commonplace vices, was not only the typical Anglo-Saxon, but the model Shakespeare held up before England; and he even thought it worthwhile pointing out that Shakespeare himself was making a large fortune while he was writing about Henry's victories. In Professor Dowden's successors this apotheosis went further; and it reached its height at a moment of imperialistic enthusiasm, of ever-deepening conviction that the commonplace shall inherit the earth, when somebody of reputation, whose name I cannot remember, wrote that Shakespeare admired this one character alone out of all his characters. The Accusation of Sin produced its necessary fruit, hatred of all that was abundant, extravagant, exuberant, of all that sets a sail for shipwreck, and flattery of the commonplace emotions and conventional ideals of the mob, the chief Paymaster of accusation.

IV

I cannot believe that Shakespeare looked on his Richard II. with any but sympathetic eyes, understanding indeed how ill-fitted he was to be King, at a certain moment of history, but understanding that he was lovable and full of capricious fancy, 'a wild creature' as Pater has called him. The man on whom Shakespeare modelled him had been full of French elegancies, as he knew from Hollingshead, and had given life a new luxury, a new splendour, and been 'too friendly' to his friends, 'too favourable' to his enemies. And certainly Shakespeare had these things in his head when he made his King fail, a little because he lacked some qualities that were doubtless common among his scullions, but more because he had certain qualities that are uncommon in all ages. To suppose that Shakespeare preferred the men who deposed his King is to suppose that Shakespeare judged men with the eyes of a Municipal Councillor weighing the merits of a Town Clerk; and that had he been by when Verlaine cried out from his bed, 'Sir, you have been made by the stroke of a pen, but I have been made by the breath of God,' he would have thought the Hospital Superintendent the better man. He saw indeed, as I think, in Richard II. the defeat that awaits all, whether they be Artist or Saint, who find themselves where men ask of them a rough energy and have nothing to give but some contemplative virtue, whether lyrical phantasy, or sweetness of temper, or dreamy dignity, or love of God, or love of His creatures. He saw that such a man through sheer bewilderment and impatience can become as unjust or as violent as any common man, any Bolingbroke or Prince John, and yet remain 'that sweet lovely rose.' The courtly and saintly ideals of the Middle Ages were fading, and the practical ideals of the modern age had begun to threaten the unuseful dome of the sky; Merry England was fading, and yet it was not so faded that the Poets could not watch the procession of the world with that untroubled sympathy for men as they are, as apart from all they do and seem, which is the substance of tragic irony.

Shakespeare cared little for the State, the source of all our judgments, apart from its shows and splendours, its turmoils and battles, its flamings out of the uncivilized heart. He did indeed think it wrong to overturn a King, and thereby to swamp peace in civil war, and the historical plays from *Henry IV.* to *Richard III.*, that monstrous birth and last sign of the wrath of Heaven, are a fulfilment of the prophecy of the Bishop of Carlisle, who was 'raised up by God' to make it; but he had no nice sense of utilities, no ready balance to measure deeds, like that fine instrument, with all the latest improvements, Gervinus and Professor Dowden handle so skilfully. He meditated as Solomon, not as Bentham meditated, upon blind ambitions, untoward accidents, and capricious passions, and the world was almost as empty in his eyes as it must be in the eyes of God.

> 'Tired with all these, for restful death I cry;—
>   As, to behold desert a beggar born,
> And needy nothing trimm'd in jollity,
>   And purest faith unhappily forsworn,
> And gilded honour shamefully misplaced,
>   And maiden virtue rudely strumpeted,
> And right perfection wrongfully disgrac'd,
>   And strength by limping sway disabled,
> And Art made tongue-tied by authority,
>   And folly, doctor-like, controlling skill,
> And simple truth miscalled simplicity,
>   And captive good attending captain ill:
> Tired with all these, from these would I begone
>   Save that, to die, I leave my love alone.'

V

The Greeks, a certain scholar has told me, considered that myths are the activities of the Daemons, and that the Daemons shape our characters and our lives. I have often had the fancy that there is some one Myth for every man, which, if we but knew it, would make us understand all he did and thought. Shakespeare's Myth, it may be, describes a wise man who was blind from very wisdom, and an empty man who thrust him from his place, and saw all that could be seen from very emptiness. It is in the story of Hamlet, who saw too great issues everywhere to play the trivial game of life, and of Fortinbras, who came from fighting battles about 'a little patch of ground' so poor that one of his Captains would not give 'six ducats' to 'farm it,' and who was yet acclaimed by Hamlet and by all as the only befitting King. And it is in the story of Richard II., that unripened Hamlet, and of Henry V., that ripened Fortinbras. To poise character against character was an element in Shakespeare's art, and scarcely a play is lacking in characters that are the complement of one another, and so, having made the vessel of porcelain Richard II., he had to make the vessel of clay Henry V. He makes him the reverse of all that Richard was. He has the gross vices, the coarse nerves, of one who is to rule among violent people, and he is so little 'too friendly' to his friends that he bundles them out of doors when their time is over. He is as remorseless and undistinguished as some natural force, and the finest thing in his play is the way his old companions fall out of it broken-hearted or on their way to the gallows; and instead of that lyricism which rose out of Richard's mind like the jet of a fountain to fall again where it had risen, instead of that phantasy too enfolded in its own sincerity to make any thought the hour had need of, Shakespeare has given him a resounding rhetoric that moves men, as a leading article does today. His purposes are so intelligible to everybody that everybody talks of him as if he succeeded, although he fails in the end, as all men great and little fail in Shakespeare, and yet his conquests abroad are made nothing by a woman turned warrior, and that boy he and Katherine were to 'compound,' 'half French, half English,' 'that' was to 'go to Constantinople and take the Turk by the beard,' turns out a Saint, and loses all his father had built up at home and his own life.

Shakespeare watched Henry V. not indeed as he watched the greater souls in the visionary procession, but cheerfully, as one watches some handsome spirited horse, and he spoke his tale, as he spoke all tales, with tragic irony.

VI

The five plays, that are but one play, have, when played one after another, something extravagant and superhuman, something almost mythological. Those nobles with their indifference to death and their immense energy seem at times no nearer the common stature of men than do the Gods and the heroes of Greek plays. Had there been no Renaissance and no Italian influence to bring in the stories of other lands English history would, it may be, have become as important to the English imagination as the Greek Myths to the Greek imagination; and many plays by many poets would have woven it into a single story whose contours, vast as those of Greek myth, would have made living men and women seem like swallows building their nests under the architrave of some Temple of the Giants. English literature, because it would have grown out of itself, might have had the simplicity and unity of Greek literature, for I can never get out of my head that no man, even though he be Shakespeare, can write perfectly when his web is woven of threads that have been spun in many lands. And yet, could those foreign tales have come in if the great famine, the sinking down of popular imagination, the dying out of traditional phantasy, the ebbing out of the energy of race, had not made them necessary? The metaphors and language of Euphuism, compounded of the natural history and mythology of the classics, were doubtless a necessity also, that something might be poured into the emptiness. Yet how they injured the simplicity and unity of the speech! Shakespeare wrote at a time when solitary great men were gathering to themselves the fire that had once flowed hither and thither among all men, when individualism in work and thought and emotion was breaking up the old rhythms of life, when the common people, no longer uplifted by the myths of Christianity and of still older faiths, were sinking into the earth.

The people of Stratford-on-Avon have remembered little about him, and invented no legend to his glory. They have remembered a drinking-bout of his, and invented some bad verses for him, and that is about all. Had he been some hard-drinking, hard-living, hard-riding, loud-blaspheming Squire they would have enlarged his fame by a legend of his dealings with the devil; but in his day the glory of a Poet, like that of all other imaginative powers, had ceased, or almost ceased outside a narrow class. The poor Gaelic rhymer leaves a nobler memory among his neighbours, who will talk of Angels standing like flames about his death-bed, and of voices speaking out of bramble-bushes that he may have the wisdom of the world. The Puritanism that drove the theatres into Surrey was but part of an inexplicable movement that was trampling out the minds of all but some few thousands born to cultivated ease.

1903—George Bernard Shaw. "To Arthur Bingham Walkley," from the dedication epistle to *Man and Superman*

George Bernard Shaw (1856–1950), who was awarded the Nobel Prize for literature in 1925, began his writing career as a journalist and a failed novelist. During the 1880s, his reputation as a music and theater critic grew, but Shaw only found real success after he turned to playwrighting in the 1890s. The prefaces that he wrote to the published versions of his plays, one of which provides the follow excerpt, have proved to be influential critical statements in themselves.

That the author of Everyman was no mere artist, but an artist-philosopher, and that the artist-philosophers are the only sort of artists I take quite seriously, will be no news to you. Even Plato and Boswell, as the dramatists who invented Socrates and Dr Johnson, impress me more deeply than the romantic playwrights. Ever since, as a boy, I first breathed the air of the transcendental regions at a performance of Mozart's Zauberflote, I have been proof against the garish splendors and alcoholic excitements of the ordinary stage combinations of Tappertitian romance with the police intelligence. Bunyan, Blake, Hogarth and Turner (these four apart and above all the English classics), Goethe, Shelley, Schopenhaur, Wagner, Ibsen, Morris, Tolstoy, and Nietzsche are among the writers whose peculiar sense of the world I recognize as more or less akin to my own. Mark the word peculiar. I read Dickens and Shakespear without shame or stint; but their pregnant observations and demonstrations of life are not co-ordinated into any philosophy or religion: on the contrary, Dickens's sentimental assumptions are violently contradicted by his observations; and Shakespear's pessimism is only his wounded humanity. Both have the specific genius of the fictionist and the common sympathies of human feeling and thought in preeminent degree. They are often saner and shrewder than the philosophers just as Sancho-Panza was often saner and shrewder than Don Quixote. They clear away vast masses of oppressive gravity by their sense of the ridiculous, which is at bottom a combination of sound moral judgment with lighthearted good humor. But they are concerned with the diversities of the world instead of with its unities: they are so irreligious that they exploit popular religion for professional purposes without delicacy or scruple (for example, Sydney Carton and the ghost in Hamlet!): they are anarchical, and cannot balance their exposures of Angelo and Dogberry,Sir Leicester Dedlock and Mr Tite Barnacle, with any portrait of a prophet or a worthy leader: they have no constructive ideas: they regard those who have them as dangerous fanatics: in all their fictions there is no leading thought or inspiration for which any man could conceivably risk the spoiling of his hat in a shower, much less his life. Both are alike forced to borrow motives for the more strenuous actions of their personages from the common stockpot of melodramatic plots; so that Hamlet has to be stimulated by the prejudices of a policeman and Macbeth by the cupidities of a bushranger. Dickens, without the excuse of having to manufacture motives for Hamlets and Macbeths, superfluously punts his crew down the stream of his monthly parts by mechanical devices which I leave you to describe, my own memory being quite baffled by the simplest question as to Monks in Oliver Twist, or the long lost parentage of Smike, or the relations between the Dorrit and Clennam families so inopportunely discovered by Monsieur Rigaud Blandois. The truth is, the world was to Shakespear a great "stage of fools" on which he was utterly bewildered. He could see no sort of sense in living at all; and Dickens saved himself from the despair of the dream in The Chimes by taking the world for granted and busying himself with its details. Neither of them could do anything with a serious positive character: they could place a human figure before you with perfect verisimilitude; but when the moment came for making it live and move, they found, unless it made them laugh, that they had a puppet on their hands, and had to invent some artificial external stimulus to make it work. This is what is the matter with Hamlet all through: he has no will except in his bursts of temper. Foolish Bardolaters make a virtue of this after their fashion: they declare that the play is the tragedy of irresolution; but all Shakespear's projections of the deepest humanity he knew have the same defect: their characters and manners are lifelike; but their actions are forced on them from without, and the external force is grotesquely inappropriate except when it is quite conventional, as in the case of Henry V. Falstaff is more vivid than any of these serious reflective characters, because he is self-acting: his motives are his own appetites and instincts and humors. Richard III, too, is delightful as the whimsical comedian who stops a funeral to make love to the corpse's widow; but when, in the next act, he is replaced by a stage villain who smothers babies and offs with people's heads, we are revolted at the imposture and repudiate the changeling. Faulconbridge, Coriolanus, Leontes are admirable descriptions of instinctive temperaments: indeed the play of Coriolanus is the greatest of Shakespear's comedies; but description is not philosophy; and comedy neither compromises the author nor reveals him. He must be judged by those characters into which he puts what he knows of himself, his Hamlets and Macbeths and Lears and Prosperos. If these characters are agonizing in a void about factitious melodramatic murders and revenges and the like, whilst the comic characters walk with their feet on solid ground, vivid and amusing, you know that the author has much to shew and nothing to teach. The comparison between Falstaff and Prospero is like the comparison between Micawber and David Copperiield. At the end of the book you know Micawber, whereas you only know what has happened to David, and are not interested enough in him to wonder what his politics or religion might be if anything so stupendous as a religious or political idea, or a general idea of any sort, were to occur to him. He is tolerable as a child; but he never becomes a man, and might be left out of his own biography altogether but for his usefulness as a stage confidant, a Horatio or "Charles his friend"—what they call on the stage a feeder.

Now you cannot say this of the works of the artist-philosophers. You cannot say it, for instance, of The Pilgrim's Progress. Put your Shakespearian hero and coward, Henry V and Pistol or Parolles, beside Mr Valiant and Mr Fearing, and you have a sudden revelation of the abyss that lies between the fashionable author who could see nothing in the world but personal aims and the tragedy of their disappointment or the comedy of their incongruity, and the field preacher who achieved virtue and courage by identifying himself with the purpose of the world as he understood it. The contrast is enormous: Bunyan's coward stirs your blood more than Shakespear's hero, who actually leaves you cold and secretly hostile. You suddenly see that Shakespear, with all his flashes and divinations, never understood virtue and courage, never conceived how any man who was not a fool could, like Bunyan's hero, look back from the brink of the river of death over the strife and labor of his pilgrimage, and say "yet do I not repent me"; or, with the panache of a millionaire, bequeath "my sword to him that shall succeed me in my pilgrimage, and my courage and skill to him that can get it." This is the true joy in life, the being used for a purpose recognized by yourself as a mighty one; the being thoroughly worn out before you are thrown on the scrap heap; the being a force of Nature instead of a feverish selfish little clod of ailments and grievances complaining that the world will not devote itself to making you happy. And also the only real tragedy in life is the being used by personally minded men for purposes which you recognize to be base. All the rest is at worst mere misfortune or mortality: this alone is misery, slavery, hell on earth; and the revolt against it is the only force that offers a man's work to the poor artist, whom our personally minded rich people would so willingly employ as pandar, buffoon, beauty monger, sentimentalizer and the like.

1920—Benedetto Croce. "Shakespeare's Interest in Practical Action," from *Ariosto, Shakespeare and Corneille*

The philolosopher Benedetto Croce (1866–1952), who served in the Italian government as both a member of parliament and the education minister, was among the most important Italian intellectuals of the first half of the twentieth century. He is known for, among other things, developing an aesthetic theory that argued art was an aesthetically independent fact that is associated with intuition rather than material objects.

The third conspicuous aspect of Shakespeare's genius corresponds to what are known as the "historical plays." Only here and there do we find a critic who takes them to be the loftiest form of Shakespearean poetry, while the majority on the other hand hold them to be merely a preparatory form for other poetry, and the general view (always worthy consideration) is that they are less happy or less intense than the "great tragedies."

It is also said of them that they represent the period of the "historical education," which Shakespeare undertook, with a view to acquiring a full sense of real life and the capacity for drawing personages and situations with firmness of outline. One critic has defined them as a series of "studies," studies of "heads," of "physiognomies," of "movements," taken from historical life or reality, in order to form the eye and the hand, something like the sketchbooks and collections of designs of a future great painter.

The defect of such critical explanations lies in continuing to conceive of the artistic process as something mechanical, and the unrecognised but understood presumption of some sort of "imitation of nature." Had Shakespeare intended to educate himself "historically," by writing the historical plays, (assuming, but not admitting, that to run through the English chronicles, and even Plutarch's lives, can be called historical education), he would have developed and formed his historical thought and become a thinker and a critic, he would not have conceived and realised the scenes and personages of the plays. Neither Shakespeare nor any other artist can ever attempt to reproduce external nature or history turned into external reality (since they do not exist in a concrete form) even in the period of first attempts and studies; all he can do is to try to produce and recognise his own sentiment and to give it form. We are thus always brought back and confined to the study of sentiment, or, as in the present case, to the sentiment which inspired what are known as the historical plays.

Among these are to be numbered all those that deal with English history, *The Life and Death of King John, Richard II, Henry IV, V, VI,* and *Richard III,* setting aside for certain reasons *Henry VIII*, but including among the plays from Roman history (or from Plutarch as they are also called), *Coriolanus*, while *Julius Caesar* and *Anthony and Cleopatra* are connected with the great tragedies. The historical quality of the material, in like manner, with every other material determination, is not conclusive as to the quality of the poetic works, and is therefore not independently valid in the estimation of the critic, as a criterion for separation or conjunction. A reconsideration of the plays mentioned above and their prominent characteristics, does not lead to accepting them as a kind of "dramatised epic," or as "works which stand half way between epic and drama" (Schlegel, Coleridge), not that there is any difficulty in the appearance of epic quality in the form of theatrical dialogue, but just because epic quality is absent in those dramas. It would indeed be strange to see epic quality appearing in an episodic manner in an author, during the period of youth alone. Epicity, in fact, means feeling for human struggles, but for human struggles lit with the light of an aspiration and an ideal, such as one's own people, one's own religious faith and the like, and therefore containing the antitheses of friends and foes, of heroes on both sides, some on the side finally victorious, because protected by God or justice, others upon that which is to be discomfited, subjected, or destroyed. Now Shakespeare, as has already been said and is universally recognized, is not a partisan; he marches under no political or religious banner, he is not the poet of particular practical ideals, *non est de hoc mundo*, because he always goes beyond, to the universal man, to the cosmic problem.

Commentators have, it is true, laboured to extract from these and others of his plays, the ideals which they suppose him to have cultivated, concerning the perfect king, the independence and greatness of England, the aristocracy, which in their judgment was the mainstay and glory of his country. They have discovered his Achilles (in the double form of "Achilles in Sciro" and of "Achilles at Troy") in Prince Henry, and his *pius Aeneas*, in the same prince become Henry V, who, grown conscious of his new duties, resolutely and definitely severs himself, not from a Dido, but from a Falstaff. They have discovered his paladins in the great representatives of the English aristocracy, and as reflected in the Roman aristocracy, by a Coriolanus, and on the other hand the class which he suspected and despised, in the populace and plebeians of all time, whether of those that surrounded Menenius Agrippa or who created tumult for and against Julius Caesar in the Forum, or those others who bestowed upon Jack Cade a fortune as evanescent as it was sudden. Finally, his Trojans or Rutulians, enemies of his people, are supposed by them to be the French. But if the epic ideal had possessed real force and consistency in the mind of Shakespeare, we should not have needed industrious interpreters to track it down and demonstrate it. On the other hand, it is clear that the author of *Henry VI*, in treating as he did Talbot and the Maid of Orleans, and the author of *Henry V*, in his illustration of the struggles between the English and the French and the victory of Agincourt, restricted himself to adopting the popular and traditional English view, without identifying that with his spiritual self, or taxing it as his guide to the conception of the English and Roman plays.

Nor is there any value in another view, to the effect that Shakespeare in these plays set the example and paved the way for what was afterwards called historical and romantic drama. Had he sought this end, he would not only have required some sort of political, social and religious ideal, but also historical reflection, the sense of what distinguishes and gives character to past times in respect to present, and also that nostalgia for the past, which both Shakespeare and the Italian and English Renaissance, were altogether without. About two centuries had to elapse before an imitator of Shakespeare, or rather of some of his external forms and methods, arose, in the composer of *Goetz von Berlichingen*. He had assimilated the new historical curiosity and affection for the rude and powerful past, and there provided the first model of what was soon afterwards developed as historical romance and drama, especially by Walter Scott.

Whoever tries to discover the internal stimulus, the constructive idea, the lyrical motive, which led Shakespeare to convert the Chronicles of Holinshed and the Lives of Plutarch into dramatic form, when his possession of the epic ideal and nostalgia for the past have been excluded, finds nothing save an interest in and an affection for practical achievement, for action attentively followed, in its cunning and audacity, in the obstacles that it meets, in the discomfitures, the triumphs, the various attitudes of the different temperaments and characters of men. This interest, finding its most suitable material in political and warlike conflicts, was naturally attracted to history and to that especial form of it, which was nearest to the soul and to the culture of the poet of his people and of his time, English and Roman history. This material had already been brought to the theatre by other writers and was in this way introduced to the attention and used by the new poet. A psychological origin of this sort explains the vigour of the representations, which Shakespeare derived from history, incomprehensible, if as philologists maintain, he had simply set himself to cultivate, a "style" that was demanded in the theatre and known as *chronicle plays*, or had there set himself a merely technical task, with a view to attaining dexterity.

That psychological interest, too, in so far as separated from a supreme end or ideal, towards which actions tend, or rather in so far as it remains uncertain and vague in this respect, limiting itself to questions of loss or gain, of success or failure, of living or dying, is not a qualitative, but a *formal* interest. It can also be called political, if you will, but political in the sense of Machiavelli and the Renaissance, in so far as politics are considered for themselves, and therefore only formally. Hence the impression caused by the historical plays of Shakespeare, of being now "a gallery of portraits," now "a series of personal experiences," which the poet is supposed to have achieved in imagination.

It is certain that their richness, their brilliancy, their attraction, lie in the emotional representation of practical activity. Bolingbroke ascends the throne, by the adoption of violent and tortuous means, knowing when to withdraw himself and when to dare. Later he recounts to his son how artfully he composed and maintained the attitude, which caused him to be looked upon with sympathy and reverence by the people, affecting humility and humanity, but preserving at the same time the element of the marvellous, so that his presence, *like a robe pontifical,* was *ne'er seen but wondered at.* He causes the blood of the deposed king to be shed, while protesting after the deed his great grief *that blood should sprinkle me to make me grow,* and promising to undertake a voyage of expiation to the Holy Land. Facing him is the falling monarch, Richard II, in whose breast consciousness of his own sacred character as legitimate sovereign and of the inviolable dignity attached to it, the sense of being to blame, of pride humiliated, of resignation to destiny or divine decree, of bitterness, of sarcasm towards himself and towards others, succeed, alternate and combat one another, a swarm of writhing sentiments, an agony of suffocated passions.

> "O, that I were as great
> As is my grief, or lesser than my name!
> Or that I could forget what I have been!
> Or not remember what I must be now!
> Swell'st thou, proud heart? I'll give thee scope to beat...."

Elsewhere we find the same inexorable conqueror, Bolingbroke, as Henry IV, triumphant on several occasions against different enemies, now infirm and approaching death, raving from lack of sleep, and envying the meanest of his subjects, blindly groping in the vain shadows of human effort, as once his conquered predecessor, and filled with terror, as he views the whole extent of the universe and the

> "Revolution of the times
> Make mountains level, and the continent,
> Weary of solid firmness, melt itself
> Into the sea! ...
> And changes fill the cup of alteration
> With divers liquors! O, if this were seen,
> The happiest youth,—viewing his progress through
> What perils past, what crosses to ensue,—
> Would shut the book and sit him down and die."

And hearing of some friends becoming estranged and of others changing into enemies, he is no longer indignant nor astonished:

"Are these things then necessities?
Then let us meet them as necessities."

Henry V meditates upon the singular condition of kings, upon their majesty, which separates them from all other men and by thus elevating, loads them with a weight equal to that which all men together have to carry, while taking from them the joys given to others, and depriving them of hearing the truth or of obtaining justice.

He feels himself to be more than a king in those moments when he tears off his own kingly mask and mirrors himself in his naked reality as man. Facing the enemies who are drawn up on the field of battle and ready to attack him, he murmurs to himself the profound

"Besides they are our *natural consciences,*
And preachers to us all; admonishing
That we should dress us fairly for our end."

Death reigns above all else in these dramas, death, which brings every great effort to an end, all torment of burning passion and ambition, all rage of barbarous crimes, and is therefore received as a lofty and severe matron; in her presence, countenances are composed, however ardently she has been withstood, however loudly the brave show of life has been affirmed. Death is received thus by all or nearly all the men in Shakespeare, by the tortured and elegiac Richard II, by the great sinner Suffolk, by the diabolic Richard III, down to the other lesser victims of fate. The vileness of the vile, the rascality of rascals, the brutal stupidity of acclaiming or imprecating crowds, are felt and represented with equal intensity, without once permitting anything of the struggle of life to escape, so vast in its variety.

The personages of these plays arise like three-dimensional statues, that is to say they are treated with full reality, and thus form a perfect antithesis to the figures of the romantic plays. These are superficial portraits, vivid, but light and vanishing into air; they are rather types than individuals. This does not imply a judgment of greater or lesser value or a difference in the art of portraying the true; it only expresses in other words and formulas the different sentiment that animates the two different groups of artistic creations, that which springs from delight in the romantic and that due to interest in human action. A Hotspur, introduced upon the scene of the romantic dramas, would break through them like a statue of bronze placed upon a fragile flooring of boards and painted canvas. He is the true "formal" hero, volitional, inrushing, disdainful, impatient, exuberant; we walk round him, admiring his lofty stature, his muscular strength, his potent gestures. He is like a splendid bow, with its mighty string drawn tight to hurl the missile, but wherefore or whither it will strike, we cannot tell. He is all rebellion and battle, yet his wit and satire is worthy of an artist; he loves, too, with a pure

tenderness. But wit and satire and the words of love, alike, bear even the imprint
and are hastened by impetuosity, as of a man engaged in conversation between
one combat and another, still joyful and hot from the battle that is over, already
hot and joyful for that which is to begin. "Away, away, you trifler," he says to his
wife, "you that are thinking of love. Love! I love thee not,

> I care not for thee, Kate: this is no world
> To play with memmets and to tilt with lips:
> We must have bloody noses and cracked crowns,
> And pass them current too. Gods me, my horse!
> What say'st thou, Kate? What would'st thou have
> with me?"

His parallel (perhaps slightly inferior artistically), is the Roman Coriolanus,
as brave, as violent and as disdainful as he, a despiser of the people and of the
people's praise; he too rushes over the precipice to death and is also a "formal" hero,
because his bravery is not founded upon love of country, or upon a faith or ideal
of any kind, one might almost say that it was without object or that its object was
itself. Nor, on the other hand, is Coriolanus a superman, in the sense suggested
by the works of some of the predecessors and contemporaries of Shakespeare.
He is not less tenderly demonstrative towards his mother or his silent wife *("my
gracious silence"),* than is Hotspur to Kate, or when, yielding to a woman's prayers,
he stays the course of his triumphant vengeance. It would be tedious to record
all the personages of indomitable power that we meet with in these historical
dramas, such as the bastard Faulconbridge, in *King John,* and most popular of
all, though not the most artistically executed, Richard III, replete with iniquity,
who clears the way by dealing death around himself without pity, and dies in the
midst of combat with that last cry of desperate courage, "A horse, a horse! My
kingdom for a horse!" At their side stand, not less powerfully delineated, and set
in relief, those queens Constance and Margaret: deprived of their power and full
of maledictions, terrible in their fury, they are either ferocious or shut themselves
up in their majestic sorrow. Queen Constance, when she sees herself abandoned
by her protectors in the face of her enemies, who have become their allies, says,
as she lets herself fall to the ground:

> "Let kings assemble; for my grief's so great
> That no supporter but the huge firm earth
> Can hold it up: here I and sorrows sit;
> Here is my throne: bid kings come bow to it."

This gallery of historical figures is most varied; we find here not only the vigorous and proud, the sorrowful and troubled, but also the noble and severe, like

Gaunt, the touching, like the little princes destined to the dagger of the assassins, Prince Arthur and the sons of Edward IV, down to the laughing and the credulous, to those who defy prejudice to wallow in debauch.

Sir John Falstaff is the first of these latter, and it is important not to misunderstand him, as certain critics have done, especially among the French. They have looked upon him as a jovial, comic type, a theatrical buffoon, and have compared him with the comic theatrical types of other stages, arriving at the conclusion that he is a less happy and less successful conception than they, because his comicality is exclusively English, and is not to be well understood outside England and America. But we must on the other hand be careful not to interpret the character moralistically, as an image of baseness, darkly coloured with the poet's contempt, as one towards whom he experienced a feeling of disgust. Falstaff could call himself a "formal" hero in his own way: magnificent in ignoring morality and honour, logical, coherent, acute and dexterous. He is a being in whom the sense of honour has never appeared, or has been obliterated, but the intellect has developed and become what alone it could become, namely, *esprit,* or sharpness of wit. He is without malice, because malice is the antithesis of moral conscientiousness, and he lacks both thesis and antithesis. There is in him, on the contrary, a sort of innocence, the result of the complete liberty of his relation toward all restraint and towards ethical law. His great body, his old sinner's flesh, his complete experience of taverns and lupanars, of rogues male and female, complicates without destroying the soul of the boy that is in him, a very vicious boy, but yet a boy. For this reason, he is sympathetic, that is to say, he is sympathetically felt and lovingly depicted by the poet. The image of a child, that is to say of childish innocence, comes spontaneously to the lips of the hostess, as she tells of how he died: "Nay, sure, he's not in hell: he's in Arthur's bosom, if ever man went to Arthur's bosom. 'A made a fine end, and went away, an it had been any Christom child. . . ."

Shylock the Jew also finds a place in the historical gallery, for the very reason that he is a Jew, "the Jew," indeed, a historical formation, and Shakespeare conceives and describes him with the characteristics proper to his race and religion, one might almost say, sociologically. It has been asserted that for Shakespeare and for his public Shylock was a comic personage, intended to be flouted and laughed at by the pit; but we do not know what were the intentions of Shakespeare and as usual they matter little, because Shylock lives and speaks, himself explaining what he means, without the aid of commentaries, even such as the author might possibly have supplied. Shylock crying out in his desperation: "My daughter! O my ducats! . . ." may have made laugh the spectators in the theatre, but that cry of the wounded and tortured animal does not make the poetical reader laugh; he forms anything but a comic conception of that being, trampled down, poisoned at heart and unshakeable in his desire for vengeance. On the other hand the pathetic and biassed interpretations of Shylock that have been given during the nineteenth century, are foreign to the ingenuousness of a creation, without a shadow of humanitarianism or of polemic. What Shakespeare has created, fusing his own impressions and experiences in the crucible of his attentive and thoughtful humanity, is the Jew, with his firm cleaving to the law and to the written word, with his hatred for Christian feeling, with his biblical language, now sententious now sublime, the Jew with his peculiar attitude of intellect, will and morality.

Yet we are inclined to ask why Shylock, seen in the relations in which he is placed in the *Merchant of Venice*, arouses some doubt in our minds; he would seem to require a background which is lacking to him there. This background cannot be the romantic story of Portia and the three caskets, or of the tired and melancholy Antonio. The reader is not convinced by the rapid fall of so great an adversary, who accepts the conversion to Christianity finally imposed upon him. But apart also from the particular mixture of real and imaginary, of serious and light, which we find in the *Merchant of Venice*, it does not appear that the characters of the strictly historical plays find the ideal complement which they should find in the plays where they appear. The reason for this is not to be found in the looseness and reliance upon chronicles for which they have so often been blamed, since this is rather a consequence or general effect of Shakespeare's attitude towards the practical life, described above. This attitude, as we have seen, lacks a definite ideal, is indeed, without passion for any sort of particular ideals, but is animated with sympathy for the varying lots of striving humanity. For this reason, it is entirely concentrated, on the one hand upon character drawing, and on the other is inclined to accept somewhat passively the material furnished by the chronicles and histories. On the one hand it is all force and impetus, while on the other it lacks idealisation and condensation. The marvelous Hotspur appears in the play, in order that he may confirm the glory of youthful Prince Hal, that is to say, that he may provide a curious anecdote of what was or appeared to be the scapegrace youth of a future sage sovereign; that is, he is not fully represented. Coriolanus runs himself into a blind alley; and even if the poet portrays with historical penetration, the patricians and plebeians of Rome, it would be vain to seek in the play for the centre of gravity of his feelings, of his predilictions, or of his aspirations, because both Coriolanus, the tribunes and his adversaries are looked upon solely as characters, not as parts and expressions of a sentiment that should justify one or other or both groups. Finally, Falstaff is sacrificed, because, like Hotspur, he has been used for the purpose of enhancing the greatness of the future Henry V; for this reason, he declines in prestige from the first to the last scenes of the first part of Henry IV, not to speak of the *Merry Wives of Windsor*, where we find him reduced to being a merely farcical character, flouted and thrashed. And when his former boon companion, Prince Hal, now on the throne, answers his advances, familiar and confidential as in the past, with hard, cold words, we do not admire the new king for his seriousness, because we are sensible of a lack of aesthetic harmony. Aesthetically speaking, Falstaff did not deserve such treatment, or at least Henry V, who inflicts it upon him, should not be given the credit of possessing an admirable moral character, which he does not possess, for it cannot be maintained that he is a great man, lofty in heart and mind, when he shows us that he has failed to understand Falstaff, and to grant him that indulgence to which he is entitled, after so lengthy a companionship. Falstaff's friends know that poor Sir John, although he has tried to put a good face on his cruel reception by his young friend, is unconsolable in the face of this inhuman estrangement, this chill repulse:

> "The king hath run bad humours in the knight,
> His heart is fracted and corroborate."

And Mistress Quickly, although a woman of bad character and a procuress, shows that she possesses a better heart and a better intellect than the great king, when she attends the dying Sir John with feminine solicitude. The narrative, of which we had occasion to quote the first phrase above, continues in the following pitiful strain:

   "'A parted even just between twelve and one, even at the turning of the tide: for after I saw him fumble with the sheets, and play with flowers and smile upon his fingers ends, I knew there was but one way; for his nose was as sharp as a pen, and 'a babbled of green fields. 'How now, Sir John,' quoth I, 'what, man! be o' good cheer.' So 'a cried out 'God, God, God,' three or four times. Now I, to comfort him, bid him 'a should not think of God; I hoped there was no need to trouble himself with any such thoughts yet. So 'a bade me lay more clothes on his feet: I put my hand into the bed and felt them, and they were as cold as any stone; then I felt to his knees, and so upward and upward, and all was as cold as any stone." And since the friends of the tavern have heard that he raved of sack, of his favourite sweet sack, Mistress Quickly confirms that it was so; and when they add that he raved of women, she denies it, thus defending in her own way the chastity of the poor dead man.

1950—Paul A. Jorgensen. "The Courtship Scene in Henry V," from *Modern Language Quarterly*

Paul A. Jorgensen (1916–2000), an English professor at the University of California at Los Angeles for more than thirty years, published numerous articles and books on Shakespeare and is remembered for the light his historical research brought to the study of Shakespeare. His most important books are *Shakespeare's Military World* (1956),

Redeeming Shakespeare's Words (1962), *Lear's Self-Discovery* (1967), and *Our Naked Frailties: Sensational Art and Meaning in Macbeth* (1971).

Henry V's inept manner of courtship, though successful as far as the French princess is concerned, has been unlucky in its appeal to critics of literature. Doctor Johnson disliked its "military grossness"; to Swinburne it had "the savour rather of a ploughman than a prince"; Mark Van Doren was reminded of a "hearty undergraduate with enormous initials on his chest"; and John Palmer found in Henry's conduct the undesirable characteristics which "are most admired in the legendary Englishman."[1] Such strictures have been, however, less convincing than the practical observation that "the wooing scene itself . . . must have been enough to float the play."[2] Proof of the episode's unusual appeal is to be found in the enduring popularity of its comic theme: the difficulties of the bluff soldier in relationship with women.

For it is not as a "legendary Englishman" that Henry proposes to Katherine. His ineptness in courtship is constantly related to the conventional soldierly temperament. "I speak to thee plain soldier," he tells the princess; and again, "take me, take a soldier."[3] The very outset of the wooing stresses the plain soldier's inability to command the niceties of language. "Fair Katherine, and most fair!" the king essays,

> Will you vouchsafe to teach a soldier terms
> Such as will enter at a lady's ear . . . ?

Henry then proclaims his inability to "mince it in love." He has "neither the voice nor the heart of flattery" about him. And, equally characteristic of the soldier, he wants the graces of poetry and dancing: "For the one I have neither words nor measure; and for the other I have no strength in measure, yet a reasonable measure in strength." If his apology does not appear convincingly humble, it is because he regards the lack of these polite virtues not as a disgrace, but as credentials for his fitness as a lover. "And while thou liv'st," he advises the princess,

> take a fellow of plain and uncoined constancy; for he perforce must do
> thee right, because he hath not the gift to woo in other places.

Abundant parallels for each of the traits claimed by Henry may be found in Elizabethan depictions of the soldier. One prominent aspect of the king's "plain" appearance is notably common. Henry makes several deprecatory references to his face. It is "not worth sunburning." He "never looks in his glass for love of anything" he sees there. When he comes to woo ladies, he frights them. But his comfort is, "that old age, that ill layer-up of beauty, can do no more spoil upon [his] face"; and he dares hope that Katherine will love him "notwithstanding the poor and untempering effect of [his] visage."

Now there is no historical evidence to justify Henry's slur upon his own beauty.[4] But we need not seek far to justify the severest of judgments upon the soldier's face. Traditionally it was "bearded like the pard."[5] It was characterized by "a Crab-tree looke, a sowre countenance, and a hard favoured visage."[6] Commenting upon types known to physiognomy, Ben Jonson pays detailed attention to "your souldiers face, a menacing, and astounding face, that lookes broad, and bigge: the grace of this face consisteth much in a beard."[7] It would obviously frighten ladies; and in Fletcher's *The Captain* Jacomo's "rusty swarth Complexion" affords women both alarm and amusement.[8]

Henry's supposedly bad face was but one signal aspect of the soldierly convention. Detail by detail, to the verge of monotony, Shakespeare has exploited this low comedy convention throughout the courtship scene.

For this conclusion to the play the dramatist was not significantly indebted to the acknowledged sources. None of the nondramatic histories dealing with Henry V offered justification for the king's inept wooing. In *The Famous Victories of Henry the Fifth*, the crude play which gave Shakespeare the general idea for the scene, the king does indeed propose to Katherine bluntly:

> Tush Kate, but tell me in plaine termes,
> Canst thou love the King of England?
> I cannot do as these Countries do,
> That spend halfe their time in woing. . . .

But here is no reference to the soldier, nor, for that matter, any convincing reason for the king's rudeness.

Shakespeare's reinterpretation of this scene apparently relied for its success upon popular appreciation of the plain soldier as a literary convention. But the popularity of the convention is less important than its trend. And it is in evaluating the play in relation to this trend that we meet an arresting difficulty; for in the Elizabethan drama prior to 1599, the plain soldier in contact with women is commonly exposed as a clownish ruffian. He is especially censured if, like Shakespeare's Henry V, he proclaims his incivility in swaggering fashion. It is necessary to scrutinize this attitude toward the soldier, since Shakespeare could scarcely have wished the hero of his most ardently patriotic play to be finally an object of ridicule.

Basis for the contemptuous attitude toward the rough soldier—particularly one who behaves uncouthly in the presence of women—is to be sought in courtly tradition; and for Elizabethan purposes this is best illustrated in Castiglione's *Courtier*. One of Count Lewis' most felicitous anecdotes—and it is forcefully rendered by Hoby's translation—serves as a reproof to the graceless warrior:

For unto such may well be said, that a worthie gentle woman in a noble assemblie spake pleasantly unto one . . . whom she to shew him a good countenance, desired to daunce with her, and hee refusing it, and to heare musicke, and many other entertainments offered him, alwaies affirming such trifles not to be his profession, at last the gentlewoman demaunding him, what is then your profession? he answered with a frowning looke, to fight.

Then saide the Gentlewoman: seeing you are not now at the warre nor in place to fight, I would think it best for you to be well besmered and set up in an armory with other implements of warre till time were that you should be occupied, least you waxe more rustier then you are. Thus with much laughing of the standers by, she left him with a mocke in his foolish presumption.[10]

It is appropriate that from so civilized a group, the plain soldier should be dismissed with urbane derision.

Thomas Churchyard gave early encouragement in England to the attitude rebuked in the *Courtier*:

Dance after drom, let tabber goe, the musyck is nott good
that maeks men loek lyck gyriss, and mynce on carpaytts gaye . . .
The sownd off trompett suer, wyll change your maydens face
A gallant stoering hors, that maeks a manneg ryghtt
wear fytter than a lady fyen, for myghtty marssys Knightt.[11]

Such misguided manliness, lamentable in a genuine soldier like Churchyard, was contemptible in men who adopted uncivil behavior to prove themselves stalwart, and it was towards such that Ascham directed the following rebuke:

And in greater presens, to beare a brave looke: to be warlike, though he never looked enimie in the face in warre: yet som warlike signe must be vsed. . . .

But Ascham comforts himself in the knowledge that such counterfeit soldiers are not truly representative of his country, that

England hath at this time, manie worthie Capitaines and good souldiours, which be in deede, so honest of behaviour, so cumlie of conditions, so milde of maners, as they may be examples of good order. . . . [12]

John Lyly made of his Sir Thopas just such a one as Ascham deplores. Thopas is not a mere borrowing from Latin comedy. Lyly has enriched the traditional vices of the *miles gloriosus* by a generous infusion of unromantic sentiments. Thopas condescendingly admits that ladies well may love him, but his "tough

heart receiveth no impression with sweet words." He is, by virtue of his warlike
nature, incapable of gentle sentiments:

> There commeth no soft syllable within my lips . . . that pelting word Ioue,
> how watrish it is in my mouth, it carrieth no sound; hate, horror, death, are
> speaches that nourish my spirits.[13]

Lyly also finds occasion to condemn this churlish attitude in genuine soldiers.
The warrior Martius advises Midas to scorn the felicities of love as "a pastime
for children, breeding nothing but follie, and nourishing nothing but idleness."[14] Although many of Martius' arguments are persuasive and are not totally
foreign to the attitude taken by Henry V, the significant aspect of his conduct
is that it is authoritatively rebuked, whereas Henry's conduct decidedly is not.
Lyly's noblest warriors, such as Alexander, are gentle as well as stalwart; in
keeping with the chivalric ideal in general, they join "letters with launces" and
"endevor to be as good Philosophers as soldiers, knowing it no lesse praise to be
wise, then commendable to be vailiant"[15]

In the plays of Robert Greene, likewise, will we look in vain for sympathetic
depictions of the uncourtly soldier. There is, to be sure, an approximation to the
Henry V of the *Famous Victories* in Greene's portrait of Sacrepant, a confirmed
warrior who suddenly discovers his love for Angelica. Like Henry V of the early
play, Sacrepant resolves to get the romantic business done with a minimum of
ceremony:

> Then know, my love, I cannot paint my grief.
> Nor tell a tale of Venus and her sonne . . .
> It fits not Sacrapant to be effeminate.[16]

These words, not particularly engaging in themselves, are the utterance of an
unscrupulous warrior, and the reader is in little doubt that Greene approved of
neither the wooer nor the wooing.

Of the earlier plays, that which comes closest in spirit to the courtship
episode in *Henry V* is *A Pleasaunt Comedie of Faire Em*. William the Conqueror
proposes to Mariana as follows:

> I cannot, Madam, tell a loving tale . . .
> That am a soldier sworn to follow arms—
> But this I bluntly let you understand—
> I honour you with such religious zeal
> As may become an honourable mind.[17]

Unlike the *Famous Victories*, this play thus attributes, though casually, the lover's
lack of eloquence to his military calling. Equally important is the fact that

William is throughout the play a likable character, and this brief episode is not intended to discredit him. Rather, it shows his sincerity. It must be admitted, however, that this plainness is unconvincing. There are none of Shakespeare's well-chosen details to impress upon the audience the fact that a rough soldier is speaking.

We shall, in the main, search vainly through the Elizabethan drama prior to *Henry V* for sympathetic depictions of the soldier who boasts of his defects as a lover or who proposes with convincing inelegance. But there is a nondramatic work which, I believe, influenced Shakespeare's treatment of the courtship scene. In the collection of tales entitled *Riche His Farewell to Militarie Profession* (1581), soldiers are given prominent and favorable attention. The reason is not far to seek. The author, Barnabe Riche, was a professional soldier, was genuinely devoted to the occupation which he supposedly was leaving, and ultimately became "the most prolific writer of the period on the soldier and the soldier's wrongs."[18] Almost certainly Shakespeare knew the *Farewell*. Probably its story "Of Apolonius and Silla" influenced the structure of *Twelfth Night*. And, a fact more pertinent to the present discussion, good evidence has recently been adduced why "Of Two Brethren and Their Wives," a story in the *Farewell*, should be considered an important source of *The Merry Wives*.[19] Since *Henry V* and *The Merry Wives* probably were written within a year of each other, it is not at all unlikely that Shakespeare had the *Farewell* fresh in his mind when he composed *Henry V*.

One of Riche's most vigorous characters is a soldier appearing in "Two Brethren." This ungainly personage has just "lately retourned from the warres, I gesse aboute the same tyme that Kyng Henry the Fift was retourned from the winnyng of Agincourt feelde."[20] Happening to espy a beautiful woman, he is "sodainly stroken into a greate[r] make to see this lampe of light, then ever he had been in the feelde to see the ensignes of his enemies."[21] He at first plans to make known his love by means of a letter.

> But then he knewe not how to beginne his letter, because souldiours are
> verie seldome accustomed to endite, especially any of these lovyng lines; and
> to speake unto her, he was likewise to learne how to use his tearmes....

He nevertheless is able to make a forthright declaration of his love, at which the woman shows seemly alarm. Disturbed but not routed by her modesty, the soldier confesses his inability to meet her on a sophisticated level. "Gentlewoman," he announces,

> I am not able to encounter you with wordes, because it hath not been my
> profession, nor trainyng up, but if you doubte of my love and good likyng,
> please it you to make triall....

The gentlewoman, who

had never been apposed with such a rough hewen fellowe, that was so blunt and plaine, aswell in his gesture as in his tearmes, beganne to thinke with herself that he might well bee a Souldiour, for she knewe that thei had little skill in the courting of gentlewomen. . . . [22]

The significant aspect of this rather obvious episode is that the soldier's suit is successful, and that he is favored over two more sophisticated individuals, a doctor and a lawyer. What is even more unusual, the woman accepts the soldier because of his very "plainesse," for "she perceived by his countenaunce the vehemencie of the love he bare unto her. . . ."[23] Her choice proves to be both gratifying and wise. The soldier makes a faithful lover, and later, by means of a cudgeling administered to both doctor and lawyer, he convincingly vindicates her good name.

Riche's endorsement of the soldier's behavior in "Two Brethren" owes much of its sincerity to the manner in which this episode parallels the author's personal endeavor in the book as a whole. Riche, himself a soldier, is self-consciously trying to please "the right courteous Gentlewomen, bothe of Englande and Ireland," to whom he dedicates the *Farewell*. In this undertaking he is sensitive concerning his social deficiencies. He finds in himself "no one maner of exercise, that might give me the least hope to win your good likinges."[24] In a passage suggesting Henry V's misgivings about dancing, he confesses his ineptness in "measures":

although I like the measures verie well, yet I could never treade them aright, nor to use measure in any thyng I went aboute. . . . [25]

Again, like Henry, he laments his inability to "discourse pleasauntly, to drive away the tyme with amorous devises"; nor is he able "to propone pretie questions, or to give readie aunsweres. . . ."[26]

But although in his suit to the gentlewomen readers he lays claim to all conceivable courtly disabilities, he obviously means to prosper. "Grosse" and "blunt" though his profession may make him, there is never any question throughout the *Farewell* as to the worth and dignity of the soldier's calling, or as to the superiority of soldiers to courtiers. Riche's noblest hero, Sappho Duke of Mantona, "had no skill in courting trade"; "his voice served hym better to cheare his souldiors in the feeld, then either to fayne or syng ditties in a ladies chamber."[27] Nothing could be further from the author's intentions than that we should deride Sappho for his plainness. Riche's contempt is directed at the courtiers who libeled the duke and procured his banishment.

We see, then, in the *Farewell* a significant reversal of the usual attitude toward the plain soldier. He is not drawn into the picture merely that we may laugh at his ungainly appearance or deride his hostility to the niceties of romance. In Riche the soldier is the hero. He will make, clearly, the best husband; and it is to be regretted that gentlewomen are deceived by accomplished "love makers, suche as can devise to please women with newe fangles, straunge fassions, by praisyng of their beauties."

As unofficial laureate of the English plain soldier, Riche may well have provided—more so than any other one source—the justification for Shakespeare's treatment of the courtship scene. At any rate Riche offered, to whoever would read him, both the most detailed account of the soldier's conventional disabilities and the strongest advocacy of the soldier's worthiness in love.

But whatever may have been Shakespeare's indebtedness to Riche or others in this respect, such indebtedness is scarcely more noteworthy than what happened to the stage soldier in the years following the first performance of *Henry V.* From 1599 forth, the plain soldier of the Elizabethan stage seems to have enjoyed a decisive rise in popular esteem. Contempt was reserved for the sham warrior; and the courtier, no longer the knightly hero of Castiglione, became generally a typed figure of dandyism, appropriately serving as a despicable antagonist for the noble soldier.

In 1599, Dekker gave sympathetic treatment to the difficulties of Orleans, a professedly plain soldier, in love. When his rival for the hand of Agripyne makes the conventional slighting remark, "Me thinkes, souldiers cannot fal into the fashion of love," Agripyne defends her unskillful suitor:

Me thinkes, a Souldier is the most faithfull lover of all men els: for his affection stands not upon complement: his wooing is plaine home-spun stuffe; theres no outlandish thred in it, no Rethoricke: a Souldier casts no figures to get his mistris heart, his love is like his valour in the field, when he payes downeright blowes.[29]

Orleans has opportunity to prove, as Henry V did not, that the soldier's boast of constancy is well founded, for he, of all Agripyne's suitors, continues to seek her love after she has suffered deformity.

If we accept the evidence of the Commendatory Verses in the First Folio, no Beaumont-Fletcher characters were more highly esteemed than the numerous plain soldiers created by these dramatists. As lovers, these men may be the object of good-natured chaffing. The attitude taken toward them by one mischievous young lady is typical:

I had as lieve be courted by a Cannon.
As one of those.[30]

There is some basis for her distaste in the ill-favored person of Captain Jacomo, whose ferociousness and limited personality show the realistic imprint of years of battle. Music, after a brief period of discomfort, puts the captain to sleep, and his polite conversation with women is limited to asking "what their shooes cost."' But even Jacomo is loved by a young lady, one who rids him of his self-distrust and makes of him a satisfactory lover. Then there is Memnon of *The Mad Lover,* mentioned more frequently than any other character in the Commendatory Verses. This "old rude Souldier," at first the victim of feminine banter, wins respect by offering his heart to the princess whom he loves. This offer is given singular attention because, in Memnon's meaning, it is no figure of speech; his friends barely prevent self-administered surgery. It is such men as Memnon who won for Fletcher's plays this commendation: "Souldiers may here to their old glories adde."[32]

That the Beaumont-Fletcher drama was not extreme in its glorification of the rude soldier is evidenced by the tribute paid by Massinger to Captain Belgarde. This "cast captain" is invited to a ceremonious banquet on condition that he appear in a new suit of clothes. Undaunted, the captain appears "in armor a case of Carbines by his side." "Who stops me now," he asks the admiring assemblage,

> Or who dares only say that I appear not
> In the most rich and glorious habit that
> Renders a man compleate?[33]

Authoritative comment on such behavior is made by his noble host:

> I commend,
> This wholesome sharpnesse in you, and prefer it
> Before obsequious tameness, it shewes lovely.[34]

Not merely cast captains were commended for their plainness. Some of the noblest Beaumont-Fletcher warriors are ill at ease in court. And Sir Thomas Overbury, drawing the Character of "A Worthy Commander in the *Warres,*" states:

> He is so honourably mercifull to women in surprisall, that onely that makes him an excellent Courtier. He knowes, the hazards of battels, not the pompe of Ceremonies are Souldiers best theaters.[35]

The persistent voices of men like Riche had done much to free from popular contempt the quality which Doctor Johnson termed "military grossness" and to transfer disdain to the simplified courtier type, a figure for whom the provincial Elizabethan temperament felt instinctive distrust. And although Henry V was not fundamentally a rough warrior, Shakespeare was doubtless wise to present him finally and memorably in the role of the plain soldier. No behavior could more aptly symbolize the crude, physically exciting theme of much of the play:

French sophistication coming under the heel of English manliness. No behavior could more happily befit the hero of Agincourt, who prevailed

> without stratagem,
> But in plain shock and even play of battle.

>   (IV, viii, 113–14)

NOTES

1. "Notes on *Henry V,*" *Plays of William Shakespeare* (London, 1765), Vol. 4; *A Study of Shakespeare,* 3rd ed. (London, 1895), p. 105; *Shakespeare* (New York, 1939), p. 176; *Political Characters of Shakespeare* (London, 1945), p. 245.

2. E. E. Stoll, *Poets and Playwrights* (Minneapolis, 1930), p. 45.

3. I have used the *Complete Works,* ed. Kittredge (Boston, 1936).

4. "He had an oval, handsome face with a broad, open forehead and straight nose, ruddy cheeks and lips, a deeply indented chin, and small well-formed ears." C. L. Kingsford, *Henry V: The Typical Medieval Hero* (New York, 1903), p. 81.

5. *As You Like It,* III, vii, 150.

6. Barnabe Riche, *The Fruites of Long Experience* (London, 1604). p. 52.

7. *Cynthias Revells,* II, iii, 26–29. *Ben Jonson,* ed. Herford and Simpson (Oxford, 1932), IV, 70.

8. II, I and ii. For Beaumont-Fletcher references I have used *Works of Francis Beaumont and John Fletcher,* ed. Glover and Waller (Cambridge, 1905–1912).

9. *Shakespeare's Library,* ed. W. C. Hazlitt, 2nd ed. (London, 1875), V, 371.

10. Everyman edition (London, 1937), pp. 36–37.

11. Commendatory Verses to Barnabe Riche's *Allarme to England* (London, 1578).

12. *The Scholemaster. English Works,* ed. W. W. Wright (Cambridge, 1904), p. 207.

13 *Endimion,* II, ii, 124–27. All Lyly references are to the *Complete Works,* ed. R. W. Bond (Oxford, 1902).

14. Midas, I, i, 27–28.

15. *Campaspe,* I, i, 82–84.

16 *Orlando Furioso,* II, i, 443–46. *Plays and Poems of Robert Greene,* ed. J. C. Collins (Oxford, 1905), 1, 235–36.

17. Lines 721–26. *The School of Shakspere,* ed. Richard Simpson (New York, 1878), II, 437.

18. Lily B. Campbell. *Shakespeare's "Histories"* (San Marino, California, 1947), p. 245.

19. Dorothy Hart Bruce. *"The Merry Wives* and *Two Brethren," SP,* XXXIX (1942), 278. Since completing this study, I have learned of T. M. Cranuill's forthcoming edition of the *Farewell,* a work which will do ampler justice to Riche's far-reaching effect on Shakespeare and the drama generally, and which, I believe, will support the Shakespearean indebtedness proposed in the present study.

20. Shakespeare Society edition (London, 1846), p. 134.

21. *Farewell,* p. 135.

22. *Ibid.,* p. 136.

23. *Idem.*

24. *Ibid,* p. 4.

25. *Idem.*

26. *Farewell*, p. 5.

27. "Sappho Duke of Mantona," *Farewell*, p. 23.

28. *Ibid.*, p. 22. Cf. *The Second Tome of the Travailes and Adventures of Don Simomdes* (London, 1584), Sig. S1, in which Riche gives fuller reasons for preferring the soldier to the courtier as lover.

29. *Olde Fortunatus. Dramatic Works* (London, 1873), I, 130. Whether either *Henry V* or *Old Fortunatus* influenced the other in the depiction of soldier as wooer is difficult to judge because of closeness of dates. *Henry V* was performed sometime between March 27 and September 28, 1599. And, according to Chambers *(Elizabethan Stage* [1923], III, 291), *Fortunatus* was played at court on December 27, 1599. But the advantage given to *Henry V* by date of performance is inconclusive, as the Stationers Register entry for *Fortunatus* suggests that the 1599 play was a revision of the earlier (1596) play on the same subject. Assuredly, however, the episode in Dekker's production could have offered only the slightest of inspiration to Shakespeare.

30. *The Captain*, I, ii.

31. *Ibid.*, III, iii.

32. Richard Lovelace, "To Fletcher Reviv'd." Commendatory Verses, First Folio, *Works of Beaumont and Fletcher*, I, xxiv.

33. *The Unnatural Combat*, ed. Talfer (Princeton, 1932), III, iii, 37. For an analogous situation see *The Noble Spanish Soldier* (1634), II, i, Tudor Facsimile Texts (1913).

34. *Ibid.*, III, iii, 106.

35. *New Characters* . . . (London, 1615), ed. Paylor (Oxford, 1936), pp. 47–48.

1969—Marilyn L. Williamson.
"The Episode with Williams in Henry V,"
from *Studies in English Literature, 1500–1900*

Marilyn L. Williamson (1927–) is Distinguished Professor Emerita of English at Wayne State University, where she also served as provost. Her publications include numerous journal articles as well as *Infinite Variety: Antony and Cleopatra in Renaissance Drama and Earlier Tradition* (1974) and *The Patriarchy of Shakespeare's Comedies* (1986).

The episode in which Henry goes disguised among his troops on the night before Agincourt, the subsequent quarrel with the soldier Williams, and its eventual result after the battle need scrutiny because they yield insight into characteristics Shakespeare develops in Henry from Richard II through Henry V. In the episode Henry reveals vestiges of his habits as Prince Hal: the disguise repeats those used to trick Falstaff and the consciousness of ceremony in the soliloquy recalls that in the planned reformation by Hal. The quarrel with Williams shows Henry still learning to be king: we discover that as king he has special privileges (being ransomed); his word cannot be trusted like other men's. In extricating himself from the oath to Williams, Henry tries to pay him off, but what would have worked in Eastcheap works no longer. The exchange of gloves echoes Hal's travesty of chivalric values in Richard II. Survival of old habits modifies the official view of Henry's reformation and rejection of Falstaff described by the Archbishop and the Chorus. Shakespeare did not jettison the character he had created, but made Henry a more complex and interesting character than we have thought.

We have been so busy deciding whether Shakespeare's portrait of Henry is satiric or heroic that we have not bothered to look closely at some of the complexity Shakespeare has put into the figure of Henry after his ascension to the throne. We know that Prince Hal is complicated by two sides of his character—the madcap and the Prince, but we tend to assume that once Henry rejects Falstaff, he has accepted his kingly role entirely and his character simply flattens out.[1] My suggestion is that the episode in which Henry goes disguised among his troops on the night before Agincourt, the subsequent quarrel with the soldier Williams, and its eventual result after the battle need scrutiny because they yield insight into characteristics of Henry which Shakespeare develops over virtually the whole tetralogy.

One of the first things that may strike us about the Chorus's introduction to the episode, "a little bit of Harry in the night," is that the Chorus arouses an expectation that Henry's behavior never fulfills:

> For forth he goes and visits all his host,
> Bids them good morrow with a modest smile,
> And calls them brothers, friends and countrymen.
> Upon his royal face there is no note
> How dread an army hath enrounded him;
> Nor doth he dedicate one jot of colour
> Unto the weary and all-watched night;
> But freshly looks and over-bears attaint
> With cheerful semblance and sweet majesty;
> That every wretch, pining and pale before,
> Beholding him, plucks comfort from his looks.[2]

Going about in disguise as Harry Le Roy of Sir Thomas Erphingham's company is simply not the same as cheering your men by moving among them as their king who is confident of victory and communicates his feeling to his troops. A possible explanation of the contradiction may lie in Shakespeare's greater interest in what the subsequent scene will reveal about Henry than in squaring his behavior with the details of the official picture of him consistently presented by the Chorus. The emphasis in the scenes where the disguised Henry passes among his men is on their effect on him, rather than the reverse. His encounters present Henry with his predicament as a man who is a ruler of men, and as such they carry on the central issue of *Henry IV, 1 and 2*.[3]

If we follow the suggestion of connections of this episode with the *Henry IV* plays, we are rewarded with several insights. We see that Prince Hal is still with us, the lover of disguises and of tricks. Twice in the earlier plays he disguises himself to trick Falstaff, and once he confronts Falstaff with the scurvy things the knight has said about him and the fat man has to use escape wit to regain good graces (*2 Henry IV*. II. iv).

In the earlier play the effect is simply that of two rogues joshing each other, but what Henry discovers after he becomes king is that the old tricks have new results, that instead of having the fun of discomfiting Falstaff, he himself is deeply shaken at the feelings his men reveal as they wait for the morning's battle. In his opening remarks Henry shows us that he knows a king's subjects hide their feelings from him, that Sir Thomas Erphingham would not betray to Henry how desperate he thinks the English predicament. Yet paradoxically Henry cannot resist the impulse to masquerade as "but a man." In doing so he helps us feel what it is like to be a king, something that Shakespeare has been exploring with him all along the way.

Although Henry's arguments may not entirely convince his critics, they do serve to convince his men that "every subject's duty is the king's; but every subject's soul is his own," but the interesting point the men boggle at is Henry's assumption that the king is a man like other men. When Henry raises the unhappy issue of the ransom (a privilege of a king) and of trusting the king's word about refusing it, Williams shows a healthy skepticism:

K. Hen. I myself heard the king say he would not be ransomed.
Will. Ay, he said so, to make us fight cheerfully; but when our throats
are cut, he may be ransomed, and we ne'er the wiser.
K. Hen. If I live to see it, I will never trust his word after.
Will. You pay him then! That's a perilous shot out of an elder-gun, that
a poor and a private displeasure can do against a monarch. You may
as well go about to turn the sun to ice with fanning in his face with a
peacock's feather. You'll never trust his word after! Come, 'tis a foolish
saying. (IV.i.202–215)

The questions of the ransom, of paying someone off, of Henry's keeping his word are to echo through the action resulting from this quarrel. William's attitude angers Henry to the point where he agrees to a quarrel, if they both live, and they exchange gloves. It is ironic that Henry's subjects know something he cannot seem to face: that the king is not just another man, that you do not trust his word in the same way, that he has privileges you do not have. How accurate they are we find out as a result of the quarrel. If we look back to Shakespeare's portrait of Henry in the other plays of the tetralogy, we see that as Prince Hal he enjoyed just such a double role as he is assuming here. He was able to hobnob with Falstaff and company as a man among men while at the same time using his position as heir apparent whenever necessary, as when the sheriff came to the Boar's Head after the Gadshill robbery (1 Henry IV. II. iv). Indeed, Falstaff reminds us constantly of Hal as both Prince and man:

> Prince. I say 'tis copper. Darest thou be as good as thy word now?
> Falstaff. Why, Hal, thou knowest, as thou art but a man, I dare; but as thou art Prince, I fear thee as I fear the roaring of the lion's whelp. (1 Henry IV. III.iii.163–167)

The quarrel with Williams shows that though Henry's old habits are still with him, they do not work in the same way.

The king's reaction to his conversation with the soldiers is the famous soliloquy on ceremony, which, though it contains some puzzling elements, fits the dramatic context better than some commentators say it does.[4] In the first lines, for example, Henry forgets that he has talked his soldiers out of doing precisely what he now accuses them of: "Upon the king! let us our lives, our souls, / Our debts, our careful wives, / Our children, and our sins lay on the king!" (IV. i. 247–249). The contradiction, however, also reveals to us how shaken Henry is by the encounter and how sorry for himself he feels about it. We also notice that the speech carries on the idea already explored in the scene itself: the difference between the king and private men. But, we may say, many kings in Shakespeare meditate about this theme: Henry's father's famous soliloquy on sleep comes immediately to mind. And, I suggest, it should, for both the similarities and the differences in the two speeches are instructive and significant. Though the speeches have in common the emphasis on the cares the king endures which common men do not share, the focus of each is adapted to the character of the speaker. It is suitable that, like other usurpers in Shakespeare, Henry IV cannot sleep, ringed round as he is by potentially rebellious lords, to whom he has given a notable example. It is equally suitable that his son, who has spent his youth flouting royal station and the values that go with it, and who loves a masquerade, should emphasize in his soliloquy the hollowness of ceremony and the outward forms of kingship. One who has built his career on the dramatic value of an astonishing reformation is bound to be especially sensitive to the show of greatness.

One could argue that because both soliloquies end with an elaborate picture of a poor wretch who can sleep while the king cannot and because a great lover of battles mentions maintaining the peace, Henry's speech is a set piece "of detached eloquence on a subject on which Shakespeare had long meditated with interest and fervour."[5] It is certainly possible that Shakespeare is simply following a similar poetic pattern appropriate to his theme rather than to the dramatic context. But I would rather explore another possibility, that the strong echo of Henry IV's speech fits with what comes shortly after the soliloquy—the prayer that refers specifically to "the fault / My father made in compassing the crown" (IV. i. 310–311). In the prayer Henry reveals that, like his father, whose sentiments he has just repeated in the soliloquy, he also is doing penance for the crime against Richard. In short, Henry is finding out how his father felt, which is another way of saying what it means to be a king. The soliloquy and the prayer form strong links to 2 Henry IV, and in doing so encourage us to recall the earlier play.

The episode does not end with the prayer, however. There remains the question of Henry's keeping his word with Williams. After the battle we witness the meeting with Williams in which Henry inquires about the gage in the soldier's hat, and Williams replies that the glove belongs to "a rascal that swaggered with me last night" (IV. vii. 130), and that he is determined to keep his oath if he can find the man alive. The implications of his angry impulse of the previous night are beginning to dawn on Henry for he asks Fluellen if the soldier should keep his oath even if "his enemy is a gentle-man of great sort, quite from the answer of his degree" (141–142). When Fluellen answers that the soldier should keep his oath if it was made to the devil himself, and it is clear that a confrontation lies ahead, Henry follows his Eastcheap habits and compounds the trick by giving Fluellen Williams's glove, telling Fluellen it is Alencon's, arranging for Fluellen and Williams to meet, while sending Warwick and Gloucester along to be certain the dupes do not injure each other. The trickery harks back to Gadshill, but as we soon see, the escape wit must be Henry's and not his victim's.

By the time Henry overtakes them, Fluellen and Williams are already quarreling, and the king finally tells Williams, "'Twas I, indeed, thou promised'st to strike; / And thou hast given me most bitter terms" (IV. viii. 42–43), and Fluellen adds, "Let his neck answer for it." Back in the Boar's Head Williams would be squirming by now, but Agincourt is not the Boar's Head, and Williams's reply makes us squirm for Henry:

> Your majesty came not like yourself: you appeared to me but as a common
> man; witness the night, your garments, your lowliness; and what your
> highness suffered under that shape, I beseech you, take it for your own
> fault and not mine: for had you been as I took you for, I made no offence;
> therefore, I beseech your highness, pardon me. (IV.viii.53–60)

Whether Williams has taught Henry the lesson which we thought the Chief Justice had taught him by sending him to prison is a moot question; I believe Shakespeare implies that he did not,[6] for Henry instantly takes refuge in a tactic that would have delighted any of the Eastcheap crowd: he pays Williams off, echoing in action Williams's words in their quarrel. The difference is that it is impossible to imagine those cronies saying to Fluellen as Williams does,

"I will none of your money." And the difference between Williams and the cronies makes all the more apparent to us the fact that Henry is still operating on Eastcheap terms.

If we look at the dramatic context, it also seems that Henry's paying off Williams is an action that has significance beyond simply being an escape from a trick that has backfired. The point of argument between Henry and Williams was the question of whether Henry might ransom himself to the French, and the matter is constantly kept before us in the surrounding action by the repeated trips of the French herald Montjoy to the English camp to offer that Henry pay ransom to stop the war. Though Henry does not pay off that quarrel, he does fulfill Williams's prophecy about him in small by stopping their quarrel with payment. He does not, then, ransom his life to the French, but his oath to Williams. We may recognize that Henry had to do so, that he could not possibly have fought with Williams. But that is just the point: his initial impulse to do so shows that he is still learning to be a king, and his solution for the problem created is more suitable to Eastcheap than Agincourt, as the behavior of Williams and Fluellen implies.

Shakespeare began his portrait of Henry in Richard II when Henry IV inquires for his "unthrifty son." Percy, that flower of chivalry and foil to Hal, replies that when the Prince was told there would be triumphs at Oxford,

> His answer was, he would unto the stews,
> And from the commonest creature pluck a glove
> And wear it as a favour, and with that
> He would unhorse the lustiest challenger. (V.iii.16–19)

Our first account of Henry connects him with a travesty of chivalric custom that is amazingly like the travesty of a similar custom with which he closes our episode in Henry V:

> Here, uncle Exeter, fill this glove with crowns,
> And give it to this fellow. Keep it, fellow;
> And wear it for an honour in thy cap
> Till I do challenge it. (IV.viii.61–65)

We seem to be dealing with very much the same characteristic in Henry as Prince and King.

One episode does not make a play, yet this one seems more than usually important because it is not only entirely Shakespeare's but also by common consent the finest small drama within a play that has had its share of detractors.[7] If my interpretation of the episode is substantially correct, it has several implications for our view of the play as a whole. The survival of old habits in Henry should be taken to modify the official view of his reformation and the rejection of Falstaff as an absolute change of the sort the Archbishop describes. Indeed, the gradual disappearance of the Eastcheap gang throughout Henry V would suggest itself as a counterpart in dramatic action to a longer process in which old habits, like old cronies, do not die instantly upon Henry's ascent to the throne. If we recognize that Shakespeare did not jettison "the character he had created,"[8] we may also see that Henry is a more complex and interesting character than we have thought[9] and that if we must continue to imagine Shakespeare's creative intensity flagging as he perfunctorily finished the tetralogy, it revived splendidly in this instance.

NOTES

1. See E. M. W. Tillyard, *Shakespeare's History Plays* (London, 1959), p. 306; R. A. Law, "Links between Shakespeare's History Plays," SP, L (1953), 184; the most extended such treatment of Henry's conversion occurs in J. H. Walter's introduction to *King Henry V*, The Arden Edition (London, 1954), pp. xviii-xxiii.

2. Chorus. 32–42; all references are to the Neilson and Hill edition (Boston, 1942).

3. See John Dover Wilson, *The Fortunes of Falstaff* (Cambridge, 1948), p. 22. 276.

4. Tillyard, p. 309; H. C. Goddard, *The Meaning of Shakespeare* (Chicago, 1951), pp. 243–244.

5. Tillyard, p. 309.

6. Mark Van Doren believes that he did not: "Henry has not learned what Williams knows," *Shakespeare* (New York, 1939), p. 150. 280

7. Especially Van Doren, pp. 143–152, and Tillyard, pp. 304–314.

8. Tillyard, p. 306.

9. Walter says, "If Henry has proved less interesting a man than Richard, it is because his problems are mainly external. The virtuous man has no obvious strife within the soul, his faith is simple and direct, he has no frailties to suffer in exposure," p. xxxii.

1977—Norman Rabkin. "Rabbits, Ducks, and Henry V," from *Shakespeare Quarterly*

Norman Rabkin (1930–) is a professor emeritus of the University of California, Berkeley, where he taught in the English department. His two most important contributions to Shakespeare studies are *Shakespeare and the Common Understanding* (1967) and *Shakespeare and the Problem of Meaning* (1981).

The greater plays leave us knowing we should be perplexed. No explication satisfies us that *Macbeth* or *King Lear*, *Hamlet* or *Othello* or *The Winter's Tale* has been safely reduced to a formula that answers all our questions. Such plays tell us that mystery is their mode; the questions aroused by them seem unanswerable, because each play in its own way creates an image of a world that is unfathomable where we most need to understand it.

Henry V is no such play. Rather, it repeatedly elicits simple and wholehearted responses from its critics, interpretations that seem solidly based on total readings of a consistent whole. This is not to say, however, that the critics agree with each other. As a matter of fact, they could hardly disagree more radically. "For some" of them, a recent writer remarks, "the play presents the story of an ideal monarch and glorifies his achievements; for them, the tone approaches that of an epic lauding the military virtues. For others, the protagonist is a Machiavellian militarist who professes Christianity but whose deeds reveal both hypocrisy and ruthlessness; for them, the tone is predominantly one of mordant satire."[1]

One way to deal with a play that provokes such conflicting responses is to try to find the truth somewhere between them. Another is to suggest that the author couldn't make up his mind which side he wanted to come down on and left us a mess. A third is to interpret all the signals indicating one polar reading as intentional, and to interpret all the other signals as irrepressible evidence that Shakespeare didn't believe what he was trying to say. All of these strategies have been mounted against *Henry V*; and all of them are just as wrong as most critics now recognize similar attempts to domesticate the greater plays to be.

I am going to argue that in *Henry V* Shakespeare creates a work whose ultimate power is precisely the fact that it points in two opposite directions, virtually daring us to choose one of the two opposed interpretations it requires of us. In this deceptively simple play Shakespeare experiments, perhaps more shockingly than elsewhere, with a structure like the gestaltist's familiar drawing of a rare beast. Gombrich describes the experience of that creature in memorable terms:

We can see the picture as either a rabbit or a duck. It is easy to discover both readings. It is less easy to describe what happens when we switch from one interpretation to the other. Clearly we do not have the illusion that we are confronted with a "real" duck or rabbit. The shape on the paper resembles neither animal very closely. And yet there is no doubt that the shape transforms itself in some subtle way when the duck's beak becomes the rabbit's ears and brings an otherwise neglected spot into prominence as the rabbit's mouth. I say "neglected," but does it enter our experience at all when we switch back to reading "duck"? To answer this question, we are compelled to look for what is "really there," to see the shape apart from its interpretation, and this, we soon discover, is not really possible. True, we can switch from one reading to another with increasing rapidity; we will also "remember" the rabbit while we see the duck, but the more closely we watch ourselves, the more certainly we will discover that we cannot experience alternative readings at the same time. Illusion, we will find, is hard to describe or analyze, for though we may be intellectually aware of the fact that any given experience must be an illusion, we cannot, strictly speaking, watch ourselves having an illusion.[2]

I

If one considers the context of *Henry V*, one realizes that the play could scarcely have been anything but a rabbit-duck.

Henry V is, of course, not only a free-standing play but the last part of a tetralogy. Some years earlier, when his talent was up to Titus Andronicus rather than to Hamlet, Shakespeare had had the nerve, at the very beginning of his career, to shape the hopelessly episodic and unstructured materials of his chronicle sources not into the licensed formlessness of the history play his audience was used to, but rather into an integrated series of plays each satisfying as a separate unit but all deriving a degree of added power and meaning from being parts of a unified whole. It is scarcely credible that, with this tetralogy behind him, Shakespeare should have approached the matter of Lancaster without thinking of the possibility of a second unified series of plays. I can think of no other explanation for the fact that already in *Richard II* Hotspur—a character completely unnecessary to that play—has been made practically a generation younger than his model. The implication of the change is that in 1595 Shakespeare already intended a play about Prince Hal. And as one notices the innumerable cross-references and links and parallels among the plays of the second tetralogy, one feels more confidently than in the first cycle that such connections are not afterthoughts, backward indices in one play to what already existed in earlier plays, but evidence of conscious through-composition.

In any event, whether or not, as I think, Shakespeare knew four or five years beforehand that he would write *Henry V*, he certainly did know in 1599 that this drama would be the capstone to an edifice of plays tightly mortared to one another. And as with each part of *Henry IV*, he must have derived enormous power from the expectations his audience brought from the preceding plays. In each of the first three plays the audience had been confronted at the beginning with a set of problems that seemed solved by the end of the preceding play but had erupted in different forms as soon as the new play began. Thus the meaning of each of the plays subsequent to *Richard II* had been enriched by the audience's recognition of the emergence of old problems in a new guise. By the time the cycle reached *Henry V*, the recurrent and interlocking set of problems had become so complex that a reflective audience must have found it impossible to predict how the last play could possibly resolve them.

The unresolved thematic issue at the end of *Richard II* is the conflict of values embodied in the two kings who are its protagonists: Bullingbrook's talent as opposed to Richard's legitimacy; Bullingbrook's extroverted energy and calculating pursuit of power as opposed to Richard's imagination, in-wardness, and sense of mortality. Richard's qualities make possible in him a spiritual life that reveals him as closer—even in his inadequacy—to the ideal figures of the comedies than is his successor, who none the less has the sheer force to survive and to rule to his country's advantage. If the play is structured to force one by the end to choose Bullingbrook as the better king—one need only contrast his disposition of Exton at the close with Richard's of Mowbray at the opening—one nevertheless finds one's emotions rather surprisingly committed to the failed Richard. *Richard II* thus poses a question that arches over the entire tetralogy: can the manipulative qualities that guarantee political success be combined in one man with the spiritual qualities that make one fully open and responsive to life and therefore fully human? Or, to put it more accurately, can political resourcefulness be combined with qualities more like those of an audience as it sees itself?

I Henry IV moves the question to a new generation, asking in effect whether the qualities split between Richard and Bullingbrook can be united in Hal. And in the manner of a comedy, it suggests optimistically that indeed they can. Thus Hal's famous schematic stance between the appropriately dead Hotspur and a Falstaff equally appropriately feigning death indicates not so much a compromise between their incompatible values as the difference between Hal's ability to thrive in a world of process by employing time as an instrument and Hotspur's and Falstaff's oddly similar unwillingness to do so.

For Hotspur, there is only the present moment. Even an hour is too long for life if honor is not its definition, and a self-destructive recklessness leads Hotspur to fight his battle at the wrong time, hoping naively thereby to gain more glory. For Falstaff, time is equally irrelevant. Like the Forest of Arden he needs no clock, since he has nowhere to go. He lives cyclically, recurring always to the same satisfactions of the same appetites, playing holiday every day, denying the scars of age and the imminence of death. Both of Hal's alter egos preposterously deny time, Hotspur to meet his death characteristically in midphrase—a phrase that Falstaff has already completed as "Food for powder"—and Falstaff to rise emblematically from his own death and shamelessly assert once again his will to live.

But Hal's affection for both men, so symmetrically expressed, suggests that he is in tune with something in each of them. Unlike his heavy father, but like both Hotspur and Falstaff, he is witty, ebulliently verbal, social, warmly responsive to others. For one illusory moment Shakespeare suggests the possibility of a public man who is privately whole. If the Prince's soliloquy has vowed an amputation he sees from the beginning as necessary, if the play extempore has ended in a suddenly heartbreaking promise to banish plump Jack and banish all the world, followed by the knock of the real world on the door, *I Henry IV* nevertheless puts us in a comic universe in which Hal need never reject Falstaff in order to reach his father's side in the nick of time; it entices us with the hope of a political world transformed by the life of comedy.

But the end of *Henry IV, Part One* marks only the halfway point, both in this massive tetralogy and in the study of Prince Hal, and Part Two brutally denies the comic optimism we might have expected to encounter once again. With the exception of Hotspur, all the ingredients of Part One seem to be present again, and in some respects they seem stronger than ever. Falstaff is given a scene (II. iv) perhaps even more endearing than Gadshill and its aftermath; he captivates Doll Tearsheet and, against her better knowledge, the Hostess. Ancient Pistol, who adds fresh attraction to the tavern world, performs one of the functions of the missing Hotspur by giving us a mocking perspective on the rhetoric and pretensions of the warrior.

And yet, despite all this and more, the effect of *Henry IV, Part Two* is to narrow possibilities. The rejection of Falstaff at its end seems to be both inevitable and right, yet simultaneously to darken the world for which the paradise of the Boar's Head must be lost. Hotspur's absence, emphasized by the dramatic device of the series of rumors from which his father must pick it out at the beginning, roots out of the political world the atmosphere of youth, vigor, charm, and idealistic commitment that Hotspur almost alone had lent it before. And Hotspur's widow's just reproaches of her father-in-law stress the old man's ugly opportunism. Northumberland's nihilistic curse—

> Let heaven kiss earth! now let not Nature's hand
> Keep the wild flood confin'd! let order die!
> And let this world no longer be a stage
> To feed contention in a ling'ring act;
> But let one spirit of the first-born Cain
> Reign in all bosoms, that each heart being set
> On bloody courses, the rude scene may end,
> And darkness be the burier of the dead! (I. i. 153–60)[3]

—that curse makes clear the destructiveness of his rebellion, a thing far different from his late son's chivalric quest, and it creates an unequivocal sense that Hal has no choice but to oppose it as effectively as he can. No longer can we assent to Falstaff's observation, plausible in Part One, that the rebels "offend none but the virtuous" (III. iii. 191), so that opposing them is almost a game. The harshness of the rebels' cause and company in Part Two demands of the audience a Hotspurrian recognition that this is no world to play with mammets and tilt with lips.

Yet the attractiveness of the King's cause is reduced too. If in some moments—as in his sensitive meditation on the crown and his emotional final reunion with Hal—Henry IV is more likable in Part Two than he was in Part One, he is no longer an active character (he doesn't even appear until the third act). And his place is filled by Prince John, as chilling a character as Shakespeare would ever create. Many a villain has more superficial charm than Hal's upright brother, and the priggish treachery by which Prince John overcomes the rebels arouses in us a distaste for political action, even when it is necessary, such as no previous moment in the plays has occasioned.[4] If Shrewsbury implied that a mature politics was compatible with the joy of life lived fully and spontaneously, Gaultree now shows political responsibility as masked and sinister, an ally of death.

Given this characterization of the political world as joyless and cruel whether right or wrong, one might expect Falstaff to carry the day. But in fact Shakespeare reduces him as much as he reduces the workaday world. It was a delicate paradox in Part One that allowed us to admire Falstaff for his ridiculous denial of mortality—"They hate us youth"; "young men must live." Falstaff might worry about how he was dwindling away, but we had no fear of losing so eternal a companion. Or, to put it more accurately, we loved him for allaying such fears; for all his grumbling at Gadshill, he could run when he had to. But in Part Two, Falstaff is mired in gross physicality and the ravages of age, obsessed with his diseases and bodily functions, commanding that the Jordan be emptied, confirming as Doll caresses him ("I am old, I am old") his stage audience's observation that desire has outlasted performance. He is the same Falstaff, but the balance is altered.

As if to reenact his great catechism on honor in Part One, Falstaff is given a similar aria in Part Two. But the praise of sherris sack, funny as it is, is no more than a witty paean to alcohol, and a description at that of the mechanical operation of the spirit, whereas the rejection of honor in Part One was convincing enough almost to undo our respect for anyone who subordinates life to ideals. Or again, the charge of foot for whom Falstaff is responsible in Part One never becomes palpable, except to elicit his sympathetic "Food for powder," which puts him essentially on their side. In Part Two, however, we are introduced to his men by name, we see him choosing them (for the most self-serving reasons), and we are aware of the lives and families that Falstaff is ruining. No longer can we see him as the spokesman of life for its own sake; his ego is self-serving, as not before, at the expense of others.

If the tavern world is no longer alluring for us, it is even more unattractive for Hal. Physically separated from Falstaff in Part Two as not in Part One, the Prince is ready at any moment to express his discomfort, his guilt, his eagerness to be away. The flyting he carries on with Poins is unpleasant: if Hal feels so out of place consorting with commoners, why doesn't he simply stop doing it? We are tempted to agree with Warwick, who tells the King that Hal's only reason for spending time with his companions is his opportunistic scheme to use them:

> The Prince but studies his companions
> Like a strange tongue, wherein, to gain the language,
> 'Tis needful that the immodest word
> Be look'd upon and learnt, which once attain'd,
> Your Highness knows, comes to no further use
> But to be known and hated. (IV. iv. 68–73)

The diseases literally corrupting Falstaff's body are endemic in *2 Henry IV.* Sickness and death pervade every element of the plot, virtually every scene, and it is no accident that it is here, not in Part One, that we meet Justice Shallow, in senile debility only a step beyond the aged helplessness of Northumberland and the King. If the medium of action in Part One was time seen as hidden road that leads providentially toward a fulfilling moment, the medium of Part Two is repetitious and meaningless process drawing relentlessly to universal annihilation. Could one "read the book of fate," the moribund King reflects, one would have to

> see the revolution of the times
> Make mountains level, and the continent,
> Weary of solid firmness, melt itself
> Into the sea, and the other times to see
> The beachy girdle of the ocean
> Too wide for Neptune's hips. (III. i. 45–51)

What we recognize here is the time of the sonnets, of Ecclesiastes; and Warwick can cheer the King only by reminding him that at least time is inevitable. The sickness that infects both Falstaff and the body politic is the sickness of life itself, joyless and rushing to the grave. In such a world Prince Hal cannot play. He must do what he can for his kingdom, and that means casting Falstaff aside.

About the necessity for the rejection we are not given the chance to have any doubts: Falstaff, after all, has just told his companions that the law is his now, and, as A. R. Humphreys notes,[5] Richard II had assured his own fall by making precisely this Nixonian claim. Yet we are forced to feel, and painfully, what an impoverishment of Hal's life the rejection causes.[6] And we recognize another aspect of that impoverishment in the drive that moves Hal to take the crown prematurely from his dying father: his commitment to political power has impelled him, as the King recognizes bitterly, to a symbolic gesture that reveals an unconscious readiness for parricide. At the end of Henry IV, Part One, Hal seemed able to accommodate all of England into his family as he moved toward its symbolic fatherhood. By the end of Part Two, in order to become King of England he has reached out to murder both of his fathers.

II

If we fancy ourselves arriving, on an afternoon in 1599, for the first performance of *Henry V*, we must imagine ourselves quite unsure of what to expect. Some months earlier the Epilogue to *2 Henry IV* had promised that "our humble author will continue the story, with Sir John in it, and make you merry with fair Katherine of France, where (for any thing I know) Falstaff shall die of a sweat, unless already 'a be kill'd with your hard opinions; for Oldcastle died [a] martyr, and this is not the man." This disingenuous come-on allows for both sympathetic and hostile readings of Falstaff, while disclaiming any knowledge of the author's intentions. But the plays that precede *Henry V* have aroused such ambivalent expectations that the question of the Epilogue is trivial. If *Henry V* had followed directly on *I Henry IV*, we might have expected to be made merry by the comedy such critics as Dover Wilson have taken that play to be,[7] for we have seen a Hal potentially larger than his father, possessing the force that politics requires without the sacrifice of imagination and range that Bullingbrook has had to pay. But Part Two has told us that Part One deceived us, for the day has had to come when Hal, no longer able to live in two worlds, would be required to make his choice, and the Prince has had to expel from his life the very qualities that made him better than his father. Have we not, after Part Two, good reason to expect in the play about Hal's kingship the study of an opportunist who has traded his humanity for his success, covering over the ruthlessness of the politician with the mere appearance of fellowship that his past has endowed him with? Surely this is what Goddard means when he calls *Henry V* "the golden casket of *The Merchant of Venice*, fairer to a superficial view than to a more searching perception."[8]

As we watch the Prologue stride across the stage of the Curtain, then, we are ready for one of two opposed presentations of the reign of the fifth Henry. Perhaps we hope that the play now beginning will resolve our doubts, set us right, give us a single gestalt to replace the antithetical images before our mind's eye. And that, as is demonstrated by the unequivocal interpretations good critics continue to make, is exactly the force of the play. We are made to see a rabbit or a duck. In fact, if we do not try obsessively to cling to memories of past encounters with the play, we may find that each time we read it it turns from one shape to the other, just as it so regularly does in production. I want to show that *Henry V* is brilliantly capable of being read, fully and subtly, as each of the plays the two parts of *Henry IV* had respectively anticipated. Leaving the theatre at the end of the first performance, some members of the audience knew that they had seen a rabbit, others a duck. Still others, and I would suggest that they were Shakespeare's best audience, knew terrifyingly that they did not know what to think.

III

Think of *Henry V* as an extension of *I Henry IV*. For the generation who came to know it under the spell of Olivier's great film, it is hard to imagine *Henry V* any other way, but Olivier's distortions, deletions, and embellishments only emphasized what is already in the play. The structure of the entire cycle has led from the beginning of conflict in a quarrel to its end in a wedding, from the disruption of royal power to its unchallenged reassertion. If *Richard II* at the beginning transformed the normally episodic chronicle form into tragedy, *Henry V* at the end turns it into comedy: the plot works through the troubles of a threatening world to end in marriage and the promise of a green world. Its protagonist, like Benedick returned to Messina, puts aside military exploits for romance, and charms even his enemies with his effervescent young manhood. Its prologue insists, as the comedies always do, on the importance of imagination, a faculty which Bullingbrook, wise to the needs of a tragic world, had rejected in *Richard II* as dangerous. And as in all romantic comedy providence guides the play's events to their desired conclusion.[9]

To be sure, Olivier's camera and Walton's music prettied up the atmosphere, transporting their war-weary audience to the fairy-tale world of the Duc de Berry. But they found their cues in the play—in the Chorus's epic romanticizations of land and sea, his descriptions of festooned fleets and nocturnal campfires and eager warriors, and his repeated invitations to imagine even more and better. Nor did Olivier invent his film's awe at the spectacle of the past. In *Henry V*, as nowhere before in the tetralogy, Shakespeare excites us by making us conscious that we are privileged to be watching the very moments at which event transforms itself into history:

> Mont.   The day is yours.
> K. Hen. Praised be God, and not our strength, for it!
> What is this castle call'd that stands hard by?
> Mont. They call it Agincourt.
> K. Hen. Then call we this the field of Agincourt,
> Fought on the day of Crispin Crispianus. (IV. vii. 86–91)

Ultimately, it was not Olivier's pictures but the play's language that made his *Henry V* so overwhelming, and the rhetoric of the play is extraordinary, unprecedented even in Shakespeare. Think, for example, of the King's oration to his troops on Saint Crispin's day (IV. iii. 19–67). Thematically, of course, the speech is a tour de force, subjecting motifs from the tetralogy to Aeschylean or Wagnerian transmutations. Like the dying John of Gaunt, Harry is inspired by a vision of England, but one characteristically his own, made as romantic by the fantasy of neighborhood legionnaires and domestic history lessons as by the magical names of England's leaders. Unlike Richard II, Harry disprizes trappings, "outward things." Like Hotspur, he cares only about honor and wants to fight with as few troops as possible in order to acquire more of it: "the fewer men, the greater share of honor." Like Falstaff, he is finicky about the kind of company he adventures with: "we would not die in that man's company / That fears his fellowship to die with us." Again like Falstaff, he thinks of the "flowing cups" to come when the day's work is done and sees the day's events in festival terms. Gaily doing battle on the Feast of Crispian, he is literally playing at war like Hotspur, paradoxically uniting the opposed principles of the two most enchanting characters of the cycle.

Such echoes and allusions give Henry's speech a satisfying finality, a sense of closure. He is the man we have been waiting for, the embodiment of all the virtues the cycle has made us prize without the vices that had accompanied them before. "He is as full of valor as of kindness," we have heard just before the speech, "Princely in both," and the Crispin's day exhortation demonstrates precisely the combination of attributes that Sherman Hawkins has pointed out as belonging to the ideal monarch postulated by Elizabethan royalism.[10] But even more powerful than its thematic content is the stunning rhetoric of the King's tirade: its movement from the King's honor to his people's; its crescendo variations on St. Crispin's day, reaching their climax in the last line; its rhythmic patterns expanding repeatedly from broken lines to flowing periods in each section and concluding climactically in the coda that begins "We happy few"; its language constantly addressed to the pleasures, worries, and aspirations of an audience of citizens. As Michael Goldman perceptively argues, such a speech almost literally moves us. We recognize it as a performance; we share the strain of the King's greatness, the necessary effort of his image-projecting. "We are thrilled," Goldman says, "because he is brilliantly meeting a political challenge that has been spelled out for us. . . . It is a moment when he must respond to the unspoken needs of his men, and we respond to his success as we do when a political leader we admire makes a great campaign speech: we love him for his effectiveness."[11]

The fourth act of *Henry V,* in the third scene of which this speech has its place, is a paradigm of the King's virtues. It begins with the Chorus's contrast between the "confident and over-lusty French" and the thoughtful and patient Englishmen at their watchful fires on the eve of Agincourt, visited by their generous, loving, brave, and concerned royal captain—"a little touch of Harry in the night." The act moves, first through contrasting scenes in the two camps, then through confrontations of various sorts between the opposing sides, to the victory at Agincourt and the King's call for the charitable treatment of the dead as he announces his return to England. In the course of the act we see Harry, constantly contrasted to the stupid and corrupt French, in a triumphant show of bravery and high spirits. But we see him also in a kind of inwardness we have seldom observed in his father, listening as neither Richard II nor Henry IV could have done to the complaints and fears of a common soldier who knows what kings impose on their subjects that they do not themselves have to risk. His response is a soliloquy as powerful in its thematic and rhetorical complexity as the public address we have just considered (IV. i. 230–84).

In some respects this soliloquy, which precedes by only a few moments the Crispin's day speech, is the thematic climax of the entire tetralogy, showing us that at last we have a king free of the crippling disabilities of his predecessors and wise in what the plays have been teaching. Recognizing that all that separates a king from private men is ceremony, Harry has escaped Richard's tragic confusion of ceremony with reality: "Is not the King's name twenty thousand names?" Unwittingly reenacting his father's insomniac soliloquy in the third act of 2 Henry IV, Harry too longs for the heart's ease of the commoner. But where the old King could conclude only, "Uneasy lies the head that wears a crown," recurring despairingly to his posture of perennial guiltiness and to his weary sense of mortality, his young son ends by remembering his responsibility, his life of service, and sees that—"what watch the King keeps to maintain the peace"—as the defining mark of the King. Moreover, in his catechistic questioning of ceremony Harry shows that he has incorporated Falstaff's clearsightedness: like honor in Falstaff's catechism, ceremony consists only in what is conferred by others, bringing no tangible good to its bearer, unable to cure disease, no more than a proud dream. But the lesson is not only Falstaff's; for, in the dark backward and abysm of time, before Hal ever entered the scene, a young Bullingbrook had anticipated his son's "Thinks thou the fiery fever will go out / With titles blown from adulation?" with a similar repudiation of comforting self-deception:

> O, who can hold a fire in his hand
> By thinking on the frosty Caucasus?
> Or cloy the hungry edge of appetite
> By bare imagination of a feast? (Richard II, I. iii. 294–97)

These multiple allusions force us to see in Henry V the epitome of what the cycle has taught us to value as best in a monarch, indeed in a man; and the King's ability to listen to the soldier Williams and to hear him suggests, like his subsequent fooling with Fluellen in the same fourth act, a king who is fully a man. All that is needed to complete him is mature sexuality, scarcely hinted at in the earlier portraits of Hal, and the wooing of Princess Katherine in the fifth act brings finality to a lively portrayal of achieved manhood, a personality integrated in itself and ready to bring unity and joy to a realm that has suffered long from rule by men less at ease with themselves and less able to identify their own interests with those of their country.

It was such a response to *Henry V* that led me years ago to write:

> In only one play in his entire career does Shakespeare seem bent on
> making us believe that what is valuable in politics and in life can
> successfully be combined in a ruler as in his state. . . . There can be no
> doubt that [the play] is infectiously patriotic, or that the ideal of the
> harmonious commonweal . . . reflects the highest point of Shakespeare's
> civic optimism. And Henry is clearly presented as the kind of exemplary
> monarch that neither Richard II nor Henry IV could be, combining
> the inwardness and the sense of occasion of the one and the strength of
> the other with a generous humanity available to neither. . . . In *Henry V*
> Shakespeare would have us believe what hitherto his work in its genre
> has denied, that in the real world of the chronicles a man may live who
> embodies the virtues and experiences the fortune of the comic hero.[12]

Reading the play thus optimistically, I had to note nevertheless how many readers respond otherwise to it, and I went on to observe that the play casts so many dark shadows—on England after Agincourt, for instance—that one can scarcely share its optimism, and that "in this respect Henry V is the most melancholy of the history plays." But I have now come to believe that my acknowledgment of that darker aspect of the play hardly suggested the terrible subversiveness with which Shakespeare undermines the entire structure.

IV

Taking the play, as we have just done, to be an extension of the first part of *Henry IV,* we are almost inevitably propelled to optimism. Taking it as the sequel of the second part of Henry IV, we are led to the opposite view held by critics as diverse as H. C. Goddard, Roy W. Battenhouse, Mark Van Doren, and H. M. Richmond. Think of those dark shadows that cloud the comedy. The point of the stock ending of romantic comedy is, of course, its guarantee of the future: marriage secures and reinvigorates society while promising an extension of its happiness into a generation to come. Like *A Midsummer Night's Dream, Henry V* ends in a marriage whose blessing will transform the world:

> K. Hen. Now welcome, Kate; and bear me witness all,
> That here I kiss her as my sovereign queen. Flourish.
> Q. Isa. God, the best maker of all marriages,
> Combine your hearts in one, your realms in one!
> As man and wife, being two, are one in love,
> So be there 'twixt your kingdoms such a spousal,

That never may ill office, or fell jealousy,
Which troubles oft the bed of blessed marriage,
Thrust in between the [paction] of these kingdoms,
To make divorce of their incorporate league;
That English may as French, French Englishmen,
Receive each other. God speak this Amen!
All. Amen!
K. Hen. Prepare we for our marriage; on which day,
My Lord of Burgundy, we'll take your oath,
And all the peers', for surety of our leagues.
Then shall I swear to Kate, and you to me,
And may our oaths well kept and prosp'rous be! *Sennet. Exeunt.*

We don't really know very much about what was to happen in Theseus's Athens. But we know a good deal about Plantagenet England; and in case any member of the audience has forgotten a history as familiar to Elizabethans as our Civil War is to us, the Chorus appears immediately to remind them—both of what would soon happen, and of the fact that they have already seen a cycle of Shakespearean plays presenting that dismal story:

Small time, but in that small most greatly lived
This star of England. Fortune made his sword;
By which the world's best garden he achieved,
And of it left his son imperial lord.
Henry the Sixt, in infant bands crown'd King
Of France and England, did this king succeed;
Whose state so many had the managing,
That they lost France, and made his England bleed;
Which oft our stage hath shown; and for their sake,
In your fair minds let this acceptance take.

"But if the cause be not good," Williams muses on the eve of Agincourt (IV. i. 134–42), "the King himself hath a heavy reckoning to make, when all those legs, and arms, and heads, chopp'd off in a battle, shall join together at the latter day and cry all, 'We died at such a place'—some swearing, some crying for a surgeon, some upon their wives left poor behind them, some upon the debts they owe, some upon their children rawly left. I am afeard there are few die well that die in a battle." Replying to Williams, the King insists that the state of a man's soul at the moment of his death is his own responsibility. Though to Dr. Johnson this appeared "a very just distinction,"[13] the King's answer evades the issue: the suffering he is capable of inflicting, the necessity of being sure that the burden is imposed for a worthy cause. The end of the play bleakly implies that there is no such cause; all that Harry has won will be lost within a generation. The Epilogue wrenches us out of the paradise of comedy into the purgatory of Shakespearean time, where we incessantly watch

> the hungry ocean gain
> Advantage on the kingdom of the shore,
> And the firm soil win of the wat'ry main,
> Increasing store with loss, and loss with store.

Contemplation of "such interchange of state, / Or state itself confounded to decay" (Sonnet 64) does not incline one toward attempting apocalyptic action. It is more likely to encourage reflections like those of *Henry IV* about the "revolution of the times," or of Falstaff in the very next scene of *2 Henry IV:* "let time shape, and there an end" (III. ii. 332).

But the implication that the cause is not good disturbs us well before the aftermath of Agincourt. The major justification for the war is the Archbishop of Canterbury's harangue on the Salic Law governing hereditary succession, a law the French are said to have violated. The Archbishop's speech to the King follows immediately on his announcement to the Bishop of Ely that he plans to propose the war as a means of alleviating a financial crisis in the Church. The speech itself is long, legalistic, peppered with exotic genealogies impossible to follow; its language is involuted and syntactically loose. The very qualities that make its equivalent in Shakespeare's sources an unexceptionable instrument of statecraft make it sound on the stage like doubletalk, and Canterbury's conclusion that it is "as clear as is the summer's sun" that King Henry is legitimate King of France is a sardonic bit of comedy.[14] Olivier, unwilling to let on that Shakespeare might want us to be less than convinced, turned the episode into farce at the expense of the Elizabethan actor playing the part of Canterbury. Denied the resources of a subsidized film industry, scholars who want to see the war justified must praise the speech on the basis of its content, ignoring its length and style. Thus in the words of one scholar, "The Archbishop discharges his duty faithfully, as it stands his reasoning is impeccable apart from any warrant given by the precedent of Edward III's claims. Henry is not initiating aggression."[15] Bradley, whose argument the critic just cited was answering, is truer to the situation: "Just as he went to war chiefly because, as his father told him, it was the way to keep factious nobles quiet and unite the nation, so when he adjures the Archbishop to satisfy him as to his right to the French throne, he knows very well that the Archbishop wants the war, because it will defer and perhaps prevent what he considers the spoliation of the Church."[16]

J. H. Walter points out that Henry's reaction to the insulting gift of tennis balls from the Dauphin is strategically placed, as not in the play's sources, after the King has already decided to go to war, and he argues that Shakespeare thus "uses [the incident] to show Henry's Christian self-control."[17] This is an odd description of a speech which promises to avenge the gift with the griefs of "many a thousand widows" for their husbands, of mothers for their sons, and even of "some [who] are yet ungotten and unborn" (I. ii. 284–87). Since the tennis balls are a response to a challenge already issued, Henry's claim that France is his by rights, the King's rage seems just a little self-righteous. Henry's insistence throughout the scene that the Archbishop reassure him as to his right to make the claim insures our suspicion that the war is not quite the selfless enterprise other parts of the play tempt us to see.

Our suspicions are deepened by what happens later. Harold C. Goddard has left us a devastating attack on Henry V as Shakespeare's model Machiavellian.[18] Goddard's intemperate analysis, as right as it is one-sided, should be read by everyone interested in the play. I want to quote only one brief excerpt, his summary of the "five scenes devoted to" the battle of Agincourt; the account will be particularly useful to those who remember the battle scenes in Olivier's film.

> 1. Pistol captures a Frenchman.
>
> 2. The French lament their everlasting shame at being worsted by slaves.
>
> 3. Henry weeps at the deaths of York and Suffolk and orders every soldier to kill his prisoners.
>
> 4. Fluellen compares Henry with Alexander and his rejection of Falstaff to the murder of Cleitus. Henry, entering angry, swears that every French prisoner, present and future, shall have his throat cut. . . . The battle is over. The King prays God to keep him honest and breaks his word of honor to Williams.
>
> 5. Henry offers Williams money by way of satisfaction, which Williams rejects. Word is brought that 10,000 French are slain and 29 English. Henry gives the victory to God. If Shakespeare had deliberately set out to deglorify the Battle of Agincourt in general and King Henry in particular it would seem as if he could hardly have done more.[19]

Admittedly, Goddard's analysis is excessively partisan. He ignores the rhetoric we have admired, he sees only the King's hypocrisy on Agincourt eve, and he refuses the Chorus's repeated invitations to view the war as more glorious than what is shown. But the burden of Goddard's argument is difficult to set aside: the war scenes reinforce the unpleasant implications of the Salic Law episode. Consider the moment, before the great battle, when the King bullies the citizens of Harfleur, whose surrender he demands, with a rapacious violence that even J. H. Walter does not cite as an instance of "Henry's christian self-control":

If I begin the batt'ry once again,
I will not leave the half-achieved Harfleur
Till in her ashes she lies buried.
The gates of mercy shall be all shut up,
And the flesh'd soldier, rough and hard of heart,
In liberty of bloody hand, shall range
With conscience wide as hell, mowing like grass
Your fresh fair virgins and your flow'ring infants.
What is it then to me, if impious War,
Arrayed in flames like to the prince of fiends,
Do with his smirch'd complexion all fell feats
Enlink'd to waste and desolation?
What is't to me, when you yourselves are cause,
If your pure maidens fall into the hand
Of hot and forcing violation?
What reign can hold licentious wickedness
When down the hill he holds his fierce career? (III. iii. 7–23)

In such language as Tamburlaine styled his "working words," the King, like the kind of aggressor we know all too well, blames the rapine he solicits on his victims. The alacrity of his attack makes one understand Yeats's description of Henry V as a "ripened Fortinbras"; its sexual morbidity casts a disquieting light on the muted but unmistakable aggressiveness of his sexual assault on Katherine in the fifth act.

Henry's killing of the French prisoners inspires similar uneasiness. Olivier justified this violation of the putative ethics of war by making it a response to the French killing of the English luggage boys, and one of the most moving moments of his film was the King's passionate response: "I was not angry since I came to France / Until this instant." After such a moment one could hardly fault Henry's

Besides, we'll cut the throats of those we have,
And not a man of them that we shall take
Shall taste our mercy. (IV. vii. 55–65)

In the same scene, indeed, Gower observes that it was in response to the slaughter of the boys that "the King, most worthily, hath caus'd every soldier to cut his prisoner's throat. O, 'tis a gallant king!" But the timing is wrong: Gower's announcement came before the King's touching speech. In fact, Shakespeare had presented the decision to kill the prisoners as made at the end of the preceding scene, and while in the source it has a strategic point, in the play it is simply a response to the fair battlefield killing of some English nobles by the French. Thus the announcement comes twice, first as illegitimate, second as if it were a spontaneous outburst of forgivable passion when it actually is not. In such moments as this we feel an eloquent discrepancy between the glamor of the play's rhetoric and the reality of its action.

Henry IV, Part One is "about temperance and fortitude," Part Two is "about wisdom and justice," and Shakespeare's "plan culminates in *Henry V.*" So argues Sherman Hawkins.[20] "Henry's right to France—and by implication England—," he claims, "is finally vindicated by a higher power than the Archbishop of Canterbury."[21] God's concern that France be governed by so ideal a monarch culminates, of course, in the ruins so movingly described in Act V by the Duke of Burgundy, to whose plea the King responds like the leader of a nation of shopkeepers with a demand that France "buy [the] peace" it wants according to a contract Henry just happens to have had drawn up. What follows is the King's coarse wooing of his captive princess, with its sexual innuendo, its repeated gloating over Henry's possession of the realm for which he sues, and its arch insistence on his sudden lack of adequate rhetoric. Dr. Johnson's judgment is hardly too severe: the King "has neither the vivacity of Hal, nor the grandeur of Henry. . . . We have here but a mean dialogue for princes; the merriment is very gross, and the sentiments are very worthless."[22]

Henry's treatment of France may suggest to the irreverent that one is better off when providence does not supply such a conqueror. And his impact on England is scarcely more salubrious. The episodes in which the King tricks Fluellen and terrifies Williams recall the misbehavior of the old Hal, but with none of the old charm and a lot more power to do hurt. In *2 Henry IV* it was the unspeakable Prince John who dealt self-righteously with traitors; in *Henry V* it is the King himself. In the earlier plays wars were begun by others; in *Henry V* it is the King himself, as he acknowledges in his soliloquy, having apparently decided not to go on pinning the blame on the Archbishop of Canterbury. And England must pay a high price for the privilege of the returning veterans to show their wounds every October 25.

We do not have to wait for the Epilogue to get an idea of it. At the end of Act IV, as we saw, the King calls for holy rites for the dead and orders a return to England. The Chorus to the ensuing act invites us to fantasy the King's triumphant return, his modesty, and the outpouring of grateful citizens. But in the next scene we find ourselves still in France, where Fluellen gives Pistol, last of the company of the Boar's Head, the comeuppance he has long fended off with his shield of preposterous language. Forced to eat his leek, Pistol mutters one last feeble imprecation ("all hell shall stir for this"), listens to Gower's final tonguelashing, and, alone on the stage at last, speaks in soliloquy:

Doth Fortune play the huswife with me now?
News have I that my Doll is dead i' th' spittle
Of a malady of France,

And there my rendezvous is quite cut off.
Old do I wax, and from my weary limbs
Honor is cudgell'd. Well, bawd I'll turn,
And something lean to cutpurse of quick hand.
To England will I steal, and there I'll steal;
And patches will I get unto these cudgell'd scars,
And [swear] I got them in the Gallia wars. (V. i. 80–89)

The pun on "steal" is the last faint echo of the great Falstaff scenes, but labored and lifeless now as Pistol's pathetic bravura. Pistol's Exit occasioned Dr. Johnson's most affecting critical comment: "The comick scenes of the history of Henry the Fourth and Fifth are now at an end, and all the comick personages are now dismissed. Falstaff and Mrs. Quickly are dead; Nym and Bardolph are hanged; Gadshill was lost immediately after the robbery; Poins and Peto have vanished since, one knows not how; and Pistol is now beaten into obscurity. I believe every reader regrets their departure."[23] But our regret is for more than the end of some high comedy: it is for the reality of the postwar world the play so powerfully conjures up—soldiers returned home to find their jobs gone, falling to a life of crime in a seamy and impoverished underworld that scarcely remembers the hopes that accompanied the beginnings of the adventure.

It is the "duty of the ruler," Hawkins says, "to make his subjects good."[24] For the failure of his subjects, the play tells us, we must hold Henry V and his worthless war responsible. Unsatisfactory though he was, Henry IV was still the victim of the revolution of the times, and our ultimate attitude toward him, hastened to his death by the unconscious ambition of his own son, took a sympathetic turn like that with which we came at the end to regard the luckless Richard. But Henry V, master manipulator of time, has by the end of the cycle immersed himself in the destructive element. The blows he has rained on his country are much more his than those of any enemy of the people, and all he has to offer his bleeding subjects for the few years that remain is the ceremonial posture which he himself has earlier had the insight to contemn. Like the Edmund of King Lear, another lusty and manipulative warrior who wins, woos, and dies young, Henry might have subscribed himself "in the ranks of death."

V

Well, there it is. Should one see a rabbit or a duck? Along the way I've cited some critics who see an exemplary Christian monarch, who has attained, "in the language of Ephesians, both the 'age' and 'stature' of a perfect man."[26] And I have cited others who see "the perfect Machiavellian prince,"[27] a coarse and brutal highway robber.[27] Despite their obvious differences, these rival views are essentially similar, for each sees only a rabbit or a duck. I hope that simply by juxtaposing the two readings I have shown that each of them, persuasive as it is, is reductive, requiring that we exclude too much to hold it.

Other positions, as I suggested at the outset, are possible. One of them began with Dr. Johnson, was developed by some of the best critics of a generation ago, among them Tillyard and Van Doren, and found its most humane expression in a fine essay in which Una Ellis-Fermor argued that by 1599 Shakespeare no longer believed what he found himself committed to create.[28] Having achieved his portrait of the exemplary public man, she suggests, Shakespeare was already on the verge of a series of plays that would ever more vexingly question the virtue of such virtue. Never again would Shakespeare ask us to sympathize with a successful politician, instead relegating such men to the distasteful roles of Fortinbras and the two Octavii, Alcibiades and Aufidius. The success-to-be Malcolm is a terrible crux in *Macbeth*. Between quarto and Folio texts of Lear, Shakespeare or his redactor is unable to devote enough attention to the surviving ruler of Britain for us to be able to identify him confidently. The governance of Cyprus and Venice are slighter concerns in Othello than the embroidery on the Moor's handkerchief. "Not even Shakespeare," Dr. Johnson said of what he considered the failure of the last act of Henry V, "can write well without a proper subject. It is a vain endeavour for the most skilful hand to cultivate barrenness, or to paint upon vacuity."[29]

A. P. Rossiter's seminal essay "Ambivalence—the Dialectic of the Histories" sensitively shows Shakespeare's doubleview of every important issue in the earlier history plays. But when he comes to *Henry V*, Rossiter abandons his schema and decides that Shakespeare momentarily lost his interest in a problematic view of reality and settled for shallow propaganda on behalf of a character whom already he knew enough to loathe.[30] But *Henry V* is too good a play for criticism to go on calling it a failure. It has been performed successfully with increasing frequency in recent years, and critics have been treating it with increasing respect.

A third response has been suggested by some writers of late: *Henry V* is a subtle and complex study of a king who curiously combines strengths and weaknesses, virtues and vices. One is attracted to the possibility of regarding the play unpolemically. Shakespeare is not often polemical, after all, and a balanced view allows for the inclusion of both positive and negative features in an analysis of the protagonist and the action. But sensitive as such analysis can be—and I especially admire Robert Ornstein's study in *A Kingdom for a Stage*[31]—it is oddly unconvincing, for two strong reasons. First, the cycle has led us to expect stark answers to simple and urgent questions: is a particular king good or bad for England? can one be a successful public man and retain a healthy inner life? has Hal lost or gained in the transformation through which he changes name and character? does political action confer any genuine benefit on the polity? what is honor worth, and who has it? The mixed view of Henry characteristically appears in critical essays that seem to fudge such questions, to see complication and subtlety where Shakespeare's art forces us to demand commitment, resolution, answers. Second, no real compromise is possible between the extreme readings I have claimed the play provokes. Our experience of the play resembles the experience Gombrich claims for viewers of the trick drawing: "We can switch from one reading to another with increasing rapidity; we will also 'remember' the rabbit while we see the duck, but the more closely we watch ourselves, the more certainly we will discover that we cannot experience alternative readings at the same time."

VI

The kind of ambiguity I have been describing in *Henry V*, requiring that we hold in balance incompatible and radically opposed views each of which seems exclusively true, is only an extreme version of the fundamental ambiguity that many critics have found at the center of the Shakespearean vision[32] and that some years ago, borrowing a bit of jargon from physics, I called "complementarity."[33] What we are talking about is the perception of reality as intransigently multivalent. Though we are poignantly convinced of basic truths—complementarity is a far cry from skepticism—we know that rabbits are always turning into 'ducks before our eyes, bushes into bears.

Such ambiguity is not a theme or even the most important fact in many plays in which it figures. I have argued that it is extraordinarily important in *Hamlet*, but to reduce *Hamlet* to a statement about complementarity is to remove its life. Though one perceives it informing plays as different from one another as *A Midsummer Night's Dream* and *King Lear*, one cannot say that it is what they are "about," and readings of Shakespearean plays as communicating only ambiguity are as arid as readings in which the plays are seen to be about appearance and reality. But in *Henry V*, it seems to me, Shakespeare's habitual recognition of the duality of things has led him, as it should lead his audience, to a point of crisis. Since by now virtually every other play in the canon has been called a problem play, let me add *Henry V* to the number. Suggesting the necessity of radically opposed responses to a historical figure about whom there would seem to have been little reason for anything but the simplest of views, Shakespeare leaves us at a loss.

Is it any wonder that *Julius Caesar* would follow in a few months, where Shakespeare would present one of the defining moments in world history in such a way that his audience cannot determine whether the protagonist is the best or the worst of men, whether the central action springs from disinterested idealism or vainglorious egotism, whether that action is virtuous and necessary or wicked and gratuitous? Nor is one surprised to see that the most romantic and comic of Shakespeare's history plays was created at the moment when he was about to abandon romantic comedy, poised for the flight into the great tragedies with their profounder questions about the meaning of action and heroism. The clash between the two possible views of the world of *Henry V* suggests a spiritual struggle in Shakespeare that he would spend the rest of his career working through. One sees a similar oscillation, magnified and reemphasized, in the problem plays and tragedies, and one is tempted to read the romances as a last profound effort to reconcile the irreconcilable. The terrible fact about *Henry V* is that Shakespeare seems equally tempted by both its rival gestalts. And he forces us, as we experience and reexperience and reflect on the play, as we encounter it in performances which inevitably lean in one direction or the other, to share his conflict.

Henry V is most valuable for us not because it points to a crisis in Shakespeare's spiritual life, but because it shows us something about ourselves: the simultaneity of our deepest hopes and fears about the world of political action. In this play, Shakespeare reveals the conflicts between the private selves with which we are born and the public selves we must become, between our longing that authority figures can be like us and our suspicion that they must have traded away their inwardness for the sake of power. The play contrasts our hope that society can solve our problems with our knowledge that society has never done so. The inscrutability of *Henry V* is the inscrutability of history. And for a unique moment in Shakespeare's work ambiguity is the heart of the matter, the single most important fact we must confront in plucking out the mystery of the world we live in.

NOTES

1. Karl P. Wentersdorf, "The Conspiracy of Silence in Henry V," SQ, 27 (1976), p. 265. See Wentersdorf's notes 3 and 4 for representatives of both points of view. Though inconclusive itself, Wentersdorf's essay presents evidence apparently intended to suggest that the truth lies somewhere between, a position to be discussed below.

2. E. H. Gombrich, *Art and Illusion: A Study of the Psychology of Pictorial Representation* (New York: Pantheon Books, 1960), pp. 5–6. 280

3. My text is *The Riverside Shakespeare*, ed. G. B. Evans et al. (Boston: Houghton Mifflin, 1974).

4. Sherman H. Hawkins astutely describes Prince John in "Virtue and Kingship in Shakespeare's *Henry IV*," *English Literary Renaissance*, 5 (1975), 335–36.

5. A. R. Humphreys, ed., *The Second Part of King Henry IV, The Arden Shakespeare* (London: Methuen, 1966), p. 176.

6. See Jonas A. Barish, "The Turning Away of Prince Hal," *Shakespeare Studies*, 1 (1965), 9–17.

7. J. Dover Wilson, *The Fortunes of Falstaff* (Cambridge: Cambridge Univ. Press, 1943).

8. Harold C. Goddard, *The Meaning of Shakespeare* (Chicago: Univ. of Chicago Press, 1951), I, 266.

9. Whether or not the King is hypocritical, as Goddard claims, in crediting his victory to God, this is certainly one reason for the assertion.

10. Hawkins, pp. 313–20 and passim

11. Michael Goldman, *Shakespeare and the Energies of Drama* (Princeton: Princeton Univ. Press, 1972), p. 70.

12. Norman Rabkin, *Shakespeare and the Common Understanding* (New York: The Free Press, 1967), pp. 98–100.

13. Arthur Sherbo, ed., *Johnson on Shakespeare*, Yale Edition of the Works of Samuel Johnson, VIII (New Haven: Yale Univ. Press, 1966), p. 552.

14. Goddard (I, 219–21) brilliantly analyzes the speech to show how self-defeating the argument is, and how it undercuts Henry's claim to his own throne in England as well.

15. J. H. Walter, *King Henry V*, The Arden Shakespeare (London: Methuen, 1954), p. xxv.

16. A. C. Bradley, "The Rejection of Falstaff," Oxford Lectures on Poetry, second edition (London: Macmillan, 1909), p. 257. Hawkins (p. 341) sees Henry as "the true inheritor of Edward the Black Prince," the genealogy as "not ironic," and "Henry's right to France . . . vindicated by a higher power than Canterbury."

17. Walter, p. xxv; sic.

18. Goddard, I, 215–68.

19. Goddard, I, 256.

20. Goddard, p. 340.

21. Goddard, p. 341.

22. Johnson on Shakespeare, p. 566.

23. Johnson, p. 563.

24. Johnson, p. 346.

25. Hawkins, p. 321.

26. Goddard, I, 267

27. Goddard, I, 260.

28. Una Ellis-Fermor, "Shakespeare's Political Plays," *The Frontiers of Drama* (London: Methuen, 1945).

29. Johnson on Shakespeare, p. 556.

30. A. P. Rossiter, "Ambivalence-The Dialectic of the Histories," *Angel with Horns* (New York: Theatre Arts Books, 1961).

31. Robert Ornstein, *A Kingdom for a Stage: The Achievement of Shakespeare's History Plays* (Cambridge: Harvard Univ. Press, 1972).

32. E.g., Michael McCanles, *Dialectical Criticism and Renaissance Literature* (Berkeley and Los Angeles: Univ. of California Press, 1975), Bernard McElroy, *Shakespeare's Mature Tragedies* (Princeton: Princeton Univ. Press, 1973), Marion B. Smith, *Dualities in Shakespeare* (Toronto: University Press, 1966), and Janet Adelman, *The Common Liar: An Essay on Antony and Cleopatra* (New Haven: Yale Univ. Press, 1973).

33. Rabkin, pp. 20–26.

1987—Paul M. Cubeta. "Falstaff and the Art of Dying," from *Studies in English Literature, 1500–1900*

Paul M. Cubeta is College Professor Emeritus of Humanities at Middlebury College. He was the director of the Bread Loaf School of

English from 1964 to 1989 and is credited with creating the Bread Loaf creative writing program. Cubeta edited *Twentieth Century Interpretations of Richard II: A Collection of Critical Essays* (1971).

Once the historical myths and dramatic concerns of The Henriad served by Falstaff's comic vision have been resolved by his legendary repudiation, Falstaff the character can no longer exist: "Reply not to me with a foolborn jest" (Shakespeare, 2H4 V.v.55).'[1] On that command to silence, the newly crowned king has destroyed his fool and jester. Falstaff could undergo a mock-magical death and resurrection at the end of *I Henry IV*, and he essentially "dies of a sweat" at the end of *2 Henry IV*, when he races recklessly to Westminster Abbey "to stand stain'd with travel, and sweating with desire to see" Hal newly crowned (V.v.24–25). But Falstaff the man cannot be dismissed or lie forgotten in Fleet Prison, abandoned by king and playwright. The Shakespearean investment in the saving grace of that comic spirit in his Lancastrian world has been too great. And so in *Henry V* he redeems Epilogue's promise in *2 Henry IV* to continue the story "with Sir John in it" (Epi., 28) with a vividly realized, yet non-existent death scene, both comic and pathetic, private and demonstrated, dedicated to the spirit of Falstaff the man.

Never allowed securely to grasp this protean giant even when his comic imagination and ironic vision die, the audience participates in the immediacy and intensity of the deathbed scene but not by observing those who stand at Falstaff's bedside. Simultaneously the audience is kept at double distance from the mystery of Falstaff's dying thoughts. Instead of a sentimental farewell in the cold, pragmatic Lancastrian world, Shakespeare seeks instead a resolution in which tragedy and comedy, doubt and belief, clarity and confusion are bound in a manner historically appropriate, morally satisfying, and psychologically dazzling. The theatrical gamble of creating a character by not creating him, of giving him life by destroying him yields the most memorable scene of the play.

To achieve the dense texture of this recollected deathbed scene, Shakespeare does not turn to his usual source for things even vaguely Falstaffian in *The Henriad—The Famous Victories of Henry V* (1598). In the life of Falstaff, Shakespeare has embodied rituals, folk tales, conventions, festivals as familiar to an Elizabethan audience as those he may now be suggestively recalling in the medieval and Renaissance tradition of *ars moriendi*, or the art of dying. To design a coherent structure and meaning to Falstaff's dying moments of introspection and memory, which appear as merely broken, delirious fragments, Shakespeare may also give Falstaff the occasion to attempt a private meditation on his life in the manner of a Renaissance meditation for Wednesday night.

Reported in an intensely moving yet uncertain retelling, Falstaff's mode of dying is as mysterious and as hauntingly perplexing as any circumstance in his life. The only words directly attributed to him, the great inventor of language, are "God, God, God!" (H5 II.iii. 19). But what this punster, this parodist and unparalleled player with the rhythms of spoken language means or what tone the repetitions are spoken in is not ours to hear. The challenger of the moral, social, political, and religious values on which civilization rests dies with a word, the Word, on which pun cannot prevail. Like his heart, which Pistol avers, was "fracted and corroborate" (II.i.124), the scene recollecting Falstaff's death is a kind of transitory memorial moment, broken, unfocused, contradictory, unchronological and impossible to recreate for even their listeners by his bedside mourners, who are then about to be swept up into events in France and propelled to their own deaths.

For the old man's allegedly delirious dying moments as told by a grieving companion whose control of the English language was never firm, Shakespeare needed some kind of intelligible inner structure not available to him in the limited theatrical possibilities of an undramatic scene of dubious recollection. All that is really necessary to complete the exposition of the Falstaff story is Pistol's opening declaration and exhortation, "for Falstaff he is dead, / And we must ern therefore" (H5 II.iii. 5–6). The flexible strategies of the meditative exercises on *ars moriendi* allow Shakespeare the undergirding of a coherent traditional structure familiar to a Renaissance audience, with its fascination for deathbed scenes. Thus he can both shape rhetorically the dramatized design of the brief scene of companionable reminiscence and give meaning to the interior monologue and meditation of the dying Falstaff. Not rheumatic, as the Hostess suggests, he is also not incoherent, only seeming so in her narrative. In this shaky account, Shakespeare illuminates for his theater audience thoughts and intentions which even in happier times Falstaff could not always share with these companions. Yet Falstaff's voice must now be the Hostess's, hopelessly literal-minded and completely antithetical to his own.

Falstaff's mocking pledges of repentance, comically counterpointing Lancastrian political guilt, may at the hour of his death, no longer counterfeited, be transformed into another attempt at reformation. But this one is more ambiguous than those extending from Hal's first soliloquy promising to redeem the time to his father's dying plea for divine forgiveness: "How I came by the crown O God forgive" (2H4 IV.v.218).[2] By prince or whore Falstaff is constantly reproached to repent, to remember his day of reckoning. His friends often sound as though they were repeating the conventional pieties of Thomas Lupset in his *Waye of Dyenge Well* (1541) or Robert Parsons's *The First Booke of the Christian Exercise, Appartayning to Resolution* (1582), in which chapter 8 is entitled "The daye of deathe Of what opinion and feelinge we shalbe, touching these matters, at the tyme of our deathe,"[3] or Gaspar Loarte's *The Exercise of a Christian Life* (1579). The moral exhortations Loarte insistently makes are typical:

take then a zelous and feruent desire to liue a new here after, and striue
to get other new behauiours, & to liue far otherwise than thou hast done
tofore. . . . Eschewe al occasions of sinne, especially the companie of
wicked men, but muche more of women, such as may prouoke thee to
noughtines, and geue thee loose and lewd example. . . . Thou must flye suche
places where God is customably offended, as be dising houses, tauernes,
dauncing schooles, and such like. . . . Thou must take hede of al excesse in
eating, drinking, sleping and clothing, and indeuour thy self to obserue a
mediocritie and temperance in eche of them.[4]

These books of Renaissance meditation, among others, Catholic and
Protestant, published in numerous editions in fifteenth- and sixteenth-century
England, all explored like good-conduct books the ways in which the devout
or those whose faith was more fragile should prepare for a final reckoning.[5]
The admonitions of sin, death, and judgment were so common as Renaissance
homilies that an English audience could have warned Falstaff as well as Hal or
Doll. "Live now as you will wish to have lived when you come to that sorrowful
day" is the kind of exhortation that runs through Parsons's *First Book*. He would
find a curious moral ally in Doll: "when wilt thou leave fighting a' days and foining
a' nights, and begin to patch up thine old body for heaven?" (2H4 II.iv.231–33).
Hal, newly crowned, is only more austerely puritanical in chastising the Falstaff
he abandons: "Leave gormandizing, know the grave doth gape / For thee thrice
wider than for other men" (V.v.53–54).

For Falstaff, playing the penitent is a subject for infinite amusement.
In plays which find their moral center in redeeming the time, repentance,
reformation, and reckoning, Hal and Falstaff can counterpoint their pledges.
"I'll so offend, to make offense a skill, / Redeeming time when men think
least I will" (1H4 I.ii.216–17) is Hal's first promise to himself and to the
audience as he rationalizes his manipulation of his tavern friends both to learn
about the potential corruption of fleshly indulgence and to prepare for a public
apotheosis in good time. The language may be spiritual, but the hours of study,
more active than contemplative, are more for his brilliant political future than
for the salvation necessary for his eternal life. For Falstaff, on the other hand,
the language of moral reformation in *I* and *2 Henry IV* carries economic, not
political or spiritual ambiguities. Hal, ironically amused, notes the rapidity
with which Falstaff transforms his pledge to "give over this life, . . . and I do
not, I am a villain, I'll be damned for never a king's son in Christendom" (1H4
I.ii.95–97) into a plan to take purses at Gadshill: "I see a good amendment of
life in thee, from praying to pursetaking" (102–103). Falstaff's instant moral
defense is that it is "no sin for a man to labor in his vocation" (104–105). His
pun on vocation as profession and religious conversion is echoed at Shrewsbury
when Hal tells Falstaff to prepare for battle and say his prayers, for he "owest

God a death" (V.i.126). Falstaff's rejoinder picks up the homophonic pun on debt, as he is determined that this is not the day to prepare to die well or at all: "'Tis not due yet. I would be loath to pay him before his day" (127–28). Let those who value honor do so. "A trim reckoning" (135). Playful language then can redeem all moral questions.

One of the deliberately unresolved mysteries of The Henriad is whether Falstaff does finally make a good end, for we have only the Hostess's not unbiased judgment that "'A made a finer end, and went away and it had been any christom child" (H5 II.iii. 10–12). An audience comes to this scene after another one of public confession and repentance so carefully orchestrated that the broken and uncertain fragments of Falstaff's only private meditation are made more resonantly convincing. Scroop, Cambridge, and Gray, trapped into confessing their treason and sentencing themselves to death, seem relieved that they have been caught. Each in turn thanks God for "the discovery of most dangerous treason" (II.ii.162), asks for divine and monarchial forgiveness, and seem almost to parody the assertion of Lupset and others that in *ars moriendi* "this dyenge well is in effecte to dye gladlye":[6]

Cam[bridge:] But God be thanked for prevention,
Which [I] in sufferance heartily will rejoice,
Beseeching God, and you, to pardon me. (158–60)

The traitors, "poor miserable wretches" (178), are borne off to their execution at the moment when Falstaff also dies, betrayed by his king, who, says the Hostess, "kill'd his heart" (II.i.88). The perspectives of betrayer betrayed, parodied and balanced, continue as a Lancastrian legacy from the time of Bolingbroke and Northumberland in *Richard II*.

For a brief interlude, almost outside the time of Henry V, as Henry dispatches his traitors and exultantly moves to France "to busy giddy minds / With foreign quarrels" (2H4 IV.v.213–14), Shakespeare elusively distances the dramatic scene of Falstaff's death by recessing it into an interior moment, a scene-within-a-scene and then within that a memory-within-a-memory. Those last friends of Falstaff—Hostess, Boy, Pistol, Nym, and Bardolph—try to recapture Falstaff's deathbed hour as a last memory. But so equivocal is their disagreement that an audience cannot even be sure who was there besides the Hostess, the Boy, and Bardolph. Nym has heard another account of Falstaff's death: "They say he cried out of sack" (II.iii.27). But who are these anonymous bedside witnesses whose story is as quickly challenged as are the contradictory reports of those who now botch the telling of their witnessed accounts? The distorted perspective of each seems finally to return the memory of Falstaff only to the security of the theater audience which can only intuit the manner of his death.

The design of the scene that is played is constructed from ambiguities of time, imagery, and theme inherent in the history plays: order/disorder, bawdy/sentimental, innocence/experience, youth/age, physical/spiritual, salvation/damnation, time/sea, life/death. Falstaff's dying like his living remains beyond precise description or adequate dramatization, imbedded in the structure of its telling. The Hostess, as the primary witness, does not herself understand the import of her account. In the confusion, distancing, and failure of Falstaff's last story lies its dramatic achievement.

To the extent that there are facts, they suggest that an emaciated Falstaff developed a sudden sweat and a high fever and died shortly after midnight. Although delirious, he seemed aware that he was on his deathbed. He apparently saw a flea on Bardolph's nose and said it was a black soul burning in hell. He inveighed against sack and prostitutes whom he called devils incarnate. He talked about the Whore of Babylon. He fumbled with his sheets, smiled at his fingertips, apparently mumbled something about green fields, called out "God" three or four times. As his feet grew cold, he asked the Hostess for more bedclothes and died.

If Falstaff is making a determined effort to die well by attempting a deathbed repentance, it is one only his Maker could be sure of. No character has been advised more insistently to remember his end, nor promised more persistently to do so when the time was right. Yet at the moment of Falstaff's dying the Hostess urges upon him as a dubious theological comfort not to think of God: "I hop'd there was no need to trouble himself with such thoughts yet" (II.iii.21–22). Her words express Falstaff's long-standing determination to postpone any day of spiritual reckoning. Nonetheless, Falstaff may be attempting a meditation in the Renaissance manner of *ars moriendi*, perhaps as broken and as incomplete as the narrated account of it. Whether spiritually efficacious or not remains beyond the limits of the play. But the dramatic, ritualistic, and psychological appropriateness of such a spiritual moment fulfills the design of Falstaff's creation and existence.

The paradoxical symmetry of Falstaff's life has always been mythic, not realistic,[7] as it embodies rituals, folk tales, and festivals. For a man who lives out of all time, the hours of his birth and death are recorded as nowhere else in Shakespeare. As he tells the Chief Justice, "My Lord, I was born about three of the clock in the afternoon, with a white head and something a round belly" (2H4 I.ii.187–89). Born allegedly an old, fat man, he dies "ev'n just between twelve and one, ev'n at the turning o' th' tide" (H5 II.iii. 12–13) like a "christom child," newly christened and now shrouded in his white baptismal clothes. From corrupted old age he moves in death to appearing as an innocent child, even as the play returns to the first time an audience saw Falstaff as he emerged at noon from bed in *1 Henry IV*. The first mythic definition of Falstaff is reinforced in his death scene. It is, as Hal says, superfluous to ask

Falstaff the time of day, for he has nothing to do with these symbols of order, political responsibility, or personal self-discipline. It is also superfluous to ask the Hostess how she could have been certain when high tide occurred on the Thames that last night. Like the fertility festival and the ritual games of the purged scapegoat, this moment is haunted by an aura of folklore and superstition. It was an old English belief, according to Sir James Frazer, held along the east coast of England that most deaths occur as the tide ebbs, a natural "melancholy emblem of failure, of weakness, and of death."[8] An audience would not have known which turning of the tide, or which twelve and one without a sense of the symbolic rightness that would remove the verbal ambiguity of the Hostess's sense of time and tide. The death of the dubiously legitimate king, Henry IV, who dies repentant in the Jerusalem Chamber as the Thames "thrice flowed, no ebb between" (2H4 IV.iv.125) parallels that of player-king Falstaff, who once mocked him for Hal's amusement in Eastcheap and now dies in Eastcheap no longer playing penitent. These balanced moments suggest again Christian rituals intertwined with folk tales, from the death of newly christened babies to those of kings and errant knights.[9]

If the Hostess, forgiving soul, believes that Falstaff is in Arthur's bosom, she is secure in her belief that Falstaff has not been judged and damned. It makes little difference whether she means the Christian heaven of Abraham's bosom as defined in Luke 16:22 or the pagan heaven of King Arthur's Avalon. And if Henry IV's belief in the prophecy that he would die in Jerusalem on his "voyage to the Holy Land, / To wash this blood off from my guilty hand" (R2 V.vi.49–50) can be accommodated by a quibble on Jerusalem Chamber, the Hostess's malapropism should be no less certain in its intent. Falstaff has always been more a practitioner of his view of *ars vivendi* than *ars moriendi*, so if the conduct of his life has been at best morally ambiguous, then its appropriate ending would be spiritually uncertain. Medieval and Renaissance meditative rituals serve both arts for him. At Shrewsbury he prefers catechisms on honor and comic resurrections that leave the body intact; rather than the grinning honor of dead Sir Walter Blunt, he declares, "Give me life, which if I can save, so" (1H4 V.iii.59–60). Salvation is a matter of preserving the body in time present. When at Eastcheap he promises, "I must give over this life, and I will give it over" (I.ii.95–96), the words would suit a Puritan preacher better than does their context in the midst of battle. "But to counterfeit dying, when a man thereby liveth, is to be no counterfeit, but the true and perfect image of life indeed" (V.iv.1 17–19).

One of Falstaff's most agile verbal games is that in his profane parody of the language of *ars vivendi* he plays a secular *ars moriendi*. As Hal tells Poins, "He will give the devil his due" (I.ii.119). He constantly protests his fear of damnation, of being corrupted by Hal even if he were a saint; he delights in refuting the charge that he is "that villainous abominable misleader of youth,

Falstaff, that old white-bearded Sathan" (II.iv.462–64). He wishes, he says, that he could have been a puritan weaver so he could sing penitential psalms. He declares to the Chief Justice that he lost his voice "hallowing and singing of anthems'" (2H4 I.ii. 189–90). Whether he is playing Lord of Misrule, Antic, Miles Gloriosus, Comic Satan, or Corrupter of Youth, his archetypal roles make a travesty of the traditional posture of the penitent who must think of his sins and prepare for the hour of his dying. Robert Parsons indeed writes his First Booke of the Christian Exercise for readers "so carelesse, or so carnallie geeuen" that like Falstaff they would hardly do more than glance at his opening pages. He asks, therefore, only for their patience while he tries to persuade them of the error of their ways and so to move them to the "necessarie resolution, of leauinge vanities to serue God."[10] Falstaff knows Parsons's text—and Lupset's, Bunny's, and Luis de Granada's—and quotes them as liberally and as cavalierly as he does Scripture, whenever they accommodate his chameleon-like purposes of serving himself while pleasing a prince in whose earthly kingdom he has hopes of long-lasting reward. He will paraphrase a meditative counselor like Parsons to share a moment of self-mockery with his prince: "What are thow the better now to haue liued in credit with the world? in fauour of princes? exalted of men?"[11] No Renaissance leader of devotional meditation would have had the imagination to concoct for a deathbed repentance the moral inventory available to Falstaff: lying, cowardice, avarice, vanity, gluttony, drunkenness, sloth, thievery, misusing the king's press, fornication. But their ponderous spiritual guides would also have neglected to point out the love and loyalty, the wit and imagination, and the comic genius that redeem Falstaff's living.

If Falstaff's deathbed scene were simply to conclude a dissolute life as Hal, his brothers, or the Chief Justice would have it, Falstaff would fall to his prayers and seek the grace Henry urges in his repudiation of him—"How ill white hairs becomes a fool and jester!" (2H4 V.v.48). What for Luis de Granada is a metaphor of consequence for a wasted life has been Falstaff's whole reality in Eastcheap, but the Shakespearean dramatic moment of Falstaff's dying will not yield transparent spiritual conclusions to Luis de Granada's easy rhetorical questions:

> If a waiefaringe man, hauinge but one farthinge in his purse, shoulde enter
> into an inne, and placinge him selfe downe at the table, shoulde require
> of the host to bringe in Partridges, Capons, Phesauntes, and all other
> delicates, that maie be founde in the howse, and shoulde suppe with verie
> great pleasure, and contentation, neuer remembringe that at the last there
> must come a time of accompt: who woulde not take this fellowe, either
> for a iester, or for a verie foole? Now what greater folie or madnes can be
> deuised, than for men to geue them selues so looselye to all kindes of vices,
> and to sleepe so sowndlie in them, without euer remembringe, that shortly

after at their departinge out of their Inne, there shall be required of them a
verie strayt and particular accompte of all their dissolute and wicked lyfe?[12]

If Falstaff denies Luis de Granada's economic and moral premises, which are
also at the heart of the Lancastrian political enterprises, his dying moments are
brilliantly poised between accepting and rejecting those spiritual conclusions.

The undramatized scene of Falstaff's death has been ruthlessly anticipated
in *2 Henry IV* as his voice modulates from robust, zesty parody to a genuine
fear of encroaching death—"Peace, good Doll, do not speak like a death's head,
do not bid me remember mine end" (2H4 II.iv.234–35). At his end he appears
to be a shrunken, dying old man, no longer the maker and embodiment of
vital language and consummate comic actor. No longer wittily supporting his
roleplaying as the devil incarnate, his language, incoherent and disconnected,
is reduced to conventional religious platitudes, traditional pieties, and pleas for
more blankets. No longer able to hide behind the fantasies of invented language,
he cannot counterfeit kings of England nor play Lord of Misrule. He cannot
turn diseases to self-serving commodity or spiritual utility. And he is no longer
"the cause that wit is in other men" (I.ii. 10).

As a great performer in need of an audience, Falstaff has never before had
an introspective or meditative moment which might be called personal. His
soliloquies on honor in *1 Henry IV* or on sack in *2 Henry IV* are essentially public
moments, the comedian indulging himself with the theater audience rather than
his stage audience. Only in a play in which he does not exist and on his deathbed
does Falstaff have a ritualistic moment of meditation in which he is only partly
aware of those around him and in which his mind turns inward and backward
in memory.

Just before his death Falstaff may meditatively engage what Ignatius Loyola
calls "seeing the spot," recalling the scene upon which one is meditating with
the immediacy of actually being present in it.[13] This conventional "composition
of place," which begins a meditation, would invoke the first of the "three powers
of the soul"—memory, understanding, and will.[14] Falstaff may remember a
romantic moment when he picked flowers in a green meadow, although the text
remains as brilliantly insecure as the telling of the babbling. That lost innocence
bears no resemblance to other memories recollected in Shallow's orchard of those
nights when old classmates recall having heard the chimes at midnight. Other
reminiscences are also unambiguous emblems of his lifesack and women; but
those memories seem now touched with the recognition of some kind of moral or
spiritual understanding, the second stage of the meditative process. Now Falstaff
no longer cries out for sack but against it, and he calls the women of Eastcheap
"dev'ls incarnate" (H5 II.iii.31–32). The Hostess's well-meaning denial, based on
the fact that he "could never abide carnation" (33), was repudiated from the first
when Falstaff admits that he would enjoy the sun only if it were "a fair hot wench

in flame-color'd taffata" (1H4 I.ii.9–10). The identification of his whores with the Whore of Babylon may suggest that Falstaff is thinking of the Apocalypse in Rev. 17:3–6: "and I saw a woman sit upon a scarlet colored beast. . . . And the woman was arrayed in purple and scarlet colour." Or perhaps as a dubiously reformed Puritan he is attacking the Catholic Church, as Edmund Bunny would have him do in his meditation. The Hostess's possible pun on "rheum" for Rome—"but then he was rheumatic" (H5 II.iii.38)—may reinforce the allusion without clarifying Falstaff's "understanding." Seeing a flea land on Bardolph's nose may be only the last flicker of the endless jokes at his expense—"his face is Lucifer's privy kitchen" (2H4 II.iv.333)—or a deathbed prophecy of Bardolph's impending sacrilege and punishment.

Is Falstaff like Hal seeking a reformation that will glitter o'er his fault as he tries without parody to redeem the time? The fragmented and disconnected structure of his last words, the ambiguity of his observations, and the malapropisms of the Hostess deny resolution as Falstaff may drift to the third and final step in the meditative process, the engaging of the affections, or the will, which traditionally concludes with a colloquy. A meditation on *ars moriendi* would appropriately end in an invocation or prayer to God. And Falstaff calls out to God. But what does he mean? Is this only a feverish cry of fear? Is he trying to make an act of contrition and asking for divine forgiveness? Is this the cry of a man who believes that he has been abandoned by God—as by friend and king—in his last hour? Is one perhaps to hear an elusive echo of Christ's last words on the Cross, a moment Renaissance spiritual advisors urged for deathbed meditations; as, for example, Thomas More in *Four Last Things*: "But whan the poynt approched in which his sacred soule shold depart out of his blessed bodye, at that pointe he cryed loude once or twice to his father in heuen"?[15] Luis de Granada in his *ars moriendi* exercise for Wednesday night would be secure in his spiritual interpretation of this colloquy, but Shakespeare's audience is denied that certainty:

> And as well herein, as in the other thinges, thou hast to consider what great greiffe and anguishe of mynde the sycke person shall then abide in callinge to minde his wicked and synfull life: and how gladly he wishethe at that time that he had taken a better waie: and what an awstere kinde of lyfe he woulde then determine to leade, if he might haue time to doe the same: and how fayne he woulde then enforce himselfe to call vpon almightie God, and to desier him of helpe and succour. Howbeit the verie paine, greife, and continuall increasinge of his sickenes and death will scarcely permitte him so to doe.[16]

The Hostess is equally certain that she knows, but she urges Falstaff to get his mind off death and an afterlife. This, the only time any one tells Falstaff not to worry about his end, physical or spiritual, would be an ironic comfort, indeed, if Luis de Granada's precepts were attended to:

The first stroke wherewith death is wont to strike, is the feare of death. Suerlie this is a very great anguishe vnto him that is in loue with his lyfe: and this forewarninge is such a great greife vnto a man, that oftentimes his carnall friendes doe vse to dissemble it, and will not haue the sicke man to beleue it, least it shoulde vexe and disquiet him: and this they will doe sometimes although it be to the preiudice and destruction of his miserable sowle.[17]

The Hostess's spiritual purposes may be a miscalculation, but this is her finest moment, not just in the innocence of her double entendres, the humor of her verbal blunders, or her sentimental recollecting of Falstaff's death. If ever there was a woman who had been sorely abused and put upon and "borne, and .. been fubb'd off" (2H4 II.i.34), it is she who has been victimized by Falstaff, who has indeed "handled" her most outrageously. Yet at the end she loves and comforts, forgives by forgetting. There is in her a Christian charity starkly missing in Falstaff's monarch. Her ministrations may also be reminiscent of those of Socrates' friends at the onset of the death of their companion, condemned as another alleged villainous, abominable misleader of youth and a threat to the established political order: "I put my hand into the bed and felt them, and they were as cold as any stone; then I felt to his knees, and so up'ard and up'ard, and all was as cold as any stone" (H5 II.iii.23–26). At the beginning of his "Remembrance of Death" in *Four Last Things*, Thomas More recalls Plato's account of Socrates' death in the Phaedo—"For some of the olde famous philosophers, whan thei wer demaunded what facultie philosophy was, answerd that it was the meditacion or exercise of death"—and then urges us to "fantasy" our own death in a detailed vision that may bear resemblance to some of the Hostess's recollection: "lying in thy bedde, . . . thy nose sharping, thy legges coling, thy fingers fimbling, . . . and thy death drawing on." Even if Shakespeare is recalling More, the unintended bawdy is characteristically the Hostess's own in gesture and simile. Falstaff's stones are cold. Desire no longer outlives performance, as Poins once ridiculed the old man. And his nose, now as sharp as a pen, makes Falstaff's gloriously hyperbolic epithets of Hal—"you starveling, you [eel]skin, you dried neat's tongue, you bull's pizzle, you stockfish" (IH4 II.iv. 244–45)—an inverted echo mocked by death, which has finally dethroned surrogate king and father.

The Hostess's vivid recollection of the approaching coldness of death suggests the unrelenting descriptions constantly set out by Loarte, Parsons, Bunny, and Luis de Granada as they urge one to meditate on the moment of dying with a calculatedly precise enumeration. If Shakespeare had their admonitions in mind, he has transformed the macabre and morbid into a bittersweet and humorous account worthy of Falstaff's vital comic spirit. He has detached the spiritual implications and left instead only the poignant corporeal reality, as the scene moves from meditation and remembrance to those who witness or learn of the event with limited understanding and qualified affection. As Parsons lugubriously imagines the inevitable moment:

Imagine, what the violent mortyfiinge of all the partes together will doe. For we see that first the sowle is driuen by death to leaue the extreamest partes, as the toes, feete and fyngers: then the legges and armes, and so consequentlye one parte dyeth after an other, vntill lyfe be restrained onlye to the harte, which holdeth out longest as the principall parte, but yet must finallye be constrained to render it selue.[19]

Not so, however, with Falstaff. His heart was fracted and corroborate and killed first.

This final creating of a character thematically and dramatically dead at the end of *2 Henry IV* is thus theatrically and structurally achieved through a transformation of an ars moriendi meditation composed of the fragments of the disintegrating comic world of The Henriad. It is a memorial to a real and mythic character whose essential ambiguity remains as mysteriously allusive in dying as in living. The Shakespearean mode of dramatization is far more affective in its indirectness than any threatening exhortation of a Renaissance spiritual counselor. For us who are invited to meditate on Falstaff the loss of Falstaffian life leads to a diminution of theatrical richness. Consolation is not to be found in any recognition that Falstaff tried to die well.

In the Hostess's disjointed narrative it is possible that some in Shakespeare's audience might recall some of the popular block wood cuts of the *Ars Moriendi* that circulated in hundreds of editions and unknown numbers of copies throughout the fifteenth and sixteenth centuries.[20] In the Editio Princeps an emaciated Moriens lies naked in bed with a blanket pulled up to his waist and his arms extended over it. He is variously surrounded by friends, family, servants, doctors, and nurses as well as grotesque little demons.[21] Such an engraving precedes Luis de Granada's Wednesday night meditation on *ars moriendi* in *Of Prayer, and Meditation*. To a Renaissance audience the realistic and the symbolic, the mythic or the allegorical could co-exist in art and could perhaps be recalled in this traditional mode as a model for the moment that Shakespeare is dramatizing through narration. The Hostess is surely an attentive nurse; Boy, a loyal young servant. Bardolph would have made a good devil; he has been advised of that often enough. Possibly at the end the shrunken Falstaff might, in addition to all his other mythic and traditional roles, unwittingly adopt that of Moriens. But whereas Moriens is shown to have died well as his soul, a young child, leaves his mouth and ascends, we are left only with the Hostess's sentimental assurance of Falstaff's "finer end."

The Hostess's lament brings only a brief truce to erstwhile companions who were at swordpoints earlier that evening. Falstaff's memory now yields to their economic self-serving calculation and suspicion even before the scene is over. By the day of Agincourt his name is forgotten. Swept up in the nationalistic fervor of war against France, this ironic band of brothers shogs off to turn a profit in a world where thievery and whoring have at least moral and mortal consequences.

Nym and Bardolph are hanged by order of the King, and Nell dies disease-ridden "i' the spittle / Of a malady of France" (V.i.82–83). And there is none to mourn their passing who would argue that they died well.

NOTES

1. Quotations are taken from *The Riverside Shakespeare*, ed. G. Blakemore Evans (Boston: Houghton Mifflin, 1974).

2. For a persuasive exploration of the parallelisms in the Henry IV plays and the two historical tetralogies, see Sherman H. Hawkins, "Henry IV: The Structural Problem Revisited," SQ 33 (1982):278–301.

3. The work of the English Jesuit Parsons was modified by the Puritan Edmund Bunny in *A Book of Christian Exercise* (1584), but with his admonitions on the Christian necessity for repentance in preparation for death virtually unchanged.

4. Gaspar Loarte, *The Exercise of a Christian Life*, trans. James Sancer (pseudo. Stephen Brinkley), (Rheims, 1584), pp. 8–10.

5. When Caxton translated in 1490 the early fifteenth-century anonymous *Latin Tractus* as the *Ars Moriendi*, or the *Crafte of Dying Well*, he was making available a text that was to become immensely popular over the next two centuries. For a full discussion of the tradition of *Ars Moriendi* in England during the sixteenth century, see Nancy Lee Beatty, *The Craft of Dying: A Study in the Literary Tradition of the 'Ars Moriendi' in England* (New Haven: Yale Univ. Press, 1970), chs. 2 and 4. See also Louis L. Martz, *The Poetry of Meditation* (New Haven: Yale Univ. Press, 1954), pp. 135–44, and Sister Mary Catharine O'Connor, *The Art of Dying Well: The Development of the Ars Moriendi* (New York: Columbia Univ. Press, 1942).

6. Thomas Lupset, *The Waye of Dyenge Well* (London, 1541), fol. 1lv.

7. Morgann's *Essay on the Dramatic Character of Sir John Falstaff*, ed. William Arthur Gill (London, 1912), p. 184.

8. Sir James Frazer, *The Golden Bough* (New York: Macmillan, 1942), abridged edn., pp. 34–35. Noted in J. I. M. Stewart, *Character and Motive in Shakespeare* (London: Longman, Green, 1949), p. 137.

9. Philip Williams, "The Birth and Death of Falstaff Reconsidered," SQ 8 (1957):362.

10. Robert Parsons, *The First Booke of the Christian Exercise* (Rouen, 1582), pp. 8, 9, 14, 25, and passim.

11. Parsons, p. 107.

12. Luis de Granada, *Of Prayer, and Meditation*, trans. Richard Hopkins (Paris, 1582), fol. 188r. An English edition was published in London in 1592.

13. "Thou must understand, that they are in such wise to be be meditated, as though they happed euen in that instant before thine eyes, in the selfe same place where thou art, or within thy soule: or otherwise imagining thou were in the very places where suche thinges happed, if haply this waies thou shalt feele better deuotion" (Loarte, p. 67).

14. W. H. Longridge, *The Spiritual Exercises of Saint Ignatius of Loyola* (London: Robert Scott, 1919), pp. 52–57.

15. *The Workes of Thomas More . . . wrytten by him in the Englysh tonge*, ed. William Rastell (London, 1557), p. 78.

16. Luis de Granada, fols. 183V-84r.

17. Luis de Granada, fol. 190r.

18. Rastell, pp. 77–78.

19. Parsons, p. 102. Edmund Bunny's account (*A Book of Christian Exercise,* [London, 1584], p. 90) is essentially the same. Luis de Granada (fol. 184') is no less explicit in his urging our attention:

> Consider then also those last accidentes, and panges of the sicknes, (which be as it were messingers of death) how fearfull and terrible they be. How at that time the sicke mans breast panteth: his voyce waxeth hoarce: his feete begynnge to die: his knees to waxe colde, and stiffe: his nostrels ronne out: his eies sincke into his head: his countenace looketh pale and wanne: his tonge faultereth, and is not able to doe his office; finally by reason of the hast of the departure awaye of the sowle out of the bodie, all his senses are sore vexed, and troubled, and they doe vtterlie leese their force, and virtue.

20. O'Connor, pp. 114–71. Of nearly 300 extant copies of block books, Sister Mary Catharine saw sixty-one of the *Ars Moriendi* in twenty-one printings from thirteen distinct sets of blocks. The series of eleven block prints depicting Moriens's deathbed temptations were printed in England by Wynkyn de Worde in the early sixteenth century and were copied and modeled with many adaptations in costume and character until Shakespeare's day, but always, as in the Wednesday night illustration in Luis de Granada's *Of Prayer, and Meditation*, with Moriens at the heart of each print in each set.

21. In block cut I a demon with a long nose hooked upward leans menacingly over Moriens. In VIII there is a representation of the mouth of hell, signified by flames with three figures writhing in agony. In IX the long-nosed demon appears with another devil pointing to a cellar where a boy is stealing a jug of wine from one of four casks—memories of past pleasures now to be forsaken? In X a man extends a scroll to Moriens "Ne intendas amicis"—"Do not concern yourself with your friends," *The Ars Moriendi*, ed. W. Harry Rylands (London: Wyman and Sons, 1881).

1998—Harold Bloom. "Henry V," from *Shakespeare: The Invention of the Human*

Harold Bloom is the longtime Sterling Professor of the Humanities at Yale University. He is the author of more than 30 books, the most influential of which are *The Anxiety of Influence, A Map of Misreading, The Western Canon, Shakespeare: The Invention of the Human,* and *Genius: A Mosaic of One Hundred Exemplary Creative Minds.*

This brilliant and subtle work will always be popular; I could say "for the wrong reasons," except that all reasons for Shakespeare's eternal popularity are correct, one way or another. And yet *Henry V* is clearly a lesser drama than the two parts of *Henry IV.* Falstaff is gone, and King Henry V, matured into the mastery of power, is less interesting than the ambivalent Prince Hal, whose potential was more varied. The great Irish poet W. B. Yeats made the classic comment on this aesthetic falling away in his *Ideas of Good and Evil*:

> [Henry V] has the gross vices, the coarse nerves, of one who is to rule among violent people, and he is so little "too friendly" to his friends that he bundles them out of door when their time is over. He is as remorseless and undistinguished as some natural force, and the finest thing in his play is the way his old companions fall out of it broken-hearted or on their way to the gallows.

I read the play that Yeats read, but much Shakespeare scholarship reads otherwise. *Henry V* is now most widely known because of the films quarried from it by Laurence Olivier and Kenneth Branagh. Both movies are lively, patriotic romps, replete with exuberant bombast, provided by Shakespeare himself, with what degree of irony we cannot quite tell but are free to surmise:

> We few, we happy few, we band of brothers;
> For he to-day that sheds his blood with me
> Shall be my brother; be he ne'er so vile
> This day shall gentle his condition:
> And gentlemen in England, now a-bed,
> Shall think themselves accurs'd they were not here,
> And hold their manhoods cheap whiles any speaks
> That fought with us upon Saint Crispin's day.
>   [IV.iii.60–67]

That is the King, just before the battle of Agincourt. He is very stirred; so are we; but neither we nor he believes a word he says. The common soldiers fighting with their monarch are not going to become gentlemen, let alone nobles, and "the ending of the world" is a rather grand evocation for an imperialist land grab that did not long survive Henry V's death, as Shakespeare's audience knew too well. Hazlitt, with characteristic eloquence, joins Yeats as the true exegete of Henry V and his play:

> He was a hero, that is, he was ready to sacrifice his own life for the pleasure of destroying thousands of other lives. . . . How then do we like him? We like him in the play. There he is a very amiable monster, a very splendid pageant. . . .

his cannot be bettered, but is that all Prince Hal matured into: an amiable monster, a splendid pageant? Yes; for this, Falstaff was rejected, Bardolph was hanged, and a great education in wit was partly thrown away. Shakespeare's ironic insight remains highly relevant; power keeps its habit through the ages. Our nation's Henry V (some might say) was John Fitzgerald Kennedy, who gave us the Bay of Pigs and the enhancement of our Vietnam adventure. Some scholars may moralize and historicize until they are purple with pride, but they will not persuade us that Shakespeare (playwright *and* man) preferred his amiable monster to the genius of Falstaff, and his splendid pageant to the varied and vital *Henry IV* plays.

In *Henry V,* the two religious caterpillars, Canterbury and Ely, finance the French wars so as to save the Church's secular estates from royal confiscation; both praise Henry's piety, and he is careful to tell us how Christian a king he is. At Agincourt, he prays to God for victory, promising yet more contrite tears for his father's murder of Richard II, and he then proceeds to order the throats cut of all the French prisoners, a grace duly performed. Some recent attention has been devoted to this slaughter, but it will not alter Henry V's popularity with both scholars and moviegoers. Henry is brutally shrewd and shrewdly brutal, qualities necessary for his greatness as a king. The historical Henry V, dead at thirty-five, was an enormous success in power and war, and undoubtedly was the strongest English king before Henry VIII. Shakespeare has no single attitude toward Henry V, in the play, which allows you to achieve your own perspective upon the rejecter of Falstaff. My stance I derive from Yeats, whose views on Shakespeare and the state deliciously share little with old-style scholarly idealists and new-wave cultural materialists:

> Shakespeare cared little for the State, the source of all our judgments, apart from its shows and splendors, its turmoils and battles, its flamings-out of the uncivilized heart.

When Shakespeare thought of the state, he remembered first that it had murdered Christopher Marlowe, tortured and broken Thomas Kyd, and branded the unbreakable Ben Jonson. All that and more underlies the great lament in Sonnet 66:

> And right perfection wrongfully disgraced,
> And strength by limping sway disabled,
> And art made tongue-tied by authority.

The censor, external and internal, haunted Shakespeare, made cautious by Marlowe's terrible end. I agree, therefore, with Yeats's conclusion, which is that *Henry V,* for all its exuberance, is essentially ironic:

> Shakespeare watched Henry V not indeed as he watched the greater souls in the visionary procession, but cheerfully, as one watches some

handsome spirited horse, and he spoke his tale, as he spoke all tales, with tragic irony.

It is so much Henry V's play that the irony is not immediately evident: there is no substantial role for anyone except the warrior-king. Falstaff's death, narrated by Mistress Quickly, does not bring that great spirit upon stage, and ancient Pistol is only a shadow of his leader. Fluellen, the other comic turn, is a fine characterization but limited, except perhaps where Shakespeare slyly employs the Welsh captain to give us a properly ironic analogue for the rejection of Falstaff:

> *Flu.* I think it is in Macedon where Alexander is porn. I tell you, captain, if you look in the maps of the 'orld, I warrant you sail find, in the comparisons between Macedon and Monmouth, that the situations, look you, is both alike. There is a river in Macedon, and there is also moreover a river at Monmouth: it is called Wye at Monmouth; but it is out of my prains what is the name of the other river; but 'tis all one, 'tis alike as my fingers is to my fingers, and there is salmons in both. If you mark Alexander's life well, Harry of Monmouth's life is come after it indifferent well; for there is figures in all things. Alexander, God knows, and you know, in his rages, and his furies, and his wraths, and his cholers, and his moods, and his displeasures, and his indignations, and also being a little intoxicates in his prains, did, in his ales and his angers, look you, kill his best friend, Cleitus.
> *Gow.* Our King is not like him in that: he never killed any of his friends.
> *Flu.* It is not well done, mark you now, to take the tales out of my mouth, ere it is made and finished. I speak but in the figures and comparisons of it: as Alexander killed his friend Cleitus, being in his ales and his cups, so also Harry Monmouth, being in his wits and his good judgments, turned away the fat knight with the great-belly doublet: he was full of jests, and gipes, and knaveries, and mocks; I have forgot his name.
> *Gow.* Sir John Falstaff.
>
>   [IV.vii.23–53]

The drunken Alexander murdered his good friend Cleitus; Shakespeare ironically reminds us that Hal, "being in his right wits and his good judgments," "killed" his best friend, the man "full of jests, and gipes, and knaveries, and mocks." One great conqueror or "pig" is much like another, as Fluellen argues. *Henry V* certainly is not Falstaff's play; it belongs to "this star of England," whose sword was made by Fortune. Yet its ironies are palpable and frequent, and transcend my own fierce Falstaffianism. Urging his troops into the breach at Harfleur, King Henry had extolled their fathers as "so many Alexanders."

Distancing is not so much bewildering in *Henry V* as it is suave and beguiling. Henry V is an admirable politician, a brave basher of heads in battle, a peerless charismatic. With Shakespeare we are delighted by him, and with Shakespeare we are rather chilled also, but carefully so; we are not estranged from Falstaff's brilliant pupil. In some ways, King Henry's hypocrisy is more acceptable than Prince Hal's, since the warrior-king is in no way a clean and clever lad doing his best to get on. Henry V has England and the English, captures France and its princess, if not the French, and will die young like Alexander, another conqueror with little left to conquer. Personal fidelities are shrugged off by so ideal a monarch; Bardolph hangs, and perhaps Falstaff would too, had Shakespeare risked that comic splendor on the French expedition. Something in us, attending or reading *Henry V,* is carefully rendered beyond care.

Henry is given to lamenting that as king he is not free, yet the former Hal is himself a considerable ironist, and has learned one of Falstaff's most useful lessons: Keep your freedom by seeing through every idea of order and code of behavior, whether chivalrous or moral or religious. Shakespeare does not let us locate Hal/Henry V's true self; a king is necessarily something of a counterfeit, and Henry is a great king. Hamlet, infinitely complex, becomes a different role with each strong performer. Henry V is veiled rather than complex, but the pragmatic consequence is that no actor resembles another in the part. *Henry V or What You Will* might as well be the play's title. Shakespeare sees to it that even the most pungent ironies cannot resist the stance of the chorus, who adores "the warlike Harry," truly the model or "mirror of all Christian kings." Even if you wanted to hear duplicity in that, the chorus will charm you with: "A little touch of Harry in the night."

Shakespeare need not remind us that Falstaff, vastly intelligent and witty beyond all measure, was desperately in love with Hal. No one could fall in love with Henry V, but no one altogether could resist him either. If he is a monster, he is more than amiable. He is a great Shakespearean personality—hardly a Hamlet or a Falstaff, but more than a Hotspur. Henry V has the glamour of an Alexander who has staked everything upon one military enterprise, but this is an Alexander endowed with inwardness, keenly exploited for its pragmatic advantages. In Henry's vision, the growing inner self requires an expanding kingdom, and France is the designated realm for growth. Henry IV's guilt of usurpation and regicide is to be expiated by conquest, and the exploitation and rejection of Falstaff is to be enhanced by a new sense of the glory of Mars and kingship. The transcended fathers fade away in the dazzle of royal apotheosis. Ironies persist, but what are ironies in so flamboyant a pageant? More than Shakespeare's heart was with Falstaff; Falstaff is mind, while Henry is but policy. Yet policy makes for a superb pageant, and something in every one of us responds to the joyousness of *Henry V.* Militarism, brutality, pious hypocrisy all are outshone by England's charismatic hero-king. This is all to the good for the play, and Shakespeare sees to it that we will remember his play's limits.

—ᵃᵃᵃ— —ᵃᵃᵃ— —ᵃᵃᵃ—

1999—Grace Tiffany. "Shakespeare's Dionysian Prince: Drama, Politics, and the 'Athenian' History Play," from *Renaissance Quarterly*

Grace Tiffany is a professor at Western Michigan University. Her scholarly work includes *Erotic Beasts and Social Monsters: Shakespeare, Jonson, and Comic Androgyny* (1995) and *Love's Pilgrimage: The Holy Journey in English Renaissance Literature* (2006). Tiffany has also written such novels as *My Father Had a Daughter: Judith Shakespeare's Tale* (2003), *Will* (2004), and *The Turquoise Ring* (2005), a retelling of Shakespeare's *The Merchant of Venice* from the perspective of the women in the play.

In *Shakespeare's Festive Comedy,* C. L. Barber notes Falstaff's likeness to Bacchus, the "festival lord," as Bacchus was represented in Erasmus's *Praise of Folly*.[1] Robin Headlam Wells and Alison Birkinshaw also note the "distinctly Dionysian character" of Falstaff's "musical predilections,"[2] and John Dover Wilson writes that Falstaff "does for our imaginations . . . what Bacchus or Silenus silenus (sīlē`nƏs), in Greek mythology, part bestial and part human creature of the forests and mountains. Part of Dionysus' entourage, the sileni are usually represented as aged satyrs—drunken, jolly, bald, fat, bearded, and did for the ancients," temporarily freeing us from normally operative "codes or moral ties" and unleashing our delight in a holiday world of wine and merriment.[3] That Falstaff so frees audiences within and without the play-world of the *Henriad* is inarguable. But distinguishing between the mythic figures of Bacchus and Silenus, whom Wilson's phrase treats synonymously, may enable us to see that it is not Falstaff but Prince Hal, ultimately King Henry V, who functions as the true Bacchus, or Dionysus, of the history plays. Falstaff is his Silenus, the fat, old, drunken companion who lends humor to Dionysian celebration. According to Greek myth it was Silenus who tutored the wine-god in the god's youth and who later joined Dionysus's entourage, a pattern which in some respects prefigures Falstaff's "misleading" and following of the young Prince Hal. And it was Dionysus whose yearly theatrical festival symbolically accomplished the rejuvenation of the ancient Athenian state, just as Hal/ Henry's performative skill restores health to a late medieval England "diseas'd," "infected," and "rank" with civil strife (*2 Henry IV* 4.1.54, 58, 64).[4]

In *Henry V* Canterbury describes Hal's carefully staged transformation from rakehell to Christian king in agricultural terms, reminding us of the ancient link between theater and Dionysian fertility:

The strawberry grows underneath the nettle,
And wholesome berries thrive and ripen best
Neighbor'd by fruit of baser quality;
And so the Prince obscur'd his contemplation
Under the veil of wildness, which (no doubt)
Grew like the summer grass, fastest by night,
Unseen, yet crescive in his faculty. (1.1.60–66)

The "veil of wildness" with which, in the *Henry IV* plays, Hal masked his political pragmatism is here presented as a natural aid to wholesome growth: the prince's proximity to "fruit of baser quality" (Falstaff, Poins, and company) has strangely contributed to his moral health, and hence to his power to enliven England. Hal's own earlier description of his performative prodigality has similarly presented it as a natural phenomenon. In *I Henry IV* he vowed to

... imitate the sun, Who doth permit the base contagious clouds
To smother up his beauty from the world,
That when he please again to be himself,
Being wanted, he may be more wond'red at ... (1.2.197–201)

In this speech Hal ties the nature metaphor to the image of drama festival, continuing, "If all the year were playing holidays / To sport would be as tedious as to work; / But when they seldom come, they wish'd for come" (1.2.204–06). Line 204 carries a double meaning, signifying both "If we played holiday all year" and "If all year we celebrated 'playing' holidays": holidays consecrated to playing, like the old English rites of spring or the drama festivals of ancient Athens. The sun's reemergence, or Hal's own reformation, will be like these annual "playing holidays." And indeed, onlookers describe Hal/Henry's ensuing military exploits in terms which suggest his status as secular fertility god, who incorporates both comedy and tragedy in his celebration. Vernon's description of Hal arming for battle with Hotspur links Mayday images with much older references to satyrs and bulls, both of which are associated with Silenus and Dionysus. Hal and his comrades are "As full of spirit as the month of May" and "Wanton as youthful goats, wild as young bulls" as they prepare, paradoxically, for possible death (1HIV 4.1.101, 103). *Henry V* sustains the metaphor of joint comic and tragic theatrical festival in its prediction of Henry's French campaign. Since the king is "in the very May-morn of his youth, / Ripe for exploits and mighty enterprises," his feats will restage those of "Edward the Black Prince, / Who on the French ground play'd a tragedy" (1.2.120–21, 105–06). Thus, while Hal's deceptive traffic with Falstaff looks, from one angle, unappealingly dishonest,[5] an alternative and more optimistic perspective on political histrionics is urged on us by the language of various characters in the plays, including Hal himself. Mediated by and through images of the life-giving sun and of thriving natural organisms, Hal's strategic theatrical practices are made to appear eternally restorative Dionysian ritual.

Perceiving Hal/Henry rather than Falstaff as Dionysian festival lord and Falstaff as accompanying Silenus may enable us to appreciate another connection between the Henriad and the classical world: the association between Falstaff and Socrates—described as a "Silenus" in Plato's *Symposium* (215b)[6]—and the collateral link between Prince Hal and the Greek general Alcibiades, Socrates' brilliant pupil. The link between Falstaff and Socrates is well-known. Scholars who want to prove this connection usually cite the analogy between Mistress Quickly's description of Falstaff's death in *Henry V* (2.3) and Socrates' last moments as described in *Phaedo*,[7] a verbal echo which has led some to find deep "affinities" between the fat knight and the philosopher, "especially in the [skeptical] light in which the latter was sometimes regarded in the sixteenth century."[8] Michael Platt notes that both Falstaff and Socrates are called "misleader of youth," both are accused of "making the worse appear the better reason" in argument, and both distinguish themselves (though in radically different ways) as foot soldiers.[9] Alice Goodman first broadened the Socrates-Falstaff discussion by noting parallels between Socrates' student Alcibiades and Falstaff's "student," Hal, focusing on *Symposium* as a source for both Shakespearean characters. Goodman cites not only references to Socrates and Alcibiades in North's translation of Plutarch's *Lives,* but observes that *Symposium's* Silenic Socrates was made popularly known through Erasmus's commentary on Socrates in *Praise of Folly* and *Adages,* works which Shakespeare undoubtedly knew.[10] Following Goodman, I propose to expand the discussion further by exploring the Dionysian qualities which Hal and Falstaff inherit from Plato's Alcibiades and Socrates,[11] as well as from representations of one or both classical figures in Plutarch, Erasmus, and even Rabelais (a source overlooked by Goodman). In the introduction to *Gargantua and Pantagruel* (1534), Rabelais writes that "Praising his teacher," *Symposium's* Alcibiades calls Socrates,

> [a] Silenus: those used to be little boxes, the kind you see, today, in drugstores, painted all round with light and happy figures ... invented in good fun, just to make the world laugh (exactly as Silenus used to do, honest Bacchus's master).[12]

Like many of Erasmus's references to Socrates, Rabelais's introduction emphasizes the Bacchic or Dionysian quality of Socrates' influence, and highlights Alcibiades as source of the Silenus conceit.[13] As Michael Allen has noted, Marsilio Ficino also commented extensively on the *Symposium* passage wherein Alcibiades elevates the comic Silenus to the status of gnostic master. It is likely that the attention given by Erasmus, Rabelais, and Ficino to this *Symposium* passage directed Shakespeare toward its study, and influenced him to explore its comic potential through the drama of Falstaff and Hal. Whatever prompted Shakespeare's use of *Symposium*, his translation of Plato's Silenic Socrates into Falstaff gave him an invaluable tool for Hal's own characterization. For the Boar's Head Silenus enhances Hal's image as Dionysian festival prince and ultimately festival king.

In what follows I argue that Shakespeare's presentation of Hal/Henry recalls the Bacchanalian ideal embodied in Alcibiades in Plato's *Symposium* and elaborated in Plutarch's account of Alcibiades' life. Shakespeare's debt to Plutarch in the Henriad has recently been discussed by Judith Mossman, who catalogues the many allusions to Plutarch's "Alexander" in *Henry V.* That Shakespeare was also considering Plutarch's "Alcibiades" during this period is suggested by his reference to its companion piece, the life of Coriolanus, in the mid-1590s *Titus Andronicus.*[14] (As John W. Velz notes, Shakespeare tended "to read [and use] the Greek lives parallel to the Roman life he was using at any given moment."[15]) In presenting a dramatic rendition of a "life," Shakespeare expresses themes directly stated in Plutarch's narratives, but does so through an indirect, conversational structure derived partly from the Platonic dialogue. Thus both Plato's and Plutarch's treatments of Alcibiades are integral to Shakespeare's Dionysian prince. In *Symposium*, Alcibiades plays Dionysus to Socrates' Silenus, and engages Socrates in a conversation which shows their Dionysian rhetorical and theatrical virtuosity. Plutarch's later account of Alcibiades' career relates how Alcibiades' military and political success was intimately connected to this Dionysian association and to Alcibiades' self-presentational skill. Alcibiades' Dionysian performative strategy, which could temporarily obliterate hierarchical distinctions between himself and the company to which he spoke, brought him closer to the common multitude than did the rigid monarchical role-play of his illustrious uncle Pericles. In "Pericles" Plutarch recounts that Pericles enacted a cold, withdrawn "counterfeate" of "majestie" so that "the people should not be glutted with seeing him to ofte."[16] Similarly, Shakespeare's chameleonlike Hal/Henry V, who blends with all companies, forges a stronger bond with the English commonwealth than does his icy father, Henry IV, who cultivates aloofness, and whose regality depends on his not being "daily swallowed by men's eyes" (1HIV 3.2.70). Thus, drawing on two classical sources, Shakespeare demonstrates in the Henriad the importance of improvisational, convivial theatrics not only to successful political argument, but to enduring leadership. And while this largely verbal self-presentational skill bears the taint of sophistry, or deceptive linguistic improvisation, still, paradoxically, Shakespeare makes the skill seem predominantly positive. He does this by associating it with the god of the drama, who mediates the experiences of peace and war, life and death, through the celebratory apparatus of comedy and tragedy.

The long tavern scene in *1 Henry IV* (2.4) is a central stage by which the Henriad forges this association between Hal's role-play and Dionysian festival. This scene, during which Hal and Falstaff banter and playact the roles of Hotspur,

Lady Percy, Henry IV, and Hal himself, closely parallels the last section of *Symposium*, where the drunken Alcibiades joins the tragedian Agathon's party and comically debates Socrates. In 2.4, Hal gleefully enters the tavern bragging that he has been "drinking deep" with the Boar's Head tapsters (2.4.15), and soon after bids Ned Poins "call in Falstaff" for further entertainment (2.4.109). His high-spirited speeches recall Alcibiades' "very drunk and very loud" entrance in *Symposium* (212e): "Good evening, gentlemen. I'm plastered. . . . May I join your party?" Alcibiades announces (213a), and sits next to Socrates (213b). In both 1 *Henry IV*'s tavern scene and *Symposium*, the subsequent encounter between the young and the old men is histrionic. That is, both interactions are performative, played in front of audiences of cheering cronies in good-humored contests for best theatrical effect. And, significantly, both contests are also sophistic. In each, what is being applauded is skill at "wrenching the true cause the false way" for ulterior motives: a practice with which Socrates was charged,[17] and of which the Lord Chief Justice will ultimately accuse Falstaff (2HIV 2.1.109–11).

Falstaff exercises sophistic virtuosity when, challenged as to "what trick" he has to excuse his cowardice at the Gad's Hill robbery (1HIV 2.4.265), he replies, "Why, hear you, my masters, was it for me to kill the heir-apparent? Should I turn upon the true prince? Why, thou knowest I am as valiant as Hercules; but beware instinct—the lion will not touch the true prince" (2.4.268–72). Falstaff is sophistic again when, speaking as Prince Hal in the playlet, he verbally translates his own gluttony and dissoluteness to virtue: "If sack and sugar be a fault, God help the wicked! . . . If to be fat be to be hated, then Pharaoh's [lean] kine are to be lov'd" (2.4.470–74). In turn, Hal claims to outdo Falstaff's rhetorical and imitative skills as they vie to impersonate Henry IV. "Dost thou speak like a king?," Hal says critically after Falstaff's attempt. "I'll play my father" (2.4.433–34). As "King Henry," Hal uses Falstaffian eloquence to exaggerate Falstaff's failings, calling Falstaff "bolting-hutch of beastliness," "villainous abominable misleader of youth," and "white-bearded Sathan" (4.4.450, 462–63).

The mock insults, delivered in competitive attempts for the applause of a listening crowd of revelers ("Judge, my masters" [1. 439]), are like *Symposium*'s exchange between Alcibiades and Socrates. In *Symposium*, Alcibiades accuses Socrates of having "figured out a way to find a place next to the most handsome man in the room" (Agathon) (213c). Socrates, evading the accusation, replies, "I can't so much as look at an attractive man but he flies into a fit of jealous rage" (213d). Alcibiades counters with the dubious accolade that Socrates "has never lost an argument in his life" (213e) (what trick hast thou, Socrates?). Finally, Alcibiades agrees to join the rhetorical contest in which the symposium guests are engaged, and speaks in ambivalent praise of Socrates, thus temporarily gaining audience attention (215–222c). But Socrates fights back with the self-serving claim, "You have already delivered your praise of me, and now it's my turn to praise whoever's on my right. But if Agathon were next to you, he'd have to praise me all over again, instead of having me speak in his honor": i.e., Agathon should stay by Socrates. Alcibiades exposes this argument as sophistry: "Look how smoothly and plausibly he found a reason for Agathon to lie down next to him!" (223a–b).

Such Socratic sophistry is a chief feature of Falstaff's whenever he appears in the history plays. Michael Platt notes that Falstaff's soliloquy at Shrewsbury, which justifies his escape from battle-wounds by discounting the existence of "honor," is not only a mock-catechism but a parody of Socratic inquiries into the nature of virtue, piety, and justice: "Can honor set to a leg? No. Of an arm? No. . . . What is honor? A word" (1HIV 5.1.131–34).[18] While Socratic dialogues generally end by affirming the speciousness of the physical world and the reality of the unseen, Falstaff's "honor" speech does the opposite, and thereby justifies his own cowardice. Thus it may initially seem that Falstaff's Socratic tendencies are ironically presented: that they disclose only the contrast between the lying knight and the philosopher who, in *The Republic* and *Phaedrus*, discredits sophistry and distinguishes his own dialectical truth-seeking from rhetorical trickery. But *Symposium* does offer a model for Falstaff in its playfully sophistic Socrates, who contrasts with the radically anti-sophistic inquirer of the other dialogues. Of all Plato's representations of Socrates, that in *Symposium* comes closest to the casuistic philosopher of Aristophanes' *Clouds*. (Aristophanes' presence as a character in Symposium may owe something to this connection. Plato has Aristophanes "trying to make himself heard" just before Alcibiades' entrance and awake with Socrates at the party's end [212d, 223d].) In *The Clouds*, Socrates teaches "public speaking and debating techniques" and shows young Pheidippides—a possible caricature of Alcibiades—how rhetorically to justify evading his father's authority.[20] Erasmus's *Praise of Folly* invokes this Aristophanic Socrates, who was always "philosophizing about clouds and ideas, measuring a flea's foot," and "learning nothing about the affairs of ordinary life."[21] Thus the merging of the figures of dialectician and sophist was as current in sixteenth-century Europe as in fifth-century Athens, and as available for comic exploitation.

Yet the comic representation of sophistry, in Erasmus and Shakespeare as well as in Aristophanes and Plato, encourages us to experience sophistic confusion as Dionysian revelry, even as the rhetorical deceiver is gently mocked. Erasmus uses a theatrical term in announcing his "fancy to *play* the Sophist before" his readers [my emphasis], adding,

> and I don't mean by that one of the tribe today who cram tiresome
> trivialities into the heads of schoolboys and teach them a more than
> feminine obstinacy in disputation—no, I shall follow the ancients
> who chose the name of Sophist in preference to the damaging title of
> philosopher.[22]

Thus, largely on the basis of its entertainment value, Erasmus defends his "praise of [sophistic] folly." The Falstaffian sophistry of Shakespeare's Boar's Head dialogues is Erasmian (and, we may recall, Rabelaisian), performed for various audiences in the service of fun: "What, shall we be merry, shall we have a play extempore?," Falstaff asks Hal (1HIV 2.4.279–80), simultaneously evading further discussion of his Gad's Hill cowardice and pointing to the theatrical nature of his and Hal's whole interaction in this scene. Such "merry" sophistry is grounded in the ancient association between sophistry and comic theater. For although the Socrates of *The Clouds* is a more satirically realized figure than is Falstaff, his moral and political danger is contained by and within the licensed ritual of Dionysian festival.[23] Similarly, the more mildly sophistic Socrates of *Symposium* is rendered a cooperative "revels lord" by the festive context of his sophistry (a symposion, or drinking party). Indeed, in *Symposium* Alcibiades uses the ribbons due Agathon for Agathon's first-place play at the festival of Dionysus—the symposium's occasion—to crown Socrates (213e), an action which presents Alcibiades as Dionysus and Socrates as the divine Silenus of Alcibiades' ensuing argument ("Isn't he just like a statue of Silenus?" [215b]). Alcibiades' willingness to grant Socrates an impromptu dramatic victory because "he has never lost an argument in his life" looks toward the last act of *1 Henry IV*, when Hal gives Falstaff "honors" for the slaying of Hotspur on similar grounds (5.4.146–58).

The entertainingly theatrical aspect of rhetorical contest (and conquest) in both *Symposium* and the Henriad is enhanced by the dizzying interchangeableness of speakers' roles. *Symposium*'s last section is characterized by place-shifting and identity melding.[24] The drunken Alcibiades, trying to crown Agathon with ribbons, only pushes them "further down his [own] head" (213b); ultimately, as noted, he gives the ribbons to Socrates. After Alcibiades' speech, the argument over seating ensues between Agathon, Alcibiades, and Socrates, resulting in a musical-chairs game of "changing places." Alcibiades' speech itself dwells on the strange identity exchanges that have marked his relationship with Socrates: "So what I did was to invite [Socrates] to dinner, as if I were his lover and he my young prey! . . . he presents himself as your lover, and, before you know it, you're in love with him yourself!" (217d, 222b). Place and role alternations are similarly pervasive in the Henriad, particularly in the long tavern scene of part one. When Hal first suggests that, in sport, he "play [the rebel Harry] Percy, and that damn'd brawn [Falstaff]" play "Dame Mortimer his wife," Hal has himself just impersonated both Percys in a brief imitative dialogue (2.4.103–10). Later in the scene, Hal and Falstaff alternate the roles of king and prince (2.4.398–481), a hierarchical inversion which is, in a sense, repeated in the play's last act, when Hal allows Falstaff to claim a military victory which he himself has won,[25] and in *2 Henry IV*, when Hal waits on Falstaff at dinner (2.4.234–90).

In *Symposium*, the role inversions help express the unstable nature of erotic attraction, a central proposition in the work. But in the Henry plays, Hal's rapid identity shifts suggest the prince's carnivalesque power to unite disparate social types within the body of a single ruler (or, in Leonard Tennenhouse's words, to incorporate "a certain popular vigor within the legitimate body of the state").[26] As Stephen Greenblatt has shown, Hal's ability to "drink with any tinker in his own language" (1HIV2.4.19), learned at the tavern, earns him the support of even the lowest social classes once he comes to rule them.[27] As Warwick tells Henry IV, "The Prince but studies his companions / Like a strange tongue" with an eye to future command (2HIV4.4.68–69). The chief director of Hal's linguistic "study" is, of course, the Boar's Head Socrates, Falstaff, who indirectly trains him in the improvisational art of winning every argument. As Alice Goodman says, Falstaff's "Socratic" teaching instructs Hal in "the speeches he will make to his father, to his soldiers, to the Princess Katharine, to Falstaff himself as he renounces him."[28]

Hal/Henry's sophistic skill is evident when he twice converts his father's wrath to appreciation by a quick turn of phrase. In part one, Hal's fanciful description of Hotspur as "factor," employed to "engross up glorious deeds" on Hal's behalf (3.2.147–48), inspires Henry IV's forgiveness of Hal's comparative slackness: now "Thou shalt have charge and sovereign trust herein" (3.2.161), the king tells Hal. And in part two, Henry IV specifically praises Hal's eloquent justification of Hal's accidental theft of the crown: "God put [it] in thy mind to take it hence/That thou mightst win the more thy father's love,/Pleading so wisely in excuse of it!" (4.5.17880). The prelates in *Henry V* note the new king's power to awe listeners with his "sweet and honeyed sentences" (1.1.50), and before Agincourt Henry V effectively, if glibly persuades reluctant soldiers that death is advantageous to the honest man (4.1.147–85).

In absorbing Falstaff's sophistic skills, Hal/Henry has become a rhetorical master reminiscent of the Socrates whom Alcibiades so elaborately praises in *Symposium*. The "mute wonder" (HV 1.1.49) with which Henry's "sweet and honeyed sentences" fill listeners is a restrained version of the "Bacchic frenzy" Socrates inspires in his hearers, who are "transported" by his discourse (*Symposium* 218c, 215d). The "moment [Socrates] starts to speak," Alcibiades says, "I am beside myself: my heart starts leaping in my chest, the tears come streaming down my face" (*Symposium* 215e). As the Henriad's Alcibiades, Hal, similarly fascinated with Falstaff's rhetorical "tricks," gradually makes this Socratic and Bacchic technique his own.

As I claimed earlier, Alcibiades as source for the theatrical and Dionysian Henry is suggested not only by *Symposium*, but by Alcibiades' representation in Plutarch's *Lives*. Plutarch recounts how Alcibiades, originally transported by Socrates' discourse, eventually acquired Socrates' own talent for swaying others with language. In Alcibiades' youth Socrates' words brought tears to his eyes, "disturb[ing] his very soul"; in later years Alcibiades himself "wanne [won] the love and good willes of private men" to whom he spoke.[29] The pattern prefigures Hal/Henry's comic rhetorical training by means of Falstaff's "quips and . . . quiddities" (1HIV 1.2.45), a training which fosters the immense persuasive power he deploys in *Henry V,* most notably when he convinces the fearful privates Bates, Williams, and Court that "the King is not bound to answer for the particular endings of his soldiers" (4.1.155–56) even when it is the king who has led them to their deaths.[30] Even more significantly, Plutarch's Alcibiades is said to have had, like the theatrically resourceful Hal/Henry,

a propert[y] whereby he most robbed mens hartes: that he could frame altogether with their manners and facions of life, transforming him selfe more easely to all manner of shapes, then the Camelion. For it is reported, that the Camelion cannot take white culler: but Alcibiades could put apon him any manners, customes, or facions, of what nation soever, and could followe, exercise, and counterfeate them when he would as well the good as the bad. For in Sparta, he was very paynefull, and in continuall exercise: he lived sparingly with litle, and led a straight life. In Ionia, to the contrary: there he lived daintely and superflu-ously, and gave him self to all mirthe and pleasure. In Thracia, he dranke ever, or was allwayes a horse backe. If he came to Tissaphernes, lieutenaunt of the mightie king of Persia: he farre exceeded the magnificence of Persia in pompe and sumptuousnes. And these things notwithstanding, never altered his naturall condition from one facion to another, neither dyd his manners (to saye truely) receyve all sortes of chaunges. But bicause peradventure, if he had shewed his naturall disposition, he might in divers places where he came, have offended those whose companie he kept, he dyd with such a viser and cloke disguise him selfe, to fit their manners, whom he companied with, by transforming him selfe into their naturall countenaunce.[31]

This Athenian "Zelig," like his English counterpart Hal/Henry, ultimately used this self-transformational skill to lead armies in imperialistic military campaigns. As Plutarch reports it, it was Alcibiades who inspired the Athenians' desire to control Sicily, much as Henry sets "all the youth of England . . . on fire" to conquer France in *Henry V* (2.Pro. 1). And Plutarch's account of Alcibiades' conquest of Selybrea looks forward to Henry's siege of Harfleur, when a 43-line speech accomplishes the relatively peaceful surrender of the French town (HV 3.3). Having breached the walled city of Selybrea with only fifty men, Plutarch writes, Alcibiades parleyed for time until the rest of his army advanced to the town. He then obtained the Selybreans' offer of peace, and thus prevented his own army from pillaging them.[32] That Shakespeare had Alcibiades in mind when he wrote Henry's Harfleur negotiation is suggested not just by the obvious similarities between the Selybrea and Harfleur episodes, but also by a passage in Shakespeare's *Timon of Athens*. There, hearing of Alcibiades' threats to return and invade Athens itself, the misanthropic Timon frightens the senators with the following warning:

> . . . But if he sack fair Athens,
> And take our goodly aged men by th'beards,
> Giving our holy virgins to the stain
> Of contumelious, beastly mad-brain'd war,
> Then let him know, and tell him Timon speaks it,
> In pity of our aged and of our youth,
> I cannot choose but tell him that I care not. . . . (5.1.171–77)

The lines echo Henry V's dire description of French "fathers taken by the silver beards," and of "fresh fair virgins" given up to "the hot and forcing violation" of "impious War" (HV 3.3.36, 14, 21, 15). The Timon lines also echo Henry's disclaimer of personal responsibility in the event: "What is't to me, when you yourselves are cause . . . ?" (HV 3.3.19–21). Yet in all three instances—Henry V, Timon, and Plutarch's account of Alcibiades at Selybrea—the terrifying vision of war is rhetorically contained, serving chiefly as a theatrical method of persuading hearers to capitulate. Harfleur's governor yields out of fear, as does Athens to Alcibiades in Timon (5.4) and Selybrea to Alcibiades in Plutarch.

This is not, of course, to say that either Alcibiades or Henry achieves victory chiefly in rhetorical terms, without recourse to violence. In both Shakespeare's and Plutarch's histories, Henry and Alcibiades recurrently let slip the dogs of war. My point is simply that Shakespeare, drawing on suggestions in both Plato's and Plutarch's descriptions of Alcibiades, presents a prince and later a king whose military victories are inseparable from rhetorical power, and whose rhetorical power is inseparable from Dionysian theatricality. The language which both Alcibiades and Henry V use to sanction war and death works, paradoxically, because of its cathartic effects on its hearers, whether those hearers are soldiers or playhouse patrons, and whether the vision that moves them is tragic or comic. All participate in the theatrical translation of war to communal celebration, urged by the central Bacchic figure who both governs and participates in the dramatic experience.

Plutarch's description of General Alcibiades' triumphal return to Athens after numerous foreign victories is a further source of Henry V's combined imperialistic and Bacchic vision. Plutarch recounts how Alcibiades led an army of Athenian priests and ministers "singing the holy songe of Iaccus [Bacchus]" to reclaim a roadway from the Peloponnesians, thus triumphing "in the sight of his countrie, where the people should see and witnesse both, his valliantnes, and also his corage."[33] Conducting the religious celebrants "in battell raye [array]," Alcibiades "had as muche shewed the office of a highe bishoppe [priest], as of a noble souldier and good captaine."[34] In this description, the theatricality of Alcibiades' ploy is suggested not only by the description of the rites of Bacchus, god of the drama, but by the stress Plutarch lays on Alcibiades' self-staging before an audience: the action conducted and performed by him "in the sight of his countrie," the people witnesses of his valor. In Alcibiades' public assimilation of the roles of priest, general, and Athenian citizen, he himself seems to incarnate the half-human fertility god (whom he conspicuously displaces in Plutarch's account). Predictably, Alcibiades' priest-general act was an immense success, increasing "the peoples good opinion of his sufficiencie." Also significant in this description of Alcibiades' popularity is the proximity to Alcibiades which even the "poore" and "meaner sorte" of people enjoy: to these "he spake so fayer . . . that they wished and desired he would take upon him like a King."[35] A crucial aspect of Alcibiades' Bacchic political talent is its encouragement of such familiarity. From close interaction with the populace grows the Dionysian hero's ability to read, as well as to manipulate, communal desire.

It is, of course, this quality of Alcibiades' that chiefly connects him to Hal/Henry. That the latter's political success surpasses that of his father, Henry IV, has directly to do with Hal/Henry's status as Dionysian figure according to Plutarch's (as well as Plato's) model. While Henry IV is no less theatrical than Hal in his quest for political mastery, his role-play lacks the communal inclusiveness of his son's. Hal/Henry, like Alcibiades, uses spontaneous improvisational and sophistic talent to blend with his company, but Henry IV holds himself aloof, cultivating remoteness for spectacular effect.[36] This remoteness is evident in Henry IV's curt dismissals even of noblemen during his chilly audiences with them: "Worcester, get thee gone" (1HIV 1.3.15); "Lords, give us leave" (3.2.1). In *1 Henry IV* Henry IV recalls how, as the uncrowned Henry Bullingbrook, he courted the crowd by remaining distant from their gaze:

> Thus did I keep my person fresh and new, My presence, like a robe pontifical, Ne'er seen but wond'red at, and so my state, Seldom but sumptuous, show'd like a feast, And [won] by rareness such solemnity.
>
>   (3.2.55–59)

Henry IV resists the "enfoeff[ment] to popularity" of men like Richard II and (as he supposes) Prince Hal, who,"being daily swallowed by men's eyes," cause onlookers to "sur[feit] with honey" and begin to "[l]oathe the taste of sweetness" (ll. 69–72). Henry IV's dramaturgical strategy imitates that of Alcibiades' uncle Pericles, whom Plutarch (in "Pericles") describes as shrinking both from the society of his peers and from the common folk. Once embarked on a political career, Plutarch writes, Pericles

> gave up going to all feastes where he was bidden, and left the entertainment of his friendes, their company and familiaritie. So that in all his time wherein he governed the common weale, which was a long time, he never went out to supper

to any of his friendes. . . . For these friendly meetings at suche feastes, doe much abase any counterfeate majestie or set countenaunce: and he shall have much a doe to keepe gravity and reputation, shewing familiaritie to every knowen friende in such open places.

Similarly, to prevent that the people should not be glutted with seeing him to ofte, nor that they should come much to him: they dyd see him but at some times, and then he would not talke in every matter, neither came much abroade among them, but reserved him selfe . . . for matters of great importaunce.[37]

But what worked for Pericles doesn't ultimately work in Shakespearean history theater. Despite Henry IV's temporary success at Periclean political performance, the precariousness of authority achieved through spectacular remoteness is manifest in his predicament throughout *Henry IV*. Even as he describes his strategy to Hal, his erstwhile supporters, coldly alienated from him, amass in rebellion against him.

Thus the Henriad suggests the deeper political power of a Dionysian theatricality that, exploiting the rhetoric of companionship, presents ruler as common citizen, just as myth presents Dionysus himself as both god and man. Through "drink[ing] with any tinker in his own language," Hal/Henry inspires a celebratory, communal response to his leadership, which enables him finally to "command all the good lads in Eastcheap" in both civil and foreign military endeavors (1HIV 2.4.14–15). Further, the Dionysian ethos Hal/Henry invokes includes rather than obscures a tragic element. Just as the Black Prince "played a tragedy" on French soil, Hal predicts the deaths of English as well as French soldiers and citizens, including his own (HV 4.3.121–25), even as he looks toward England's regeneration in a vision of war stories told to sons (HV 4.3.50–56). Like the Dionysian drama festival, Shakespeare's "Athenian" Henriad mediates bloodshed and rebirth through celebratory theatrical rhetoric. And like Alcibiades, Hal/Henry uses the mediated vision for imperialism.

I have argued that the Henriad accomplishes its celebratory purpose by hybridizing the genres of narrative history and dialogue. In merging matter from Plutarch's *Lives* and Plato's *Symposium*, Shakespeare gives Plutarch's narrated plot a Platonic dialogic life, suggesting a variety of associations between Hal/Henry and Alcibiades. Henry displays the military leadership evident in Plutarch's account of Alcibiades as well as the Dionysian revelry Alcibiades, with Socrates, enacts in Plato's playful dialogue. Viewed another way, the merging of Plutarch's life of a fallen hero with *Symposium*'s light-hearted presentation of Alcibiades fuses tragic and comic genres. Similarly, as Alice Goodman has shown, the Henriad blends the comic vision of Socrates found in *Symposium* with the tragic one found in *Phaedo*, thus broadening and enriching our emotional response to Hal's "Socrates," Falstaff.[38] *Symposium* ends, in fact, with Socrates encouraging just such a synthesis, arguing that "the skillful tragic dramatist should also be a comic poet" (223d).

I suggest that this blending of tragic and comic genres is fundamental to Shakespearean history theater, which justifies and tempers war and sophistic politics by interpreting them as Dionysian play. The Henriad in particular discloses only to celebrate the verbal tactics by which war is translated to tragedy, and sophistry to comedy.

NOTES

1. Barber, 68.
2. Wells and Birkinshaw, 105.
3. Wilson, 128.
4. These and all other quotations from Shakespeare are from *The Riverside Shakespeare*. Henceforth in my main text I will refer to *1 Henry IV, 2 Henry IV*, and *Henry V* as 1HIV, 2HIV, and HV, respectively.
5. The list of scholars who deride Hal's theatrical politics is long indeed, but as sample writings see Greenblatt; Van Doren, 149; Garber; and Cartelli, 8. For optimistic readings of Hal's theatricality see Tillyard, 271–72; Toliver, 68–69; and Webber, 534.
6. Plato, 1989. All references to *Symposium* are to this edition.
7. These include Moore; Stearns; Lloyd; Scoufos; Jones, 20–21; and Cubeta, 254.
8. Fleissner, 61.
9. Platt, 180.
10. See Goodman. That Shakespeare may have known Plato's dialogues in Latin is suggested by T. W. Baldwin's demonstration of the importance of Latin even to grammar-school education in Elizabethan England (passim in Baldwin). This suggestion is supported in Thomson, 15, and Muir, 1. Although two dialogues entitled Alcibiades I and II were attributed to Plato (most notably by Ficino) during the Renaissance, these works were not commonly presented in grammar school (as were Plato's earlier and middle dialogues). Baldwin does not stress them, and Shakespeare's familiarity with them is doubtful. (I am grateful to Michael Allen for pointing out to me the doubtful authenticity of these dialogues.)
11. As Baldwin notes, knowledge of *Symposium* was readily available to sixteenth-century scholars with even "small Latin" through a Latin translation by N. Liburnius, Divini Platonis Gnomologia, published in 1555 (Baldwin, 2, 652–53).
12. Rabelais, 7. (I thank Michael Allen for calling my attention to this passage.) Mikhail Bakhtin, the most important recent commentator on Rabelais, notes the "positive, triumphant, liberating" effect of Rabelais's humor, here incarnate in the Silenic Socrates (or Socratic Silenus). See Bakhtin, 300.
13. Edgar Wind comments on the general Renaissance interest in the image of Socrates as Alcibiades' Silenus, as well as on Erasmus's specific reference to the image in Adages. See Wind, esp. 172–73.
14. An instance noted by Frank Kermode is the "curious parallel between Tamora's attempt to divert Lucius from his purpose"—his intent to sacrifice the Goth queen's eldest son—"and that of Volumnia when Coriolanus arrives at the gates of Rome with the Volscians." See Kermode, 1022.
15. The quotation from John Velz is from private correspondence. I thank Professor Velz for drawing the references to Coriolanus in Titus Andronicus to my attention. For a discussion of Shakespeare's characteristic uses of Plutarch, see Homan.
16. Plutarch, 1:9.

17. See Plato, 1981, 18c.

18. Platt, 180.

19. See especially book 1 of *The Republic*, and sections 272–74 of *Phaedrus* in Plato, 1938, on Socrates' dispute with the Sophists.

20. Aristophanes, 40, 138–39.

21. Erasmus, 97. I am grateful to Alice Goodman for pointing to the connection between the Erasmian and the Aristophanic Socrates. See Goodman, 100.

22. Erasmus, 64.

23. This argument may seem to run counter to Socrates' own words (as reported by Plato) in Apology, where in the Athenian court he defends himself against the image presented "in the comedy of Aristophanes, a Socrates swinging about there, saying he was walking on air and talking a lot of other nonsense about things of which I know nothing at all" (19c). However, since *The Clouds* was produced in 423 B.C., 24 years before Socrates' trial and execution, it seems improbable that it played any major motivating role in the state's action against him.

24. See Nehamas and Woodruff for a sustained discussion of the various identity substitutions that characterize Symposium's last section.

25. This scene ironically inverts Plutarch's account of how Socrates, having saved Alcibiades' life in a battle against Potidaea during the Peloponnesian Wars, supported the Athenian generals in giving Alcibiades the honor of having saved Socrates' life. See Plutarch, "Alcibiades," 1:93ff. Also noted in Goodman.

26. Tennenhouse, 84. Tennenhouse's argument differs in some major ways from my own, the chief difference being that he interprets Hal/Henry's theatricality as essentially comic. Instead, I see the festivity Hal/Henry incorporates as specifically Dionysian, including a tragic as well as a comic aspect. In the festival of Dionysus, both aspects of human experience are celebrated.

27. See Greenblatt.

28. Goodman, 100.

29. Plutarch, "Alcibiades," 1:93, 117.

30. Henry's casuistry in this scene is evident to a careful reader of the play. Henry argues that "every subject's soul is his own" and not the king's responsibility (4.1.177), even though in the play's second scene he has charged that the Dauphin's "soul/Shall stand sore charged" for the deaths of his soldiers (1.2.282ff).

31. Plutarch, "Alcibiades," 117–18.

32. Ibid., 129–30.

33. Ibid., 135–36.

34. Ibid., 136.

35. Ibid.

36. In this I differ with Tennenhouse, who sees Henry IV's role as similar to the one perpetuated by his son, both kings embodying an England that "incorporates the robust features of festival" (80).

37. Plutarch, 1:8–9.

38. Goodman, 100.

BIBLIOGRAPHY

Allen, Michael J. B. "De Libro Sexto Cum Commento." In *Francois Rabelais: Critical Assessments*, ed. Jean-Claude Carron, 178–212. Baltimore, 1995.

Aristophanes. *The Clouds*. Trans. William Arrowsmith. In Four Plays by Aristophanes, ed. William Arrowsmith, Richmond Lattimore, and *Douglass Parker, 21–47.* New York, 1962.

Bakhtin, Mikhail. *Rabelais and His World*. Trans. Helene Iswolsky. Cambridge, Mass., 1968.

Baldwin, T. W. *Shakspere's Small Latine and Lesse Greeke*, 2 vols. Urbana, 1944.

Barber, C. L. *Shakespeare's Festive Comedy*. Princeton, 1959.

Cartelli, Thomas. "Ideology and Subversion in the Shakespearean Set Speech." *ELH* 1 (1986): 1–25.

Cubeta, Paul M. "Falstaff and the Art of Dying." In *Falstaff* ed. Harold Bloom, 246–57. New York, 1992. First published in *SEL* 27:2 (1987), 197–211.

Erasmus, Desiderius. *Praise of Folly* and *Letter to Martin Dorp*. Trans. Betty Radice. Baltimore, 1971.

Fleissner, R. F. "Putting Falstaff to Rest: 'Tabulating the Facts'." *Shakespeare Studies* 16 (1983): 57–74.

Garber, Marjorie. "'What's Past Is Prologue': Temporality and Prophecy in Shakespeare's History Plays." *Renaissance Genres: Essays on Theory, History, and Interpretation*, ed. Barbara Kiefer Lewalski, 301–31. Cambridge, Mass., 1986.

Goodman, Alice. "Falstaff and Socrates." *English* 34:149 (1985): 97–112.

Greenblatt, Stephen. "Invisible Bullets: Renaissance Authority and Its Subversion." In *Political Shakespeare*, ed. Jonathan Dollimore and Alan Sinfield, 18–47. Manchester, 1985.

Homan, Sidney. "Dion, Alexander, and Demetrius—Plutarch's Forgotten Parallel Lives—as Mirrors for Shakespeare's Julius Caesar." *Shakespeare Studies* 8 (1976): 195–210.

Jones, Emrys. *The Origins of Shakespeare*. Oxford, 1977.

Kermode, Frank. Introduction to Titus Andronicus, by William Shakespeare. In *The Riverside Shakespeare*, ed. G. Blakemore Evans, 1019–22. Boston, 1974.

Lloyd, Roger. "Socrates and Falstaff." *Time and Tide*, 22 Feb. 1958: 219–20.

Moore, John Robert. "Shakespeare's Henry V." *Explicator* 1 (1942): item 61.

Mossman, Judith. "Henry V and Plutarch's Alexander." *Shakespeare Quarterly* 45:1 (1994): 57–73.

Muir, Kenneth. *Shakespeare's Sources: Comedies and Tragedies*. London, 1961.

Nehamas, Alexander and Paul Woodruff. *Introduction to Symposium*, by Plato, xi–xxvi. Indianapolis, 1989.

Plato. *Phaedrus, Ion, Gorgias, Symposium, Republic, Laws*. Trans. Lane Cooper. New York, 1938.

———. *Republic*. Trans. G. M. A. Grube. Indianapolis, 1974.

———. *Five Dialogues*. Trans. G. M. A. Grube. Indianapolis, 1981.

———. *Symposium*. Trans., ed., and intro. Alexander Nehamas and Paul Woodruff. Indianapolis, 1989.

Platt, Michael. "Falstaff in the Valley of the Shadow of Death." In *Falstaff*, ed. Harold Bloom, 171–202. New York, 1992. First published in *Interpretation* 8:1 (1979), 5–29.

Plutarch. *Lives of the Noble Grecians and Romans*. 6 vols. Trans. Thomas North. London, 1579. Reprint, 1895.

Rabelais, Francois. *Gargantua and Pantagruel*. Trans. Burton Raffel. New York, 1990.

Scoufos, Alice Lyle. "The 'Martyrdom' of Falstaff." *Shakespeare Studies* 2 (1966): 174–91.

Shakespeare, William. *The Riverside Shakespeare*, ed. G. Blakemore Evans. Boston, 1974.

Stearns, Monroe M. "Shakespeare's Henry V." *Explicator* 2 (1943): item 19.

Tennenhouse, Leonard. *Power on Display*. New York, 1986.

Thomson, J. A. K. *Shakespeare and the Classics*. London, 1952.

Tillyard, E. M. W. *Shakespeare's History Plays*. New York, 1944.

Toliver, Harold E. "Falstaff, the Prince, and the History Play." *Shakespeare Quarterly* 16 (1965): 63–80.

Van Doren, Mark. *Shakespeare*. New York, 1953.

Webber, Joan. "The Renewal of the King's Symbolic Role: From Richard II to Henry V." *Texas Studies in Literature and Language* 4 (1963): 530–38.

Wells, Robin Headlam, and Alison Birkinshaw. "Falstaff, Prince Hal and the New Song." *Shakespeare Studies* 18 (1986): 103–15.

Wilson, John Dover. *The Fortunes of Falstaff*. New York, 1944.

Wind, Edgar. *Pagan Mysteries in the Renaissance*. 1958. Reprint, New York, 1968.

HENRY V IN THE
TWENTY-FIRST CENTURY
❧

Referring to the feast of St. Crispin, the saint's day on which the battle of Agincourt took place, Henry predicts, "Crispin Crispian shall ne'er go by, / From this day to the ending of the world, / But we in it shall be remember'd." His words, however, have proved inaccurate; "the feast of *Crispin* passes by without any mention of *Agincourt*," Samuel Johnson observed and passes as well, in contemporary times, without much, if any, mention of Crispin. Shakespeare is not likely to suffer the fate of Crispin anytime soon, and students of his work will continue to comment on *Henry V*.

The attention *Henry V* has received in the first decade of the new millennium has led to no radical change in approaches to the play. Critics continue to engage the debates and issues that dominated the last two decades of the twentieth century. Tom McAlindon, in *Shakespeare Minus 'Theory'* (2004), devotes a chapter to illustrating the problems with Greenblatt's "Invisible Bullets," an essay that had received similar attention throughout the 1990s. McAlindon then turns to *Henry V*, revisiting the problem of the king's character and taking issue with too positive, too negative, and ambiguous versions of the character.

Two of the issues that recurred throughout that twentieth century that McAlindon reevaluates are Canterbury's motives for sanctioning the war and Henry's brutality. Canterbury's desire to prevent the bill that proposes seizing church lands, McAlindon argues, would have been seen by Shakespeare's original audience as a postponement of the coming of the Reformation; the satire is then directed against the corrupt church, not the king. Henry, by contrast, is genuinely concerned with the validity of Canterbury's explanation of the Salic law. In regard to Henry's brutality, McAlindon points out that historians of the period, including Hall and Holinshed, also acknowledge the violence of Henry's French campaign. Holinshed's "account of the 'lamentable slaughter' of the French prisoners, for example, makes it seem like a wild orgy of violence. . . . Yet Holinshed does not allow his awareness of martial savagery to affect his strongly held view that Henry was a great and good king." Holinshed records the violence unleashed on towns that, unlike Harfleur, failed to surrender and informs his readers that such acts were allowed "by the law of arms." McAlindon, however, is not trying to prove that Henry is beyond reproach; he argues that Shakespeare's representation of Henry V is positive but complex enough to acknowledge that the king has flaws, a view R. A. Foakes advocates in *Shakespeare and Violence* (2003).

John S. Mebane, while taking a different stance from McAlindon's, asserts that it is now impossible to take Henry as a positive figure. Mebane also addresses problems with Greenblatt's and Jonathan Dollimore and Alan Sinfield's formulations from the 1980s, in his 2007 essay "'Impious War': Religion and the Ideology of Warfare in *Henry V*." Mebane maintains that critics need to address aesthetic, not just ideological, concerns within literary texts. He does not undermine the value of the portrayal of Henry V put forth by those earlier critics. The king, in his view, is a negative figure, though he grants that Henry has some noble motives, "his felt need to unify Britain and forestall civil war." Mebane's problem with those whom he is following is that they deemphasize the artistic value of literary works and authorial control over texts' reflections on their culture's ideology. His interest is in establishing that Shakespeare opposed the use of religion to justify war in opposition to pacifist elements of the Bible, and he argues that "the dramatic form and artistic strategies of Shakespeare's history plays—especially *Henry V*—undercut the ideology of 'just war' by emphasizing the fear that all warfare is damnable."

In contrast to MacAlindon and Mebane, Marjorie Garber avoids overtly situating her reading of *Henry V* in relation to those of other critics. The title of her book, *Shakespeare After All*, gestures toward the idea that her focus is Shakespeare rather than the debates that rage around his work, and her essay seems to strike a neutral tone. Her view of Henry leans toward the positive, but she does not refrain from drawing attention to negative aspects of the king's character. She notes, for example, that Henry, unlike Richard II, "will not continue to foster favorites who act against the public weal" but characterizes Henry's response to traitors as the "merciless execution of malefactors," even though she is contrasting the merciless king with Richard II, whose weakness in the face of traitors led to his downfall. Garber's calling Henry "King Harry" also has positive connotations, for while the French consistently call him Harry, British characters, with the exception of the Chorus, refer to the king using that name only when Shakespeare wants to suggest the idea that Henry is a figure of communal fellowship. Harry is perhaps the king's more modest version of Hal.

It is hard to imagine that, in the future, attention will be shifted away from concerns over how we are meant to understand Henry, but what direction criticism will take is equally difficult to fathom. At the beginning of the twentieth century, it would have been impossible to foresee the direction critics would follow at the end of the century, even though we can now see relationships between early and late twentieth-century considerations of the play. The only thing that seems certain at this point is that in a hundred years, people will be reading Shakespeare, and when they turn to *Henry V,* they will absorb and analyze anew the actions of the king, the clergy, and the other characters Shakespeare has sent across the stage.

2004—Marjorie Garber. "Henry V," from *Shakespeare After All*

Marjorie Garber is the William R. Kenan Jr. Professor of English and of Visual and Environmental Studies at Harvard University. She has published on a wide variety of subjects. Her books on Shakespeare include *Dream in Shakespeare: From Metaphor to Metamorphosis* (1974), *Coming of Age in Shakespeare* (1997), *Profiling Shakespeare* (2008), and *Shakespeare and Modern Culture* (2008).

Each act of *The Life of Henry V* begins with a prologue, and each of these, as we will see, has the paradoxical effect of both bringing the audience closer to the dramatic action and marking the impossibility of conveying the "truth" of that action on the stage. The prologue to the first act is justly famous, both for its high rhetorical style and for its evocative description of the theater-space. A character called the Chorus—variously costumed, in the history of stage productions, in armor, in Elizabethan attire, in a supposedly "timeless" cloak, and as the personification of Time himself—comes forth to introduce the action, and the play:

> O for a muse of fire, that would ascend
> The brightest heaven of invention:
> A kingdom for a stage, princes to act,
> And monarchs to behold the swelling scene,
> Then should the warlike Harry, like himself,
> Assume the port of Mars, and at his heels,
> Leashed in like hounds, should famine, sword, and fire
> Crouch for employment. But pardon, gentles all,
> The flat unraised spirits that hath dared
> On this unworthy scaffold to bring forth
> So great and object. Can this cock-pit hold
> The vasty fields of France? Or may we cram
> Within this wooden O the very casques
> That did affright the air at Agincourt?
>
> Henry V *Prologue* 1–14

These are the questions the Prologue puts forth, and the answer, of course, is no. This "cock-pit" *cannot* hold the "vasty fields of France," nor can this "wooden O" contain all the soldiery and armor that fought in the Battle of Agincourt.

"Wooden O," now a celebrated phrase often used as shorthand for Elizabethan playhouses in general and for Shakespeare's Globe in particular, is an apt description of the multisided structures built in the Bankside district along the Thames. The Globe, built in 1599, was polygon with sixteen sides—essentially round. The Curtain, which may have been the site of the first performances of *Henry V*, was also a round playhouse. A "cock-pit" was originally, as the name implies, a place for the fighting of gamecocks, a popular Elizabethan sport. The buildings constructed for this purpose were sometimes used for the performance of plays, and later the term came to be used as a synonym for "theater." (Our term "orchestra pit," for a space below floor level at the front of a theater, is related to the same word.) What is being emphasized with the use of both terms, "wooden O" and "cock-pit," is the inadequate nature of the theater—any theater—to contain such intractable elements as the "vasty fields of France," where the play's battles will be set, or indeed the majesty of kingship, personated onstage by actors. The "gentles" in the audience, gentlemen and gentlewoman, are requested "[g]ently to hear" the play—that is, to make gracious allowances for its inevitable deficiencies.

This kind of apologia is familiar from the epilogues as well as the internal prologues of other Shakespearean plays. (Puck's Epilogue to *A Midsummer Night's Dream*, for example, begins, "If we shadows have offended, / Think but this and all is mended: / That you have but slumbered here.") But in the case of *Henry V*, where what is at stake is English history and English heroism, the prologues (and indeed the final and deflating Epilogue) are both more numerous and more insistent, reminding the audience at every turn that the play's illusion *is* illusion. We are asked to "[s]uppose within the girdle of these walls / Are now confined two mighty monarchies" (Prologue 19–20) and told: "Think, when we talk of horses, that you see them" (26). And in the prologue to act 5 we are asked to "behold, / In the quick forge and working-house of thought, / How London doth pour out her citizens" (5.0.22–24). The "quick forge and working-house of thought" is the mind. Thus these prologues, rather than increasing the realism and immediacy of the play, instead underscore the fact that it *is* a play. While the topic of *Henry V* is history, its mode of presentation is drama, and dramatic fiction. Yet the apparent deficiency is also an advantage. Another way of understanding the claims and disclaimers of the prologues is to see that they announce the immediacy and currency of "history" for the present day—a theme that will itself be stressed by King Henry V when he comes, on the battlefield in act 4, scene 3, to predict the future reputation of those who will have fought with him that day. History is the reputation of the soldier king and his newly united countrymen. In *Henry IV Part I* Prince Hal pledged, in his "I know you all" soliloquy, that he would fulfill his hidden promise, "[r]edeeming time when men think least I will." T. S. Eliot, perhaps remembering these lines, wrote powerfully in his *Four Quartets* about the role of the poet in culture, where "Every phrase and every sentence is an end and a beginning, / Every poem an epitaph," and where

We die with the dying:
See, they depart, and we go with them.
We are born with the dead:
See, they return, and bring us with them.
The moment of the rose and the moment of the yew-tree
Are of equal duration. A people without history
Is not redeemed from time, for history is a pattern
Of timeless moments. . . .
. . . .
History is now and England.

> *T. S. Eliot, "Little Gidding," section 5, lines 15–24*

For Shakespeare, too, and specifically for *Henry V,* history is "now and England" when it is retold, rewritten, or presented on the stage. History in the theater is to be played over and over, and it constitutes the epitaph for those who die in war. The audience is urged, by the use of its imagination, working collaboratively with the author and with the actor, to re-create the world of Henry V and to render his time-bound victory—soon to be lost through the weakness of his son and successor, the child-king Henry VI—timeless in memory and power.

As the play opens, we can observe something of both the achievements and the limitations of King Henry V's new world. For example, the bishops who are urging him to battle against France have rather mercenary motives for doing so, but the King whose "sleeping sword of war" they will awaken is, for them, clearly a redeemed man:

Consideration like an angel came
And whipped th'offending Adam out of him,
Leaving his body as a paradise.

> 1.1.29–31

The King is no longer a wild young prince called Hal, but rather a king who has reclaimed the comfortable name of Harry, a name he shared in *Henry IV Part 1* with Hotspur (Harry Percy), his chief rival. And this King Harry is a man who expressly and deliberately defines himself as a Christian king:

We are no tyrant, but a Christian king,
Unto whose grace our passion is as subject
As is our wretches fettered in our prisons.

> 1.2.241–243

From the royal plural to the disquieting image of a king's passion chained to his grace as a prisoner is chained to his prison, these are indications of necessary self-control and even self-sacrifice. It is in this somber spirit of resolve that the King receives a "tun of treasure" sent him by his opposite number, the Dauphin of France. "What treasure, uncle?" he inquires. "Tennis balls, my liege," is the answer (1.2.258). Why tennis balls? They are a symbol of frivolity, appropriate for the playboy prince the Dauphin still thinks he is confronting when he claims, in act 2, that England is, "so idly kinged, / Her sceptre so fantastically borne / By a vain, giddy, shallow, humorous youth, / that fear attacks her not" (2.4.26–28). Tennis is a "French" game, said to have originated in France in the Middle Ages; known as "jeu de paume," it is played on a "court." Several Shakespeare plays of this period mention tennis as an aristocratic entertainment, including *2 Henry IV*, where it becomes the occasion for Prince Hal to joke about Poins's lack of clean linen, and *Much Ado About Nothing*, where we are told that Benedick has shaved his beard so as to appear presentable as Beatrice's lover, and that "the old ornament of his cheek hath already stuffed tennis balls"—apparently an actual practice of the period. But King Henry V's response to the Dauphin's playful and insulting gift makes it clear that the jest is both understood and not appreciated. His language is chillingly cold (not "vain," "giddy," or "humorous"), and the royal "we" again does its job, starting as a description of the man, and moving without pause or break into the pledge of a nation, before returning to the personal "I" that marks the King's anger and his new promise. For this speech, too, is a kind of pendant to "I know you all," revisiting the narrative of a man underestimated by spectators and rivals, until he decides to let his true light shine:

> We are glad the Dauphin is so pleasant with us.
> His presence and your pains we thank you for.
> When we have matched our rackets to these balls,
> We will in France, by God's grace, play a set
> Shall strike his father's crown into the hazard.
>
> . . . .
> And we understand him well,
> How he comes o'er us with our wilder days,
> Not measuring what use we made of them.
>
> . . . .
> But tell the Dauphin I will keep my state,
> Be like a king, and show my sail of greatness
> When I do rouse me in my throne of France.
> For that I have laid by my majesty
> And plodded like a man for working days,
> But I will rise there with so full a glory
> That I will dazzle all the eyes of France.
>
> 1.2.259–279

"I will keep"; "I do rouse"; "I have laid by my majesty"; "I will rise therewith . . . glory"; "I will dazzle." This is both the voice of resolute human kingship and the voice of the self-described Christian king, who knows that he must fall to rise, must plod like a man for working days, no longer—as in his earlier youth—for "playing holidays." The prize for which he strives is "this best garden in the world, / Our fertile France" (5.2.36–37), explicitly likened to an Eden, but now choked with weeds and with corruption. The fertility of France will, in the event, be personal as well as agricultural, since part of the prize for which he angles will be a marriage with Catherine, the French princess. But that court-ship is far distant. At this moment King Henry V is all king, all soldier. He has succeeded in doing what his father, Henry IV, could never do: turn civil wars, inward wars, outward toward external enemies. ("[B]usy giddy minds / With foreign quarrels," his dying father had advised him [*2 Henry IV* 4.3.341–342].) Henry V, backed by the bishops, will now lead a battle against the French—in effect, a new religious crusade to recover a lost and fallen land.

In marked contrast to Richard II, whose death he mourns and repents, this King will not continue to foster favorites who act against the public weal. Rather, he will put aside private feelings and private friendships to become a public man. Three traitors are found among his retinue, Cambridge, Scrope, and Grey. Henry tests them by suggesting that he might offer mercy to a man who has, we are told, "railed against his person," spoken against the King. When Cambridge, Scrope, and Grey all insist that he respond not with mercy but with justice, he turns this same advice against them: "The mercy that was quick in us but late / By your own counsel is suppressed and killed" (2.2.76–77). This language of suppression and repression will characterize both the King and the play. Richard II had found Judases everywhere, and traitors in both Mowbray and Bolingbroke, but his own weakness was such that he allowed Bolingbroke to live, and to return to England—and Bolingbroke became responsible for Richard's death. Henry V, King Harry, is by contrast unyielding to the traitors in his midst, his own Judases: "I will weep for thee, / For this revolt of thine methinks is like / Another fall of man" (2.2.137–139).

Again and again in this play we will hear language and see actions that echo and correct the pattern of *Richard II*. Richard's inward wars become outward wars. Richard's weakness with traitors becomes a necessary and merciless execution of malefactors. Just as *Henry IV Part 2* echoed and balanced *Part 1*, so will *Henry V* repeatedly echo and balance *Richard II*. (1) the King who thought he was Christ ("Arm, arm, my name!"; "you Pilates / Have here delivered me to my sour cross" [*Richard II* 3.2.82; 4.1.230–231]) will be contrasted with the King who followed the example of Christ (eating and drinking with commoners; going in disguise, as an ordinary man, among his fellows) without self-conscious theatricality; (2) the narcissistic, private, inward-looking moment when Richard

II calls for a mirror in the deposition scene, only to dash it to the ground in anger, frustration, and self-disgust, is transmuted into the triumphantly public moment when Henry V is described, by the choric voice of the prologue in the play's second act, as "the mirror of all Christian kings" (2.0.6); (3) the pattern of banishment and exclusion, sometimes playful and sometimes dead serious (and sometimes both at once), is continued and expanded; and (4) the new King's stern sense of political necessity has been prefigured in the previous plays. In *Henry IV Part 1*, in reply to Falstaff's lighthearted "Banish plump Jack, and banish all the world," we heard the chilling monosyllables of resolute reply: "I do; I will"—a lesson Falstaff did not, and would not, learn. In *Part 2* that ominous promise of kingly self-control became an overt rejection: "I know thee not, old man. Fall to thy prayers" (*2 Henry IV* 5.5.45). In *Henry V* the world of "working days" replaces the "playing holidays" of *1 Henry IV*. Thus, too, the execution of Prince Hal's old tavern companion Bardolph, who has robbed a church, is accompanied by a terse admonition: "We would have all such offenders so cut off" (3.6.98). So much for old friendships.

In fact, the whole of yet another old order is dying off in this history play: the old order, or "old disorder," of the tavern world and the world of Misrule. Corporal Nim, whose name is an Old English word meaning "to steal," warns darkly that "[m]en may sleep, and they may have their throats about them at that time, and some say knives have edges" (2.1.18–20); he is hanged like Bardolph. By the end of the play Mistress Quickly, too, is dead, having succumbed, appropriately in this play about French-English wars, to a "malady of France" (5.1.73)—an English term for venereal disease. Most shocking of all, Falstaff is dead, Falstaff who throughout two entire plays steadfastly asserted his youth, and who seemed to be, in his way, an eternal energy, an eternal spirit. "The King has killed his heart" (2.1.79), says Mistress Quickly, and later she poignantly describes the moment when he ascended to the place she calls "Arthur's bosom," a splendidly "English" malapropism for the biblical phrase "in Abraham's bosom" (Luke 16:22):

> "How now, Sir John?" quoth I. "What, man? Be o' good cheer." So a cried out, "God, God, God," three or four times. Now I, to comfort him, bid him a should not think of God; I hoped there was no need to trouble himself with any such thoughts yet. So a bade me lay more clothes on his feet. I put my hand into the bed, and felt them, and they were as cold as any stone. Then I felt to his knees, and so up'ard, and up'ard, and all was cold as any stone.
>
> 2.3.16–23

This little Shakespearean "unscene," not witnessed by the audience but reported to us, is both comical and poignant. To feel a man from the knees "up'ard, and up'ard" is, for the Hostess, perhaps the surest test of telling life from death (the pun on "stone," meaning "testicle," underscores the point), and for Falstaff, about whom Poins had jested in *Part 2* that his desire had for so many years outlived performance, it is a fitting, if also fittingly bathetic, final encomium.

What has died with Falstaff? It is useful to compare the death of this Sir John to that of another iconic figure, John of Gaunt, in *Richard II*. The old fat man and the old thin man have a good deal in common. Both deaths signal the passing of an order long in power, the "other Eden" world of John of Gaunt, medieval, feudal, and hierarchical, and the world of Misrule of Sir John Falstaff. The death of Falstaff reported in the second act of *Henry V* is a counterpart, and fallen echo, of that earlier defining moment.

We will again encounter this vision of kingship as a role that necessitates coldness, rigid self-control, and fettered passions in Shakespeare's later plays, where calculating characters like Octavius Caesar prevail over more robustly heroic, if flawed, figures like Julius Caesar and Antony of *Antony and Cleopatra*. But the figures that survive and thrive from this play are the eccentric and aberrant ones: Pistol, Fluellen, even the absent Falstaff. Falstaff seemed to die at the end of *Henry IV Part 1*, but he rose up again with a lie. We are told that he has died early in this play, that the King has killed his heart, and yet again he rose up, in the city comedy *The Merry Wives of Windsor*. So comedy will always do, for it is "timeless" and "boundless"—until it comes face-to-face with death.

Increasingly, however, the new King resembles, not the discredited Falstaff, but his chief competitor in the realm of "honour," Hotspur, the Harry Percy whose ambitious heroism and valor in *Henry IV Part 1* have now become part of this Harry's persona and role. As we have seen, the French Dauphin miscalculates fatally in sending the English King his taunting gift of tennis balls. The Dauphin, we learn, has written a sonnet in praise of his horse, and he proudly claims, "[M]y horse is my mistress" (3.7.40). What is this but an enormously funny parody of Hotspur in *Part 1*, who says, half-jokingly, to his wife, "That roan shall be my throne" (*1 Henry IV* 2.4.64)? In King Harry, though, the intrinsic values for which Hotspur stood now find a sudden and appropriate place. We hear him declare, in the final wooing scene with Catherine the French princess, that he is no orator—this same witty wordsmith who has been delighting audiences with his nimble tongue for the length of three plays. "I speak to thee plain soldier," he will tell her (5.2.145–146). And the lady he woos is now, like Hotspur's wife, addressed as "Kate." He is like Hotspur, and also like his more ruthless self, in the words he speaks to his troops at Harfleur:

Once more unto the breach, dear friends, once more,
Or close the wall up with our English dead.

3.1.1–2

And this line, we are clearly given to understand, has become a rallying cry and a public slogan, since Bardolph parodies it in the following scene: "On, on, on, on, on! To the breach, to the breach!" (3.2.1). (During World War II, Laurence Olivier, then in uniform as a lieutenant of the Fleet Air Arm, delivered a number of patriotic addresses that closed with a stirring version of "Once more unto the breach.") But most of all, King Harry is the reincarnation of Hotspur's ambitious and capacious spirit in his wonderful speech in act 4 on the occasion of St. Crispin's Day. This speech, often recited out of context, became so popular in England as a patriotic set piece that it was frequently performed on its own. (Olivier's stirring delivery of it in 1942, on a radio program called "Into Battle," became the genesis for the 1944 film of *Henry V.*) Like Hotspur, King Harry now praises the quest for honor, and he expresses the view, as Hotspur had done on the field at Shrewsbury in *Henry IV Part 1,* that if there are fewer soldiers to fight, more glory will accrue to each:

> King Harry By Jove, I am not covetous for gold,
> Nor care I who doth feed upon my cost;
> It ernes me not if men my garments wear;
> Such outward things dwell not in my desires.
> But if it be a sin to covet honour
> I am the most offending soul alive.
> . . . .
> We would not die in that man's company
> That fears his fellowship to die with us.
> This day is called the Feast of Crispian.
> He that outlives this day and comes safe home
> Will stand a-tiptoe when this day is named
> And rouse him at the name of Crispian.
> He that shall see this day and live t'old age
> Will yearly on the vigil feast his neighbours
> And say, "Tomorrow is Saint Crispian."
> Then will he strip his sleeve and show his scars
> And say, "These wounds I had on Crispin's day."
> Old men forget; yet all shall be forgot,
> But he'll remember, with advantages,
> What feats he did that day. Then shall our names,
> Familiar in his mouth as household words—
> Harry the King, Bedford and Exeter,
> Warwick and Talbot, Salisbury and Gloucester—
> Be in their flowing cups freshly remembered.
> This story shall the good man teach his son,
> And Crispin Crispian shall ne'er go by

From this day to the ending of the world
But we in it shall be remembered,
We few, we happy few, we band of brothers.
For he today that sheds his blood with me
Shall be my brother; be he ne'er so vile,
This day shall gentle his condition.
And gentlemen in England now abed
Shall think themselves accursed they were not here,
And hold their manhoods cheap whiles any speaks
That fought with us upon Saint Crispin's day.

    4.3.24–67

This extraordinary speech returns the play to many of the same themes raised at the beginning by the Prologue: memory, epitaph, and mortality. It proposes a kind of immortality in fame familiar from Shakespeare plays in other genres, like *Love's Labour's Lost*. But in this drama of English history the very existence of the play as a commemorative object confirms the ideology of the King's impassioned claim. Old men will remember us, as the reader and the audience remember. And, moreover, they will remember "with advantages," augmenting, expanding and embroidering upon, the facts of the battle. In this patriotic account of the transmission of feats of heroism, the tales told by veterans to their sons reverse the negative affect of "Rumour painted full of tongues" in *Part 2*, glorifying the "story" each time it is repeated. The issue of "reputation," so vital in *Richard II*, here returns with a positive result. Where King Richard II lay "in reputation sick" on the deathbed of his land, King Henry V confidently predicts that the outcome of this battle "[f]rom this day to the ending of the world" will be "freshly remembered" in annual celebration. Instead of appealing ineffectually to the angels on behalf of a theory of divine right, like Richard ("Arm, arm, my name!"), Henry appeals to a "band of brothers." The "fewness" of "[w]e few" may be a Hotspur trait, but the concept of a band of brothers is pure Hal. His education in the tavern world, his awareness of his own desire for "small beer," common comforts and common company, make him more than a vainglorious Hotspur. He has become the modern king a modern England needs. Whatever the audience may feel about his character, its calculations and self-dramatizations, the fit between this King and his circumstances is carefully crafted by the playwright, who was writing almost two hundred years after the battle of Agincourt and would have had his own modern monarch, as well as Henry V, clearly in mind.

On the eve of Agincourt, the battle in which, famously, a small group of English noblemen and archers defeated a French army of foot soldiers and knights, the King wanders among troops who are weary, hungry, and despondent. The prologue to act 4 traces this royal progress:

O now, who will behold
The royal captain of this ruined band
Walking from watch to watch, from tent to tent,
Let him cry, "Praise and glory on his head!"
For forth he goes and visits all his host,
Bids them good morrow with a modest smile
And calls them brothers, friends, and countrymen.
Upon his royal face there is no note
How dread an army hath enrounded him;

. . . .

A largess universal, like the sun,
His liberal eye doth give to everyone,
Thawing cold fear, that mean and gentle all
Behold, as may unworthiness define,
A little touch of Harry in the night.

    4.0.28–47

The cloak the King borrows is that of the old and faithful knight Sir Thomas Erpingham, and under this cloak—as under the cloak of night—the new King goes out among his subjects. To them he speaks in prose, calling himself "Harry Le Roy" (or *le roi*), a transparent alias of truth and falsehood. In this play about France and England, French lessons and English lessons, "Le Roy" have been pronounced to rhyme with "toy," but the audience, unlike Ancient Pistol, would clearly understand the ruse. Not realizing the "gentleman's" true identity, Pistol nonetheless offers up an irrepressible praise of his king:

The King's a bawcock and a heart-of-gold,
A lad of life, an imp of fame,
Of parent good, of fist most valiant.
I kiss his dirty shoe, and from heartstring
I love the lovely bully. . . .

    4.1.45–49

Like another Shakespearean braggart soldier, Don Armado in *Love's Labour's Lost*, Pistol is given to linguistic extravagance, even at the cost of linguistic accuracy. The common soldiers are less tolerant, and less effusive. They are frightened of dying in battle, and are inclined to think that the King does not understand their position. The disguised King, the king in effect come to earth among his subjects, speaks to them in words that recall, although with far more self-possession and self-knowledge, Richard II's belated and heartbroken discovery of his own mortality. "I live with bread, like you," said Richard, "feel want, / Taste grief, need friends. Subjected thus, / How can you say to me I am a king?" (Richard II 3.2.171–173). Here is this King's version, less autocratic but equally lonely, rejoicing in rather than deploring his human condition, as he speaks from his disguise as the Welshman Harry Le Roy:

> I think the King is but a man, as I am. The violet smells to him as it doth to me; the element shows to him as it doth to me. All his senses have but human conditions. His ceremonies laid by, in his nakedness he appears but a man.
>
> 4:1.99–102

And again:

> By my troth, I will speak my conscience of the King. I think he would not wish himself anywhere but where he is. . . . Methinks I could not die anywhere so contented as in the King's company, his cause being just and his quarrel honourable.
>
> 4.1.113–122

This is a doubled language that he learned from Falstaff in the Eastcheap tavern, where his great mentor likewise spoke of himself in the third person ("A goodly, portly man, i'faith, and a corpulent. . . . And now I remember me, his name is Falstaff. . . . Him keep with; the rest banish" [*1 Henry IV* 2.5.384–391])

The King is playing a role here, at the same time that he is speaking no more or less than the truth. When his soldiers begin to make dispirited observations, like "I wish he were here alone" or "That's more than we know," the audience can sense Henry's growing feeling of isolation ("His ceremonies laid by, in his nakedness he appears but a man"). Anyone who recalls *Henry IV Part 2* will trace this bittersweet sentiment to the scene at this King's father's deathbed, where the son beheld the dying king asleep beside the glittering crown on his pillow ("Uneasy lies the head that wears a crown' [*2 Henry IV* 3.1.31]). As soon as he is alone onstage, Henry V speaks for the first time in this play in soliloquy, out of the darkness:

> What infinite heartsease
> Must kings neglect that private men enjoy?
> And what have kings that privates have not too,
> Save ceremony, save general ceremony?
>
> 4.1.218–221

Ceremony, the trappings of office. Henry's rumination harks back, again, to Richard II, who said as he divested himself of the signs of kingship, "I give this heavy weight from off my head, / And this unwieldy sceptre from my hand. . . . / With mine own tears I wash away my balm, / With mine own hands I give away my crown" (*Richard II* 4.1.194–198). Again, here is Henry V:

'Tis not the balm, the sceptre, and the ball,
The sword, the mace, the crown imperial.
. . . .
The throne he sits on, nor the tide of pomp
That beats upon the high shore of this world—
No, not all these, thrice-gorgeous ceremony,
Not all these, laid in bed majestical,
Can sleep so soundly as the wretched slave
Who with a body filled and vacant mind
Gets him to rest, crammed with distressful bread.

    4.1.242–252

The mention of bread, the staple food of the poor, sounds a persistent note throughout these history plays. As Richard II had marked his ordinary humanity ("I live with bread, like you"), so the tavern bill in Falstaff's pocket recorded, as Prince Hal noted with amusement in *Henry IV Part 1*, "but one halfpennyworth of bread to [an] intolerable deal of sack" (2.5.492–493). Behind this equation of bread with the ordinary, diurnal, "working day" world, the wages of the common man, stand the words of the Sermon on the Mount, "Give us this day our daily bread" (Matthew 6:11). Henry V, already associated with "small beer," is here also linked with a taste for "daily bread," for the working-day food of working-day men. He comes to the battlefield, cloaked, disguised as Harry Le Roy, to lift the spirits of his troops. Here he fulfills his promise to be a "Christian king" in another sense. Again the play stresses the loneliness as well as the responsibility of rule. His is a task that cannot finally be shared.

It is when the King is in disguise that he finds himself caught up in a quarrel with the soldier Williams. He tells the soldiers he has heard the King say that he will not be ransomed, and Williams contends that this is mere propaganda, a public utterance to make the soldiers fight cheerfully in a dangerous cause, and that the King would certainly consent to be ransomed. "If I live to see it," says the disguised King, "I will never trust his word after." "You'll never trust his word after! Come, 'tis a foolish saying," retorts Williams. Who are you that your trust should matter, one way or the other? And so the quarrel develops, and in fact it develops into a curiously familiar shape:

Williams: How shall I know thee again?
King Harry: Give me any gage of thine, and I will wear it in my bonnet.
Then if ever thou darest acknowledge it, I will make it my quarrel.
Williams: Here's my glove. Give me another of thine.

    4.1.192–196

For a moment we are back in the world of *Richard II,* with the formal challenge between Mowbray and Bolingbroke, complete with gages, oaths, and the promise of a fight—but in how different a spirit. This conflict is based on a matter of opinion rather than a matter of treason, and it is settled by a gesture of generosity and inclusiveness. "Your majesty came not like yourself" is Williams's defense when the truth is revealed, and the King will fill his glove up with gold coins, with "crowns." Bolingbroke's glove was thrown down to gain a crown. His son, Henry V, fills up his own glove with crowns, and gives it freely to a common soldier as a sign of fellowship.

For the same reason that the stage cannot hold the "vasty fields of France," it cannot hold the entire English army massed against the French. But the play presents a representative sampling of the various constituencies the King will need to meld into a single fighting—and living—force. This is the "colonial" moment for *Henry V,* as act 3, scene 2, introduces four officers speaking in four regional accents: Gower the Englishman, MacMorris the Irishman, Jamy the Scot, and the indomitable Fluellen, the Welshman. Together they present, onstage, a microcosm of the whole nation, a living, speaking map of Britain. (We might compare this scene emblematically to the famous "Ditchley portrait" of Queen Elizabeth, by Marcus Gheeraerts the Younger, in which the Queen, the mistress of her kingdom, stands on a map of England. Painted in 1592, the portrait partakes of the same national spirit as *Henry V.* As always, Shakespeare's "history" plays are concerned as much with current history as with the historical past, and his Henry V is a close relation, as well as an ancestor, of the reigning Queen.)

It is worth noting that the Irish captain, MacMorris, takes great offense when someone refers to his nation as if it were a separate entity. "What ish my nation?" he demands. "Who talks of my nation?" (3.3.62–63). His nation is now a part of King Harry's England. The fallen, fragmented world, divided into England, Ireland, Scotland, Wales, and France, is—for a moment, at least—about to be restored. Needless to say, this is an ideological construction. These subject "nations" all declare themselves eager to be ruled. Unlike Owen Glendower, they do not stand apart from English domination. We may recall the sage advice of Henry IV to his son, that he should "busy giddy minds / With foreign quarrels." The same sentiment is voiced more generously in this play by one of the common soldiers, Bates, who intercedes in a growing quarrel between his fellow soldier, Williams, and the disguised Henry V: "Be friends, you English fools, be friends. We have French quarrels enough" (4.1.206–207).

Civil wars, whether of language or of action, must and do give way to the energies of an external war, a war that is thought of, once again, as a kind of holy war. For when the battle is concluded, and the King hears the lengthy roll call of the French who have perished, he asks for "the number of our English dead" and is given a list miraculous for its brevity:

King Harry Edward the Duke of York, the Earl of Suffolk,
Sir Richard Keighley, Davy Gam Esquire;
None else of name, and of all other men
But five-and-twenty. O God, thy arm was here,
And not to us, but to thy arm alone
Ascribe we all. When, without stratagem,
But in plain shock and even play of battle,
Was ever known so great and little loss,
On one part and on th'other? Take it God,
For it is none but thine.

     4.8.97–106

"God fought for us," says the King, calling for "holy rites" to commemorate the dead. Here an attentive Shakespearean audience might remember the far more cynical words of Prince John at Gaultres Forest as he betrayed the rebels: "God, and not we, hath safely fought today" (*2 Henry IV* 4.1.347). In this assertion, as in so many, Henry V both echoes and redeems the language and the actions of his predecessors.

    Among the several army captains, the clear audience favorite is the Welshman, Fluellen, who, with an aplomb worthy of Bottom, declares that he is not ashamed of the King:

By Jeshu, I am our majesty's countryman. I care not who knows it, I will confess it to all the world. I need not to be ashamed of your majesty, praised be God, so long as your majesty is an honest man.

    4.7.102–105

The King—who is, after all, "Harry of Monmouth" and the former Prince of Wales—has had his own praise for Fluellen: "Though it appear a little out of fashion, / There is much care and valour in this Welshman" (4.1.82–83). It is Fluellen who stresses the King's Welsh ties: "All the water in Wye [a Welsh river] cannot wash your majesty's Welsh plood out of your pody, I can tell you that" (4.7.97–98). Here yet again we can note an echo of *Richard II*, the pendant to this play: "Not all the water in the rough rude sea / Can wash the balm from an anointed king." But King Harry is anointed by the people, by the Welsh "plood" in his "pody." The confusion of *p* and *b* is a stage convention associated with comic Welsh characters from Shakespeare's time to the present, and is also magnificently on display in Fluellen's learned comparison of his king to a classical model he names as "Alexander the Pig." Fluellen knows his history, and proceeds, as did many Renaissance historians, by the same comparative method exemplified in Plutarch's *Parallel Lives of the Noble Grecians and Romans*, drawing an extended historical analogy between Henry V and Alexander. When the

King gives Fluellen his "favor"—actually a glove that belongs to the common soldier Williams—and watches to see how he defends himself against a beating, it is in one sense the playful spirit of the old Prince Hal that is on display. But in another sense this gesture is King Harry's acknowledgment that one Welshman is a good as another.

Fluellen's chief opponent and polar opposite is Ancient Pistol, with whom he becomes embroiled in a comic "controversy" in act 5. It is noteworthy that *Henry V,* a play that centers on war and soldiery, concludes with two extended comic scenes. In *1 Henry IV* comedy turned to history; here history turns to comedy, and indeed to the promise of a marriage between the King of England and the Princess of France. For a brief but brilliant moment, until the sober voice of the Epilogue returns the audience to English history and to the losses sustained by the weak King Henry VI ("[w]hich oft our stage hath shown") the victory over France achieved at Agincourt is transmuted into rapprochement. This play revisits, in both scenes in the final act, a topic that has been stressed from *Richard II* through the *Henry IV* plays—the question of language and its relationship to politics and rule. At issue is not only language-learning but a respect for the multiplicity of languages, and an awareness—both comic and serious—of the dangers of translation.

The first of these two scenes features the enforced language instruction of Pistol, presided over by Fluellen, who is waiting for him with a leek, the onion-like herb that is the national emblem of the Welsh. To Pistol's astonishment and horror—and to the corresponding amusement of the audience—he is forced to eat the leek, bite by bite, while Fluellen stands over him with a club. Pistol: "I eat and eat. . . . Quiet thy cudgel, thou dost see I eat" (5.1.43–46). It is the English captain, Gower, who correctly interprets this event as a language lesson: "I have seen you gleeking and galling at this gentleman twice or thrice. You thought, because he could not speak English in the native garb, he could not therefore handle an English cudgel" (5.1.66–69). Valor, and not elaborate language or high birth, is now the mark of a gentleman—and of an English soldier. Yet our last glimpse of Pistol shows him, unfazed, swearing to turn bawd and cutpurse, and planning to return to England to make his fortune in the stews. The Pistols of this world cannot be killed in battle because they never go to battle. They represent the irreducible mischief in humankind, a mode of misrule that is not holiday, but rather anarchy and animal energy: "for, lambkins, we will live" (2.2.116).

Nonetheless, Pistol's comically discomfiting language lesson makes a serious political point. Warring populations and incomprehensible languages will divide a people just when the people most need to be united. Somewhere behind the scenes there is a faint whiff of a reference to Babel and Pentecost, the first the biblical moment when a multiplicity of languages divided mankind, and the second the moment when the capacity to speak and understand all languages enabled the

Apostles to communicate universally ("And how hear we every man in our own tongue . . . ?" [Acts 2:8]). This may be one of the reasons for the presence of the rather comic wooing scene between the French Princess and the English King. Charming in itself, it also completes and concludes the theme of language and languages that has been present throughout all these history plays.

Catherine's language lesson in act 3, scene 4 has also engaged this theme, since even in the apparent safety of the Princess's chamber, danger lurks. The innocent French words *pieds* and *robe*, when rendered in the English tongue, are transformed into the vulgar terms "foot" and "cown" (for "gown"), which bring a blush to a maiden's cheek—and which still have their cognate counterparts in vulgar French and English. The delicious sense of naughtiness marked in Catherine's response is appropriate for her rank and station, and is joined—to the audience's amusement—by a palpable sense of resolve. For the Princess and her gentlewoman Alice, having discerned the danger, bravely decide to pronounce the words. This kind of comic language-learning scene, with the inevitable, and often lewd, mispronunciation or mistranslation of "foreign" words, is used by Shakespeare in several plays, including *Love's Labour's Lost* and *The Merry Wives of Windsor*. Closely akin are other scenes of malapropism in which learned and unlearned speakers find themselves at cross-purposes (for example, Dogberry and the Watch versus the aristocrats in *Much Ado About Nothing*, or even the foolish Sir Andrew Aguecheek in *Twelfth Night*, who despite his wealth and fashionable affectations does not know the meaning of the word *pourquoi*). But in *Henry V* the comical scene between the two Frenchwomen—a nice break after all the scenes at war—is in a way a domesticated version of the linguistic squabbles on the battlefield, and prepares the Princess for her political role as an English queen. Throughout *Henry V*, in fact, the King's continuing quest to speak and be understood is counterpointed by the adventures of Fluellen, on the one hand, and Catherine, on the other, so that it is quite fitting that the final act of the play should be divided between them, the first of these two scenes presenting the humiliation of Pistol, and the second the wooing of Catherine, with the King present and active in both.

King Harry's speeches in the wooing scene are prose, a form he has used, for three plays, on the battlefield or in the tavern but never, until now, at court. His declaration of love is couched, deliberately and significantly, in plain language. He is a "plain king," a "fellow of plain and uncoined constancy," who speaks to her "plain soldier" (5.2.124, 149, 146). "Plain" in this period is a term of art in language and style, in contrast to "curious" and "pointed." "Uncoined," meaning "not fabricated or invented," reverses once more the language of counterfeiting that pursued this King's father. Each word must now mean precisely and only what it says:

King Harry: For these fellows of infinite tongue, that can rhyme
    themselves into ladies' favours, they do always reason themselves out

again. What! A speaker is but a prater, a rhyme is but a ballad; . . . but a good heart, Kate, is the sun and the moon—or rather the sun and not the moon, for it shines bright and never changes, but keeps his course truly.

5.2.151–159

"Kate" is itself the King's deliberate Englishing of the Princess's name, and it may remind the audience not only of Lady Percy (Hotspur's forthright Kate, whom he teased about swearing like a "comfit-maker's wife") but also of Kate/ Katherine in *The Taming of the Shrew*, whose bridegroom likewise lectured her about the sun and the moon. In the balance of this final scene the King speaks French as well as English, the Princess English (of a comical sort) as well as French, and the betrothal is celebrated with a kiss in which King Harry finds "more eloquence . . . than in the tongues of the French Council" (5.2.256–258). The play that started out with a narrowly construed, casuistical reading of a Latin phrase—*In terram Salicam mulieres ne succedant,* translated as "No woman shall succeed in Salic land"—concludes, apparently, with the fruitful union of French and English, Welsh and Scot in a single, hopeful nation, united by a political marriage that is also presented as a love match.

And yet that hope is deliberately undercut by the play's Epilogue, which immediately follows the betrothal scene. The Epilogue reminds the audience with brutal directness that after Henry V came his son Henry VI, and that the child king Henry VI had so many conflicting advisers that everything gained by his father's war and marriage was swiftly lost. The Epilogue, in the form a Shakespearean sonnet, returns the scenario to the playhouse, or rather to the "author" of the play and the "little room" in which his actors have performed.

Thus far with rough and all-unable pen
    Our bending author hath pursued the story
In little room confining mighty men,
    Mangling by starts the full course of their glory.
Small time, but in that small most, greatly lived
    This star of England. Fortune made his sword,
By which the world's best garden he achieved,
    And of it left his son imperial lord.
Henry the Sixth, in infant bands crowned king
    Of France and England, did this king succeed,
Whose state so many had the managing
    That they lost France and made his England bleed,
Which oft our stage hath shown—and, for their sake,
    In your fair minds let this acceptance take.

Epilogue 1–14

The triumph of *Henry V* is only a temporary one, momentary in terms of the scope of history. The history plays in Shakespeare's earlier sequence, "[w]hich oft our stage hath shown," depict in grim detail the consequences of the loss of France, the bleeding of England, and the long agony of the Wars of the Roses. The play the audience has been watching is, as the prologues have insisted, only an illusion, forged in the working-house of thought. The conventional request for applause ("let this acceptance take") returns the power to the audience, where it has always been. What we are asked to approve is a spectacle of victory, and a concept of kingship, that is finally only an idea, precariously achieved and too easily lost.

BIBLIOGRAPHY

❧

General Bibliography

Bloom, Harold, ed. *William Shakespeare's Henry V*, Modern Critical Interpretations. New York: Chelsea House, 1988.

Boyce, Charles. *Shakespeare A to Z: The Essential Reference to His Plays, His Poems, His Life and Times, and More*. New York: Facts on File, 1990.

Bradshaw, Graham. *Misrepresentations: Shakespeare and the Materialists*. Ithaca, NY: Cornell University Press, 1993.

Bullough, Geoffrey. *Narrative and Dramatic Sources of Shakespeare*. 8 vols. London: Routledge, 1957–75.

Dowden, Edward. *Shakspere [sic]: His Mind and Art*. 1872. New York: Capricorn, 1962.

Foakes, R. A. *Shakespeare and Violence*. Cambridge: Cambridge University Press, 2003.

Hattaway, Michael, ed. *The Cambridge Companion to Shakespeare's History Plays*. Cambridge: Cambridge University Press, 2002.

Highley, Christopher. *Shakespeare, Spenser and the Crisis in Ireland*. Cambridge: Cambridge University Press, 1997.

Holderness, Graham, ed. *Shakespeare's History Plays* (Richard II to Henry V), (New Casebooks). Houndmills: Macmillan, 1992

Honan, Park. *Shakespeare: A Life*. Oxford and New York: Oxford U P, 1998.

Lynch, Jack. *Becoming Shakespeare*. New York: Walker & Company, 2007.

O'Connor, John. *Shakespearean Afterlives: Ten Characters with a Life of Their Own*. London: Icon, 2003.

Quinn, Michael, ed. *Shakespeare:* Henry V. Ed. Michael Quinn. (Casebook series). London: Macmillan, 1969.

Rothwell, Kenneth S. *A History of Shakespeare on Screen*. Cambridge: Cambridge University Press, 2000.

Schoenbaum, S. *Shakespeare: His Life, His Language, His Theater*. New York: Signet: Penguin, 1990.

Sen Gupta, S. C. *Shakespeare's Historical Plays*. London: Oxford University Press, 1964.

Shapiro, James. *A Year in the Life of William Shakespeare: 1599.* New York: HarperCollins, 2005.

Sinfield, Alan, ed. *Faultines: Cultural Materialism and the Politics of Dissident Reading.* Oxford: Clarendon Press, 1992.

Vickers, Brian. *Appropriating Shakespeare.* New Haven: Yale University Press, 1994.

———, ed. *Shakespeare: The Critical Heritage.* 6 vols. London: Routledge, 1974–1981.

Henry V Through the Ages

Altieri, Joanne. "Romance in *Henry V.*" *Studies in English Literature 1500–1900* 21 (1981): 223–40.

Altman, Joel B. "'Vile Participation': The Amplification of Violence in the Theater of *Henry V.*" *Shakespeare Quarterly* 42 (1991): 1–32.

Baker, David J. "'Wildehirissheman': Colonialist Representation in Shakespeare's *Henry V.*" *English Literary Renaissance* 22 (1992): 37–61.

Barton, Anne. "The King Disguised: Shakespeare's *Henry V* and the Comical History," in *The Triple Bond: Plays, Mainly Shakespearean, in Performance.* Ed. Joseph G. Price. University Park: Pennsylvania State University Press, 1975: 92–107.

Belsey, Catherine. "Making Histories Then and Now: Shakespeare from Richard II to Henry V." In *Uses of History: Marxism, Postmodernism, and the Renaissance.* Ed. Francis Barker et al. Manchester: Manchester UP, 1991. 24–46.

Bloom, Harold. *Shakespeare: The Invention of the Human.* New York: Riverhead, 1998.

———, ed. *William Shakespeare's Henry V,* Modern Critical Interpretations. New York: Chelsea House, 1988.

Brennan, Anthony. "That Within Which Passes Show: The Function of the Chorus in *Henry V*" in *Philological Quarterly,* 58 (1979): 40–52.

Calderwood, James L. *Metadrama in Shakespeare's Henriad:* Richard II *to* Henry V. Berkeley: University of California Press, 1979.

Campbell, Lily B. *Shakespeare's Histories: Mirrors of Elizabethan Policy.* Los Angeles: The Ward Richie Press, 1947.

Danson, Lawrence. "*Henry V*: King, Chorus, and Critics." *Shakespeare Quarterly* 34 (1983): 27–43.

Dollimore, Jonathan, and Alan Sinfield. "History and Ideology: The Instance of *Henry V.*" In *Alternative Shakespeares.* Ed. John Drakakis. London, 1985.

Goddard, Harold. *The Meaning of Shakespeare.* 2 vols. Chicago: University of Chicago Press, 1951.

Granville-Barker, Harley. *From Henry V to Hamlet.* London, Oxford University Press, 1925.

Greenblatt, Stephen. *Shakespearean Negotiations: The Circulation of Social Energy in Renaissance England*. Berkeley and Los Angeles: University of California Press, 1988.

Greenburg, Bradley. "'O for a muse of fire': *Henry V* and Plotted Self-Exculpation" from *Shakespeare Studies* 36 (2008): 182–206

Hazlitt, William. *Characters of Shakespeare's Plays*. New York: Chelsea House, 1983.

Helgerson, Richard. *Forms of Nationhood: The Elizabethan Writing of England*. Chicago: University Of Chicago Press, 1992.

Holderness, Graham. *Shakespeare's History*. New York: Palgrave Macmillan, 1985.

Howard, Jean E., and Phyllis Rackin. *Engendering a Nation: A Feminist Account of Shakespeare's English Histories*. London: Routledge, 1997.

Jorgensen, Paul A. *Shakespeare's Military World*. Berkeley: University of California Press, 1956.

Knight, G. Wilson. *The Olive and the Sword: A Study in England's Shakespeare*. London: Oxford University Press, 1944.

Lane, Robert. "'When Blood is their Argument': Class, Character, and Historymaking in Shakespeare's and Branagh's *Henry V*." *ELH* 61 (1994): 27–52.

Leggatt, Alexander. *Shakespeare's Political Drama: The History Plays and the Roman Plays*. London: Routledge, 1988.

Loehlin, James N. *Shakespeare in Performance: Henry V*. Manchester: Manchester University Press, 1997.

Marx, Steven. "Holy War in *Henry V*." *Shakespeare Survey* 48 (1995): 85–99.

———. "Shakespeare's Pacifism." *Renaissance Quarterly* 45 (1992): 49–95.

McAlindon, Tom. *Shakespreare Minus 'Theory.'* Aldershot: Ashgate, 2004.

McEachern, Claire. *The Poetics of English Nationhood*. Cambridge: Cambridge University Press, 1996.

Mebane, John S. "'Impious War': Religion and the Ideology of Warfare in *Henry V*," *Studies in Philology* 104 (2007): 250–66.

Meron, Theodor. *Bloody Constraint: War and Chivalry in Shakespeare*. Oxford: Oxford University Press, 1998.

———. *Henry's Wars and Shakespeare's Laws: Perspectives on the Law of War in the Later Middle Ages*. Oxford: Clarendon Press, 1993.

Neill, Michael. "Broken English and Broken Irish: Nation, Language and the Optic of Power in Shakespeare's Histories," *Shakespeare Quarterly* 45 (1994): 1–32.

Newstrom, Scott. "'Step Aside, I'll Show Thee a President' George W as Henry V?" *Pop Politics* (2003) http://www.poppolitics.com/articles/2003/05/01/George_W_as_Henry_V?

Patterson, Annabel. "Back by Popular Demand: The Two Versions of *Henry V.*" *Renaissance Drama* 19 (1989): 29–62.

Quint, David. "'Alexander the Pig': Shakespeare on History and Poetry," *Boundary* 2 10 (1982): 49–67.

Rabkin, Norman. *Shakespeare and the Problem of Meaning.* Chicago: U of Chicago P, 1981.

Saccio, Peter. *Shakespeare's English Kings: History, Chronicle, and Drama.* Oxford: Oxford University Press, 1977.

Schwyzer, Philip. *Literature, Nationalism and Memory in Early Modern England and Wales.* Cambridge: Cambridge University Press, 2004.

Tennenhouse, Leonard. *Power on Display: The Politics of Shakespeare's Genres.* New York: Methuen, 1986.

Thorne, Alison. "Awake Remembrance of These Valiant Dead: *Henry V* and the Politics of the English History Play." *Shakespeare Studies* 30 (2002): 162–87.

Tillyard, E. M. W. *Shakespeare's History Plays.* London: Chatto and Windus, 1944.

Traversi, Derek. *Shakespeare: From Richard II to Henry V.* Stanford: Stanford UP, 1957.

Van Doren, Mark. *Shakespeare.* Intro. David Lehman New York: NYRB Classics, 2005.

Wentersdorf, K. P. "The Conspiracy of Silence in *Henry V.*" *Shakespeare Quarterly* 27 (1976): 264–87.

Wilcox, Lance. "Katherine of France as Victim and Bride," *Shakespeare Studies* 17 (1985): 61–76.

Williamson, Marilyn. "The Episode with Williams in *Henry V.*" *Studies in English Literature 1500–1900* 9 (1969): 275–82.

ACKNOWLEDGMENTS

❧

Henry V in the Twentieth Century

Paul A. Jorgensen, "The Courtship Scene in Henry V," *Modern Language Quarterly*, vol. 11, no. 2, pp. 180–81. Copyright © 1950 University of Washington. All rights reserved. Republished and used by permission of Duke University Press.

Marilyn L. Williamson, "The Episode with Williams in Henry V," *Studies in English Literature 1500–1900*, vol. 9, no. 2 (Spring 1969): 275–82. Copyright © 1969. Reprinted with permission from *SEL: Studies in English Literature 1500–1900*.

Norman Rabkin, "Rabbits, Ducks, and Henry V." *Shakespeare Quarterly*, vol. 28, no. 3 (1977): 279–96. Copyright © 1977 Folger Shakespeare Library. Reprinted with permission of the Johns Hopkins University Press.

Paul M. Cubeta, "Falstaff and the Art of Dying," *Studies in English Literature 1500–1900*, vol. 27, no. 2 (Spring 1987): 197–211. Copyright © 1987. Reprinted with permission from *SEL: Studies in English Literature 1500–1900*.

Harold Bloom, "Henry V," from *Shakespeare: The Invention of the Human*. Published by Riverhead Books/Penguin Putnam Inc. Copyright © 1998 by Harold Bloom.

Grace Tiffany, "Shakespeare's Dionysian Prince: Drama, Politics, and the 'Athenina' History Play," *Renaissance Quarterly*, vol. 52, no. 2 (Summer 1999): 366–83. Copyright © 1999 *Renaissance Quarterly*.

Henry V in the Twenty-first Century

Marjorie Garber, "Henry V," from *Shakespeare After All*, pp. 391–408. Copyright © 2004 by Marjorie Garber. Used by permission of Pantheon Books, a division of Random House, Inc.

INDEX

INDEX

❧